TORTS AND RETRIBUTION

Torts and Retribution is the first work of its kind to offer a comprehensive analytical retributive framework for punitive damages across legal jurisdictions. It expands the scope of tort theory by unchaining it from the canonically exclusive perspective of the defendant by integrating the long-overlooked perspective of victims of reprehensible wrongdoing seeking punitive awards. Its cross-disciplinary approach brings to tort theory insights from empirical research on social cognition and theoretical debates over the retributive justifications for the imposition of punishment under a conceptual framework coined *Relational Retribution*. This framework suits both the bilateral structure of tort law and the proactive role allocated to the victim in tort litigation. By recognizing the fundamental connection between the defendant and the plaintiff, *Relational Retribution* focuses both on punishment as the imposition of a deserved sanction and on the significance of the wrongdoing for the victims and their demand for denunciation and value affirmation.

María Guadalupe Martínez Alles is Associate Professor at the University of Denver Sturm College of Law.

Torts and Retribution

THE CASE FOR PUNITIVE DAMAGES

MARÍA GUADALUPE MARTÍNEZ ALLES
University of Denver Sturm College of Law

CAMBRIDGE
UNIVERSITY PRESS

CAMBRIDGE
UNIVERSITY PRESS

Shaftesbury Road, Cambridge CB2 8EA, United Kingdom

One Liberty Plaza, 20th Floor, New York, NY 10006, USA

477 Williamstown Road, Port Melbourne, VIC 3207, Australia

314–321, 3rd Floor, Plot 3, Splendor Forum, Jasola District Centre, New Delhi – 110025, India

103 Penang Road, #05–06/07, Visioncrest Commercial, Singapore 238467

Cambridge University Press is part of Cambridge University Press & Assessment, a department of the University of Cambridge.

We share the University's mission to contribute to society through the pursuit of education, learning and research at the highest international levels of excellence.

www.cambridge.org
Information on this title: www.cambridge.org/9781009567893

DOI: 10.1017/9781009567886

When citing this work, please include a reference to the DOI 10.1017/9781009567886

First published 2025

A catalogue record for this publication is available from the British Library

Library of Congress Cataloging-in-Publication Data
NAMES: Martínez Alles, María Guadalupe, 1978– author.
TITLE: Torts and retribution : the case for punitive damages / María Guadalupe Martínez Alles, University of Denver Sturm College of Law.
DESCRIPTION: Cambridge, United Kingdom ; New York, NY : Cambridge University Press, 2025. | Includes bibliographical references and index.
IDENTIFIERS: LCCN 2024048049 | ISBN 9781009567893 (hardback) | ISBN 9781009567886 (ebook)
SUBJECTS: LCSH: Exemplary damages. | Torts. | Lex talionis.
CLASSIFICATION: LCC K923 .M37 2025 | DDC 347/.077–dc23/eng/20241010
LC record available at https://lccn.loc.gov/2024048049

ISBN 978-1-009-56789-3 Hardback
ISBN 978-1-009-56791-6 Paperback

To my parents and late grandmother

Ninguna decisión es final, todas se ramifican en otras

(No decision is final, all diverge into others)

Jorge Luis Borges, La Lotería en Babilonia (1941)

Contents

Preface

Torts and Retribution offers an analytical retributive framework that allows us to think about punitive damages across jurisdictions. Searching for the proper place of punishment in private law is particularly timely because the discussions about it are at present dynamically evolving in most civil law and common law jurisdictions. Although the common law of torts has for centuries combined compensatory and punitive responses, punitive damages being the paradigmatic example of a tort institution with salient retributive elements, scant scholarly attention has been devoted to justifying the retributive dimension. Indeed, the prevailing approach in tort theory, a field dominated by variants of rights-based theories (broadly understood) and law and economics accounts, has been to promote or perfect the rectificatory and deterrence dimensions of tort law, sometimes by rejecting outright or, more often, by remaining candidly indifferent to the institution's retributive facet. For their part, rights-based approaches to tort law have emphasized its rectificatory dimension, which leads them to either plainly reject punishment as anomalous or to somehow corset it, however ill-fittingly, within tort law's rectificatory framework, although recently some effort has been made to formulate rights-based justifications for the practice of awarding punitive damages in tort cases where there is evidence of willful or wanton misconduct by the defendant. Several of these recent reconstructions hazard some ideas to justify retribution's place in tort law, but only in qualified manners that do not offer an adequately thorough retributive rationale of punitive damages. Instrumentalist approaches to tort law (e.g., law and economics accounts) take a different yet analogous tack by focusing exclusively on the deterrent effect of punitive damages. These accounts directly reduce punishment to deterrence, thereby wholly neglecting the relevance of the retributive dimension of the institution. The global trends followed by tort scholars and theorists in these respects reflect a general academic reticence to take up plausible theoretical groundings for the place of retribution in tort law. *Torts and Retribution* overcomes these shortcomings traversing tort theory with a novel, sorely missing theoretical justification of the retributive dimension of tort law that is embedded in punitive damages, which I coin *Relational Retribution*. The time has come to consider tort responses in a manner that more accurately reflects the significance and meaning of the specific circumstances of the wrongdoing for the private parties involved as well as for society as a whole.

This project takes the uneasy yet unavoidable observation of tort law's retributive dimension very seriously. It respectfully scrutinizes the most compelling reconstruction of the widely accepted definition of the function of punitive damages as a combination of "retribution and deterrence." Justifying retribution in torts is daunting in part because it requires reassessing the widely accepted assumption underlying our understanding of tort law that attributes the mechanism an exclusively private rectificatory function. First of all, justifying retribution in torts requires questioning the classic formalistic depiction of victims as seeking restoration to their former state before the tort occurred. To replace this depiction, I posit the victims as seeking richer, textured, and value-laden responses that capture the significance of the wrongdoing by communicating the situated meaning of the impact of reprehensible wrongs on them and their complex motivations for resorting to tort law and its process for private redress. My reading of the private actor incorporates insights from social psychology and other social sciences that empirically test the true roots and causes of the motivation to punish reprehensible wrongdoing. These findings elicit difficult questions on the desirability of making room for intuitive–emotive reactions to wrongdoing in the classic rationalistic model of legal reasoning. They also invite doubt with regard to the widespread view that victims' motivations to sue, particularly their retributive motivations, are so subjective as to render them rationally suspect and to be shunned because of their proximity to desire for private revenge or retaliation, both of which are considered morally objectionable bases for a normative justification of punitive damages. Most significantly, findings from the social sciences question the supposedly crystalline monopoly of the state over the administration of punishment through criminal law and procedure. *Torts and Retribution* embarks on this multifaceted probe of the retributive quest in torts with a fresh examination of alternative yet persuasive readings of tort law's assumptions. Ultimately, this book extends an invitation to both tort and criminal law scholars to engage jointly in a conversation on the forms of punishment in our democratic societies that fall outside the confines of criminal law and procedure. Hopefully, readers looking for a fresh approach to the topic will appreciate this work, and those less persuaded by the argument will still find the book valuable for its detailed survey of the classic and contemporary works that inform current debates, perhaps by helping them to reinforce their own position or even to improve it.

Acknowledgments

This journey has certainly been long and challenging. *Torts and Retribution* draws on over a decade of research that began during my doctoral studies at Yale Law School in 2011 and has continued ever since. Understandably, my willingness to dig deep into the punitive drive and explore alternative readings of widespread assumptions, which I find persuasive, has encountered at almost every turn some skepticism. Yet during this journey, I have also been fortunate to enjoy the support and encouragement of scholars from many different legal traditions who generously and genuinely engaged with my work. Their engagement and support have made all the difference to me. Writing a book is a collective enterprise – however lonely the process felt much of the time. *Torts and Retribution* is much more than an individual achievement thanks to Doug Kysar who took a chance and generously agreed to serve as the supervisor of the original thesis on which this book is based. He was a source of inspiration and a mentor, and his influence on my thinking is difficult to understate. I am deeply grateful for his kindness, continuous support, and encouragement over the years. My gratitude to John Witt also runs deep, for his generous and genuine engagement with the project since its inception, for extraordinary substantive feedback, and for constant support and encouragement when it was most needed. I am grateful to Diego Papayannis, for reading several segments of the emerging manuscript and offering invaluable feedback for improvement. He has never failed to provide encouragement, support, and friendship over the years. The manuscript has also benefited enormously from the efforts, discussions, feedback, conversations, and comments of Alberto Pino Emhart, Esteban Pereira Fredes, Alexander Vargas Tinoco, Martín Juárez Ferrer, Sebastián Figueroa, Martín Hevia, Magdalena Bustos, Gregory Keating, Felipe Jiménez, Douglas Husak, Gideon Yaffe, John Goldberg, Paul Miller, Arthur Ripstein, Anita Bernstein, Crescente Molina, Cedric Vanleenhove, Lotte Meurkens, Claudio Michelon, John Macleod, Amalia Amaya, Tsampika Taralli, James Goudkamp, Donal Nolan, Rafael Peteffi da Silva, Francisco de Elizalde, Leon Anidjar, Patricio Nazareno, Alejandro Chehtman, Ezequiel Monti, Horacio Spector, Eduardo Rivera López, Eduardo Stordeur, Yanina Pantiga, and Adrian Kuenzler. I am particularly grateful to Matthew Dyson for his generosity and support with this project. Furthermore, I thank four anonymous reviewers for their extremely helpful comments that pushed me to refine the manuscript. Also, thanks to my wonderful colleagues at IE Law School and to IE University for their support.

It was a privilege to present and discuss some of the ideas of the manuscript at different stages of development in diverse academic forums. For this, I am particularly grateful to Amalia Amaya, James Goudkamp, Reihnard Zimmermman, Paul Miller and John Oberdiek, Cedric Vanleenhove and Lotte Meurkens, Sebastián Figueroa, and Alejandro Chehtman for allowing me to benefit from the feedback and exchange of thoughts with the participants in the Edinburgh Legal Theory Workshop (Edinburgh University), the Obligations Discussion Group (Oxford University), the Aktuelle Stunde (Max Planck Institute for Comparative and International Private Law), the Conference on Civil Wrongs and Justice in Private Law (Rutgers Law School), the M-EPLI Roundtable on Punitive Damages (Maastricht University), the Legal Theory Workshop (Autonomous University of Madrid), and the Faculty Workshop (Torcuato Di Tella University), respectively. I am grateful beyond words to my colleagues from Latin America, a truly extraordinary group of private law theorists who have generously included me in numerous workshops and initiatives where I was able to discuss, further develop, and improve this project from its outset. Their support and camaraderie meant much to me. Special thanks go to Alberto Pino, Esteban Pereira, Alexander Vargas, Martín Juárez, Martín Hevia, and Carlos de la Rosa Xochitiotzi. For first encouraging me to jump into the conversations on torts, I thank Manuel Cornet and Daniel Pizarro, private law professors at my alma mater, The National University of Córdoba (Argentina), who generously gave me the space, support, and confidence to initiate my academic career when I was just starting out. I owe special thanks to Sharon McCann, whose engagement and professionalism as an editor are exceptional and, above all, for seeing the manuscript's potential and embarking with me on this project, as well as various of her colleagues at Cambridge University Press. Also, thanks to Bradley Hayes, whose persistent copy-editing has helped me find some balance between the exactitude demanded by the discipline and specific subject and sympathy for nonspecialists.

Several of the preliminary ideas (significantly revised and developed) upon which parts of the book build appeared in the previously published articles: "Moral Outrage and Betrayal Aversion: The Psychology of Punitive Damages," "Tort Remedies as Meaningful Responses to Wrongdoing," and "Punitive Damages: Reorienting the Debate in Civil Law Systems."

Lastly and most of all, I must acknowledge the importance of those closest to me. I should start with my parents Gustavo and Margarita, lifelong advocates of all my projects just because they were mine, my late grandmother Margarita, whose belief in me never faltered, and my brother Juan, whose support was constant. I will not list everyone in my family whose support has also meant more than I can express, but I trust you know who you are. I must also acknowledge the debt I owe my childhood friends from Córdoba and my adulthood friends from Buenos Aires. Their friendship has been a constant reminder of what ultimately matters in life. I save my final acknowledgment for Adrian, for his love, unconditional support, and invaluable wisdom across all these years, without which I would never have managed to turn this manuscript into a book.

Introduction

Tort Law Punishes

The depiction of punitive damages as "a monstrous heresy" that has deformed the law of torts since their very introduction set from that very moment the tone of the theoretical inquiry on the place of punishment in private law. The tension then instilled and the theoretically motivated recoil against punitive damages has long made many tort scholars and tort theorists across jurisdictions reluctant to sound out plausible theoretical groundings for the place of punishment in tort law. As a result, scholarly attention has largely focused on the anomalous, exceptional, and foreign nature of punitive damages in torts. Many scholars have defended the theoretical inconsistency of punitive damages with tort theory more forcefully, often to the point of calling for the institution's abolition (or limitation) in common law jurisdictions or outright rejecting it in civil law legal systems. Doubtlessly, this defensive tendency is not uniform across jurisdictions. Genuine scholarly efforts attempting to offer explanations of and justifications for punitive damages are already prolific and on the rise in the United States, are observable and steadily increasing in England (and other Commonwealth countries), and are gradually taking hold in civil law jurisdictions as well.

None of the arguments against punitive damages raised during this long history have as yet proven persuasive enough to accomplish their abolitionist aims. Quite the contrary, punitive damages, at least in practice, are here to stay. They are widely recognized in common law jurisdictions and are gradually gaining recognition in civil law systems. The United States is without doubt the paradigmatic common law jurisdiction where punitive damages are prominent in the law of torts, both in theory and practice. However, recent trends show that they are also gaining prominence in other theoretical and dogmatic domains, even in legal systems where their availability was originally constrained (such as in England) or historically resisted or denied (as in most civil law jurisdictions). For instance, there are now English law scholars who currently contemplate expanding the availability of punitive damages beyond the restrictive "categories test" and "forms of actions" constraints. They argue that the traditional, formalistic approach to the institution prevents the law from substantively responding to behaviors that are equally as reprehensible but fall outside the current restrictive categories. Similarly, in civil law legal systems, Argentina, Mexico, and Chile being the primary pioneers, punitive damages have been expressly recognized. In Europe, the initial attitude of outright rejection is also changing. Punitive damages have been included in the recent draft proposal for civil code reform in France and Italy, Spain, France, and Greece have started to demonstrate more permissiveness to the enforceability of foreign court judgments that include punitive damages. These developments have led to fresh conversations and scholarship on punitive damages in other European jurisdictions – even in Germany where punitive damages have been fiercely resisted and foreign punitive judgments have been to date considered contrary to domestic public policy and thereby unenforceable. As all these examples should have made evident, the punitive quest in private law has a dynamic quality in that it finds expression even in systems that expressly deny their validity. Most importantly, tort scholars, both from civil and common law legal traditions, widely acknowledge the pervasiveness of punitive components in tort law, having identified practices by which classic compensatory damages (such as increasing compensatory awards for pain and suffering) covertly or indirectly demonstrate responsiveness to punitive concerns in addition to the strictly compensatory award. Underlying this observation is dissatisfaction with the widespread practice in tort law of imposing poorly hidden yet openly denied punishment. Alongside this dissatisfaction is the conviction that, if tort law is truly condoning and imposing punishment, the practice must have reasoned, legal justification and be carried such that any punishment meted can be identified, treated, and controlled as such. Implicit in these observations is also the notion that regarding punishment in tort as some dependent, parasitic, or subsidiary component of compensation (i.e., when compensation is not enough) is misleading. Treating punishment as some add-on to compensation misses the point that punishment and compensation are distinctive responses to wrongdoing and demand independent and differentiated treatment.

In this overall, even global state of affairs, the time seems ripe for a wide-ranging, thorough, and meaningful quest for the theoretical and legal justification of punishment in tort law. For as much as punitive damages represent the paradigmatic example of a tort institution with salient retributive elements, scant scholarly attention has been devoted to justifying the persistence of the retributive dimension. The starting point for this project is my understanding that a genuinely scholarly attitude should willingly acknowledge the insufficiency of the classic theoretical account of tort law as an exclusively private rectificatory mechanism that is made evident by the pervasiveness of its punitive components. In addition, such an attitude also mandates a more profound discussion regarding the proper place for punishment in modern tort law, one that is neither constrained by the traditional treatment of punishment as an "anomaly" nor a corollary regulatory mechanism whose exclusive aim is "deterrence." As I aim to demonstrate over the course of this expedition, none of these scholarly approaches have as yet proven conducive in terms of elucidating the role of punishment in tort law (or in what way it is embedded in punitive damages). While many accounts for punishment in tort law compete for dominance, none clarifies its justifications in a way that properly distinguishes the punitive, compensatory, and deterrent dimensions of the law of torts. Here again, the time seems ripe to fill that gap.

This project takes seriously the observation that tort law punishes. It takes seriously the most compelling reconstruction of the widely accepted double "punish and deter" function of punitive damages, which posits that their purpose is "retribution and deterrence." *Torts and Retribution* adds a new dimension to the current narrative by fleshing out missing retributive ingredients in a robust alternative theory to the dominant deterrence accounts of punitive damages. Put another way, this project departs from the contention that, if retribution does have a place in tort law, then we should ask what that place is and ought to be. It is this simple yet highly controversial and long misunderstood idea that I aim to explore, to recast, and to ultimately vindicate. *Torts and Retribution* unchains the classic approach to punishment in torts from the exclusive and unilateral perspective of the defendant (wrongdoer perspective), taking a novel tack that purports full integration of the long-overlooked perspective of the victim of reprehensible wrongdoing who seeks the imposition of a punitive award through tort law (wrongdoer-victim perspective). As the title of this book suggests, the goal is reconciling torts and retribution in a manner that responds to both the relational significance of the role of the victim in expressing *condemnation* and to the importance of maintaining institutional modes of moral communication that convey *value affirmation* between the private parties involved in a tortious situation. My argument boils down to the claim that retribution in torts is relational. Following a cross-disciplinary approach that enriches tort law with insights from the literature on social cognition regarding victims' retributive motivations and from criminal law debates over the retributive justifications for the imposition of punishment, *Torts and Retribution* devises the novel notion of *Relational Retribution*. This notion comfortably suits both the interpersonal structure of tort law and the proactive role traditionally allocated to the victim in tort litigation. By recognizing the necessary interconnection between defendant and plaintiff, *Relational Retribution* offers a much more holistic account of retribution in torts, which recognizes the necessary interconnection between the reprehensible character of the defendant's conduct as deserving of punishment and the rich correlative retributive motivations of the tort victim who initially seeks the imposition of the monetary sanction (the punitive award) for purposes of *condemnation* and *value affirmation*.

Taking retribution in torts seriously is certainly daunting. It necessarily demands reassessment of widely accepted assumptions underlying the understanding of tort law as an exclusively private rectificatory mechanism. To begin, it requires questioning the classic formalistic depiction of victims as seeking restoration to their former state before the tort occurred, however imperfect that rectification may be. In its place, I depict the victims as seeking richer, textured, and value-laden responses that also capture the significance of the wrongdoing in a way that communicates the situated meaning of the impact of reprehensible wrongs on them and their complex motivations for resorting to tort law and its procedure for private redress. My reading of the tort victim feeds on insights from social psychology and social sciences into the true motives that drive people to punish reprehensible wrongdoing as well as from the "reactive attitudes" distinctively involved in holding others morally accountable that are discussed in moral philosophy. These findings elicit difficult questions on the desirability of making room for intuitive-emotive reactions to wrongdoing in the classic rationalistic mold of legal reasoning. They also invite doubt over the widespread view that victims' motivations to sue, particularly their punitive or retributive motivations, are a suspiciously subjective factor that tort law ought not consider given their proximity to a desire for private revenge or retaliation, both of which are considered morally objectionable bases for a normative justification for punitive damages. Most controversially, the research defies the supposed monopoly of the state in administering and imposing punishment through criminal law and procedure. As I should have expected, I myself have had to struggle to square the theoretical and empirical sources with my own understanding and legal training. On the other hand, I do understand the resistance I encountered to my willingness to push the retributive quest further and offer alternative readings of widespread assumptions that I find more persuasive. It has been a long journey. Hopefully, readers looking to engage in a fresh conversation on the topic will appreciate this work, while those less persuaded by the new reading will find among the classic and contemporary works surveyed resources that help them reinforce their position or perhaps even improve it.

◊ ◊ ◊

A few clarifications on scope, terminology, and methodology are in order. I focus exclusively on punitive damages because they represent the paradigmatic punitive institution in torts that primarily responds to retributive concerns. However, this does not mean that the question regarding the place of punishment in tort law should be exclusively confined to punitive damages. Indeed, some tort law scholars have recently argued that a range of other remedies (for instance, general damages awarded for defamation, the relaxation of the remoteness of damage rule where the wrongful behavior is deliberate, accounts of profits, among others), even if covertly or informally, also manifest a concern with punishment in torts. These are insightful claims that certainly deserve attention, but, since they do not directly concern retribution, at least not in the relational terms in which retribution is reconstructed in this book, I opted to maintain my original focus on punitive damages.

Because punitive damages are sought against individuals and corporations alike, I contend that assessing retribution in the mass-market setting becomes relevant in the enterprise of understanding the ultimate justification for punitive responses in the product liability context. I am aware that many tort scholars, mostly from outside the United States, resist the idea of categorizing product liability as tort law. However plausible this objection may or may not be, it does not undermine my argument. My aim is to elucidate the retributive rationale of punitive responses to reprehensible wrongdoing whether the defendant's behavior is exercised as an individual or as an individual acting collectively (e.g., a corporation). Ignoring retributive responses to egregious corporate wrongdoing that occurs within mass-market contexts would mean failing to account for relevant instances of wrongful behavior which causes significant harm to victims and leads to similar demands for a punitive response. Whether classified as tort law or not, product liability litigation against corporate defendants is similarly informed by questions of accountability, private redress, and relational justice. Those are the core values that ultimately matter.

I am also aware that punitive damages in product liability litigation have mostly been awarded in the United States (and, very recently, Argentina). However, I do not believe the relative isolation of the United States experience impairs my argument either. In the present global economy, reprehensible corporate behavior manifesting systematic mistreatment of consumers and reckless indifference for their rights and well-being is so commonplace that we cannot afford to ignore it. Paying judicious attention to the relevant debates on punitive damages in the American product liability context could contribute not only to a better understanding of the fundamental retributive rationale of the institution but also help identify the relevant markers in a global discussion of the proper place for punishment in mass markets beyond the jurisdiction of the United States. The significance of this timely conversation is reinforced by recent developments in Europe (and beyond), where active efforts to adapt the EU Product Liability Directive (1985) to the digital age are at the center of the debates over AI liability.

As regards terminology, because punitive damages are also known as exemplary damages in England and other Commonwealth jurisdictions, I use the terms "punitive damages" and "exemplary damages" interchangeably throughout the book. Moreover, because the most compelling reconstruction of the widely accepted "punishment and deterrence" double function of punitive damages is that they are aimed at "retribution and deterrence," I will use the terms "punishment" and "retribution" interchangeably as well. Last, since punitive damages operate in the context of reprehensible wrongdoing conveying some degree of mistreatment, indifference, open disregard, demeaning, or disrespect from the wrongdoer to another person, I often use the term "victim" to refer to the wronged party and "offender" to refer to the wrongdoer.

Methodologically speaking, the aim of the book is to determine the best theoretical grounding for punitive damages. I do not attempt to show that my reconstruction of the justification for retribution in torts best accommodates or fits the theoretical accounts already available in the tort law literature. Certainly, several aspects of

Relational Retribution fit the civil recourse theory understanding of tort law as relational wrongs with its underlying ideas of accountability, obtaining private redress, and responsive behavior following a wrong better than it fits the insistent focus of the corrective justice approach on allocation back or the exclusive emphasis of economic analysis on deterrence, but seeking the greatest degree of accommodation with these competing tort theories is not central to the book's aim.

The aim is to provide a more robust, sturdy theoretical grounding capable of guiding us when the question is what the proper place and justification for punishment in tort law is and ought to be across jurisdictions. Likewise, I do not intend to interpret, account for, criticize, or justify any particular doctrine, statute, precedent, or practice of awarding punitive damages. The goal is to provide solid theoretical grounding from which jurists and scholars from diverse jurisdictions and legal traditions might better conceptualize the retributive rationale operative in tort law, independently of the particularities and actual shape of the practices of awarding punitive damages in their legal community. For that reason, I cite statutes, case law, restatements of the law, and other relevant legal materials on punitive damages in many different legal systems only with the purpose of illustrating, discussing, challenging, developing, and advancing the arguments that this book presents. Ultimately, the point is that jurisdictions across the world will benefit from learning from each other and, most importantly, from a robust theoretical retributive framework that better informs domestic discussions on whether to adopt punitive damages (and how) or whether to improve their current application and institutional design going forward (and how).

While the book does predominantly rely on references to Anglo-American case law and scholarship, this reliance is simply explained by the historically much more widespread and diverse nature of the practice of awarding punitive damages in that tradition (i.e., they are generally available in a broad range of cases, from product liability to privacy torts to sexual harassment lawsuits, among many others) as compared to other common law jurisdictions (such as England, where the availability of punitive damages is tightly restricted to certain categories of torts). Two factors in particular have created an environment that has given rise to heated debate and rich discussions on the punitive institution, ultimately fueling the salience of punitive damages as a central feature of Anglo-American tort law. First is the decades-long push for tort reform in the United States, which has habitually accused punitive damages as a tort institution "out of control" (i.e., one that has become excessively unpredictable and produced exorbitant awards, and was therefore in need of reform). This factor is compounded by the influence of legal realism and, particularly, the flourishing of law and economics accounts of tort law that situated the theoretical debate over punitive damages' rationale in dominant terms of efficient deterrence. Additionally, the book's predominant engagement with Anglo-American sources reflects the preponderant influence of the Anglo-American experience and scholarly debates on the topic in most civil law legal traditions that have either recently introduced punitive damages or are currently debating whether to do so. The review and assessment of the existing punitive damages practice and scholarship in the most representative jurisdictions will provide a valuable resource not only to those seeking an in-depth understanding of the common law practice and its shortcomings but also to legal scholars, practitioners, lawmakers, and judges in countries outside the common law tradition in various stages of considering the adoption of punitive damages within their legal systems.

◊ ◊ ◊

In the remainder of this Introduction, I preview the central themes of the book to provide readers with a sense of its overall approach and what to expect. To that end, I highlight the core ideas, some substantive, others methodological, that underpin the foundations of the theoretical retributive framework that I explore, introduce, develop, and defend throughout the book.

PERSISTENT QUESTIONS

Punitive damages have long been considered a complex remedial institution that stands somewhere between the civil and the criminal law or – to put it more precisely – an institution oriented toward punition within a private-law context. Its focus on punishment is in fact what leads to the most perplexing puzzles associated with it. Although awarded as damages for harm done to a plaintiff by a defendant in a private lawsuit, the purpose of such awards in most jurisdictions is explicitly conceived as punitive in nature and therefore noncompensatory. Nevertheless, because the gravamen behind such damage awards is considered civil, the procedural safeguards of the criminal law (such as proof "beyond a reasonable doubt" of responsibility and prohibitions against double jeopardy, excessive fines, and compulsory self-incrimination) are not generally held to apply. The mix of criminal and civil law objectives and effects ensures that controversy will always surround the institution.

From a theoretical standpoint, the recurrent problem is whether there exists any normative space for punishment within a civil action or if punishment should be reserved for the public-law realms of either criminal or administrative and regulatory law. The notion that private law remedies, reflecting the underlying logic of civil claims, are to be compensatory and nonpunitive is so well established that it may be seen as the core distinction between public and private law. The evident tension created by this dual aspect of punitive damages leads to, at least, two fundamental questions: (1) What place, if any, do punitive damages have in the law of tort? And, if they do have a place in tort law, (2) should they be subject to differentiated treatment in virtue of their hybrid nature? The threat that punitive elements in tort law pose to the long-standing distinction between public and private law is so powerful that tort theorists have generally responded with arguments that in one way or another can be seen as an attempt to circumvent the fundamental punitive quest. Some reject punishment as an anomaly to be tolerated or ignored; others force it into tort law's compensatory framework. Still others equivocate punishment with deterrence or offer a refashioning of the victims' right to demand punishment as a legal power for private redress. These reactions from tort theorists to the question of punishment largely explain the scarcity of theoretical reflection on the place of retribution in tort law. In fact, the scholars who follow these approaches have shown very little interest in developing the retributive dimension of tort law because the notion of just retribution is either inconsistent with the notion of justice in the framework they propose or because they are indifferent to the matter, for the questions that preoccupy them would not enrich from its development. Only recently has more effort been made to provide justifications for the practice of awarding punitive damages that evoke some notion of retribution, but only in highly qualified manners that do not convincedly advance a thorough retributive rationale of the institution. By taking the punitive quest seriously, this book undertakes the long-overdue enterprise of building a robust theoretical grounding for the retributive dimension of tort law embedded in punitive damages.

Besides the strange mix of civil and criminal law objectives and effects that operate in punitive damages, a second distinctive aspect, which also raises important challenges for theorists, is related to the double function served by the institution, that of "punishment and deterrence." All legal actors seem to understand punitive damages as an award that goes beyond compensation for the actual harm inflicted both in order to punish defendants and deter them (and others) from engaging in similar misconduct in the future. In a notable show of consensus, the scholars, lawyers, and judges all openly agree: punitive damages both "punish and deter." Despite the near unanimity of this understanding of the double purpose of punitive damages – punishment and deterrence – what legal actors and scholars specifically mean when they refer to either punishment or deterrence is ambiguous. Indeed, the duality of the concept that the label "punishment and deterrence" is meant to capture is often used to defend conflicting views on punitive damages. Many, if not most, scholars fail to recognize the tension between and under-specification of the most common explanations.

For instance, punishment can be plausibly thought of as retribution. Yet this notion is sufficiently abstract to accommodate quite varied conceptions, such as private retribution (where the relevant wrong is that done to an individual plaintiff seeking vindication of her rights) or public retribution (where the focus is on a wrong caused to society in general). As for the scholars who hold deterrence to be the primary goal of punitive damages, this approach also leaves room for divergent understandings, for deterrence too can be specific, general, or both (depending on whether the aim is dissuading the particular defendant from reoffending, or dissuading others from engaging in similar tortious conduct by way of example or warning). Deterrence can also be complete or optimal, depending on whether the intent is to discourage completely or to a certain degree the defendant's engagement in a specific activity or behavior. Because of the special role that the double function plays in the debates over punitive damages, it is tempting to conceptualize the competition for predominance of different theories as an interpretive dispute – one that revolves around the different possible conceptions of punishment and deterrence. Accordingly, each author could be understood as arguing for the particular interpretation of "punish and deter" that, in her view, best captures and justifies the practice of awarding punitive damages. This interpretation would then provide the most solid foundation on the basis of which proposals for particular adjustments to regulate the practice of punitive damage awards would be oriented.

That both functions are to some extent interconnected does not mean that one of the functions cannot be understood as the core of the institution to the detriment of the other. It could be the case that punishment is seen as a secondary or as a necessary attribute of deterrence, or that deterrence is a secondary, necessary effect of punishment. The large and sophisticated body of scholarship on the deterrence aspect of punitive damages has not yet been matched by a similarly thorough account of its dominant retributive dimension. By taking seriously the most compelling reconstruction of the widely accepted double "punish and deter" function of punitive damages, which posits that their purpose is "retribution and deterrence," this book argues that stripping punitive damages of their retributivist content would deprive them of a fundamental element. The interconnectedness of retribution and deterrence makes the relevant question not whether to embrace "retribution" or "deterrence" but instead examining the interplay between the two (i.e., how "retribution" and "deterrence" interact). Following this approach, the book identifies the types of deterrence that are compatible with *Relational Retribution*.

VALUING THE VICTIM'S PERSPECTIVE

Torts and Retribution is meant to invite readers to rethink and resignify the role of the private actor in the articulation of tort law and the tort process. Taking retribution seriously means shifting the attention from the classic formal, utterly abstract depiction of the victim in a tortious situation as seeking individual restoration in order to comprehend a much more substantive, contextual, and textured account of what motivates victims to assume the considerable cost, in both financial and personal terms, of pursuing a punitive response to the wrongdoing they suffered. The foundation for the reconstruction I propose is a richly complex understanding of tort victims who hold dear values that impinge on their own sense of self-worth as well as the other-regarding norms they believe should be enforced in their political community. This understanding of the tort victim is responsive to the moral significance of the wrongdoing for the victim and to the importance that is attributed to the values (or dignitary interests) that the defendant's reprehensible behavior encroached or invaded. Ultimately, this approach argues for abandoning the nearly exclusive and unilateral focus on the reprehensibility of the defendant's behavior and the notion of deservedness or "just deserts" for the imposition of a monetary sanction. Instead, it proposes a relational approach to retribution which is able to better connect the defendant and victim in a more holistic fashion and better capture the correlative significance of the victim's motivations to punish reprehensible wrongdoing. Once we delve more deeply into the victim's retributive motivations and establish their relational dimension, retribution solely conceived as "just desert" no longer seems an accurate representation of what tort victims seek to achieve by filing a punitive lawsuit. Instead, it turns out that alternative motives for retribution such as "denunciation" and "value affirmation" often better explain the victim's perspective. In this book, I develop this insight by exploring, identifying, and refining the expressive content of *Relational Retribution* in torts as an institutional mode of moral communication between the private parties. Underlying the analysis is the idea that, assuming we care about individuals' ability to engage meaningfully with their peers and community, we should make sure legitimate, official channels for expression are available to them. Tort lawsuits provide in an important sense a means for developing and articulating collective standards of conduct. Punitive damages themselves are a meaning-producing institution that embraces the values embodied in the condemnatory legal message that the wrongdoer is not somehow worth more than the victim and is not entitled to treat the victim in a manner that diminishes her value.

THE VICTIM'S (LEGAL) POWER TO BE PUNITIVE

Any book that challenges the prevailing view that punishment exclusively pertains to the state's monopoly over coercion that is embodied in the domestic context by the criminal law and procedure might understandably assume a position of resistance. I ask those prone to such a stance to consider the contention that the initial uneasiness with this project mainly stems from the particular framing of the public–private divide by tort scholars themselves. The objection most often raised is that punitive damages represent a dangerous privatization of the state's power to punish. This objection is predicated on an understanding that one of the greatest accomplishments of the modern state is the massive reduction in violence that it brought to everyday life. This triumph was partly if not largely achieved through the prohibition and prosecution of various forms of private violence (duels, honor killings, etc.). The theoretical foundation for the prohibition of those forms of violence was the principle barring individual citizens, following the universalist Enlightenment principles that inspired the French and American Revolutions, from punishing reprehensible wrongdoing themselves. Ever since, embracing private revenge has been anathema in our societies, however accepted and even condoned in exceptional circumstances. Still, the clear-cut eighteenth-century divide between public and private law is not only simplistic but, now at least, largely unconvincing. No one denies that citizens should not enjoy the power to punish directly other citizens or that the desire for vengeance is a normatively inappropriate basis for legal action. The question for or against punishment in tort law, however, is quite different. It is not about whose business it is to exact punishment on others. It is about the relative virtues and vices of channeling punishment through privately controlled yet judicially regulated processes (tort law) or through publicly controlled judicial processes (criminal law). When framed this way, those initial objections start to fade, for the role of the state in the former is patent. Following this approach, this book explores the meaning and significance of the victim's power to demand punishment through tort law and what it means and what it takes to seek the imposition of punishment through the articulation of the tort judicial processes.

PLURALITY OF COMPETING VALUES

Tort law gives concrete expression to important values in our society. The tort process, where judgments weighing rights and responsibility are central, is where accountability is assigned, harms are aired, and collective standards of conduct and levels of care are enforced, refined, challenged, and redefined as our societies evolve. As a community, we should put some focus on how tort law and its procedure, in addition to providing ex post remedies, might help us to proactively contribute to the process of constructing other-regarding meaning in our society by voicing the values and beliefs that inform our understanding of what we owe to each other as members of the same community; by voicing our collective intuitions regarding risk, trust, and truth that reflect the nature and depth of our interpersonal relationships with one another. The tort process provides a channel for private individuals to appeal to the other-regarding values they esteem of great social importance in a judicial forum for which other legitimate, effective avenues are extremely scarce. For decades now, jurisdictions have, for different reasons, increasingly sought recourse from alternative mechanisms of dispute resolution that depersonalize the tort victim. Social compensation systems and settlement processes have been devised that operate on a bureaucratic model that minimizes consideration of the right to redress in order to expedite compensation and the adjudication process. Adjudication is also moved outside the courts with the rise of what are called "settlement mills," private entities who promise quick awards by eagerly pursuing out-of-court settlements. In the face of these (and other) developments, we ought to focus more than ever on better understanding the role of the tort victim and the courts in shaping tort law. Tort victims are specially situated to convey the moral significance and impact of the defendant's wrongful behavior on their lives and expose the underlying social and cultural implications of the wrongdoing. Preserving tort law's sensitivity to the rich moral insights that tort victims provide when they articulate the tort process is worthwhile, I will argue. Following this line of thinking, this book favors approaches to tort law that are sensitive to the plurality of the competing values involved in the articulation of tort law and the tort process rather than deducing implications from the grand theories of tort law that attempt to explain and justify it under a single unifying principle. It is my view that these theoretical reconstructions sacrifice too much for the sake of coherence, elegance, and simplicity. In doing that they lose touch with the richness of the complexity, fluidity, and diversity that characterize tort law and the tort victims who resort to it for distinct responses to a variety of different instances of tortious wrongdoing.

A CROSS-DISCIPLINARY APPROACH

I undertake the enterprise of elaborating a theoretical retributive grounding of punitive damages in torts by disentangling two interrelated but nonetheless different aspects that require separate evaluation. On one hand is (1) the victim's retributive motivations for punishment; on the other, (2) the actual justifications for the imposition of punishment on the wrongdoer. The latter has understandably been predominantly studied by criminal law theorists. The former has been mostly taken up by social psychologists interested in the influence of lay retributive intuitions on judgment and decision-making and by moral philosophers interested in the "reactive attitudes" that drive us to hold others morally accountable for their actions. The ultimate proposal is that exploring and integrating the variety of insights and perspectives on punishment afforded by those disciplines does a service to tort law by opening new, constructive dimensions from which tort law's retributive facet can be grasped. It is my belief that there is much to be gained from this approach – and that it is one that has not been fully explored in the tort law literature.

On one side, reaching out to criminal law theorists for insights on retribution recognizes a certain fluidity between crimes and torts that releases the tight-fisted tension of the dogmatic boundary between private law and public law. A broad search for retributive motivations beyond the confines of private law cases reveals that the retributive rationale of punishment has been predominantly discussed by criminal law scholars in the particular context of the criminal law and procedure. Unless the topic has been staked off for exclusive use by criminal law theorists, what prevents tort scholars from devising a sound retributive rationale for tort law on the basis of their work? In this sense, the idea of cross-disciplinarity that I embrace does not take the form of a "transplant" from the criminal law to tort law. Rather, I ask how the debates over punitive damages in tort law might benefit from the insights on retribution that have long been discussed and developed in the criminal law context and if they might be recast within the particularities of the tort context. The underlying belief that inspires this approach is the suspicion that too often we, as ordinary citizens but also as lawyers, judges, and legal scholars, encounter long-standing assumptions that appear unquestionable. Too often, legal scholars treat long-standing assumptions as static and untouchable truths. That the right to exact punishment is exclusive to the criminal law is just one of them, however pervasive it is. This book invites all of us to rethink this assumption by examining the possibility that punishment has a proper place in tort law as well. Might there be a way to accommodate punitive damages such that any democratic legal system or jurisdiction need not cower before the justification for imposing sanctions for reprehensible misbehavior that, although not strictly criminal, merits condemnation? This interdisciplinary approach also invites tort and criminal law scholars to engage in a joint conversation on the alternative forms of punishment in our societies that fall outside the realm of the criminal law and the criminal procedure.

On the other side, the insights provided by the social sciences on laypeople's retributive motivations for punishment and the literature on "reactive attitudes" afford a new reading of another long-standing assumption: that emotive-intuitive reasoning opposes rationalistic legal reasoning in some irreconcilably dichotomous relation. I contend that if retribution plays a significant role in the lay understanding of punishment, before repressing or rejecting emotive-intuitive reactions to instances of reprehensible wrongdoing, we should first strive to better analyze, break down, and understand them. Findings from the fields of cognitive and social psychology on the retributive motivations that shape victims' punitive reactions to reprehensible wrongdoing reveal the richness of the moral insights that they express with regard to the proper treatment that members of a community owe to each other in particular circumstances of wrongdoing. These findings bring to light the underlying values that motivate the retributive reactions of the victims of reprehensible wrongdoing. They offer valuable insight into two particularly powerful cognitive motivations, moral outrage and betrayal aversion, for the motivation to punish those who wrong us in a reprehensible manner. These dynamics form a logic and structure that distinguishes them, in particular circumstances, from irrational (senseless) or excessively emotional (rash or unthinking) reactions, and, in such circumstances, tort law should afford them complementary validity. Ultimately, these insights from the social sciences offer a new constructive space for rethinking punishment and deterrence in alignment with public intuitions of justice and as such make a valuable contribution to the debates over the retributive dimension of tort law.

GREATER CONTEXTUAL SENSITIVITY

Torts and Retribution does not content itself with spotlighting the underappreciated retributive dimension of tort law alone. It further argues that because punitive damages are sought against individuals and corporations alike, assessing the specific pathway of the retributive motivations in each context of wrongdoing leads to a better understanding of what ultimately motivates people to seek them. In developing this approach, *Torts and Retribution* untangles retributive motivations that seek to address individual invasions of dignitary interests from those that respond to violations of societal trust. It maps these two kinds of retributive motivations onto egregious wrongdoing that occurs, respectively, within interpersonal contexts and within mass market contexts. The difference implies that the substantive content of our retributive motivations toward individuals or corporations is affected by contextual factors in distinctive ways. Asymmetrical access to information, structural power dynamics, aggregate decision-making processes, and large-scale impact on society are some of the central factors in the context where corporate wrongdoing usually occurs. Conversely, interpersonal interaction with another individual and conduct directed toward a specific person are typically the prime factors in the context of wrongdoing that involves individual value-diminishing behavior by the wrongdoer toward the victim. Identifying the relevant characteristics in the different contexts of wrongdoing where punitive damages are sought will help us elucidate how victims' punitive responses to reprehensible wrongdoing are constructed differently when directed toward corporations or toward individual human agents. Ultimately, this approach highlights the relevance of conceptually distinguishing among distinct types of legal actors (the natural versus legal nature of the wrongdoer) and distinct manners through which individuals and legal entities typically engage in reprehensible tortious behavior (the interpersonal versus impersonal nature of the wrongdoing), bringing to light a contextual and layered reconstruction of tort victims' retributive motivations that remains unexplored in the tort law literature.

THE SIGNIFICANCE OF THE EXCEPTIONAL

Another understandable source of skepticism would be the primary focus of this project on a small fraction of tort cases, which are, almost by definition, exceptional. Here again, I take the point. Yet I am not sure we should attach less significance to the relatively scarce "exceptional" cases than to most "regular" cases. Why are quantity and regularity so important for legal theory? Understanding tort law representativeness in solely quantitative terms is misguiding in that it diverts our attention from the much scarcer yet more fundamental torts involving reprehensible violations of substantive interests of great social significance. These (fortunately) rare instances of gross disregard do not fall neatly into criminal offenses but do demand an institutional response that matches the seriousness of the behavior, recognizes the significance of the interests invaded, and has the potential to trigger meaningful conversations over what we as members of the same political community understand the proper norms should be for the regard of others. Overlooking the importance of this relatively slim category of tortious cases just because there are less of them risks mistaking the true value and actual role of tort law and tort victims in our society. Whether or not *Relational Retribution* takes hold as a guiding principle for rethinking the theory behind our "anomalous" embrace of punitive damages, I hope this book will persuade skeptics that we should be more open to the possibility that the most compelling reasons to embrace tort law at all are perhaps found in those scarce exceptional cases. *Torts and Retribution* invites us to look at tort law more qualitatively rather than quantitatively.

LOOKING AHEAD: PRODUCT LIABILITY AND NEW TECHNOLOGIES

News of significant harms caused by reckless corporations that should have done better are unfortunately nothing new. Headline examples cover a wide range of industries, from tobacco companies engaging in orchestrated deception for decades to car manufacturers that market vehicles with fatal mechanical defects, breast implants made using adulterated silicone, pharmaceutical companies that hide the carcinogenic effects of their drugs or the addictiveness of opioids, and on down the line. Meanwhile, rapidly evolving technologies are bringing novel safety concerns surrounding artificial intelligence (AI). A recent example is self-driving cars that fail to avoid fatal, preventable accidents. Another involves the possibility that AI-enabled robotic surgical tools could cause avoidable harm to patients. At the same time, consumers are growing more aware of – and preoccupied with – their limited access to information about the products they consume, which is also related to the exponential rise in risk of significant harm due to new technologies.

Product liability regimes have predominantly been understood as a protective mechanism enabling consumers to obtain ex post private redress for harm caused by a defective product. By exploring the place of retribution in the mass market context, this book offers instead a broader, novel, and interdisciplinary understanding of product liability as a complementary and legitimate avenue for consumers to participate in the construction of the meaning of (un)acceptable risk in our society, which goes beyond the sole aim of seeking ex post redress. It offers a reading of product liability that acknowledges the significance and richness of the consumer's perspective and relevant role in bringing the punitive lawsuit. Under this new light, product liability litigation provides a channel for private individuals to express substantive values of great importance in a judicial forum for which few alternative legitimate or effective avenues exist. The underlying idea is that, in order to avoid becoming a society that rejects utter reliance on experts, we should find an official forum for expert and layperson understandings of risk to speak to each other and interact. This would allow lay people to have a voice in the construction of the significance of risk in our society and foment a culture in which experts identify with the people they serve. This proposal does not diminish the importance of encouraging regulatory and legislative activities to be more responsive to the insights and convictions of laypersons but acknowledges that the complementary avenue for participation provided by private tort litigation has its own distinctive advantages.

This book thus invites us not only to rethink the proper place and scope of punitive damages in product liability litigation but also, and perhaps more importantly, to initiate a fresh discussion about product liability regimes that might influence the behavior of market actors such that societal trust in experts grows stronger. To take a single example, such a discussion could lead to a greater definition of product defectiveness and proper standards of liability for product design defects that are responsive to the immediate challenges of the evolving risks posed by AI to consumer safety.

PART I

The Place of Punishment in Torts

OVERVIEW

Imagine the following scenarios. A former client maliciously defames you by making false allegations about your professional competence and personal character for more than a year, damaging your professional credibility and impairing your career prospects. Or a work colleague deliberately exposes intimate aspects of a relationship that you would rather have kept private in order to embarrass you and diminish your standing among your peers and colleagues, which negatively affects your interpersonal relationships with them as well as your work environment and opportunities for promotion. Last, what if the wrongdoer is not an individual person but a collective entity? Say the manufacturer of your car callously betrays your expectation of safety by knowingly marketing a vehicle with a defective ignition switch, causing the motor to stall in traffic without functioning airbags, ultimately leading to a road accident where you suffer devastating injuries, or the manufacturer of your favorite health-care products deliberately markets a talc-based powder containing asbestos, which eventually causes you to develop ovarian cancer. Or maybe your insurance company's corporate policy is to reflexively deny, in bad faith, requests for costly chemotherapy treatment, which allows your cancer to advance to the point of fatal metastasis while you struggle with the bureaucratic hurdles. In each of these scenarios, as in countless other imaginable and, unfortunately, actual ones that occur day in and day out, which responses available through the legal system properly address the harm you have suffered? In particular, what type of recourse should tort law afford the victims of these wrongs as against those who have wronged them?

In the earlier situations and many others, the perceived need for a rectificatory response for the harm suffered (i.e., compensatory damages) frequently coexists with the perceived need for a condemnatory response to the reprehensible behavior (e.g., punitive damages). Reprehensible wrongs that affect victims' interests, such as their individual dignity, physical integrity, or individual autonomy, do not only involve acts of rectification; instead, reprehensible wrongs also require a response that helps victims to denounce the gravity of the disregard with which those interests were infringed and demand some reaffirmation of their own self-worth, including reaffirmation of other-regarding values in society. In each of the earlier cases, tort victims act upon a complex, value-laden set of reasons that drive them to request not only compensation for their injuries; rather, tort victims also (and perhaps primarily) seek a condemnatory response capable of incorporating the meaning and significance of having been wronged in a reprehensible fashion by the malicious client, the mean colleague, or the callous corporation. To put it more succinctly, in the context of egregious wrongdoing, tort law responses often go beyond rectification, demanding condemnation as well.

To begin disentangling the punitive quest, Part I sets the stage by reassessing the place of punishment in torts across common law and civil law jurisdictions. Chapter 1 begins by acknowledging the role of punitive damages as the paradigmatic proof of punishment's place in the law of torts. After a brief overview of current global punitive damages practices, one which demonstrates that the debates over the place of punishment in tort law are no longer only of interest to common law scholars, Chapter 1 offers a detailed description of the understanding, scholarly treatment, and judicial availability of punitive damages in two major common law jurisdictions (England and the United States) and in civil law legal traditions (in particular, Latin America and Continental Europe). In mapping the unique contours and idiosyncratic features of the scholarly debates and judicial availability of punitive damages of those jurisdictions, the chapter identifies a common pattern that begs further inquiry: In most jurisdictions, the tendency is to frame the debate on the place of punishment in tort law such that, in one way or another, attempts are made to circumvent the fundamental retributive quest instead of addressing it head-on.

From the arguments that "smuggle" punitive damages using other civil law institutions, Chapter 2 takes up the historical resistance from tort theorists to the very idea of punishment in tort law. The perceived threat of punitive elements in tort law to the long-standing distinction between private and public law is so powerful that tort theorists have generally responded by resisting punitive awards as an anomaly. They have corseted punishment within tort law's rectificatory framework, equated punishment with deterrence, and refashion the victim's right to be punitive as a formal legal power for private redress. Chapter 2 takes a close look at these guarded reactions from tort theorists to the question of punishment and how they explain not only the scarcity of theoretical reflection on the place of retribution in tort law but, additionally, that those theoretical reconstructions are unsuitable for a productive delineation and justification of the punitive, compensatory, and deterrent dimensions of the law of torts. The chapter ultimately argues that this gap in tort theory should be addressed by seeking a place for punishment in tort law that is neither constrained by the traditional treatment of punishment as an "anomaly," as "compensation," nor as a corollary regulatory mechanism whose exclusive aim is "deterrence."

1

Punishment Is Part of Tort Law

Punitive damages represent the paradigmatic manifestation that punishment has a place in the law of torts.[1] They are firmly entrenched in most common law jurisdictions where they have been granted for centuries.[2] In recent decades, punitive damages have been the object of debates in civil law jurisdictions as well – particularly, although not exclusively, in Latin America and Continental Europe.[3] Indeed, few private law institutions arising from the common law tradition have fascinated civil law scholars as much as punitive damages. Enticed by the Anglo-American practice of awarding punitive damages, scholars of tort law, consumer law, antitrust law, intellectual property law, and antidiscrimination law have all actively discussed introducing the common law institution in civil law legal systems. As a result, punitive damages have recently been incorporated into the Consumer Protection Statutes of Argentina (2008)[4] and Chile (2019).[5] They were included in draft proposals for major civil code reform initiatives in

1 For the argument that various other species of damages are also concerned with punishment, see P. Cane, *The Anatomy of Tort Law* (Hart Publishing, 1997), pp. 116–19; J. Goudkamp and E. Katsampouka, "Punitive Damages and the Place of Punishment in Private Law" (2021) 84 *Modern Law Review* 1257, 1258. However, see J. Murphy, "Anomalies in Tort Law: A Cause for Concern?" (2023) 86 *Modern Law Review* 872, 886–91 (casting doubt on those claims).

2 For instance, Australia, Canada, New Zealand, United Kingdom (except for Scotland), and United States provide for punitive damages in their respective legal systems.

3 For debates on punitive damages in other civil law jurisdictions, see C. Vanleenhove and L. Meurkens (eds.), *The Recognition and Enforcement of Punitive Damages Judgments across the Globe: Insights from Various Continents* (Eleven International Publishing, 2023).

4 Consumer Protection Act 2008 (Argentina), No. 26.361, arts. 52 bis and 8 bis.

5 Consumer Protection Act 2018 (Chile), No. 21.081, art. 53(c) (note that they are not called "punitive damages" which gives room for alternative interpretations. Indeed, some scholars have suggested that they are more similar to the English "aggravated damages" than to "punitive damages."). For this stance, see S. Gamonal Contreras and A. Pino Emhart, "The Role of Human Dignity in Private Law: An Interpretation from the Concept of Dignity as Status" (2022) 43 *Revista de Derecho Privado* 45, 60.

Argentina (2015)[6] and France (2017)[7] and were in effect introduced in China's new Code of Civil Law (2021).[8] Mexico recently introduced them through a landmark Supreme Court decision (2014),[9] while the Brazilian Superior Court of Justice ruled, for the very first time, that a foreign court's decision awarding punitive damages should not be considered, per se, contrary to domestic public policy and thereby unenforceable (2022).[10] Furthermore, the Italian Court of Cassation also recently recognized them as enforceable (2017),[11] reversing its previous understanding that punitive damages granted by foreign courts were against the Italian "public order."[12] From these developments, it can be inferred that the overall attitude and sentiment toward the proper place for punishment in private law is a dynamic, evolving feature of most civil law jurisdictions.[13] Moreover, overtly punitive civil sanctions such as penalty clauses as well as covertly punitive sanctions in nonpecuniary damages awards have been widely

6 Civil Code Reform Project 2015 (Argentina), art. 1713.

7 The proposal would introduce a form of civil punishment (amende civile) in the Code Civile for profit-seeking wrongs (faute lucrative) (Project de Réforme du Droit de la Responsabilité Civile 2017, art. 1266-1). For a status update, see J. Knetsch, "France" (2022) 11 *European Tort Law Yearbook* 174. For the argument that the proposed amende civile is seen as a middle ground between punitive and gain-based damages, see S. Rowan, "Punishment and Private Law: Some Comparative Observations," in E. Bant, W. Courtney, J. Goudkamp and J. M. Paterson (eds.), *Punishment and Private Law* (Hart Publishing, 2021), p. 71.

8 Civil Code (China), arts. 179, 1185, 1207, 1232.

9 SCJN, Primera Sala, Amparo Directo 30/2013, February 26, 2014.

10 STJ HDE 586/CA, Min. Raul Araújo, May 16, 2022, *Apotex* v. *Kalinka*.

11 Corte di Cassazione [Cass] July 5, 2017, N° 16601, AXO *Sport SpA* v. NOSA *Inc*. This is also the current position in Spain, France, and Greece.

12 Until 2017, the prevailing criteria in Italy was established in Corte di Cassazione [Cass] January 19, 2007, No. 1183. Note that the highest courts of other European countries have generally refused to enforce foreign judgments (particularly American ones) imposing punitive damages on defendants because of their incompatibility with "public order." Notable examples are: Germany, BGH (Bundesgerichtshof), June 4, 1992, case IX ZR 149/91, BGHZ (Entscheidungen des Bundesgerichtshofs in Zivilsachen) 118, 312; and the Netherlands, Gerechtshof's-Hertogenbosch August 31, 2021, ECLI:NL:RBOBR:2019:4987, nos. 3.7.3–3.7.5. Similarly, outside Europe, the Supreme Court of Japan has recently ruled that punitive damages are incompatible with Japanese public policy (*Hondaya Inc.*, May 25, 2021, *Minshū*, 75(6), 2022, 2935). But see M. G. Martínez Alles, "Punitive Damages in Argentina and Mexico: Rethinking the Scope of the Public Policy Exception," in C. Vanleenhove and L. Meurkens (eds.), *The Recognition and Enforcement of Punitive Damages Judgments across the Globe: Insights from Various Continents* (Eleven International Publishing, 2023), p. 132 (arguing that the approach to the classic "public policy exception" in cases of enforcement of foreign punitive judgments is shifting [particularly, in jurisdictions where punitive-like instruments, either overly or covertly, are recognized in their domestic tort law] from outright rejection as against the "public order" to a focus on questions of proportionality and excessiveness of the foreign punitive award).

13 Note that common law jurisdictions are not exempt. For instance, an ongoing discussion in English law questions the restrictiveness of the classic "categories test" originally introduced in *Rookes* v. *Barnard*, subsequently arguing for expansion in the scope of application of exemplary damages. I explore this scholarly trend in Section A (a).

acknowledged across many civil law jurisdictions[14] and, more recently, in common law jurisdictions as well.[15]

Certainly, widespread recognition of punitive damages in the common law of torts and more recent gradual recognition in civil law systems does not mean that they are uncontested. Quite the contrary, probably no area of the law of torts has generated as much controversy over the decades as that of punitive damages. Under both legal traditions, punitive damages have been persistently depicted as an "anomaly" or even as a "monstrous heresy" that introduces alien criminal law notions (from public law) into the law of torts (private law).[16] This stigma, which is closely related to the classic public–private divide, has been predominant in English legal reasoning and led Lord Devlin to devise the restricted "categories test" that persists to this day (and which, according to some English scholars, long posed an obstacle to expansion).[17] Similarly, the powerful threat to the fundamental distinction between private law (tort law) and public law (criminal law) has

[14] E. Büyüksagis, I. Ebert, D. Fairgrieve, R. C. Meurkens and F. Quarta, "Punitive Damages in Europe and Plea for the Recognition of Legal Pluralism" (2016) *European Business Law Review* 137, 157 (arguing, based upon scholarly work and case law from Germany, Italy, the Netherlands, France, and Switzerland, that "extra-compensatory damages are frequently applied by national judges, albeit not always in an overt manner, and that such a phenomenon should not be deemed a priori in conflict with the principles of European law."). For more references, see Section B.

[15] On this point, see Goudkamp and Katsampouka, "Punitive Damages and the Place of Punishment in Private Law," 1288–91.

[16] W. P. Keeton, D. B. Dobbs, R. E. Keeton and D. G. Owen, *Prosser and Keeton on Torts*, 5th ed. (West Publishing, 1984), p. 9 (the standard reaction of tort-law scholars to punishment is that "the ideas underlying the criminal law have invaded the field of torts."). For ancient judicial antipathy to punitive damages in English and American case law: "[punitive damages] confuse the civil and criminal functions of the law" and referring to the "anomaly inherent in exemplary damages": *Rookes* v. *Barnard* [1964] AC 1129, 1126–27 (Lord Devlin); "the function of the civil law which is to compensate with the function of the criminal law which is to inflict deterrent and punitive penalties": *Broome* v. *Cassell & Co Ltd* [1972] AC 1027, 1086 (Lord Reid); "the idea [of exemplary damages] is wrong. It is a monstrous heresy. It is an unsightly and unhealthy excrescence, deforming the symmetry and body of the law.": *Fay* v. *Parker* [1873] 53 NH 342, 382 (Foster J). Also, see Lord Scott's opinion in *Kuddus* v. *Chief Constable of Leicestershire Constabulary* [2001] UKHL 29; [2002] 2 AC 122 [95]: "an award of exemplary damages, the intention of which is not to compensate the victim of a wrong but to punish its perpetrator, is an anomaly."). For scholarly work along these lines, see C. Morris, "Punitive Damages in Tort Cases" (1993) 44 *Harvard Law Review* 1173, 1176 ("The doctrine [of punitive damages] is widely denounced as an 'anomaly'."); A. Beever, "The Structure of Aggravated and Exemplary Damages" (2003) 23 *Oxford Journal of Legal Studies* 87, 110 ("Exemplary damages [...] are logically an anomaly that should be expunged from the law."). But see Goudkamp and Katsampouka, "Punitive Damages and the Place of Punishment in Private Law," 1268–87 (challenging the anomaly stigma in English law). However, see Murphy, "Anomalies in Tort Law," 889 (casting doubt on Goudkamp's and Katsampouka's efforts "to show that exemplary damages are *not* anomalous within private law") (emphasis in the original).

[17] See generally J. Goudkamp and E. Katsampouka, "Form and Substance in the Law of Punitive Damages," in A. Robertson and J. Goudkamp (eds.), *Form and Substance in the Law of Obligations* (Hart Publishing, 2019), pp. 331–52 (arguing that Lord Devlin's real motive for establishing the "categories test" was his desire to restrict to the greatest possible extent a remedy that he considered anomalous).

dominated the debate on whether to introduce punitive damages among scholars in Europe and Latin America for decades to the present day.[18] In the United States, where the rise of legal realism helped to soften the public–private divide, the predominant legal reasoning behind the need of restrictions on punitive damages has been framed not in terms of "anomaly" but instead in terms of "reasonableness" and "proportionality" under the constitutional clause of due process.[19] This clause prohibits courts from employing standard tort procedures to award punitive damages that can only be justified on a regulatory rationale, since such an award would represent a sanction imposed without the due process of law.[20] This scholarly emphasis has been largely fueled by the prominent discussions over punitive damages awards of the early 1990s, when the United States Supreme Court engaged the constitutional grounds of this common law institution for the first time.[21] Since then, scholarly efforts in the United States to understand, reconstruct, reinterpret, and ultimately justify the practice of awarding punitive damages have been on the rise.[22]

Following these discussions, some tort scholars and policymakers argued for directly rejecting or abolishing punitive damages while others mounted concerted efforts to restrict the scope of their applicability and the size of their amounts.[23] Clearly, abolitionists have failed in their repeated attempts to eliminate punitive damages since they remain part of the common law of torts and the support for maintaining (or even expanding them) is considerable in most common law jurisdictions (even in England).[24] Similarly, fierce attempts to reject them outright

[18] See the scholarly works cited in Section B.

[19] See, for example, *State Farm Mut Auto Ins Co* v. *Campbell*, 538 US 408 (2003) 426 ("courts must ensure that the measure of punishment is both reasonable and proportionate to the amount of harm someone suffers"). Note, however, that in the mid nineteenth century, the anomaly argument (derived from the private–public law divide) was in fact the main objection invoked by Simon Greenleaf to categorically reject punitive damages. See S. Greenleaf, A *Treatise on the Law of Evidence*, 2nd ed. (Little and J. Brown, 1848), para. 253, p. 242 n2.

[20] For scholarly discussions on this point, see Section A (b).

[21] The three most important cases are: *BMW of North America Inc* v. *Gore*, 517 US 559 (1996); *State Farm Mut Auto Ins Co* v. *Campbell*, 538 US 408 (2003); *Philip Morris USA* v. *Williams*, 549 US 346 (2007).

[22] To clarify: I am not suggesting that tort scholars in other common law jurisdictions have not made efforts to meaningfully engaged with the institution; quite the contrary, my point is rather that scholarship along these lines is much scarcer outside of the United States.

[23] For scholarly examples of abolition, see Beever, "The Structure of Aggravated and Exemplary Damages," 87; W. K. Viscusi, "The Social Costs of Punitive Damages against Corporations in Environmental and Safety Torts" (1998) 87 *Georgetown Law Journal* 285 (arguing that abolishing punitive damages would improve social welfare). For a recent work arguing for limits on punitive damages, see B. J. McMichael and W. K. Viscusi, "Bringing Predictability to the Chaos of Punitive Damages" (2022) 54 *Arizona State Law Journal* 471. For an account of efforts to reduce corporate exposure to litigation in the United States, see M. Gilles, "'A Force Created': The U.S. Chamber of Commerce and the Politics of Corporate Immunity" (2023) 72 *DePaul Law Review* 139.

[24] On this point, see A. Burrows, "Reforming Exemplary Damages: Expansion or Abolition?" in P. Birks (ed.), *Wrongs and Remedies in the Twenty First Century* (Clarendon Press, 1996), p. 173 (arguing that

in civil law jurisdictions have also failed since, as mentioned earlier, punitive damages have been at the center of legal debates for decades and are gradually gaining recognition (either through revisions that introduce them in effect or, indirectly, through enforcement of foreign punitive judgments awards) in those legal traditions as well. Certainly, some civil law jurisdictions (e.g., Germany and The Netherlands) have historically maintained fierce resistance to punitive damages, yet commentators have repeatedly noted the presence of punitive elements in their domestic tort laws – observations that might, in the years to come, spark a change of posture in those jurisdictions.[25] Moreover, the conventional indictments of punitive damages as out of control, unpredictable and exorbitant, and counterproductive deterrents of socially desirable economic activity that impose disproportionate burdens on businesses have recently been challenged.[26] Empirical studies in the United States,[27] England,[28] and Australia[29] have demonstrated that punitive damages are in fact rarely awarded and that, far from exorbitant or out of control, they are for the most part uniform and moderate. Even though there is still disagreement regarding the question of overdeterrence, this empirical contention becomes less persuasive if punitive awards are both infrequent and moderate.

As global concerns over punitive damages in tort law are both undeniably persistent and divergent in common law and civil law jurisdictions, a closer look at the distinctive contours of the scholarly debates over them in the specific context of the different legal traditions seems warranted. This section briefly characterizes each of them.

even though, as a matter of principle, the abolition of exemplary damages is more convincing, "a *pragmatic* case can be made for [their] retention.") (emphasis in the original).

25 See the scholarly works cited in Section B.

26 Arguing that punitive damages pose a threat of corporate insolvency, see generally Viscusi, "The Social Costs of Punitive Damages."

27 For classic studies showing that concerns about punitive damages unpredictability is unwarranted, see T. Eisenberg, J. J. Rachlinski and M. T. Wells, "Reconciling Experimental Incoherence with Real-World Coherence in Punitive Damages" (2002) 54 *Stanford Law Review* 1239; T. Eisenberg, P. L. Hannaford, M. Heise, N. LaFountain, B. Ostrom, M. T. Wells and G. T. Munsterman, "Judges, Juries and Punitive Damages: Empirical Analyses Using the Civil Justice Survey of State Courts 1992, 1996, and 2001 Data" (2006) 3 *Journal of Empirical Legal Studies* 263. Similarly, see M. Rustad, "In Defense of Punitive Damages in Products Liability: Testing Tort Anecdotes with Empirical Data" (1992) 78 *Iowa Law Review* 1, 42–45 (discussing how colossal punitive damages are much rarer than assumed). But see A. M. Polinsky, "Are Punitive Damages Really Insignificant, Predictable, and Rational? A Comment on Eisenberg et al." (1997) 26 *Journal of Legal Studies* 663, 664 (challenging Eisenberg et al.'s studies that punitive damages are insignificant, predictable, and rational). For a recent recognition that "requests for punitive damages are often denied, and even when they are granted, the awards frequently do not add much to compensatory damage," see D. Kahneman, O. Sibony and C. R. Sunstein, *Noise. A Flaw in Human Judgment* (William Collins, 2021), p. 190.

28 J. Goudkamp and E. Katsampouka, "An Empirical Study of Punitive Damages" (2018) 38 *Oxford Journal of Legal Studies* 90.

29 F. Maher, "An Empirical Analysis of Exemplary Damages in Australia" (2019) 43 *Melbourne University Law Review* 694.

A COMMON LAW SYSTEMS: ENGLAND AND THE UNITED STATES

Punitive damages have enjoyed recognition as a common law tort remedy for centuries – going back to the first recorded exemplary damage awards in England in 1763.[30] Criticism has also surrounded punitive damages from the very outset, and the forms they have taken over time and across common law jurisdictions has varied greatly. Punitive awards were first instituted in North America during the colonial era but have evolved following their own path in the new nation's jurisprudence and scholarship, resulting in a practice that differs starkly from its current counterpart in England and other common law jurisdictions.[31] For this reason, I treat the two separately. As they represent the two major common law jurisdictions, the focus in what follows is primarily on the understanding, scholarly treatment, and judicial availability of punitive damages in England and the United States. Occasionally, reference is made, mainly for comparative purposes, to relevant aspects of the practice in other common law jurisdictions such as Australia, Canada, New Zealand, and Singapore.

a *The English Approach*

While punitive damages are generally available in the United States whenever the defendant's conduct reaches a certain degree of "reprehensibility," England's exemplary damage awards are much more confined in their range of application.[32] Their availability has been restricted from the very outset to specific categories of torts – what is called the "categories test." As explained by Lord Devlin in the leading case *Rookes* v. *Barnard*, exemplary damages can only be awarded in cases involving (1) "oppressive, arbitrary or unconstitutional action by the servants of the government"; (2) when "the defendant's conduct has been calculated by him to make a profit for himself which may exceed the compensation payable to the plaintiff"; and (3) where such award is "expressly authorised by statute."[33] In addition to these

[30] *Huckle* v. *Money* [1763] 95 ER 768 and *Wilkes* v. *Wood* [1763] 98 ER 489. For the historical significance of *Huckle* and *Wilkes*, see J. Taliadoros, "The Roots of Punitive Damages at Common Law: A Longer History" (2016) 64 *Cleveland State Law Review* 251. For a challenge to the well-settled narrative that before 1763 juries only increased damages in aggravated tort cases to further compensate plaintiffs for intangible injuries, see N. Sinanis, "Aggravation in Tort before 1763" (2022) 43 *Journal of Legal History* 24 (arguing that pre-1763 juries may have applied punitive and exemplary principles when increasing financial liability of aggravated tortfeasors).

[31] For an overview of punitive damages and their historical roots in the United States, see L. L. Schlueter, *Punitive Damages*, 8th ed. (LexisNexis, 2020). For the historical roots of exemplary damages in England, see J. Edelman (ed.), *McGregor on Damages*, 20th ed. (Sweet & Maxwell, 2017), para. 13-002.

[32] When I refer to "England" I mean all the United Kingdom save Scotland, which does not recognize punitive damages.

[33] *Rookes* v. *Barnard* [1964] AC 1129, 1226–27.

conditions (and other restrictions),[34] exemplary damages are considered "a remedy of last resort" in that they are only awarded if the sum awarded in compensation inadequately punishes or deters the defendant.[35]

A direct consequence of such a restrictive approach, one which persists to the present day, is the preclusion of exemplary damage awards in tortious cases of contumelious conduct that warrants punishment and deterrence even if the defendant is not a public servant or did not seek profit from the wrong. Later courts and scholars criticized the strictly categorical approach so defined on the grounds that it constituted an "unprincipled" and "formalistic" restraint of a tort remedy.[36] More recently, James Goudkamp and Eleni Katsampouka have argued that "[g]iven that the sole source of support for the categories test is the belief that precedent requires its recognition, the case for abolishing the test is irresistible."[37] This criticism was patently manifested in the *Kuddus* decision. In this case, exemplary damages were released from the restrictions of further formal cause of action because the "cause of action test" (or "pre-1964 test"), which restricted exemplary damages to causes of action recognized before 1964, "represented in practice an arbitrary and irrational restriction on the availability of exemplary damages."[38]

A parallel line of thinking can be found in a recent scholarly trend arguing for substantively expanding the availability of exemplary damages in English law.[39] The underlying claim is that the availability of exemplary damages and the remedy's rationale (i.e., to punish and deter) should be coextensive rather than constrained by arbitrary "categories" and formal "cause of action" restrictions.[40] Whether English courts and legislators will willingly expand availability to exemplary damages is not

34 For a detailed analysis of the hurdles that claimants need to clear before punitive damages can be awarded in English law, see Goudkamp and Katsampouka, "Punitive Damages and the Place of Punishment in Private Law," 1261–65.

35 *Kuddus* v. *Chief Constable of Leicestershire Constabulary* [2001] UKHL 29; [2002] 2 AC 122 [63] (Lord Nicholls). This "if but only if" test was first introduced in *Rookes* 1128 (Lord Devlin).

36 *Uren* v. *John Fairfax & Sons Pty Ltd* [1966] 117 CLR 118, 137–38 [HCA] (Taylor J) (questioning that the different treatment between profit-seeking and wanton conduct lacks any rational justification); *Kuddus* 67 (Lord Nicholls) (similar). Also see A. Burrows, *Remedies for Torts and Breach of Contract*, 3rd ed. (Oxford University Press, 2004), p. 424.

37 See J. Goudkamp and E. Katsampouka, "Punitive Damages: Ten Misconceptions," in E. Bant, W. Courtney, J. Goudkamp and J. M. Paterson (eds.), *Punishment and Private Law* (Hart Publishing, 2021), p. 216.

38 *Kuddus* 63.

39 See, for example, Goudkamp and Katsampouka, "Form and Substance in the Law of Punitive Damages," pp. 331–52; A. Roberts and M. Richardson, "Privacy, Punishment and Private Law," in E. Bant, W. Courtney, J. Goudkamp and J. M. Paterson (eds.), *Punishment and Private Law* (Hart Publishing, 2021), pp. 83–103 (arguing for expansion to breach of privacy cases).

40 This is in line with the Law Commission for England and Wales (Law Commission, *Aggravated, Exemplary and Restitutionary Damages*, Law Com 247 [1997] 1.20) recommendation to reject the restricted categories test in favor of a new approach in which punitive damages would be available in exceptional cases of "deliberate and outrageous disregard of the plaintiff's rights."

yet clear.[41] At the same time, it should be noted that the restricted approach thus far favored in England has not been followed by the Commonwealth jurisdictions in New Zealand, Australia, Canada, and Singapore, all of which have restricted exemplary damages much less.[42] Canada, for instance, represents the common law jurisdiction with the most flexibility for exemplary awards – even allowing them for breach of contract,[43] which sets it apart from England, Australia, Singapore, and New Zealand.[44]

In the midst of the tension between those who argue for "broadening" the scope of exemplary damages and those who insist on "maintaining" the status quo, scant scholarly attention has been devoted to the actual role and effect of the salient retributive rationale of the institution, which has been openly recognized as such since the very beginning of the common law of torts,[45] subsequently acknowledged by the English Law Commission,[46] and ultimately justifies them. Yet predominant in English tort scholarship remains the traditional focus on the bilateral relationship between the tort victim and the tortfeasor in terms of interpersonal justice.[47] This is reflected, on one hand, in the insistent search for comprehensive explanations

41 The United Kingdom Government has rejected expansionary proposals on the availability of exemplary damages arguing that "[t]he purpose of the civil law on damages is to provide compensation for loss, and not to punish" and that exemplary damages "should not be the subject of new statutory provisions." Department of Constitutional Affairs, The Law on Damages [CP 9/07, 2007] 198. But see *Kuddus*, however, which is certainly an example of the expansive trend.

42 Courts have declined to follow *Rookes* in New Zealand (*Taylor* v. *Beere* [1982] 1 NZLR 81, 93), Australia (*Uren* v. *John Fairfax & Sons Pty Ltd* [1966] 117 CLR 118, 138 [HCA]), and Canada (*Vorvis* v. *Insurance Corp of British Columbia* [1989] 1 SCR 1085, 1108). More recently, the Singapore Court of Appeal in *ACB* v. *Thomson Medical Pte Ltd* [2017] SGCA 20; [2017] 1 SLR 918 [173] joined that trend arguing that "punitive damages may be awarded in tort where the totality of the defendant's conduct is so outrageous that it warrants punishment, deterrence, and condemnation."

43 *Whiten* v. *Pilot Insurance Co.* [2002] SCC 18; [2002] 1 SCR 595.

44 In English law, there is no direct evidence that punitive damages can be awarded for breach of contractual rights or for equitable wrongs. However, it is debatable whether contract law truly forbids these awards. On this point, see J. Goudkamp, "Exemplary damages," in G. Virgo and S. Worthington (eds.), *Commercial Remedies: Resolving Controversies* (Cambridge University Press, 2017), pp. 321–29. In Australia, *Harris* v. *Digital Pulse Pty Ltd* [2003] NSWCA 10; [2003] 44 ACSR 390 is the authority invoked for not allowing punitive damages for breach of contract.

45 See Cane, *The Anatomy of Tort Law*, p. 114 ("the law currently contains no rational principle governing the availability of punitive damages"). Similarly, see Murphy, "Anomalies in Tort Law," 890 (noting that is "telling that [commentators] support for the continued availability of exemplary damages tends to be expressed in carefully limited ways, and on grounds of *pragmatism* rather than on grounds of *principle*" (emphasis added).

46 The Law Commission for England and Wales (Law Commission, *Aggravated, Exemplary and Restitutionary Damages*, Law Com 247 [1997] 5.22) concluded in its final report that "it is coherent to pursue the aims of punishment (retribution, deterrence, disapproval) through the civil law."

47 For an overview of the interpersonal approach to English tort law, see generally D. Nolan and A. Robertson (eds.), *Rights and Private Law* (Hart Publishing, 2012). For a comparison of instrumental and interpersonal conceptions of punishment, see M. Cappelletti, "Comparative Reflections on Punishment in Tort Law," in J. S. Borghetti and S. Whittaker (eds.), *French Civil Liability in Comparative Perspective* (Hart Publishing, 2019), pp. 329–51.

of and justifications for the rectificatory rationale of tort law in ways that depict the retributive aspect of exemplary damages as "alien" to the correlative structure of tort law.[48] It can also be seen, on the other hand, in the persistent depiction of punitive damages as an "anomalous" feature that actually belongs to criminal law but must nonetheless be tolerated in tort law out of respect for judicial precedent and legislative mandates.[49] As will be thoroughly explored in Chapter 2, the "structural" critique and the "anomaly" stigma, which underlie most scholarly work on exemplary damages, have each impeded theoretical work on the vindication of punishment (retribution and deterrence) in English tort law and pre-empted meaningful debate over possible justifications.[50] Even English scholars who recognize the retributive aspect of exemplary damages hesitate to advance a thorough defense of retribution in tort law (i.e., in interpersonal terms), attempting instead to explain them away as a form of "substitutive damages" for contumelious violations of rights.[51] Still other scholars have primarily tackled retribution either in unilateral terms of "just desert"[52] or through an exclusive focus on "deterrence,"[53] which has proven difficult to square with the dominant focus on the transactional relationship between the tort victim seeking the punitive award and the wrongdoer whose contumelious conduct allegedly warrants judicial imposition of punitive damages. The emphasis on the interpersonal character of torts usually leads to deny any room for retributive punishment in tort law.[54]

Certainly, what makes an interpersonal (or private) retributive rationale of exemplary damages difficult to articulate are the fundamental challenges it poses for the legal order rooted in the long-standing divide between private law and public law.[55] Such a rationale also questions the established assumption regarding the vertical

48 See generally J. Gardner, "Torts and Other Wrongs" (2011) 39 *Florida State University Law Review* 43, and "What Is Tort Law For? Part 1. The Place of Corrective Justice" (2011) 30 *Law and Philosophy* 1.

49 See Beever, "The Structure of Aggravated and Exemplary Damages," 109, n91 (stating that there is "an almost universal sense [that exemplary damages] are anomalous."). Similarly, Murphy, "Anomalies in Tort Law," 891 ("[e]xemplary damages may fairly be regarded as anomalous.").

50 See Section A of Chapter 2.

51 R. Stevens, *Torts and Rights* (Oxford University Press, 2007), pp. 85–88. I explore Stevens's reconstruction in Section B of Chapter 2.

52 See K. Barker, "Punishment in Private Law – No Such Thing Anymore," in E. Bant, W. Courtney, J. Goudkamp and J. M. Paterson (eds.), *Punishment and Private Law* (Hart Publishing, 2021), pp. 44–47. Moreover, see N. J. McBride and R. Bagshaw, *Tort Law*, 6th ed. (Pearson Education, 2018), p. 767, n157 (arguing that through punitive damages the tort victim is provided with an avenue of redress to satisfy her "natural desire to see the defendant pay for treating her in such an outrageous fashion.").

53 See, for example, J. Edelman, "In Defence of Exemplary Damages," in C. E. F. Rickett (ed.), *Justifying Private Law Remedies* (Hart Publishing, 2008), pp. 225–48.

54 For this stance, see Barker, "Punishment in Private Law," p. 61 (directly arguing that there is no such thing as retributive punishment in modern private law).

55 See J. Penner, "Punishments and Penalties in Private Law, with Particular Reference to the Law Governing Fiduciaries," in E. Bant, W. Courtney, J. Goudkamp and J. M. Paterson (eds.), *Punishment and Private Law* (Hart Publishing, 2021), p. 117 (arguing that the right to punish is conceptually a public right).

and public character of punishment as only legitimately exercised by the state by virtue of its monopoly over coercive means.[56] Moreover, recognizing retribution as a valid ground for sanction raises serious concerns regarding the desirability of assigning normative value to retribution in tort law, a branch of private law.[57] These concerns are understandable, reasonable, and explain, in part, the scholarly reluctance to explore deeply the retributive dimension of tort law and the insistence on its rectificatory rationale. These factors may also partially explain the persistence of English tort scholars who distinguish the compensatory nature of "aggravated damages" from the punitive nature of "exemplary damages," although both types of awards are triggered by contumelious conduct and translate into an additional sum of money granted to the victim.[58] As will be detailed in Part II, "aggravated damages" were introduced by Lord Devlin in *Rookes* to qualify awards meant to compensate the injury to the plaintiff when she suffered through wrongful conduct that was aggravated by the manner – malice, arrogance, malevolence, insolence, or spite – with which it was done. "Exemplary damages," on the other hand, were confined by Lord Devlin in *Rookes* to the purpose of punishing the defendant for wrongful conduct in restricted categories of contumelious torts.[59]

The overall reluctance to admit retribution may also explain the attempts to directly transform exemplary damages into something else. A telling example of such efforts is the recently created category of "vindicatory damages."[60] Such awards purportedly aim to vindicate the right breached and express public outrage, not to punish the wrongdoer. These awards are "vindicatory" in that they provide tangible force to the formal declaration of the right and formal recognition of the wrong.[61]

[56] On this point, see A. Burrows, "The Scope of Exemplary Damages" (1993) 109 *Law Quarterly Review* 358, 361 ("punishment demands a state-individual relationship: it is not something for one individual to exact from another").

[57] For the argument that tort law loses some internal coherence (due to incompatibility) if it attempts to fulfill both a retributive and a reparative agenda at the same time, see Murphy, "Anomalies in Tort Law," 891.

[58] For examples of scholarly works along these lines, see generally J. Murphy, "The Nature and Domain of Aggravated Damages" (2010) 69 *Cambridge Law Journal* 353; Stevens, Torts and Rights; Beever, "The Structure of Aggravated and Exemplary Damages." But see, however, Cane, *The Anatomy of Tort Law*, p. 79 (arguing that they are indistinguishable); Goudkamp and Katsampouka, "Punitive Damages and the Place of Punishment in Private Law," 1278 (arguing that "[t]he understanding that aggravated damages are at least sometimes awarded to punish is widely accepted.").

[59] See Section B of Chapter 5.

[60] On vindication in private law, see K. Barker, "Private and Public: The Mixed Conception of Vindication in Torts and Private Law," in S. G. A. Pitel, J. W. Neyers and E. Chamberlain (eds.), *Tort Law: Challenging Orthodoxy* (Hart Publishing, 2013), pp. 59–93. For a discussion on vindication in tort law, see J. N. E. Varuhas, "The Concept of 'Vindication' in the Law of Torts: Rights, Interests and Damages" (2014) 34 *Oxford Journal of Legal Studies* 253. Note that "vindicatory damages" may be awarded in certain jurisdictions for violations of constitutional rights; see, for example, *Attorney-General of Trinidad and Tobago* v. *Ramanoop* [2005] UKPC; [2006] 1 AC 328.

[61] See, for example, J. Varuhas, *Damages and Human Rights* (Hart Publishing, 2016), pp. 125–29 (arguing that vindicatory damages "mark the sense of public outrage" at the serious violation of an important human right).

However, it is difficult to understand how exactly the expressive purpose (signaling a wrong or affirming the importance of a right) differs from punishment when all is said and done. After all, as Antony Duff points out, "vindicatory damages are [….] essentially punitive, in that they can serve their expressive, symbolic purpose only if they are burdensome for the defendant."[62] It may however provide insight on the occasional tendency of English judges to impose punishment covertly via mechanisms other than exemplary damages as a way to circumvent the restrictions on them.[63]

In sum, these scholarly trends demonstrate the constant struggle with the punitive aspect of tort law on the one hand (since the very outset by *Rookes*) and, on the other, the hesitation of scholars to tackle, directly and meaningfully, the more fundamental question of the independent role of punishment in tort law and its retributive justifications. This reticence persists even though English courts themselves have affirmed that "the availability of exemplary damages should be co-extensive with its rationale" and subsequently recognized that "[t]he underlying rationale [of exemplary damages] lies in the sense of outrage which a defendant's conduct sometimes evokes, a sense which is not always assuaged fully by a compensatory award of damages."[64] As Goudkamp and Katsampouka have observed, "[t]he absence of a properly developed rival perspective regarding [English] punitive damages is unhealthy."[65]

b *The Anglo-American Approach*

In the United States, punitive damage awards are a relatively frequent practice and, in principle, are broadly available whenever the defendant's conduct displays a certain degree of "reprehensibility."[66] Some of the typical formulations employed by courts to describe the type of grossly unacceptable or morally offensive conducts that call for an interest in punishment and deterrence are "wanton," "outrageous," "egregious," or "reckless indifference to other's rights."[67] However, such general availability should not lead us to believe that the treatment and application of punitive damages by courts, or their regulation by legislatures, are uniform across the many jurisdictions that comprise the United States. Indeed, despite the spread of certain

62 R. A. Duff, "Torts Crimes and Vindication: Whose Wrong is it?," in M. Dyson (ed.), *Unravelling Tort and Crime* (Cambridge University Press, 2014), p. 153.

63 On this point, see Goudkamp and Katsampouka, "Punitive Damages and the Place of Punishment in Private Law," 1288–91 (arguing that this represents a "substitution phenomenon").

64 *Kuddus* 65 (Lord Nicholls).

65 Goudkamp and Katsampouka, "Punitive Damages and the Place of Punishment in Private Law," 1258.

66 Note that punitive damages are not generally available in Louisiana, Massachusetts, Nebraska, New Hampshire, and Washington.

67 For an overview of the practice of awarding punitive damages in the United States, see Schlueter, Punitive Damages.

general conceptions to the point of commonplace sloganeering (e.g., "punitive damages serve the purposes of punishment and deterrence"), any thorough foray into the case law and statutes reveals that punitive damages are approached and applied quite differently from state to state within the American federation. For instance, while in many states punitive damages are insurable as a matter of public policy, others prohibit the practice of taking out insurance to protect from potential punitive awards on principled grounds.[68] Then again, some states assign the entire amount of punitive damage awards to the plaintiff, while others have recently enacted split-recovery statutes that mandate a percentage of the award to the state as a means to disincentivize spurious lawsuits in search of windfall gains for plaintiffs.[69] Similar disparities are observed with regard to the size of punitive damages awards (a handful of states have enacted statutes that cap punitive awards)[70] and procedural safeguards, including stricter evidentiary standards in some jurisdictions where the institution serves a purpose similar to that of the criminal law.[71]

This is the context in which the debates have focused on a disparate variety of legal issues concerning controversial features of practical significance (such as who should receive the award, whether split-recovery statutes should be enacted, whether stricter evidentiary standards should be implemented, the arguments for and against insurability, and so on). At first glance, the predominance of these debates over particular legal aspects may be a sign that the disagreements over punitive damages primarily lie at the concrete level of practical implications. However, this hypothesis collapses under the realization that the debate over practical legal implications cannot possibly be resolved without first addressing the most fundamental theoretical grounding for punitive damages and the functions they serve. The genuine source of disagreement ultimately lies with the relation between the two purposes of punishment and deterrence and the circumstances in which one trumps the other.[72]

This foundational issue has given rise to many interesting questions and led many scholars to develop more theoretically grounded inquiries in the field to advance these debates. Certainly, offshoots of the United States school of legal realism,

[68] On punitive damages insurability across the United States, see J. Kircher and C. Wiseman, *Punitive Damages: Law and Practice*, 2nd ed., 2 vols. (Clark Boardman Callaghan, 2023), vol. 1, ss. 7:14–28.

[69] Two states that have enacted such statutes are, for example, Utah, which apportions first $50,000 to the injured party, but any subsequent amounts are split equally between the state and injured party [Utah Code Ann. §78B-8-201(3)(a)]; Alaska, which apportions 50 percent to the state's general fund [Alaska Stat. §09.17.020(j)].

[70] For instance, Alaska established a cap "at the greater of three times the amount of compensatory damages or $500,000" [Alaska Stat. §09.17.020(f)].

[71] For instance, Alaska requires a standard of "clear and convincing evidence" [Alaska Stat. §09.17.020(b)], while Colorado demands an even higher standard of "beyond a reasonable doubt" [Colo. Rev. Stat. Ann. §13-25-127(2)].

[72] On this point, see T. Colby, "Clearing the Smoke from *Philip Morris* v. *Williams*: The Past, Present and Future of Punitive Damages" (2008) 118 *Yale Law Journal* 392, 394 (noting that "in two centuries of issuing punitive damages decisions, the Supreme Court has never adequately answered the most simple and fundamental of questions: What, exactly, are punitive damages? What is their purpose?").

particularly that embodied in the law-and-economics approach to tort law, played an influential role in framing the modern debate over punitive damages. The legal realists' relative disregard for the public law-private law distinction set the precedent for the embrace of deterrence in tort law by the law and economics school that situates theoretical debate over punitive damages in terms of an optimally "efficient" balance between compliance and economic development rather than in the theoretical imperatives that derive from the division between tort law (private law) and criminal law (public law), which, as referred earlier, is patent in the English scholarly approach to the institution.[73] Against this background, Anglo-American tort law was shaped by the academic tension between the dominant regulatory approach introduced by law and economics scholars in the 1970s and the rights-based corrective justice critique of that approach in the 1980s, a debate that gave punitive damages scant attention. To begin with, justifying punitive damages has proven challenging for corrective justice theorists,[74] and their difficulty to come up with a satisfactory account has in turn ceded room for instrumentalist conceptions developed primarily from economic analyses that appear, at least on the surface, attractive.[75] The struggle led to a division of scholars into two camps, one emphasizing corrective justice over deterrence and the other downplaying corrective justice in favor of deterrence.[76] Consequently, most Anglo-American scholars who take up the common law of torts take some position with respect to the merits of a private or regulatory understanding of tort law.

Current discussions on the theoretical justifications of punitive damages awards clearly reveal this dichotomy. Private approaches to tort law have, from the outset, either rejected outright punitive damages, arguing there is no justification whatsoever for punishment in private law, or attempted to accommodate them by

73 For the claim that law and economics deny the significance of a principled distinction between public law and private law, preferring to see the law through the lens of economic efficiency, see N. B. Oman, "The Honor of Private Law" (2011) 80 *Fordham Law Review* 31, 36; A. Harel, "Public and Private Law," in M. Dubber and T. Hörnle (eds.), *The Oxford Handbook on Criminal Law* (Oxford University Press, 2014), pp. 1040–63. For the classic discussion on the private–public law divide, see L. Green, "Tort Law: Public Law in Disguise" (1959–60) 38 *Texas Law Review* 257, 269 (according to his view, private law is "public law in disguise"). Also see M. J. Horwitz, "The History of the Public/Private Distinction" (1982) 130 *University of Pennsylvania Law Review* 1423, 1426 (arguing that "the division of law into public and private realms" is arbitrary and that all categories of private law are delegations of public power that can only be justified by public purposes). For a recent reconstruction of the distinction between private and public law, see H. Dagan and B. C. Zipursky, "Introduction: The Distinction Between Private Law and Public Law," in H. Dagan and B. C. Zipursky (eds.), *Research Handbook on Private Law Theory* (Edward Elgar Publishing, 2020), pp. 1–21.

74 See E. J. Weinrib, "Civil Recourse and Corrective Justice" (2011) 39 *Florida State University Law Review* 273, 290 (arguing that the place of one-sided considerations such as punishment and deterrence structurally pertains not to private but to criminal law). I explore corrective justice theorists' uneasy relationship with punishment in tort law in Section A of Chapter 2.

75 I explore instrumental accounts of punitive damages in further detail in Section E of Chapter 2.

76 For a chronicle of the dispute in the late 1990s, see G. T. Schwartz, "Mixed Theories of Tort Law: Affirming Both Deterrence and Corrective Justice" (1997) 75 *Texas Law Review* 1801.

building them into traditional rectificatory frameworks.[77] Only recently, and partly inspired by the steady development of John Goldberg and Benjamin Zipursky's civil recourse theory,[78] more efforts have been made by American tort scholars to provide a variety of deontological justifications for the practice of permitting juries to award punitive damages in tort cases where there is evidence of willful or wanton misconduct by the defendant.[79] The dominant regulatory approaches, for their part, have mainly focused on the institution's deterrent effect (i.e., pursuing optimal or societal deterrence goals) and limiting (and splitting) award amounts to maximize efficiency.[80]

Several Anglo-American scholars have tried to provide an account of punitive damages from different theoretical perspectives. While the sheer diversity of viewpoints may represent one of the most interesting features of American tort law, it exacerbates the task of compiling a comprehensive account of the punitive institution, for different approaches generally imply different scholarly projects, which in turn bring methodological choices into question. A brief account of some of the theories that currently enjoy purchase in scholarly circles will illustrate the divergences, gaps, and mismatches.

One of the most representative conceptions of punitive damages from the law and economics approach is Mitchel Polinsky and Steven Shavell's "multiplier" formula, which stresses the deterrence function of the institution.[81] These scholars see punitive damages as a tool enabling cost internalization aimed at achieving optimal deterrence.[82] They propose multiplying compensatory damage awards (thus yielding punitive damage awards) in situations where the defendant enjoys good odds of

77 I explore this scholarly approach in further detail in Section A of Chapter 2. Note that the private–public law divide underlies most corrective justice theorists' rejection of punitive damages in torts.

78 For their latest account of civil recourse theory, see J. C. P. Goldberg and B. C. Zipursky, *Recognizing Wrongs* (Harvard University Press, 2020).

79 For scholarship along these lines, see, for example, B. C. Zipursky, "A Theory of Punitive Damages" (2005) 84 *Texas Law Review* 105; T. B. Colby, "Beyond the Multiple Punishment Problem: Punitive Damages as Punishment for Individual, Private Wrongs" (2003) 87 *Minnesota Law Review* 583; A. J. Sebok, "Punitive Damages: From Myth to Theory" (2007) 92 *Iowa Law Review* 957; E. Encarnacion, "Resilience, Retribution, and Punitive Damages" (2022) 100 *Texas Law Review* 1025. I explore these accounts in further detail in Sections F and G of Chapter 2.

80 For scholarship along these lines, see, for example, A. M. Polinsky and S. Shavell, "Punitive Damages: An Economic Analysis" (1998) 111 *Harvard Law Review* 869; C. M. Sharkey, "Punitive Damages as Societal Damages" (2003) 113 *Yale Law Journal* 347. I explore these accounts in further detail in Section E of Chapter 2.

81 Polinsky and Shavell, "Punitive Damages: An Economic Analysis," 869. Arguments on economic deterrence have been further developed by others, such as R. Craswell, "Deterrence and Damages: The Multiplier Principle and Its Alternatives" (1999) 97 *Michigan Law Review* 2185; K. L. Hylton and T. J. Miceli, "Should Tort Damages be Multiplied?" (2005) 21 *Journal of Law, Economics, and Organization* 388.

82 For a variant, within cost-internalization approaches, which understands punitive damages as achieving the goal of societal general deterrence, see Sharkey, "Punitive Damages as Societal Damages," 347.

escaping detection by legal authorities.[83] From their point of view, the defendant's state of mind and the degree of reprehensibility of the wrongful conduct in question are irrelevant because the objective is not punishing wrongdoing, but rather maximizing the deterrent effect of the award on future conduct. By consequence, the problematic nature of some entrenched features of punitive damage awards under some theories (when, for example, a portion of the award is allocated to the state or people are allowed to take out insurance to protect themselves from such awards) dissipates under an optimal deterrence framework. As a matter of fact, this deterrence-focused approach removes the normative qualms that have led some jurisdictions to prohibit insurance policies against punitive damage awards (in fact, this framing might even stimulate such policies). Similarly, no concrete predefinition of the award's beneficiary – the plaintiff, special funds, or the state – would be required as long as the plaintiff had sufficient incentives and legal standing to bring the lawsuit. Moreover, to the extent that punitive damages are dictated as a function of optimal deterrence, they would not be subject to United States Supreme Court review for constitutional due process or excessiveness.[84]

Approaching punitive damages from another perspective, that of civil recourse theory, Zipursky argues that the plaintiff is entitled to seek beyond what would represent equivalent compensation for the harm incurred (i.e., more than mere self-restoration) when the defendant's wrong was either willful or wanton. This is what Zipursky calls the plaintiff's "right to be punitive" and accounts for what he refers to as the "civil aspect" of the institution.[85] To be more precise, this "civil aspect" does not involve any authorization by the state for private individuals to perform the role of prosecutor or attorney general. Rather, it involves empowering the victims of a certain kind of egregious wrong to punish wrongdoers by seeking a penalty through civil remedy.[86] Zipursky maintains that the "civil aspect" represents the most fundamental expression of the practice within the common law of torts, which is understood as distinctively private.[87] One practical implication of this conception is that

[83] For a similar proposal, see R. D. Cooter, "Economic Analysis of Punitive Damages" (1982) 56 *Southern California Law Review* 79; "Punitive Damages for Deterrence: When and How Much?" (1989) 40 *Alabama Law Review* 1143; and "Punitive Damages, Social Norms, and Economic Analysis" (1997) 60 *Law and Contemporary Problems* 73, 91 (building on Becker (1968), Cooter proposes the "rule of the reciprocal": to determine total damages, one should multiply harm to the plaintiff by the enforcement error).

[84] See C. M. Sharkey, "Punitive Damages Transformed into Societal Damages," in E. Bant, W. Courtney, J. Goudkamp and J. M. Paterson (eds.), *Punishment and Private Law* (Hart Publishing, 2021), p. 185 (alluding to the very same implications as the ones that follow from her "societal general deterrence" reconstruction of punitive awards).

[85] See Zipursky, "A Theory of Punitive Damages," 106–7 (arguing that "[i]t is the plaintiff's right to be punitive, not the system's need to punish the defendant, that explains the special status of punitive damages within American tort law.").

[86] Ibid 151–52.

[87] On this point, see B. C. Zipursky, "*Palsgraf*, Punitive Damages, and Preemption" (2012) 125 *Harvard Law Review* 1757, 1771 ("the court has failed to appreciate the ways in which punitive damages might

insurability against punitive damages becomes untenable and should be prohibited or considered unenforceable, for they effectively allow the wrongdoer to escape punishment. In this approach, it is also of utmost importance that the plaintiff herself collect the award (not the state nor anyone else) and that such lawsuits not trigger the special constitutional scrutiny afforded to criminal defendants (namely, the procedural safeguards of the criminal law) because, understood in the "civil way," punitive damages are "basically civil, and not about criminal punishment."[88]

There is, however, another family of theories that advances the idea of punishment as social sanction, that is, as public rather than private. Reprehensible and wanton behavior remains extremely relevant in these theories, but the underlying idea differs from the notion of the plaintiff's right to be punitive operative in Zipursky's private variant. The idea behind this approach is that the central aim of punitive damage awards is to punish the defendant for the total harm that her wrongful conduct has caused to all of society, not just the harm that it caused to the plaintiff appearing before the court. This account posits that punitive damages should punish public wrongs (wrongs to society) and therefore reflect the full scope of harm that the defendant's conduct visited upon all of society. This view has been predominant in judges' opinions and comments on them for the last several decades.[89] Among the practical implications of this approach, I would like to emphasize support for split-recovery statutes (which have recently been enacted in several states) that divide punitive damage awards between the plaintiff and some designated public fund or the government.[90] Despite the recent trend, this conception has been questioned on important constitutional grounds involving judicial excessiveness review and due process (namely concerning multiple punishments for a single instance of wrongdoing, the stricter standards of proof required in public law, and so on).[91] Furthermore, in an attempt to resolve the contradictory implications presented by the public punishment and optimal deterrence perspectives, Catherine Sharkey has recently suggested "societal compensation" as a

once have fit into a conception of tort law as private law, and that failure has contaminated its entire approach to the subject.").

88 Zipursky, "A Theory of Punitive Damages," 107.

89 Describing this consensus as one that emerged without reason or explanation over the last several decades, see Colby, "Beyond the Multiple Punishment Problem," 603–6. Also see Zipursky, "*Palsgraf*, Punitive Damages, and Preemption," 1770–71 (arguing that "[a]t the core of a wide variety of tort thinking today is the assumption that a plaintiff in a tort case is, at least in part, performing a private attorney general role" and that there is "[a] proclivity of the Justices of the Supreme Court to see punitive damages as a private attorney general mechanism for delivering punishment and deterrence.").

90 For a discussion on split-recovery statutes in the United States, see Sharkey, "Punitive Damages as Societal Damages," 375–80, 444.

91 See, for example, *Philip Morris USA* v. *Williams*, 127 USSC 1057, 1063 (2007) (where the Supreme Court held that "the Constitution's Due Process Clause forbids a State to use a punitive damages award to punish a defendant for injury that it inflicts upon nonparties."). Also see B. C. Zipursky, "Punitive Damages After Philip Morris USA v. Williams" (2007) 44 *Court Review* 134, 135 (where he offers an interpretive reconstruction that accommodates what he calls the "non-harm rule" doctrine introduced by the Supreme Court in Williams).

nonretributive goal of punitive damages.[92] Sharkey claims that the social dimension of punitive damages has not garnered sufficient acknowledgment.[93]

To take another attempt to theorize the justification for punitive damages on the basis of court decisions, the relatively recent United States Supreme Court opinions in *State Farm* v. *Campbell*[94] and *Philip Morris* v. *Williams*[95] provoked a wave of scholarship that defended victim vindication as the core value of punitive damages to address the constitutional issues raised in those highly resonant cases. For instance, theorists such as Thomas Colby hold up private punishment as the main purpose of punitive damages, emphasizing individualized punishment for highly wrongful conducts (where the wantonness of the behavior is one of the most salient elements). According to Colby, punitive damages function as private sanctions operating in a private law setting (i.e., punitive damages represent a form of legalized private revenge).[96] Punitive damage awards therefore cannot be equated with criminal penalties (public sanctions), and, for this reason, Colby concludes that the criminal procedural safeguards are not necessarily applicable to punitive damages cases.[97] Similarly, Mark Geistfeld has argued in favor of a rationale vindicating the position of plaintiffs to demonstrate that punitive damages satisfy the constitutional requirements of both substantive and procedural due process.[98]

As is evident, each of these approaches to punitive damages is distinctive and considerable disagreement divides them on key issues. We can, notwithstanding, identify a common pattern in the contours of the Anglo-American scholarship on the institution. As the most common lines of research and argument pursued by authors clearly demonstrate, the prevailing punitive damages scholarship in the United States has – as should be expected – been closely connected to domestic experience.[99] To diagnose the structure of the actual disagreements on punitive damages, I would

92 See Sharkey, "Punitive Damages as Societal Damages," 368–70. Sharkey's proposal purports to correct the errors of internalization introduced by the multiplier model. I take up her proposal in Section E of Chapter 2.

93 Ibid 352.

94 538 US 408 (2003).

95 549 US 346 (2007).

96 Colby, "Clearing the Smoke from Philip Morris v. Williams," 423 n125. Similarly, see Sebok, "Punitive Damages: From Myth to Theory," 1031 (arguing that punitive damages are a way of providing "state-sanctioned revenge").

97 Colby, "Clearing the Smoke from Philip Morris v. Williams," 396. Note that Colby has attempted to justify punishment in tort law on the basis of the distinction between wrongs to society (which are the domain of criminal punishment achieving the State's interest in retribution and deterrence) and wrongs to private parties (which are the domain of private punishment achieving the victim's interest in seeking revenge), ibid 424–27, 436–40.

98 See M. A. Geistfeld, "Punitive Damages, Retribution, and Due Process" (2008) 81 *Southern California Law Review* 263, 264.

99 On this point, see A. J. Sebok, "Normative Theories of Punitive Damages: The Case of Deterrence," in J. Oberdiek (ed.), *Philosophical Foundations of the Law of Torts* (Oxford University Press, 2014), p. 314 (arguing that "the debate over the positive law of punitive damages [...] has been complicated by an obsession with constitutional law [which had suppressed] a more explicitly normative discussion of punitive damages in the United States.").

start with their portrayal. As I understand them, the disagreements can be graphically represented by a tree following Ronald Dworkin's well-known characterization. In general terms, all agree on the more general and abstract propositions regarding punitive damages – the "trunk" of the tree – but deeply disagree over the more refined sub-interpretations of those abstract propositions – the "branches."[100] In fact, as most scholars and judges seem to agree, at the tree trunk level, punitive damages are an extra-compensatory award imposed to punish defendants and deter them (and others) from engaging in similar misconduct in the future. They also all agree on the general source of the predicament, namely, that punitive damages are imposed precisely for the purposes of punishment and deterrence.[101] However, there is considerable dispute among scholars over the interpretation and specific definition of punishment and deterrence, that is, over exactly what in Dworkin's metaphor the branches of the tree represent.[102]

With this scheme in mind, the idea of "extra-compensatory awards imposed in order to punish and deter" comprises the concept of punitive damages, while the theoretical positions on how punishment and deterrence should be understood in order to justify its extra-compensatory character represent the different conceptualizations of the concept of punitive damages. The relevance of this contrast between concept and conception is important to understand because, as Dworkin explains, it represents "a contrast between levels of abstraction at which the interpretation of the practice can be studied";[103] which is to say, "at the first level agreement collects around discrete ideas that are uncontroversially employed in all interpretations; at the second the controversy latent in this abstraction is identified and taken up."[104]

As demonstrated, most scholarly work on punitive damages has accepted the general predicament posed by the purposes of punitive damages (punishment and deterrence) as the self-evident and uncontroversial starting point for any plausible

[100] See R. Dworkin, *Law's Empire* (Harvard University Press, 1986), p. 70. In the author's example, the community interprets the social practice of "courtesy," over which maintains disagreements of the same schematic structure as the one represented with the trunk and branches metaphor.

[101] For instance, see Kircher and Wiseman, Punitive Damages: Law and Practice, s. 4:12 (citing forty-four jurisdictions that justify punitive damages on both punishment and deterrence grounds). Also see Restatement (Second) of Torts §908 (1979) ("Punitive damages are damages, other than compensatory or nominal damages, awarded against a person to punish him for his outrageous conduct and to deter him and others like him from similar conduct in the future."); *BMW of North America Inc.* v. *Gore*, 517 US 559, 568 (1996) ("Punitive damages may properly be imposed to further a State's legitimate interests in punishing unlawful conduct and deterring its repetition."), among many other legal sources.

[102] Indeed, most of the time it is unclear what legal actors and scholars mean when they refer to each concept. See, for example, D. Markel, "How Should Punitive Damages Work?" (2009) 157 *University of Pennsylvania Law Review* 1383, 1391 (referring that "[u]nfortunately, although courts frequently invoke the purposes of retribution and deterrence, they often offer little analysis of these purposes or their implications.").

[103] See Dworkin, Law's Empire, p. 71.

[104] Ibid.

interpretive enterprise. From there, the scholars' primary goal has been advancing competing conceptions of punishment and deterrence, each with their differing interpretive merits, in an attempt to justify the American practice of awarding punitive damages. In other words, it is an outcome-driven interpretive approach.[105] As a result, questions concerning, for example, the extent to which punishment and deterrence are compatible (i.e., which connotations of punishment are compatible with which connotations of deterrence, and vice versa); or when one purpose is more compelling or less salient than the other; or whether both purposes are necessarily linked (i.e., whether they can ever be fully disentangled) have only been addressed from the perspective of the practice itself. The discussion of these key issues regarding the institution's main purposes of punishment and deterrence has been intertwined, it bears emphasizing, with a practice that is known to be highly complex and contradictory.

That most United States legal scholarship has been dominated by an outcome-driven interpretive approach that focuses on the purposes or functions established by case law and statutes for punitive damages in an effort to identify the best justification for extra-compensatory awards warrants questioning. Following this interpretive approach, Anglo-American scholars have attempted to provide accounts that incorporate as many of the salient characteristics of the practice of punitive damages in the United States as possible (i.e., those observable in judicial pronouncements, decisions of juries, statutes, etc.). Each author can be read as advancing their own interpretation of the rough data – an interpretation that presents these characteristics within the framework of some "point" or "value" that ultimately justifies the practice of punitive damages as socially worthwhile.[106]

As seen earlier, some claim that the practice of awarding punitive damages is best understood as a means for plaintiffs to seek punishment for wrongdoing of a specific type; others interpret the practice as the way society as a whole performs its responsibility to punish individuals whose conduct causes widespread harm. Still others see punitive damage awards as an opportunity to better society by deterring future wrongdoing, and so on and so forth. Significantly, none of these interpretations claims to account for all of the available data. Scholars usually discard some

[105] Similarly, see P. M. Gerhart, *Tort Law and Social Morality* (Cambridge University Press, 2010), p. xiii (stating that "[t]he major flaws in much existing theory [is the] excessive generality and lack of specificity […] and theory that is outcome-driven.").

[106] Some scholars explicitly acknowledge this kind of inquiry. For instance, see Sebok, "Punitive Damages: From Myth to Theory," 1023 ("This article has approached punitive damages from an interpretive point of view. The test of this theory is whether it can provide an account of the practice of punitive damages that fits its institutions and rules and provide a theoretical framework that plausibly can justify those institutions and rules."); Sharkey, "Punitive Damages Transformed into Societal Damages," p. 156 (arguing that punitive damages should be transformed into societal damages on the basis of her interpretation that what courts are saying when awarding punitive damages typically using the language of retributive punishment might actually be something else – namely, effectuating societal deterrence), among many other examples.

instances of the practice as mistakes or missteps – namely the ones that cannot be justified under the scheme that they advance (i.e., cases whose decisions cannot be construed according to the driving principle identified). This feature is characteristic of the pronounced tendency among Anglo-American scholars to draw practical implications from their analyses, ones often ultimately oriented to produce proposals for concrete legal reform.[107] However, this normative component is not rejected as a disconnect between the scholarship and the actual practice because, according to this type of reconstruction, the accounts maintain an "interpretive equilibrium." As Dworkin explains, "[t]he justification need not fit every aspect or feature of the standing practice, but it must fit enough for the interpreter to be able to see himself as interpreting that practice, not inventing a new one."[108]

It is certainly true that some accounts reflect this interpretive pattern more or less than others. Polinsky and Shavell's argument for the award multiplier, for instance, can be read along purely normative lines, and some of the most powerful criticism against it attacks not its veracity but rather its feasibility, which, for that matter, is how normative proposals are most commonly rejected. Even these authors, nevertheless, present their model as the most explicit and sophisticated account of the reasoning of many court decisions that follow essentially correct intuitions.[109] At the same time, such authors also very emphatically insist certain awards that do not align with their theories, such as that of the well-known Exxon Valdez oil spill case,[110] were erroneous – since the whole world knew about the accident, a rational actor like this large corporation would not expect to escape liability, which means punitive damages should not have been awarded in this case.[111]

Reflecting on the salient outcome-driven interpretive approach of the Anglo-American scholarship on punitive damages opened my eyes to another possibility. It could be the case – given the degree of discrepancy among different accounts and, more importantly, the considerable number of paradigmatic cases that each perspective rejects – that the Anglo-American practice of punitive damages is too complex for reasonable reconstruction by a single, coherent interpretive exercise. There appears to be a factual obstacle to the interpretative enterprise in the case of punitive damages, at least in the way this label is ordinarily used in the United States.[112]

[107] See P. W. Kahn, *The Cultural Study of Law: Reconstructing Legal Scholarship* (University of Chicago Press, 1999), pp. 7–30 (comprehensively describing this tendency to legal reform in American scholarship).

[108] See Dworkin, Law's Empire, p. 90 (where Dworkin goes on to assert that, indeed, constructive interpreters "try to show legal practice as a whole in its best light, to achieve equilibrium between legal practice as they find it and the best justification of that practice.").

[109] Polinsky and Shavell, "Punitive Damages: An Economic Analysis," 896–900.

[110] *Exxon Shipping Co* v. *Baker*, 554 US 471 (2008).

[111] Polinsky and Shavell, 'Punitive Damages: An Economic Analysis', 903–4.

[112] This has led some to suggest "a change in nomenclature" regarding extra-compensatory damages; see, for example, G. Calabresi, "The Complexities of Torts: The Case of Punitive Damages," in M. S. Madden (ed.), *Exploring Tort Law* (Cambridge University Press, 2005), pp. 346–47.

Practices as fragmented and contradictory as punitive damage awards pose a serious problem to the constructive interpreter; indeed, the fact that they exist serves as the foundation for a particular strain of skepticism regarding interpretation, one which Dworkin calls "internal."[113]

Resuming, it may be inferred that although these scholarly efforts doubtlessly possess much value, most suffer from a major flaw. They have been severely constrained by two important factors: (1) the obstacle posed by the factual mess, for the practice of awarding punitive damages in the United States is highly complex, fragmented, and not only inconsistent but often contradictory; and (2) the predominant outcome-driven interpretive approach of the scholarship that focuses on describing and evaluating the purposes or functions of punitive damages as identified in the case law and statutes in an effort to determine the most befitting justification for these extra-compensatory awards. As might be expected, taking this sort of outcome-driven interpretive scholarly approach that is directly tied to an inherently complex and contradictory practice for justifications has not yielded coherent, convincing accounts of what essentially justifies punitive damages awards.[114] Instead, as demonstrated, the reluctance to burrow below the level of institutional practice has not only added to the confusion but, more importantly, has constrained the attempts to both explain and justify punitive damages. It has unquestioningly assumed punitive damages as an indisputable part of the practice of torts and subsequently focused on one particular aspect of the institution over others without really attempting to account in a meaningful way for the theoretical grounding of their deeply embedded retributive character.[115] To be sure, the factual complexities of the Anglo-American practice cannot be circumvented, but it is still possible to employ a different scholarly approach. Given the long-standing search for a convincing account of punitive damages, should tort scholars truly aspire to elaborate one, they ought to start contemplating alternative scholarly approaches that allow them to circumvent the limitations imposed by the very complexities and contradictions of American punitive damages case law, statutes, and doctrine. They ought to consider approaches that allow room for meaningful examination of more fundamental questions regarding

113 See Dworkin, Law's Empire, pp. 78–79, 266–74 (the main contention of the internal skeptic is "that legal practice is too deeply contradictory to yield to any coherent interpretation at all."). I must acknowledge that others, though in different ways, have made comparable observations about the American practice of punitive damages. For instance, see Calabresi, "The Complexities of Torts," pp. 336–37 (arguing that punitive damages "can perform at least five very different functions" and that any attempt of rationalization is problematic because it would "concentrat[e] essentially on one [...] role.").

114 For the argument that punitive damages theory is in crisis, see Sebok, "Punitive Damages: From Myth to Theory," 959 ("[c]ourts now lack an adequate theory to explain to themselves, lawyers, and litigants the purpose of punitive damages.").

115 Note that the very few attempts by tort scholars in the United States to delve into the retributive character of punitive damages have not yet yielded any full-fledged retributive rationale for the institution. I thoroughly engage these theories in Section G of Chapter 2.

the proper place of punishment in tort law and its justifications before diving headlong into the analysis of strictly legal material (i.e., judicial pronouncements, decisions of juries, statutes, doctrines, etc.). Only then would it become possible to develop a fuller, more thorough understanding of punishment and deterrence as the stated dual purposes of the institution in the first place. It suggests that to elucidate punishment and deterrence as the core purposes of the institution, the discussion should shift from the level of the conception to that of the concept and focus on those "discrete ideas that are uncontroversially employed in all interpretations."

B CIVIL LAW SYSTEMS: LATIN AMERICA AND CONTINENTAL EUROPE

In recent decades, punitive damages have moved to the center of debates in civil law jurisdictions as well – particularly, though not exclusively, in Latin America and Continental Europe.[116] The prospect of "transplanting" the alien institution to certain civil law national jurisdictions has generated vigorous discussions among civil law scholars for the last decades.[117] The lack of any established domestic practice of punitive damage awards has forced civil law scholars to concentrate on developing two different (though slightly related) lines of scholarship. I believe the distinction between them could prove useful here: one advances descriptive claims while the other describes normative ones. Characterizations of each type of inquiry follow.

To start, *comparative* punitive damages scholarship has overwhelmingly concerned itself with one major question: Does the practice of private law in civil law countries somehow respond to the same issues that punitive damages address in the common law systems?[118] The evolution of both traditions followed different paths and has distinctive institutions. Punitive damages are a conspicuous example, yet systems of both civil and common law inspiration must address, ultimately, a similar, if not identical, range of social problems. After all, deliberately wanton, recklessly

[116] When I refer to the civil law tradition in the present section, I mean the legal systems of Continental Europe and Latin America, which represent a narrow but widespread understanding for comparative purposes. See, for example, J. H. Merryman and R. Pérez-Perdomo, *The Civil Law Tradition: An Introduction to the Legal Systems of Europe and Latin America*, 4th ed. (Stanford University Press, 2018). Moreover, I focus narrowly on Latin America and Continental Europe mainly for expertise and knowledge.

[117] In an effort to make this presentation more concise, all references to specific countries are included in the footnotes that follow.

[118] The most prominent comparative studies on punitive damages are H. Koziol and V. Wilcox (eds.), *Punitive Damages: Common Law and Civil Law Perspectives* (Springer, 2009), and L. Meurkens and E. Nordin (eds.), *The Power of Punitive Damages. Is Europe Missing Out?* (Intersentia, 2012). Although these studies do not prescribe a single line of inquiry – they actually combine them – most country reports are written from a comparative perspective. These works have been of significant help in my survey of scholarship in continental Europe, and I will refer to many of them in the following footnotes.

indifferent, outrageous, and reprehensible behavior is not unique to common law countries. In every civil law jurisdiction are defendants who deserve punishment and behavior that must be marked as unacceptable.

Looking at how different legal institutions respond to similar situations constitutes a classical comparative law functionalist approach in which the scholar's attention is caught by a peculiar institution linked with a robust practice that does not yet exist in other systems.[119] The scholar then tasks herself to explain why the institution does not exist in both jurisdictions.[120] Work on punitive damages along this line of inquiry has typically followed two distinctive patterns: (1) on one side, many authors have sought to identify civil law institutions that more or less resemble punitive damages. They direct our attention to mechanisms by which defendants are condemned to pay sums above the level of the harm caused to the plaintiffs, as punitive damages do in common law systems[121]; (2) on the other side, scholars have sought to show how, in actual practice, tort litigation in certain civil law jurisdictions covertly awards extra-compensatory damages. One covert manner is the practice of inflating compensatory damages where outrageous behavior is involved, as in the case of "generous" awards for "pain and suffering," which theoretically should be strictly compensatory in nature. Such practices of disguising damage awards with a punitive component as compensatory awards (most commonly under the heading of nonpecuniary damages for physical injury, personality, or privacy rights infringements) have been widely identified in most civilian jurisdictions where punitive damages are not yet properly recognized in the law of torts.[122]

[119] For a description of different modes and critiques of functionalism, see R. Michaels, "The Functional Method of Comparative Law," in M. Reimann and R. Zimmermann (eds.), *The Oxford Handbook of Comparative Law* (Oxford University Press, 2006), pp. 339–82.

[120] For a thoughtful analysis of this method and its difficulties, see D. Kennedy, "New Approaches to Comparative Law: Comparativism and International Governance" (1997) 1997 *Utah Law Review* 545, 561, 588–90.

[121] This argument has been made in the following legal systems: France, see J. S. Borghetti, "Punitive Damages in France," in Koziol and Wilcox, *Punitive Damages*, pp. 56–58 (noting that "[a]lthough punitive damages do not officially exist as such under French law, some mechanisms do exist which bear some resemblance to them"); Germany, see N. Jansen and L. Rademacher, "Punitive Damages in Germany," in Koziol and Wilcox, *Punitive Damages*, pp. 75–76 (noting how some German authors "point to provisions in the [German Civil Code] and other codes that intend to prevent unwanted behavior and supposedly contain elements of punishment."); Hungary, see A. Menyhárd, "Punitive Damages in Hungary," in Koziol and Wilcox, *Punitive Damages*, p. 94 (analyzing Hungarian institutions such as penalty clauses that are said to resemble punitive damages); Italy, see A. P. Scarso, "Punitive Damages in Italy," in Koziol and Wilcox, *Punitive Damages*, p. 106 (exploring how scholars have inferred elements of punitive damages from a few Italian statutory provisions that resemble them); and Spain, see P. Del Olmo, "Punitive Damages in Spain," in Koziol and Wilcox, *Punitive Damages*, pp. 140–51 (discussing "legally based arguments [that] have been proposed to show that there are some punitive elements in Spanish tort law.").

[122] Countries where this practice has been observed out by scholars include: Argentina, see M. G. Martínez Alles, "¿Para Qué Sirven los Daños Punitivos? Modelos de Sanción Privada, Sanción Social y Disuasión Óptima" (2012) 5 *Revista de Responsabilidad Civil y Seguros* 55 (identifying the use of pain and suffering awards as a punitive mechanism employed by Argentinian judges); Brazil,

Commentators have demonstrated that the courts' inquiry into the wrongfulness of the defendant's behavior plays an important role in the judge's choice of remedy, such that the size of the remedies awarded are proportional to the perceived "reprehensibility" of the defendant's conduct. This tendency suggests that judges do not merely try to compensate the injured plaintiff but additionally intend to punish wrongdoers covertly for particularly reprehensible behavior.[123] Such scholarship suggests that judges, however quietly, often demonstrate some sensitivity to proportional retribution by punishing wrongdoers in proportion to both the wrongfulness of their behavior and the relevance of the victim's protected interests infringed by the reprehensible conduct.

Coming from a different angle, many civil law scholars advance a *normative* argument that the private law in their jurisdiction lacks adequate tools for certain factual situations, which common law judges ordinarily deal with by awarding punitive damages. They assume a policy-oriented viewpoint and propose enacting statutes introducing this institution to their systems.[124] Within this discussion over the desirability of the legal transplant of punitive damages, two separate debates have become the most prominent. First is the ongoing dispute over the *compatibility* of this alien institution with the driving principles of the private law of torts in the civil law system in question, one which is dominated by the notions of compensation

see N. Rosenvald, *As Funções da Responsabilidade Civil: a Reparação e a Pena Civil*, 2nd ed. (Atlas, 2014); Chile, E. Pereira Fredes, "Un Alegato a Favor de las Consideraciones Punitivas en el Derecho Privado" (2015) 7 *Revista de Derecho. Escuela de Postgrado* 61 (arguing that the fact that Chilean judges award damages for pain and suffering to punish the defendant represents a fracture to the rectificatory rationale); France, see Borghetti, "Punitive Damages," pp. 62–67 (stating that "[i]t is widely shared belief among French lawyers and academics that French courts sometimes set damages not only on the basis of the harm suffered by the plaintiff, but also by taking into account the behavior of the tortfeasor, with the aim of punishing"); S. Rowan, "Punishment and Private Law: Some Comparative Observations," in E. Bant, W. Courtney, J. Goudkamp and J. M. Paterson (eds.), *Punishment and Private Law* (Hart Publishing, 2021), p. 66 (pointing out to "[a] tendency on the part of lower courts, consciously or otherwise, to vary the quantum of [non-pecuniary damages] in accordance with the culpability of the defaulting party."); Germany, see Jansen and Rademacher, "Punitive Damages," pp. 77–85 (pointing out that "there are authors who argue that [German] courts frequently award damages [...] that cannot seriously be considered as purely compensatory."); Italy, see Scarso, "Punitive Damages," pp. 111–13; and Spain, see M. Otero Crespo, "Punitive Damages Under Spanish Law," in Meurkens and Nordin, *The Power of Punitive Damages*, p. 300 (arguing that "[i]t is undeniable that punitive damages do really breath in [the Spanish] system, more or less camouflaged under certain compensatory clothes.").

123 Similarly, see A. Pino Emhart, "No Sólo Quieren Dinero: La Función Expresiva de la Responsabilidad Extracontractual," in R. Barría Díaz, A. Ferrante and L. C. San Martín Neira (eds.), *Presente y Futuro de la Responsabilidad Civil* (Thomson Reuters, 2017), p. 175 (pointing out that judges in Chile tend to consider the defendant's wealth when measuring the amount of pain and suffering awards).

124 For the article written from this viewpoint that has most clearly influenced Latin American scholarly debates over punitive damages, see R. D. Pizarro, "Daños Punitivos," in A. Kemelmajer De Carlucci (ed.), *Derecho de Daños: Libro en Homenaje al Prof. Félix Trigo Represas*, 2 vols. (La Rocca, 1993), vol. 2, pp. 287–337. Similarly, see Rowan, "Punishment and Private Law," pp. 63–82 (describing this pattern in the context of the recent debates toward introducing punitive damages in France).

and restitution.[125] Following this logic, punitive damages are understood as a departure from the prevailing rectificatory rationale of tort law that confines any award of damages to the sole aim of compensating the injured person and according to which no attention should be paid to the character of the tortfeasor's conduct. Indeed, one of the main arguments of this type against punitive damages claims that any expressly punitive sanction must be regulated by criminal law and that punitive damages are therefore alien to tort law. They are thus depicted as an absurd, dysfunctional mixture of civil with criminal and administrative law. As already mentioned earlier in this chapter, some superior courts have actually addressed such concerns in relation to the enforcement of foreign judgments that included punitive damage awards – mainly by arguing that such awards infringe the "public order." Taking a different tack, other civil law scholars have emphasized that punitive damages are compatible with tort law if they fulfill a deterrent function (instead of a punitive one).[126] Second, authors in virtually every jurisdiction have objected to transplant proposals because of the questionable constitutionality of punitive damages, which ranges from problems of double punishment to infringements of the principle of legality (according to which penalization is only permitted if the wrongful conduct has been precisely codified), the greater strictness of criminal standards of proof, and procedural safeguards, among others.[127] What ultimately underlies

125 Compatibility with existing regimes is probably the most prominent contention with punitive damages in the civil law world. Examples include, in Colombia, see L. V. García Matamoros and M. C. Herrera Lozano, "El Concepto de los Daños Punitivos o Punitive Damages" (2003) 5 *Revista de Estudios Socio-Jurídicos* 211, 224–26 (arguing that punitive damages are incompatible with the compensatory nature of Colombian private law); in France, see Borghetti, "Punitive Damages," pp. 68–69 (considering arguments pro compatibility – the peine privée function – and against it – the réparation intégrale principle); in Germany, see Jansen and Rademacher, "Punitive Damages," pp. 75–76 (emphasizing that "the sole functions of the German law of damages are the reparation of injury and the compensation of resulting losses, while punishment of the wrongdoer is strictly reserved for criminal law."); in Italy, see Scarso, "Punitive Damages," pp. 106–9 (considering problems of compatibility with the compensatory nature of Italian tort law); and in Spain, see Del Olmo, "Punitive Damages," p. 154 (dealing with several compatibility issues). Moreover, see H. Koziol, "Punitive Damages – A European Perspective" (2008) 68 *Louisiana Law Review* 741, 753 (arguing that punitive damages are inconsistent with the fundamental principles of the private law).

126 For this stance, see C. Wagner, "Punitive Damages," in J. Basedow, K. J. Hopt, R. Zimmermann and A. Stier (eds.), *The Max Planck Encyclopedia of European Private Law* (Oxford University Press, 2012), pp. 1403–6 (proposing a new term that better reflects the deterrence function: "preventive damages"); P. Salvador Coderch, "Punitive Damages" (2000) 1 *InDret* 1, 14. I explore this approach in Section E of Chapter 2.

127 Scholars have explored constitutionality issues in: Argentina, see M. G. Martínez Alles and P. Nazareno, "Desafíos Constitucionales de los Daños Punitivos: Los Problemas del Ne Bis in Idem," in S. Legarre, L. S. Grosman, J. C. Rivera (h) and J. S. Elías (eds.), *Tratado de los Derechos Constitucionales* (Abeledo Perrot, 2014), p. 688 (for a comprehensive study of the constitutional challenges of punitive damages in Argentina with particular emphasis on the problems of ne bis in idem); Colombia, see García Matamoros and Herrera Lozano, "Punitive Damages," pp. 227–28 (arguing that punitive damages would violate the principle nullum crime sine lege and hence have no place under Colombian constitutional law); Germany, see Jansen and Rademacher, "Punitive Damages," p. 76 (noting that punitive damages arise problems of double punishment and violate the principle

both the (in)compatibility and the (un)constitutional arguments is the pervasively proclaimed clear-cut line separating private and public law.

Before continuing, however, note should be taken of the degree to which the discussions in both these areas of inquiry have been influenced by the complexity of the Anglo-American practice and scholarly approach to the institution, both of which were described in the preceding section. Although punitive damages originated in England before spreading to most common law jurisdictions, the current perception of the institution in the civil law world is overwhelmingly dominated by the United States experience.[128] Indeed, the citations both in studies of punitive damages and in court judgments awarding them (in those jurisdictions where they are available) refer almost exclusively to case law and authors from the United States.[129]

Now, for similar reasons, both these scholarly agendas – comparative and normative – depend highly on the conception of the practice of punitive damages, one that is generally assumed rather than explored. Both discussions depart from an implicit conception of how punitive damages should be understood and the functions that they perform in tort litigation in the United States. For its part, (1) a functionalist comparative analysis typically connects institutions (e.g., punitive damages) to social problems in the legal system of origin, which allows the identification of the set of issues that in a particular system are addressed by the institutional arrangement. Once this framework for comparison is established, scholars examine the other legal system(s) to find out how those problems are handled in their jurisdictions. Since the basis for comparison hinges on the understanding of how the institution works and the functions it performs in the system of origin, problems at this level will necessarily affect the whole comparative enterprise; (2) by the same token, normative studies ineluctably assume that a determined institution (e.g., punitive damages) serves a particular function in a foreign legal system. Based on that type of understanding, scholars will contend that their own legal system fails to respond to at least some of the problems that the institution addresses in the system of origin and, hence, argue for adopting or transplanting the institution. Here as well, the understanding of the functions that are served and the role

of nullum crime sine lege); Hungary, see Menyhárd, "Punitive Damages," pp. 99–102 (discussing problems of double punishment and the principle that there is "no crime without a law" under the Hungarian Constitution).

128 See, for example, Salvador Coderch, "Punitive Damages," 3 (noting that punitive damages are "now archetypically American") (my translation).

129 For instance, the few books on punitive damages published in the civil law world clearly demonstrate this trend: E. López Herrera, *Los Daños Punitivos* (Abeledo Perrot, 2008); Meurkens and Nordin, *The Power of Punitive Damages*; Koziol and Wilcox, *Punitive Damages*; R. C. Meurkens, *Punitive Damages: The Civil Remedy in American Law, Lessons and Caveats for Continental Europe* (Kluwer, 2014). Moreover, this trend is also patent in the case law awarding punitive damages in Argentina and Mexico. For concrete references of case law citing United States sources, see Martínez Alles, "Punitive Damages in Argentina and Mexico," pp. 129–47.

that is played by the specific institutional arrangement in the system of origin is of utmost importance.

Given the complexity of the Anglo-American practice and the many different and even contradictory functions that punitive damages perform in it, both lines of scholarship present major difficulties. For instance, as the state of the debate in the United States might lead us to expect, scholars in Latin America and Continental Europe struggle to grasp the multiplicity of overlapping conceptions of punishment and deterrence that are operative in the Anglo-American practice.[130] As a result, authors end up tacitly assuming one conception of the institution that performs the referential role in their study. However, insufficient regard for the partiality of such understandings (likely due to innocent unfamiliarity) makes them more prone to confident assertions of authoritative "this-is-what-punitive-damages-are-all-about" claims. This is problematic for obvious reasons. Clearly, comparative studies that ignore the complexity of the practice are defective by their own standards. Additionally, each author's implicit subscription to a particular understanding of the practice referred to as "punitive damages" has created semantic problems that further muddle the debates.[131] Third, although it is not obvious at first sight how well articulated normative discussions may be affected by reliance on a peculiarly narrow understanding of the practice of punitive damages (after all, someone could propose that a system be reformed through the incorporation of an institution designed in a particular way, independently of any actual foreign practice), in fact, such reliance ends up creating a more severe problem. Because these scholars typically advocate a legal transplant, the presentation of the practice of origin under an arbitrarily partial characterization fails to account for all the components of the institution whose introduction they seek.[132]

[130] For a detailed description of the contradictions and inconsistencies generated by the array of overlapping conceptions of punishment and deterrence at work in the scholarly debates and in the judicial decisions awarding punitive damages in Argentina, see Martínez Alles, "¿Para Qué Sirven Los Daños Punitivos?," 62–64.

[131] For instance, I am of the view that one of the most prominent debates between Argentine scholars on punitive damages has suffered from a semantic issue of precisely this kind. For a detailed analysis of these semantic problems in the Latin American context, see M. G. Martínez Alles, "La Dimensión Sancionadora del Derecho de Daños. Los Daños Punitivos," in D. M. Papayannis (ed.), *Manual de Responsabilidad Extracontractual* (Suprema Corte de Justicia de la Nación de Mexico, 2022), pp. 601–47. For an analysis of similar problems in the European context, see, for example, B. A. Koch, "Punitive Damages in European Law," in Koziol and Wilcox, "Punitive Damages," p. 197 (pointing out that, among other factors, "the blurriness [of the status of punitive damages in Europe] is due to the ambiguous use of terminology.").

[132] The problem here, of course, is the legal-transplant strategy. Proposals for legal reform can be articulated in two different ways: (1) by designing a new institution for the purpose in question, or (2) by advocating a legal transplant. In the first case, inspiration for design could surely be taken from a foreign legal practice, but as long as noticeable effort has been made to distinctively create a new institution, legal actors should have little reason to believe that the foreign practice that inspired the reform could work as a resource in case of application problems. This is precisely the problem with legal transplants, where the content of the package being imported is significantly undetermined.

This has led to problems in the drafting of legislation and, subsequently, implementation issues.[133]

Going back to the two primary strands of punitive damages scholarship in civil law jurisdictions, it can be inferred that, in order to meaningfully participate in the punitive damages debate, civil law scholars would be better served by avoiding the temptation to improve the understanding of the Anglo-American practice together with offering country-specific compilations regarding the (in)compatibilities with the institution in the authors' own legal systems. Rather, they ought to focus first on getting the theory right. To be sure, detailed descriptions of the complexities and incongruencies of the Anglo-American practice and scholarly approach to punitive damages serve as a helpful warning to those who favor transplanting the legal institution into their local jurisdictions and provide a valuable resource to those advocating the creation of a punitive damages institution tailored to their particular legal system. However, the fundamental scholarly debate over punitive damages in civil law systems must focus on the ultimate theoretical grounding of domestic punitive elements in their own legal systems that are already operating (albeit covertly).[134] The punitive component of these practices introduces relevant questions regarding the place of punishment in tort law that challenge the classic rectificatory rationale and demand proper justification. The existence of the punitive component also reveals the deficiency of purely dogmatic arguments against punitive damages – which basically come down to the assertion that punishment and retribution are considered the exclusive domain of criminal law and therefore lie outside the scope of tort law.

Genuine scholarly debate should willingly encourage efforts to make transparent those hidden punitive elements that are patent in their domestic private law practices of awarding damages, since any legal system that imposes sanctions in a covert manner without genuine justification should be considered questionable a priori. At the same time, scholars should be engaging in a profound discussion regarding the proper place for punishment in modern tort law, one that is not only less concerned with dogmatic boundaries between private law and public law but also more

For a cautionary account of the serious difficulties of advocating for a legal transplant strategy, see V. E. Schwartz and C. E. Appel, "Exporting United States Tort Law: The Importance of Authenticity, Necessity, and Learning from Our Mistakes" (2011) 38 *Pepperdine Law Review* 2. For an analysis of the different theories of legal transplants, see generally P. Legrand, "The Impossibility of 'Legal Transplants'" (1997) 4 *Maastricht Journal of European and Comparative Law* 111.

133 This is exactly the kind of issues Argentina has been dealing with since the reform of the Consumer Protection Act in 2008, which transplanted punitive damages to the country's legal system (Law N° 26.361, arts. 52bis and 8bis). Note that draft proposals that intended to deal with these problems were discussed in 2015 (as part of the Argentinian Civil Code Reform) and in 2018 (in the context of proposals to reform the Consumer Protection Statute), both without success. For a detailed analysis of the proposals, see D. Lo Giudice, *Daños Punitivos* (El Derecho, 2024).

134 I have argued for this scholarly approach before. See M. G. Martínez Alles, "Punitive Damages: Reorienting the Debate in Civil Law Systems" (2019) 10(1) *Journal of European Tort Law* 63.

responsive to the embedded retributive character of the institution.[135] Moreover, the new global scenario, in which several civil law jurisdictions have already introduced (or are seriously considering introducing) punitive damages into their legal systems while others are actively reconsidering the scope of the traditional public policy exception in cases of enforcement of foreign punitive judgments, fundamentally undermines not only the strength of the stark public–private divide originally invoked for outright rejection but also the widespread assumption that punitive awards are an "anomalous" and "foreign" feature that is exclusive of the common law of torts. If they ever were truly anomalous and foreign, they certainly are not anymore.

[135] I have introduced such arguments in M. G. Martínez Alles, "La Dimensión Retributiva del Derecho de Daños: La Perspectiva de la Víctima," in J. A. García Amado and D. M. Papayannis (eds.), *Dañar, Incumplir y Reparar. Ensayos de Filosofía del Derecho Privado* (Palestra, 2020), pp. 107–31.

2

Punishment in Tort Theory

The mere idea of punishment in tort law has always encountered strong resistance from tort theorists mainly because, according to traditional wisdom, the right to punish has been widely understood as belonging to the exclusive monopoly of the state (in the sense that no individual has legitimate authority to exact punishment from another), and, accordingly, a clear border must be drawn in the legal order between private law (and therefore tort law) and public law (under which criminal law falls). The threat that punitive elements in tort law pose to these long-standing distinctions is so powerful that tort theorists have generally responded by resisting punishment as an anomaly, considering punishment as substitutive, corseting punishment within tort law's compensatory framework, equivocating punishment with deterrence, and refashioning the victim's right to be punitive as a legal power for private redress. These reactions from tort theorists to the question of punishment partly explain the scarcity of theoretical reflection on the place of retribution in tort law. In fact, as we will see, the scholars who follow these approaches have shown no particular interest in developing the retributive dimension of tort law because the notion of just retribution was either inconsistent with the notion of justice in the framework they proposed or because they were indifferent to the matter, for developing it would not help them to achieve their goals. For their part, more recent efforts to provide justifications for punitive damages as some form of punishment, however scarce, evoke some notion of retribution, but only in highly qualified manners that do not convincedly advance a thorough retributive rationale of the institution. Whatever flaws they might have, these theories warrant a closer look.

A PUNISHMENT AS ANOMALY

Corrective justice theories of tort law (broadly understood) argue that when someone has been wronged, injustice has been done, and the tortfeasor who committed the injustice bears an obligation to repair (make whole) the person she has wronged.[1] In simple terms, tort law is a legal mechanism for the enforcement of the tortfeasor's duty to repair (i.e., to make her victim whole). Corrective justice theorists have long resisted punitive damages.[2] Ernest Weinrib has emphatically argued that punitive damages have no place in tort law since they "are geared, not to restoring the plaintiff's rights, but to punishing the defendant for the high-handed manner in which the wrong was committed."[3] In this line of thinking, Weinrib asserts the inconsistency of punitive damages with the theoretical framework of the law of torts because of the one-sidedness of the institution, which solely focuses on the conduct of the defendant instead of the relationship between the defendant's action and the plaintiff's right.[4] Accordingly, he argues that, as a structural matter, such considerations do not pertain to private law but rather to the criminal law.[5] The criminal law concerns itself with behavior deemed inconsistent with a determined, generalized regime of rights, whereas private law applies to violations of an individual's particularized right.[6] Moreover, Alan Beever has also emphatically asserted the place of punitive damages in public law.[7] They are "foreign to the structure of private law" in that, for instance, they bestow a "windfall" on the victim (for reasons that are independent of her interaction with the defendant) who "[c]annot justly demand to be put in a *better position* than she would have been in had she not been wronged."[8] For Beever, no understanding

[1] I refer in this subsection to corrective justice theories of tort law broadly because they deal with the specific quest for punishment in torts similarly. I allude to the representative theorists in the main text and following footnotes without meaning to undermine the subtle particularities of each theoretical account of tort law. Certainly, the individual theories included in this set vary greatly. However, taking up the distinctive features of each is not necessary for the particular points I want to make in this subsection.

[2] Note that other legal theorists have also subscribed to the usual objections raised by corrective justice theorists against justifying punitive damages in private law, see, for example, J. Penner, "Punishments and Penalties in Private Law, with Particular Reference to the Law Governing Fiduciaries," in E. Bant, W. Courtney, J. Goudkamp and J. M. Paterson (eds.), *Punishment and Private Law* (Hart Publishing, 2021), p. 117.

[3] See E. J. Weinrib, *Corrective Justice* (Oxford University Press, 2012), pp. 169–83; and *The Idea of Private Law* (Harvard University Press, 1995), p. 135 n25 ("under corrective justice damages are compensatory, not punitive.").

[4] See E. J. Weinrib, "Two Conceptions of Remedies," in C. E. F. Rickett (ed.), *Justifying Private Law Remedies* (Hart Publishing, 2008), p. 24.

[5] See E. J. Weinrib, "Civil Recourse and Corrective Justice" (2011) 39 *Florida State University Law Review* 273, 290.

[6] See E. J. Weinrib, "Punishment and Disgorgement as Contract Remedies" (2003) 78 *Chicago-Kent Law Review* 55, 86 (explaining the observation that "corrective justice renders punitive damages problematic is obvious on its face.").

[7] See A. Beever, "The Structure of Aggravated and Exemplary Damages" (2003) 23 *Oxford Journal of Legal Studies* 87, 105.

[8] Ibid 107 (emphasis added) (according to Beever, punitive damages would violate the "better position" constraint). Similarly, see Weinrib, Corrective Justice, p. 97 ("Punitive damages do not restore to plaintiffs what is rightfully theirs, but instead give them a windfall."). Note that the often raised "windfall" objection as necessarily precluding punitive damages does not seem persuasive since rights-based theorists could, for instance, propose guidelines to meet that constraint or come up with other ways in

of the common law of torts is possible without the recognition that punishment (retribution) has no place in it.[9] Under this light, punitive damages clearly stand as impermissible for two related reasons. The first is their distinctively one-sided focus on the defendant's conduct. The second is connected to the role they play in protecting societal interests (whether framed in terms of deterrence or retribution) rather than the private interests tied to the particular transaction between the parties proper to private law.

Other prominent scholars have advanced similar arguments. John Gardner has argued that punitive damages exceed the reach of corrective justice.[10] This is coherent with Gardner's continuity thesis in which the award of damages seeks to restore things "to where they would have been had one not occasioned their loss."[11] Arthur Ripstein, for his part, argues that tort remedies seek to correct the wrong by giving the victims back the means that were deprived by the tortfeasor who took them.[12] When these means do not longer exist, as is usually the case in most tort cases, Ripstein claims that money "can provide the plaintiff with means that go as far as possible toward having equivalent means."[13] Accordingly, compensatory damages "give you back the means you had, however imperfectly."[14] Within Ripstein's framework, compensatory damages thus aim to "put the plaintiff back in the position that he or she would have been in had the wrong not occurred";[15] or "make it as though the wrong had never happened."[16] Following this logic, Ripstein claims that any legal imposition of punitive damages either represents a means to exact corrective justice indirectly or a vehicle for public policy. In the first sense, imposing punitive damages can be seen as an indirect form of corrective justice to the extent that such awards can be understood, according to Ripstein, as aggravated or as gain-based damages. In the second sense, they may be understood as justified by policy considerations (e.g., deterrence) that override the limits imposed by corrective

which tort systems could establish limits for such awards. On a similar line, see S. Steel, "Deterrence in Private Law," in H. Psarras and S. Steel (eds.), *Private Law and Practical Reason: Essays on John Gardner's Private Law Theory* (Oxford University Press, 2023), p. 137 (arguing that the windfall objection is only *pro tanto*).

9 See A. Beever, "Justice and Punishment in Tort: A Comparative Theoretical Analysis," in C. E. F. Rickett (ed.), *Justifying Private Law Remedies* (Hart Publishing, 2008), pp. 249–98 (Beever even praises the civil law for better grasping this point and openly reproaches civil law scholars who argue that punitive elements are present in civil law systems.).

10 See J. Gardner, "Torts and Other Wrongs" (2011) 39 *Florida State University Law Review* 43, 47–48 ("One may regret that people have come to expect, and are often granted, various kinds of awards that go beyond the strictly reparative."); and "What Is Tort Law For? Part 1. The Place of Corrective Justice" (2011) 30 *Law and Philosophy* 1, 48 (referring to the use of punitive damages by American juries as "turning the law of torts into a ridiculous combination of lottery and pillory.").

11 See Gardner, "What Is Tort Law For?," 37.

12 See A. Ripstein, *Private Wrongs* (Harvard University Press, 2016), p. 251.

13 Ibid 252.

14 Ibid.

15 Ibid 259.

16 Ibid 260.

justice, to the extent that a damage award can be framed as an incentive rather than as a remedy for the wrong that the defendant did to the plaintiff.[17]

As I understand it, corrective justice theoretical difficulties with punishment are rooted in their ambition to explain, interpret, or justify tort law from a *monist*[18] and *structural*[19] perspective. From these approaches, punishment is understood as a threat both to an exclusive rectificatory rationale of tort law and to its bilateral structure concerned with internal notions of interpersonal justice.[20] The underlying fear seems to be that devoting too much attention to punitive damages (or other "unorthodox" remedies) risks undermining all the explanatory power of the "paradigmatic" rectificatory rationale of tort law.[21] It will also introduce consideration of nonrelational purposes (i.e., punishment, deterrence) which are external to the two-party transaction, leading to the deformation of the bilateral structure of tort law by blurring the separation between the latter and the criminal law. To be sure, corrective justice theorists are aware that tort law is not all about rectification. They acknowledge as much by introducing "qualifiers" for their claims.[22] For instance, Weinrib asserts that corrective justice consists in "undoing, *to the extent possible*, the injustice that has been committed."[23] He similarly qualifies his assertion that tort law "places the defendant under the obligation to restore the plaintiff, *so far as possible*, to the position the plaintiff would have been in had the wrong not

17 Ibid 259–60.

18 For representative scholarship on this point, see, for example, P. Cane, *The Anatomy of Tort Law* (Hart Publishing, 1997), pp. 224–25 (criticizing explanatory accounts of tort law based on a single principle); S. Hershovitz, "The Search for a Grand Unified Theory of Tort Law: Review of Arthur Ripstein's Private Wrongs" (2017) 130 *Harvard Law Review* 942; S. Hedley, "The Rise and Fall of Private Law Theory" (2018) 134 *Law Quarterly Review* 214; D. Priel, "Tort Law for Cynics" (2014) 75 *Modern Law Review* 703; E. Sherwin, "Interpreting Tort Law" (2011) 39 *Florida State University Law Review* 227, 241 (contending that "[t]ort law is not a natural phenomenon that might be expected to conform to a single motivating principle, or even a coherent set of principles; rather, it is a human artifact, produced by many decision-makers over a long period of time."); J. Stapleton, *Three Essays on Torts* (Oxford University Press, 2021), pp. 1–34 (criticizing "Grand Theories" while arguing for a "reflexive tort scholarship").

19 Corrective justice theories are fundamentally structural. See, for example, Weinrib, Corrective Justice, p. 12 (arguing that "[c]orrective justice is the synthesis of two complementary abstractions: correlativity and personality"; and that "[c]orrelativity articulates at the most general level the structure of the relationship between the interacting parties as doer and sufferer of the same injustice."); and Ripstein, Private Wrongs, p. 23 (arguing for "taking [tort] structures and doctrines at face value").

20 See Weinrib, Corrective Justice, p. 97 ("Punitive damages are inconsistent with corrective justice for reasons both of structure and of content."). For an influential discussion of the structure of tort law characterizing it as bipolar, see J. L. Coleman, "The Structure of Tort Law" (1988) 97 *Yale Law Journal* 1233; E. J. Weinrib, "Understanding Tort Law" (1989) 23 *Valparaiso University Law Review* 485; and S. R. Perry, "The Moral Foundations of Tort Law" (1992) 77 *Iowa Law Review* 449.

21 See, for example, Gardner, "Torts and Other Wrongs," 55 (noting that putting too much emphasis on unorthodox tort remedies, such as punitive damages, might be misleading).

22 On this point, see S. Hershovitz, "Corrective Justice for Civil Recourse Theorists" (2011) 39 *Florida State University Law Review* 107, 115–16.

23 See Weinrib, Corrective Justice, p. 36 (emphasis added).

been committed."[24] Gardner, for his part, alludes to "restoring things, *at least in some measure*, to where they would have been had one not occasioned their loss."[25] Similarly, even Ripstein acknowledges that few people would indifferently accept receiving compensation for an injury over not having suffered the injury in the first place.[26] Certain injuries, for example, losing a leg, cannot be repaired, and therefore cannot be truly compensated.[27] However, Ripstein seems to think that the qualifier "as far as possible" does the work necessary for theoretical coherence: Compensatory damages should get their means back to the victims *as far as possible* to the position where they would be if the wrong had never happened.

Perhaps these scholars thought that by introducing such qualifiers they could elegantly avoid the problem of formulating a thorough account that confronts what is left out of the rectificatory approach.[28] Perhaps they fear that further exploration would demonstrate the limited explanatory power of rectification in the structure and practice of the existing law. Certainly, the formal formula of "restoring the victim to the position in which she would have been in the absence of a wrong" and the focus on abstractly restoring the "normative equilibrium" between defendant and plaintiff is an appealing framing of tort remedies because it fits the bilateral transactional theoretical structure of private law without really accounting for the significance of the substantive role and attitude of the victim (e.g., her value-laden motivations, her sense of outrage, her experience of injury, the significance of the wrongdoing in her life, etc.), the victim who is ultimately calling upon a defendant to respond for the wrong done.[29] The formal and abstract depiction of the tort

[24] See Weinrib, The Idea of Private Law, p. 135 (emphasis added).

[25] See Gardner, "What is Tort Law For?," 37 (emphasis added).

[26] See Risptein, Private Wrongs, p. 252 ("Compensation does not aspire to make up a welfare loss so that the plaintiff is indifferent between noninjury and injury plus compensation.").

[27] Ibid 234 (for the idea that remedies are "second best").

[28] On this point, see R. L. Rabin, "Law for Law's Sake" (1996) 105 *Yale Law Journal* 2261, 2263 (suggesting that "Weinrib's notable intellectual accomplishment in fashioning a doctrinal universe to fit his philosophical principles is undermined both by its highly conceptual normative character and by its insistent indifference to functional concerns about the impact of tort law on society."). Similarly, see N. Sage, "Relational Wrongs and Agency in Tort Theory" (2021) 41 *Oxford Journal of Legal Studies* 1012, 1035 (describing Weinrib's account of tort law's relationality as "so extraordinary abstract."); C. Essert, "Thinking Like a Private Lawyer" (2018) 68 *University of Toronto Law Journal* 166, 173 (arguing that Weinrib' and Ripstein' reconstructions are "robustly metaphysical").

[29] Among Weinrib's declared aims are to "identify[] the most abstract unifying [legal] conceptions"; to "carry[] to its extreme the tendency to abstract that marks legal thinking" by offering "the barest and most general ideas underlying … the parties' relationship," see Weinrib, Corrective Justice, pp. 13–14; Ripstein, for his part, has asserted that "[he] will unashamedly maintain that the point of tort litigation is to resolve the specific dispute between the parties currently before the court, based entirely on what transpired between them," see Ripstein, Private Wrongs, p. 23. This private-internal account transpires from Ripstein's understanding of private law as existing in isolation from the larger social context. To clarify: corrective justice theorists neither argue that the motivations of tort victims to sue are uniform nor deny that tort victims might in fact have different motivations to sue; they ignore this empirical factor altogether because their structural normative frameworks formally operate without any determination of any tort victim's particular motivation to sue.

plaintiff as detached from the substantive content of her responses to wrongdoing of this approach implies that whatever else lies beyond restoration to the plaintiff's rightful position is external and foreign to tort law. Ripstein, for instance, rules out either any consideration of the defendant's degree of culpability (i.e., the degree of her indifference to the plaintiff's safety) or of the plaintiff's attitude toward the defendant (i.e., the extent of her anger, resentment, or thirst for revenge) by asserting that such considerations are "nonrelational."[30] According to Ripstein, "the wrong that the defendant did to the plaintiff must drive the analysis, not the attitude that it does, would, or should generate in either party."[31] Certainly, avoiding examination of the victims' perspective simplifies a great deal in the sense that it is much less complex to look exclusively at the wrong suffered by the plaintiff and take for granted that what the victim seeks in response through tort law boils down to compensation. In this reading, compensation serves as some sort of abstract (or approximate) restoration to her rightful position. It does not aspire to any meaningful examination of the actual significance of the wrongdoing for the private parties involved, wrongdoing that is informed not only by the manner of the defendant's conduct but also by the victims' reactive attitudes, which are much more complex and textured and which, in many circumstances, implicate a punitive motive for compensation.[32] The bottom line is that this type of structural understanding of tort law leaves out any meaningful connection to the underlying substance of the original response to the wrongdoing. Such understandings neglect (by failing to explore empirically) not only the variety of substantive motives that drive victims to seek recourse from tort law for appropriate responses but also the broader social context in which tort law is applied. As it is argued in Chapters 3, 4, 9, and 10, neglecting these factors ultimately impairs a sound reconstruction of the subtle interplay between the range of substantive interests that are regularly intertwined in tort law's processes.

Indeed, it is very difficult to sustain the notion that torts exclusively consist of losses compensable in money and, furthermore, that the monetary remedy effectively returns the plaintiff to the position (or closer to the position) that she was in prior to the wrong.[33] In truth, compensation is much less rectificatory than private

30 See Ripstein, Private Wrongs, p. 268.

31 Ibid.

32 On this point, see M. J. Radin, "Compensation and Commensurability" (1993) 43 *Duke Law Journal* 56, 71 (suggesting that one possible reason why legal discourse "has kept making rhetorical gestures like 'coming close' to rectification may be an effort to avoid implying a punitive meaning for compensation.").

33 On this point, see, for example, S. Hershovitz, "Tort as a Substitute for Revenge," in J. Oberdiek (ed.), *Philosophical Foundations of the Law of Torts* (Oxford University Press, 2014), p. 93 ("We can never restore things to just the way they were, and all too often, we cannot restore them at all."). For a critique of corrective justice accounts of tort remedies as rectificatory, see G. C. Keating, "Is the Role of Tort to Repair Wrongful Losses?," in D. Nolan and A. Robertson (eds.), *Rights and Private Law* (Hart Publishing, 2012), p. 405 (arguing that each of us owes tort obligations to everyone else and that they are not fundamentally obligations of reparation). For the argument that the remedy sought by

law theorists tend to argue. On the most basic level, tort law generally undercompensates those who were seriously injured. The vast majority of tort remedies for irreparable injury are converted into awards for pain and suffering or other damages that can hardly be captured in purely monetary terms. In such cases, restoring the individual to her state prior to the wrongdoing (i.e., to her former position) is clearly illusionary.[34] Moreover, the broad availability of noncompensatory remedies such as punitive damages proves the de facto inexistence of any absolute, definitive objection to damages awards for beyond what the victim has suffered purely in terms of loss (i.e., more-than-compensation).[35] Further proof that no absolute prohibition of noncompensatory awards exists is found in the discretion that some legal systems allow for reducing damage awards to less than the loss suffered by the victim (i.e., less-than-compensation) in certain cases. These include instances where the loss was caused neither willfully nor by gross negligence and the payment of the compensation would leave the liable party in financial hardship.[36] By consequence, the claim that noncompensatory responses are foreign to tort law loses a second leg to stand on.

In addition, because, in practice, tort law does consider the character of the defendant's conduct more often than is recognized by tort theorists, their assertions that tort law is predominantly concerned with the objective facts of the tortfeasor's conduct over the degree of culpability or reprehensibility also come into question.[37] The fact is that in tort cases the blameworthiness of the defendant's conduct is often considered, as it is in criminal law. Indeed, the noncompensatory responses already identified necessarily reflect particular circumstances of the wrongdoing in holistic fashion, for they consider the character of the defendant's wrongful conduct toward the particular victim who suffered or experienced the loss in order to justify either the award of damages for more-than-compensation or the reduction of the award of damages for less-than-compensation. Additional damages are awarded when the defendant's conduct is particularly egregious, reprehensible, or wanton; when the tort is committed in

a harmed plaintiff is *satisfaction* from the particular defendant who wronged her, see generally J. C. P. Goldberg and B. C. Zipursky, *Recognizing Wrongs* (Harvard University Press, 2020) (civil recourse theory is not tied to a notion of restoration or making whole).

34 See, for example, S. A. Smith, "Duties, Liabilities, and Damages" (2012) 125 *Harvard Law Review* 1727, 1753 (stating that "[n]o sum of money can make it as if a rape or assault or the loss of a loved one never happened.").

35 As mentioned in Chapter 1, Argentina, Australia, Canada, Chile, China, Mexico, New Zealand, Singapore, the United Kingdom (except Scotland), and the United States, to name some of the most important jurisdictions, include punitive damages as part of their law of torts.

36 Argentina (Civil Code, art. 1742), Brazil (Civil Code, art. 944), and Switzerland [Civil Code, art. 44 (2)] allow judges to reduce the award amounts when certain conditions are met.

37 On that commonly accepted assertion, see, for example, R. A. Duff, "Torts, Crimes and Vindication: Whose Wrong Is It?," in M. Dyson (ed.), *Unravelling Tort and Crime* (Cambridge University Press, 2014), p. 155; Ripstein, Private Wrongs, p. 268 (arguing that the defendant's degree of culpability is derivative, nonrelational, and the analysis must only take into account the wrong that the defendant did to the plaintiff).

particularly humiliating or distressing circumstances; or when it shows a willful and conscious disregard of the rights or safety of others. Awards are sometimes reduced when the defendant's conduct was modestly negligent; when warranted by the personal situation of the victim (i.e., whether and how badly the victim needs compensation); or in consideration of the defendant's lack of wealth or ability to pay the damages awarded. Clearly, both kinds of noncompensatory responses are functions of the particular circumstances and the significance of the wrongdoing for the victim. These tort remedies are thus as much concerned with assessing the harm done to the victim and its significance to her (i.e., her experience of injury) as they are with assessing the character of the defendant's conduct who committed the wrong.

Certainly, responses for more-than-compensation introduce relevant questions regarding the place of punishment in tort law that challenge the classic rectificatory rationale advanced by most corrective justice accounts of tort law. However, tort theorists' rhetorical insistence on rectification as the paradigmatic guideline and on a clear-cut border between private law (tort law) and public law (criminal law) has impeded broader theoretical reflection on the significance of tort remedies beyond rectification. The frequent recourse of many commentators and courts to the argument that the aim of damages awards is compensation for loss not only contributes to the misunderstanding.[38] It also creates a dynamic in which there are almost no incentives for elaborating explanations or justifications of awards that do not fit the rectificatory framework. As a result, the rectificatory aspect of damage awards has been overemphasized by tort theorists at the expense of serious consideration of noncompensatory responses, most likely out of respect for a neat theoretical distinction between private law and public law.[39] As a result, compensation has become

[38] For examples on what courts and commentators normally say with regards to the aim of compensatory damages: *United States* v. *Hathaley*, 257 F 2d 920, 923 (10th Cir. 1958) ("The fundamental principle of damages is to restore the injured party, as nearly as possible, to the position he would have been in had it not been for the wrong of the other party"); Restatement (Second) of Torts §901 (1979) ("the law of torts attempts primarily to put an injured person in a position as nearly as possible equivalent to his position prior to the tort"); A. Burrows, *Remedies for Torts and Breach of Contract*, 3rd ed. (Oxford University Press, 2004), p. 33 ("the aim of compensatory damages is to put the claimant into as good a position as it would have been in if no tort had been committed"); D. B. Dobbs, *Dobbs Law of Remedies: Damage-Equity-Restitution*, 2nd ed. (West Publishing, 1993), p. 3 ("The damages remedy is a money remedy aimed at making good the plaintiff's losses."); D. Laycock and R. L. Hasen, *Modern American Remedies: Cases and Materials*, 5th ed. (Aspen Publishing, 2018), p. 17 (explaining that restoring the plaintiff to her "rightful position" is "the essence of compensatory damages.").

[39] See Weinrib, *The Idea of Private Law* (asserting that private law is an entirely different thing than public law); A. Ripstein, "Tort Law in a Liberal State" (2007) 1(2) *Journal of Tort Law* 1, 11 (expressing that "[o]verlooking this familiar distinction between private law and public law generates at least some of the malaise of recent tort scholarship."). Also see K. Barker, "Private and Public: The Mixed Conception of Vindication in Torts and Private Law," in S. G. A. Pitel, J. W. Neyers and E. Chamberlain (eds.), *Tort Law: Challenging Orthodoxy* (Hart Publishing, 2013), p. 75 (arguing that those legal systems that cannot remedy the personal side-effects of rights-infringements through compensation or restitution "need to work harder to expand the reach of compensatory and restitutionary remedies, not persist in the use of punitive damages awards to oblique, restorative ends.").

the paradigmatic remedy, while noncompensatory responses, such as punitive damages, have gradually evolved as a matter of practice in the law of remedies without substantial grounding in any deeper underlying theory. They have usually either been applied covertly, explained as "anomalies," or subsumed into frameworks that are less offensive to the predominant rectificatory theory.

B PUNISHMENT AS SUBSTITUTIVE DAMAGES

According to rights-based theory, tort law is solely concerned with the vindication of primary rights, and victims who suffer a wrong are entitled to a secondary right to a remedy for the violation of their primary rights. On the rights-based approach, remedies are thus straightforward in the sense that they basically enforce the primary rights by giving the plaintiff the very thing to which she is entitled – rights and remedies are understood as the two sides of the same coin. Following Robert Stevens, where the primary right cannot (or should not) be enforced, the plaintiff is entitled to an award of damages in substitution for the right (i.e., to vindicate the right that has been infringed).[40] These "substitutive damages" represent the value of the right infringed, which is independent of the victim suffering any loss (i.e., it is irrelevant whether loss is incurred or not). To be sure, when losses have been suffered by the victim, consequential compensatory damages can be added to the victim's basic substitutive award. In this way, Stevens understands the remedy, which usually takes the form of monetary compensation, as "the closest response the law can give to the wrong not having been committed in the first place."[41]

Following this logic, Stevens argues that the two-sidedness of private law imposes strict limits on the types of reasons that justify its operation, reasons that must also be bilateral in the sense that they must apply equally to both parties. For Stevens, therefore, one-sided arguments, such as the interest in deterring the defendant from future wrongdoing or the objective of compensating the claimant for his or her loss, cannot be invoked to support claims related to private law rights and duties.[42] However, when it comes to punishment (i.e., punitive damages), Stevens's position differs from most rights-based theorists. He shifts from valuing the right infringed to an argument based on the seriousness of the violation of the right.[43] According to Stevens, punitive damages can be justified "as a form of substitutive damages for the right infringed" on the basis that they are awarded in *substitution* for a right that is *seriously* infringed – or as Lord Nicholls said in *Kuddus*, "an emphatic vindication

[40] R. Stevens, *Torts and Rights* (Oxford University Press, 2007).

[41] Ibid 59.

[42] See generally R. Stevens, "Private Law and the Form of Reasons," in A. Robertson and J. Goudkamp (eds.), *Form and Substance in the Law of Obligations* (Hart Publishing, 2019).

[43] See Stevens, Torts and Rights, pp. 85–88.

of the claimant's rights."[44] The underlying claim is that "the contumacious infringement of a right is more serious" than a merely negligent one and that, as a consequence, higher damages are demandable for such violations of the right: "[t]he more outrageous the defendant's conduct, the greater the infringement of the right and the greater the substitutive award."[45]

This means that punitive damages understood as substitutes for the right depend not only on the value of the right but also on the particular manner and circumstances in which the right is infringed. However, under the rights-based approach, where the violation of the right represents sufficient grounds for an award of substitutive damages, the defendant's degree of reprehensibility does not affect the value of the right infringed. It is therefore not clear why the amount of damages imposed on the defendant (i.e., the punitive award) should be affected by the nature of the infringement.[46] In other words, if Stevens is truly concerned about the value of the right, the fact that the infringement was "contumacious" should have no impact on the extent of the substitutive award unless he is willing to acknowledge that when it comes to punitive damages, the concern is with the defendant's culpability and the consequential impact of the outrageousness of the wrong for the victim. If that is the case, then Stevens's argument for punitive damages awards is perhaps better understood as a supplement to compensatory damages rather than as a substitutive award.[47] Indeed, this understanding would align better with his suggestion to label them "retributory damages" and quantify them in "[proportion] to the gravity of the infringement of the right," which seems to involve some idea of deservedness.[48] The problem is that, having emphatically ruled out deterrence as a justification for punishment, Stevens must offer a retributive justification for why tort law cares about punishing the defendant's conduct when the tort was committed in a contumacious manner that does not rely on the one-sided arguments that, in his reconstruction, offer no justification for claims of private law rights and duties. Indeed, rights-based theorists object to retribution in tort law mostly because the principle of "just desert" (or "deservedness"), as the most widely acknowledged retributive ground for punishment, is defined in nonrelational terms. It is nonrelational because the severity of the sanction imposed on an individual is determined solely by the gravity of her wrongdoing, while tort law, in contrast, should not focus on the reprehensibility of the defendant's conduct, but instead the transaction between the two parties. Because of the bilateral (interpersonal) structure of private law, rights-based theorists deem the notion of retribution as foreign to tort law and more pertinent to criminal law.

44 Ibid 85; *Kuddus* v. *Chief Constable of Leicestershire Constabulary* [2001] UKHL 29; [2002] 2 AC 122 [29].

45 See Stevens, Torts and Rights, p. 85.

46 Similarly, see D. Nolan and A. Robertson (eds.), *Rights and Private Law* (Hart Publishing, 2012), p. 21.

47 I take inspiration here from Andrew Burrows's work on "Damages and Rights," in Nolan and Robertson, Rights and Private Law, pp. 275–308.

48 See Stevens, Torts and Rights, p. 85.

C PUNISHMENT AS (RETALIATORY) COMPENSATION

From yet another standpoint, some tort scholars have of late abandoned the traditional corrective justice approach of simply rejecting punishment as inconsistent with the bipolar, rectificatory structure of tort law in favor of arguments that punishment can be accommodated within a compensatory rationale. The starting point of these accounts is usually the acknowledgement that standard corrective justice theory is descriptively inadequate: There is a problem of fit between the stated rectificatory goal of compensation and the details of compensatory remedies in that, in the vast majority of tort injuries (e.g., pain and suffering, harms from physical injury, wrongful death, etc.), the harm done cannot be repaired monetarily, and thus compensatory remedies are not suited for the purpose of restoring the victim to her "rightful position."[49] This discrepancy between compensatory remedies and actual loss has led scholars to ask why victims sue for compensatory damages using tort law if compensation does not restore them to their rightful position – or only does so imperfectly or in limited fashion. They wonder whether there is "something else" that tort law accomplishes that is obscured in the compensatory discourse. These scholars do not deny that monetary awards are compensatory remedies that provide satisfaction for measurable losses suffered by victims but contend that victim satisfaction also involves "retaliation" against the injurer.[50] They question whether loss-focused conceptions of corrective justice deflect attention from the role and attitude of the victim in pursuing a tort lawsuit and thus fail to consider that victims frequently do not simply wish to recover their losses but actually seek to prevail over those who unjustly injured them. Loss-focused corrective justice cannot explain the retaliatory sentiments that often accompany claims to compensation.

To resolve these problems, Emily Sherwin proposes recasting the relationship between defendant and victim as one of "revenge" rather than "moral right" and "duty." In this reconstruction, Sherwin introduces what she calls "retaliatory compensation," arguing that the practice of compensation has a retaliatory function (i.e., it may also serve as an outlet of revenge) based on the genuine sentiments that move victims to pursue damage awards – the idea that "victims do not simply wish to recover for losses; they wish to prevail over their injurers."[51] She contends that the corrective justice understanding of compensation must be revised because this

[49] See E. Sherwin, "Compensation and Revenge" (2003) 40 *San Diego Law Review* 1387, 1394 (arguing that money does nothing to eliminate the harm: "compensatory remedies are helpless to restore victims to their rightful position.").

[50] Ibid 1413 (arguing that "[l]awsuits provide vehicles for retaliatory aggression."). Recently, Sherwin has put some distance from "retaliatory aggression," see E. Sherwin, "Comments on Stephen Smith's Duties, Liabilities and Damages" (2012) 125 *Harvard Law Review Forum* 164, 169 (stating that "providing the victim with a retaliatory remedy is a way to recognize, and allow the victim to reassert, moral equality").

[51] See Sherwin, "Compensation and Revenge," 1396–97.

moral component of compensation requires both refinement and recognition.[52] She therefore stipulates that, while compensatory remedies provide legal satisfaction to the victims, genuine satisfaction often demands retaliation against the injurer: Sherwin advances the idea that, through the legal process, the victim strikes back at the wrongdoer by exacting relief at the wrongdoer's expense to even the score.[53] She claims that the "outcome of the remedy is not simply correction of loss, but an adjustment in the comparative positions of the parties."[54] Under this view, the object of compensatory remedies is comparative in the sense that it "is not simply to adjust the absolute position of the claimant, but also to adjust an outcome in which the relative positions of the claimant and the wrongdoer are deemed to be unfair."[55] According to Sherwin, "this comparative element of compensation, which seeks to counterbalance rather than to simply repair the wrong done to the claimant, has a close affinity to revenge."[56] Thus may vindictiveness, she argues, be justified in the pursuit of legal compensation.

The appeal of Sherwin's approach lies in shifting attention from the wrongdoer's duty to repair to the role and attitude of the victim who initiates and pursues a tort lawsuit by identifying the deep, intuitive moralistic roots of the punitive components present in tort law. However, Sherwin's proposal goes no further than expanding the concept of compensation to encompass that "something else" (i.e., victim satisfaction and revenge) that is not captured by tort law's classic rectificatory structure. She does not analyze how patently retributive intuitions could be better captured by tort law without constraining them corset-like into the compensatory framework. As a matter of fact, Sherwin herself acknowledges the limits of her proposal by recognizing the tension between certain features of compensatory remedies and the substantive role for retribution in the practice of compensation. For instance, she points out that the indifference of compensation to fault makes revenge through claims for compensatory remedies irrational and, moreover, that purely compensatory liability does not inflict much grief on sufficiently affluent or insured defendants.[57]

In my view, as it is argued in Chapter 5 of Part II, one of the problems with compensatory approaches to punishment is that, in their efforts to make punishment fit into the classic rectificatory framework, they end up portraying punishment as dependent on and subsidiary to compensation.[58] This not only leads, paradoxically, to an overemphasis on compensation that they themselves criticize, but also, and perhaps most importantly, to dismissing the more fundamental question of whether punishment (retribution) may play an independent role in the tort context since

52 Ibid 1397.
53 Ibid 1396.
54 Ibid 1397.
55 Ibid 1389.
56 Ibid.
57 Ibid 1404.
58 See Chapter 5 where I argue for a delineation between punishment and compensation.

they offer no delineation of punishment from compensation. On the contrary, such approaches seem to reassert confidence in the view that compensatory damages can do all the work on their own.

A similar problem surfaces in those civil law jurisdictions where scholars have argued for mixed-nature (i.e., punitive and compensatory) nonpecuniary awards in order to render account of reprehensible wrongdoing. For instance, the Supreme Court of Mexico recently introduced punitive damages by interpreting them as a punitive component of pain and suffering awards.[59] Similarly, courts and commentators in Brazil have increasingly recognized a dual character of moral damages (i.e., nonpecuniary awards), namely compensatory and punitive.[60] Certainly, this approach is particularly appealing to civil law jurisdictions intricately designed around the principle that sharply separates private law (tort) and public law (crime). However, the attractiveness of such a proposal depends on the grounds it offers for disentangling the punitive and compensatory components of the nonpecuniary award. Thus far, civil law jurists have not persuasively undertaken this challenge. Yet even in those cases where the punitive and compensatory facets of nonpecuniary awards were conceptually delineated, and each prescribed through a differentiated treatment, the problem would persist. This is because the punitive award would still ride on, parasitically, the availability and actual recognition of the nonpecuniary award. Punitive awards would not be available in tortious instances where particularly reprehensible behaviors worthy of punishment and deterrence occurred but in which only pecuniary damages are available or, for any reason, the claim for nonpecuniary damages does not succeed. In sum, linking the punitive claim to the compensatory claim for nonpecuniary awards not only dilutes the conceptual distinction between punishment and compensation but also limits the scope and availability of punitive damages, diminishing its punitive rationale.[61] And it ultimately represents yet another attempt to circumnavigate the more fundamental question of whether an independent place for punishment (retribution) legitimately exists in tort law.

D PUNISHMENT AS (SUBSTITUTE FOR) REVENGE

One different perspective comes to us from Scott Hershovitz, who has recently questioned rectification as paradigmatic and abandoned the traditional tort theorist reaction of simply rejecting punishment as an anomaly. That is, he argues that

59 SCJN, Primera Sala, Amparo Directo 30/2013, February 26, 2014, 87–91. Note that there is still uncertainty on whether the Court will fully embrace this approach in the future.

60 See, for example, STJ HDE 586/CA, Min. Raul Araújo, May 16, 2022, *Apotex* v. *Kalinka*. For scholarly work noting that nonpecuniary awards have a dual compensatory and punitive character, see R. Peteffi da Silva and M. Pickersgill Walker, "Punitive Damages: United States Conceptualization of the Doctrine and Case Law Analysis of Santa Catarina Court of Appeals" (2016) 74 *Seqüência (Florianópolis)* 295.

61 For further delineation between punitive, aggravated, and pain and suffering awards, see Chapter 5.

punishment may not be as inconsistent with the bipolar structure of private and therefore tort law as is assumed because it often serves the goal of corrective justice.[62] In his early work, Hershovitz argued that tort law "can serve as an outlet for vindictive motives," positing that tort law often operates as a substitute for revenge by sending the same messages that revenge exacted personally would (probably) have sent.[63] Recently, Hershovitz has attempted to put more distance between his theory on torts and his early focus on revenge. In his latest work on torts, he focuses on the messages that tort liability sends about our relations to one another, arguing that tort law is primarily an expressive institution in that a tort judgment represents public affirmation that "this defendant wronged that plaintiff."[64] From this standpoint, Hershovitz claims that the point of corrective justice may also involve correcting the message sent by the wrongdoing with regard to the victim's social standing (i.e., a decision in favor of the plaintiff vindicates the social standing of victims). Accordingly, the monetary award is not only about altering allocations in an effort to restore the status quo ante by returning victims to a position similar to the one they would have been in absent the wrong. Surely, Hershovitz acknowledges that repair is one form of corrective justice but contends that is not the only pertinent dimension, at least not in most cases or for most injuries. For Hershovitz, both reparative and nonreparative damages serve a communicative purpose: They mark the wrong as the responsibility of the defendant.[65] Punitive damages, in his view, are also communicative in that they "help mark the gravity of the wrong."[66] Thus, Hershovitz claims that when courts go beyond pecuniary losses and, for instance, award pain and suffering or punitive damages, they are not exceeding the ambit of corrective justice. Such damage awards have every bit as much to do with corrective justice in that they contribute to correct the message that wrongdoing sends about the victim's social standing. Hershovitz acknowledges the tension between corrective justice (which requires that we vindicate the social standing of victims) and retributive justice (which requires that we condemn the people who wrong the victims) in tort law by pointing out that, to the extent that punitive damages communicate condemnation, they serve the ends of retributive justice and, as a consequence, tort law is not purely corrective, just as criminal law is not purely retributive. He goes even further by suggesting that the reason we make punitive damages available through tort law may be retributive justice (or some expression of condemnation), which may be called for to meet the dictates of corrective justice understood more broadly than in purely rectificatory terms.[67]

62 See S. Hershovitz, "Treating Wrongs as Wrongs: An Expressive Argument for Tort Law" (2017) 10(2) *Journal of Tort Law* 405.

63 See Hershovitz, "Tort as a Substitute for Revenge," pp. 96–97 (arguing that tort damages do "justice through the message that they send about the victim's standing and the wrongdoer's responsibility.").

64 See Hershovitz, "Treating Wrongs as Wrongs," 440.

65 See Hershovitz, "Tort as a Substitute for Revenge," p. 96.

66 Ibid.

67 See Hershovitz, "Treating Wrongs as Wrongs," 445.

Admittedly, Hershovitz's arguments on retribution in tort law are tentative and underdeveloped – he himself recognizes that he is not offering a full theory of retributive justice – but they are nevertheless important. They point out an understanding of tort law that is more nuanced, that comprises many dimensions and which not only opens a path to question the rigidity of the widely proclaimed division between torts and crimes but also to the rich potential of theoretical studies that fall outside the narrow lens of rectification (i.e., reflections that move beyond the abstract exercise of determining the rightful positions of the two parties).

E PUNISHMENT AS DETERRENCE

Taking a different tack to the widespread criticism of punitive damages by private law theorists as contrary to the common law structure of private law (i.e., as a heresy or a deformation), James Edelman argues that punitive damages can be defended on the basis of their goal of deterrence.[68] Inspired by the American punitive damages precedents in *Grimshaw* and *Romo*, Edelman contends that depriving private law of deterrent-based awards, such as punitive damages, would produce a serious "moral gap" in the sense that wealthy litigants would be allowed to appropriate the private law rights of others just by paying compensation.[69]

In asserting a distinction between a punitive rationale and a punitive effect, Edelman emphasizes that his defense of punitive damages is based upon a deterrence rationale even if the punitive award has a punitive effect for the defendant. He seems to argue that various damage awards have the same punitive effect in the sense that the defendant who is required to compensate for loss caused suffers a punishment on her wealth – and that there is nothing particularly special about punitive damages in this regard.[70] Then, Edelman criticizes theories of tort law that deny deterrence a legitimate role in tort law. To counter them, he argues that deterrence has deep roots in private law, so much so that punitive damages will never be easily uprooted without a compelling justification. However, Edelman's position seems to rely on the deterrence function of tort law more generally rather than a deterrence-based rationale of punitive damages.

A distinctive aspect of punitive damages, which raises important challenges for Edelman's approach, is related to the double function served by the institution: punishment and deterrence. All legal actors seem to understand punitive damages as a

68 See J. Edelman, "In Defence of Exemplary Damages," in C. E. F. Rickett (ed.), *Justifying Private Law Remedies* (Hart Publishing, 2008), pp. 225–48. Similarly, see Barker, "Private and Public," p. 82 (stating that "if [punitive damages] are to be retained [in modern private law], their function must be expressly aligned with public purposes such as deterrence, not with the private purposes of personal restoration.").

69 See Edelman, "In Defence of Exemplary Damages," p. 227.

70 Ibid 234.

sum of money beyond compensation that is awarded for the actual harm inflicted in order to both punish defendants for past behavior and deter them (and others) from similar misconduct in the future. Scholars, lawyers, and judges all openly agree on this precise conundrum, namely, that punitive damages both "punish and deter."[71] Although this understanding of the double purpose of punitive damages – punishment and deterrence – is nearly unanimous, it is often unclear what legal actors and scholars mean when they refer to either punishment or deterrence, or both. In fact, most theorists of punitive damages rely on the duality of the concept that the label "punishment and deterrence" is supposed to capture in order to defend conflicting views, even though its articulation is frequently peculiar. For instance, punishment can be plausibly understood as retribution, meaning that the grounds for punitive damages are located in the offense the defendant caused.[72] Yet this notion is sufficiently abstract to accommodate quite varied conceptions, such as private retribution (where the relevant wrong was done to the individual plaintiff seeking vindication of her rights)[73] and public retribution (where the focus is on the wrong caused to society in general).[74] Alternatively, others argue that deterrence is the primary goal of punitive damages, an approach that also leaves room for divergent understandings, for deterrence can also be both specific or general (depending on whether it is aimed at dissuading the particular defendant from reoffending, or dissuading others from engaging in similar tortious conduct by way of example or warning).[75] Deterrence can also be complete or optimal (depending on whether the intention is to discourage the defendant's engagement in a specific activity or behavior completely or to an acceptable degree).[76] Some of these theories even admit a variety of combinations between the two functions of punishment and deterrence. However, the fact that both functions are to some extent interconnected does not mean that one of the functions cannot be understood as the core element of the institution to the detriment of the other for it could be the case that punishment is understood as a secondary or necessary attribute of deterrence, or that deterrence

71 For concrete references, see above Section A (b) of Chapter 1.

72 For this view, see, for example, P. Cane, "Retribution, Proportionality and Moral Luck," in P. Cane and J. Stapleton (eds.), *The Law of Obligations: Essays in Celebration of John Fleming* (Oxford University Press, 1998), p. 169 ("[punitive damages] are unarguably retributive in the sense that they rest on a judgment that the defendant should have acted differently.").

73 Several authors in relation to both tort law and criminal law have developed this notion. I explore this in further detail in Chapter 4.

74 I explore distinct notions of retribution below in Section G.

75 For a general discussion on this distinction, see T. Colby, "Clearing the Smoke from Philip Morris v. Williams: The Past, Present and Future of Punitive Damages" (2008) 118 *Yale Law Journal* 392, 470–72.

76 For a discussion on this distinction, see K. N. Hylton, "Punitive Damages and the Economic Theory of Penalties" (1998) 87 *Georgetown Law Journal* 421, 452–54 (arguing that gain elimination, not loss internalization, is the primary goal of punitive damages). Also see D. Markel, "How Should Punitive Damages Work?" (2009) 157 *University of Pennsylvania Law Review* 1383, 1391 (arguing that courts rarely distinguish between "complete deterrence (aiming at preventing the commission of similar misconduct in the future)" and "optimal deterrence (aiming at cost internalization).").

is depicted as a secondary and necessary effect of punishment.[77] Needless to say, the different theoretical positions have very important normative implications for the way punitive damages play out in practice.

Edelman's defense can be criticized for the reasons just laid out. In fact, his exclusive defense of punitive damages on deterrence grounds fails to address what is actually entailed by the deterrence-based rationale, leaving room for divergent understandings that introduce ambiguity.[78] Admittedly, he concludes that private law does not aim for complete deterrence but for a balance between sufficient deterrence and the liberty of the individual, but, still, this does not tell us much about how punitive damages actually operate as a deterrence in tort law (i.e., to what extent, in what form, and on what grounds) or how they are at all distinct from other damages awards.[79] Moreover, Edelman does not address the relationship between deterrence and punishment as the widely accepted double function of punitive damages. Even if we interpret Edelman's account as implicitly accounting for the double aspect by assigning the main function of punitive damages to deterrence and a secondary collateral function to punishment (i.e., the punitive effect), this implicit interpretation does not tell us what, in Edelman's view, deterrence is all about.

Abstraction at the substantive level of the deterrence rationale for punitive damages is also evident in representative civil law scholarship on the institution. Eloquent examples are found in recent defenses of punitive damages, both in Latin America and Continental Europe, on exclusively deterrent grounds. Anxiety over the perceived need to resist condoning outright punishment in private law, whether because it is seen generally as foreign to the civil law legal culture or, in particular, to the rectificatory rationale of tort law, has led tort scholars of those legal traditions to argue more pragmatically that, if punitive damages are "sanctions" that can be understood as "deterrence," then they are compatible with the law of torts – meaning that there are no substantial obstacles to their introduction in their legal systems.[80] However, here again, these scholars have yet to offer an explicit account

[77] For an explanation on how deterrence can play a secondary or primary function in relation to punishment but cannot be the sole justification of exemplary damages, see Beever, "The Structure of Aggravated and Exemplary Damages," 102.

[78] This phenomenon goes beyond tort scholarship. See, for example, C. M. Sharkey, "Punitive Damages Transformed into Societal Damages," in E. Bant, W. Courtney, J. Goudkamp and J. M. Paterson (eds.), *Punishment and Private Law* (Hart Publishing, 2021), p. 159 n12 (pointing out that courts in the United States, England, Canada, and Australia stop short of offering meaningful explanations of the concept of deterrence).

[79] See Edelman, "In Defence of Exemplary Damages," p. 247.

[80] See, for example, G. Wagner, "Punitive Damages," in J. Basedow, K. J. Hopt, R. Zimmermann and A. Stier (eds.), *The Max Planck Encyclopedia of European Private Law* (Oxford University Press, 2012), pp. 1403–6 (proposing a new term that better reflects the deterrence function: "preventive damages"); P. Salvador Coderch, "Punitive Damages" (2000) 1 *InDret* 1, 14 (similar). At the EU level, see Directive (EU) 2024/1760 of the European Parliament and of the Council of June 13, 2024, on corporate sustainability due diligence and amending Directive (EU) 2019/1937 and Regulation (EU) 2023/2859 ("[d]eterrence through damages (punitive damages) [] should be prohibited.").

of the understanding of "deterrence" they are advancing in their reconstructions. This is problematic for at least two reasons. First, as explained earlier, "deterrence" can be understood in a variety of ways that are fundamentally different (i.e., specific, general, complete, optimal). The abstract approach introduces ambiguity and even more complexity into scholarly debates and the foreign legal community's understanding of what-punitive-damages-are-all-about. Of course, this does not mean that these scholars and others have not developed basic intuitions regarding the conceptions of punishment and deterrence at stake, but it is evident that a systematic exposition of the competing conceptions is practically nonexistent and the debate about their distinct normative implications mostly absent. Second, the fact that they reject outright the "punishment" aspect of punitive damages as incompatible with the rectificatory rationale of tort law as a branch of private law not only poses an obstacle to meaningful discussion of whether a place for retribution in tort law exists at all but also, and perhaps most importantly, it raises the question of why deterrence can be simply embraced as "compatible" with that same rectificatory rationale of tort law without any compelling argument – for under the rectificatory rationale both deterrence and punishment are "outliers" that demand justification.

A proposal that reduces "punishment" to "deterrence" based on an assumed (rather than explored) incompatibility of the former with private law without any further specification of the conceptions of punishment and deterrence at play (and how they are interconnected) cannot possibly be considered either persuasive or satisfactory. To that end, the current scholarly debate on the rationale of punitive damages should be reconducted at a much more concrete level by engaging in thorough discussions regarding the identification, justification, and defense of specific interpretations of the functions of punishment and deterrence and their derivative normative and practical implications.[81] Surely, the novelty of this scholarly approach will require private law scholars to recognize, on one side, the insufficiency of the traditional theoretical understanding of tort law as an exclusively private compensatory mechanism and, on the other, the constraining effect of the pervasively proclaimed yet disputable clear-cut line between private law and public law which underlies the incompatibility argument.

From another perspective, instrumentalist theories of tort law based on economic efficiency, such as law and economics,[82] have similarly focused on the exclusive deterrent rationale of punitive damages by directly reducing punishment to deterrence. Unlike the deterrent accounts described earlier, the main law and economics

[81] A recent example of this type of scholarly approach can be found in K. Barker, "Punishment in Private Law – No Such Thing Anymore," in E. Bant, W. Courtney, J. Goudkamp and J. M. Paterson (eds.), *Punishment and Private Law* (Hart Publishing, 2021), pp. 35–62.

[82] The economic analysis of law was introduced in the 1960s in the United States as a new alternative school of thought to legal doctrine. The first attempts to apply economic analysis to different areas of law were made by R. Coase, "The Problem of Social Cost" (1960) 3 *Journal of Law and Economics* 1; and G. Calabresi, "Some Thoughts on Risk Distribution and The Law of Torts" (1961) 70 *Yale Law Journal* 499, who are considered its co-founders.

approach to punitive damages embraces a specific rationale of deterrence called "optimal deterrence." The indifference toward punishment from the law and economics approach derives from that school's utilitarian approach: Tort law's purpose is promoting an efficient allocation of resources, and, accordingly, inefficient conduct (whether reprehensible or not) constitutes the wrong that must be corrected through incentives that cause people to take cost-justified precautions.[83] The irrelevance of the reprehensibility of the defendant's conduct itself indicates that punishment (or retribution) is trivial and that punitive damages are simply one of the many tools at hand to achieve the goal of optimal deterrence.

Scholars in the United States began to think about punitive damages in light of the economic principle of optimal deterrence in the 1980s.[84] The underlying idea is forcing those who perform the potentially harmful activity to assume the costs of it, which, following the economic model in which actors are rational and self-interested, will ensure that said activity will only be carried out to an economically efficient degree. Put another way, additional investments of resources will not be necessary to avoid causing harm when the cost of abstaining from the harmful action exceeds the cost of the harm that the wrongdoer will be responsible for. The inverse is also held as true: Additional investments will be necessary to prevent harm when the cost of abstaining from it is lower than the cost that would be imposed on the wrongdoer for causing it.

The problem behind this economic logic is that it does not play out in practice. Some wrongdoers, for example, speculate that they may not be held responsible for the full cost of the harm caused by their conduct. Perhaps they wager that many of the affected victims will never file a lawsuit (e.g., due to the high cost of legal counsel or mere unawareness of having been harmed). Many others who do sue may not prevail for reasons unrelated to the merit of their claims.[85] Punitive damages are thus introduced in this approach as a tool to correct this particular type of market problem. And it is intended to do so by directly attacking the source of the problem: the failure of compensatory damages to fulfill their function of incentivizing suppliers to adjust their activity to socially efficient levels. The idea is to remedy this deficiency of the compensatory system (i.e., underenforcement) by imposing

[83] See generally W. M. Landes and R. A. Posner, *The Economic Structure of Tort Law* (Harvard University Press, 1987), p. 28.

[84] For representative scholarship along these lines, see, for example, R. Cooter, "Economic Analysis of Punitive Damages" (1982) 56 *Southern California Law Review* 79; and "Punitive Damages for Deterrence: When and How Much?" (1989) 40 *Alabama Law Review* 1143; A. M. Polinsky and S. Shavell, "Punitive Damages: An Economic Analysis" (1998) 111 *Harvard Law Review* 869; W. K. Viscusi, "The Social Costs of Punitive Damages Against Corporations in Environmental and Safety Torts" (1998) 87 *Georgetown Law Journal* 285; C. M. Sharkey, "Punitive Damages as Societal Damages" (2003) 113 *Yale Law Journal* 347; K. N. Hylton, "A Theory of Wealth and Punitive Damages" (2008) 17 *Widener Law Journal* 927, among others.

[85] See G. T. Schwartz, "Empiricism and Tort Law" (2002) 2002 *University of Illinois Law Review* 1067, 1071 (discussing possible reasons for under-enforcement).

an extra-compensatory bonus (i.e., a punitive award) in cases where providers might conceivably escape liability for (at least some of) the harm that their activity causes. In the face of the threat of extra-compensatory awards, the wrongdoer, who before carrying out her activity only factors the compensation of those harms that she speculates will be successfully claimed into her cost–benefit calculation, will begin to include potential punitive damages in the cost she might be forced to pay, not only those she would have to bear out of claims for compensatory damages.

Along this line of analysis, Robert Cooter and Steven Shavell, in turn, strove to emphasize the role of punitive damages in the incentivization of efficient behavior. Optimal deterrence is achieved, according to these authors, by threatening the defendants with expected damage awards equal to the expected damages caused by their harmful conduct, that is, by ensuring that the person who carries out a conduct considers the total costs of their activity. The goal is to force the wrongdoer and others in similar situations to internalize the costs of the harm caused as a result of their behavior. The basic idea is that the complete internalization of costs, by all producers, will lead to socially efficient results.

Within these economic theories that emphasize optimal deterrence, we can identify the now classic normative theory of the multiplier proposed by Mitchell Polinsky and Steven Shavell.[86] These authors devised a special formula, which they call "the punitive damages multiplier," to calculate the amount of punitive damages that they believe are necessary for optimal deterrence.[87] Subscribing to the line of analysis that I have been describing, they understand that the agent causing the harm should pay for the harm that their conduct generates, neither more nor less, in order to achieve optimal deterrence. If the wrongdoer pays less than the harm she causes, an under-deterrence problem would result (that is, the precautionary measures taken would be inadequate, the price of the products would be very low, and more and more activities that produce risks would occur). On the contrary, if the wrongdoer pays more than the harm she causes, an overdeterrence problem would be generated (that is, unnecessary precautions would be taken, the price of products would be too high, and risky activities that are also socially beneficial would be undesirably discouraged). In this context, the crucial question considered by the authors is the following: Do actors sometimes escape to answer for the harms they cause? If they do, the quantum of the damage award imposed on them in the cases in which they are found liable should necessarily exceed the compensatory damages, so that they pay for the harm that they actually cause. Polinsky and Shavell understand that the nonimposition of this extra-compensatory bonus would result in an inadequate deterrence; their proposal is then that this "excess" be computed with respect to the compensatory award under the heading of "punitive damages." Accordingly, if the person causing harm has a certain chance of escaping

[86] Polinsky and Shavell, "Punitive Damages: An Economic Analysis."

[87] Ibid 889.

responsibility for it (that is, the probability of being held liable for the harm caused is less than 100 percent), the appropriate amount of the total award (i.e., compensatory plus punitive damages) to be imposed should equal the harm caused to the victim multiplied by the inverse of the probability of being found liable.[88] In this way, in the long run, wrongdoers would be held liable for the harm caused, leading to socially desirable behavior in terms of adopting appropriately precautionary measures (i.e., cost-effective precautions) and informing their decision to engage in risky activities.

According to Polinsky and Shavell, punitive damages are justified only on a limited spectrum, that is, only in the circumstances in which the wrongdoers have a chance to escape liability for the harm they cause. Furthermore, the authors argue that the courts are wrong to consider the reprehensibility of the defendant's conduct as a relevant factor in determining the imposition of punitive damages, for this factor is irrelevant if the objective of the institution is optimal deterrence.[89] In other words, factoring the reprehensibility of the defendant's conduct into punitive damage awards impedes optimal deterrence in two situations: (1) when punitive damages are imposed in excess, that is, in cases where the defendant's conduct is certainly reprehensible but the chances of being found liable are also nearly certain; and (2) when punitive damages are not imposed because the defendant did not display reprehensible conduct, that is, simple negligence but the chances of escaping liability were high. Thus, the only criterion that the authors clearly consider relevant for the imposition of punitive damages is the chances of evading liability, regardless of whether the defendant's conduct was reprehensible or not. This does not, of course, imply ignoring the reprehensibility of a defendant's conduct if the conduct pertains to its potential effect on the chances of escaping liability (e.g., when there is evidence that some product's defect was concealed). From a different but still economic deterrence perspective, Catherine Sharkey has recently proposed, building on her prior work on punitive damages, that we "transform punitive damages into societal damages" by reconceptualizing them in terms of the non-retributive goal of "societal general deterrence."[90] The economic rationale behind her account is once again that of loss internalization: The goal of punitive damages "is to address the under-enforcement problem by increasing damages for the harms that are detected and sanctioned by a sufficient amount to ensure that injurers' expected liability equals the social cost of their harm-producing conduct."[91] As a consequence, according to Sharkey, "punitive damages are warranted in all cases

88 Ibid 874 n124, 889.

89 For case law along this line, see *Ciraolo* v. *City of New York*, 216 F 3d 236, 246 (2d Cir. 2000) (in which Judge Calabresi asserted that an award imposed to achieve optimal deterrence should be allowed independently of whether the defendant's conduct was reprehensible).

90 See Sharkey, "Punitive Damages Transformed into Societal Damages," pp. 156–59.

91 Ibid 165.

where under-enforcement is an issue; there is no reason to distinguish between intentional and purely negligent (or even strict liability) harms."[92]

These accounts of punitive damages whose exclusive rationale is deterrence (whether optimal or societal) disregard the punitive dimension altogether opening themselves to criticism from several angles. For instance, their characterization of the conventional common law requirement of reprehensibility for punitive damage awards as normatively irrelevant certainly affects their descriptive power since ignoring its history implies failing to account for (1) the predominant and long-standing common law practice of imposing punitive awards only when reprehensibility has been determined; or for (2) why punitive damages can only be judicially claimed by an individual victim against the particular defendant when the economic logic priming efficiency would call for granting legal standing to a third party in better position to play the efficiency enforcement role qua private attorney-general. Moreover, since the relevant criterion for punitive damages is, under the optimal deterrence rationale, "the probability of escaping liability," this economic reconstruction must assume that the punitive decisions of jurors and judges tend to map more closely to optimal deterrence objectives (e.g., the chances that wrongdoing will be detected) than to punitive intuition (e.g., the more severe the conduct, the greater the sanction). However, this assumption lacks empirical support; in fact, it has been questioned by several experimental studies. The research demonstrates that jurors regularly reject the Polinsky–Shavell instructions in determining what the appropriate civil penalties are.[93] According to the studies, potential jurors rely on the reprehensibility of the conduct in assessing punitive damages in open disregard for detection rates.[94] Some studies even conclude that courts cannot successfully implement the kind of rigorous cost–benefit analysis required to achieve optimal deterrence.[95] Even scholars from the law and economics camp have begun to acknowledge that the optimal deterrence theory of punitive damages lacks any considerable force in either positive or descriptive law and economics analyses.[96]

92 Ibid.

93 See, for example, N. R. Feigenson, "Can Tort Juries Punish Competently?" (2003) 78 *Chicago-Kent Law Review* 239, 275–76.

94 See C. R. Sunstein et al., *Punitive Damages: How Juries Decide* (Chicago University Press, 2002), pp. 135–39, 151–64.

95 See, for example, A. Schwartz, "Proposals for Products Liability Reform: A Theoretical Synthesis" (1998) 97 *Yale Law Journal* 353, 386–88 (arguing that courts are incapable of applying a negligence rule that will yield efficient outcomes); K. W. Viscusi, *Reforming Products Liability* (Harvard University Press, 1991), p. 212 (conceding that courts are ill-equipped to conduct cost–benefit tests).

96 See, for example, C. M. Sharkey, "Economic Analysis of Punitive Damages: Theory, Empirics, and Doctrine," in J. Arlen (ed.), *Research Handbook on the Economics of Torts* (Edward Elgar Publishing, 2013), pp. 489–96 (discussing the difficulties of determining likelihood of detection). Moreover, see *Ciraolo* v. *City of New York*, 216 F 3d 236, 244–45 (2d Cir. 2000) (Calabresi J., concurring) (where judge Calabresi stated that "[a]lthough widely accepted by economists and acknowledged by some courts, the multiplier function of punitive damages has nonetheless been applied haphazardly at best.").

As for the societal deterrence reconstruction, it is not clear why the propounded societal purpose exclusively implicates a deterrence rationale for punitive damages. Much to the contrary, the relevant factors identified by Sharkey to measure societal deterrence (particularly, the defendant's history or pattern of repeated wrongdoing, the broader societal impact of the defendant's conduct and the defendant's financial status) may all very well support a retributive reading of the institution grounded on reprehensibility (e.g., repeated misconduct that causes widespread harm to others is more serious than an isolated instance of wrongdoing) and proportional punishment (e.g., the defendant's wealth is a relevant factor that should be considered when determining the sum of a punitive award that most appropriately conveys the gravity of the reprehensible behavior).[97] Indeed, most of the case-law examples offered by Sharkey strongly emphasize highly reprehensible behavior (e.g., a widespread pattern and practice of abuse and deceit on the part of a mega-bank directed at vulnerable victims), which, again, aligns well with a retributive rationale. Moreover, whether or not they mitigate or disincentivize windfall gains, as Sharkey argues, split-recovery schemes that divert part of the monetary sanction to the state or public funds could express the public interest of the state to punish highly reprehensible behavior that triggers the imposition of societal damages. It is also not clear why societal damages should be available in class actions as Sharkey proposes since, under a societal deterrence rationale, class action mechanisms themselves are conceptually sufficient to address the under-enforcement problem.[98] Thus, if societal damages are available in class action lawsuits, they must be doing something other than loss internalization. Certainly, Sharkey's reconstruction is rich and offers valuable insight. It brings to the fore fundamental questions that must be debated further. My point here is that making the case for an exclusive societal general deterrence rationale for punitive damages without dealing with the patently retributive elements that seem operative in it presents, a priori, certain challenges. Sharkey seems to have a point that economic deterrence goals of punitive damages resonate better in the context of corporate wrongdoing than with competing retributive rationales of the institution; however, that resonance alone does not in and of itself debunk the fundamental retributive

[97] See Sharkey, "Punitive Damages Transformed into Societal Damages," pp. 166–72. While acknowledging that courts do in fact consider "proportionate punishment factors" to gauge punitive awards, Sharkey argues that they should be directed to "societal deterrence factors" premised on loss internalization. On the proportionality of sanctions, see Section B of Chapter 4.

[98] Note that Sharkey herself acknowledges that the existence of a class action would appear to be a substitute or alternative response to the societal notion of punitive damages she is advancing, but still argues for their availability in the class action context. See Sharkey, "Punitive Damages Transformed into Societal Damages," p. 178. For the European stance, see Directive (EU) 2020/1828 of the European Parliament and of the Council of November 25, 2020, on representative actions for the protection of the collective interests of consumers and repealing Directive 2009/22/EC ("the awarding of punitive damages [in representative actions] should be avoided").

underpinnings of punitive damages.[99] Last, the lack of any conclusive empirical studies confirming the effectiveness of either optimal deterrence or societal deterrence puts their feasibility into question, which undoubtedly diminishes the force of normative proposals such as those offered by Polinsky and Shavell (i.e., the punitive damages multiplier) and Sharkey (i.e., societal damages).[100]

F PUNISHMENT AS (A LEGAL POWER FOR) PRIVATE REDRESS

John Goldberg and Benjamin Zipursky's civil recourse theory offers an alternative that purports to unseat both corrective justice and law and economics accounts of tort law. Under civil recourse, the law of torts represents, in the first instance, a law of relational wrongs.[101] Tort law is about a victim's legal power to respond to the wrongs done to her, and to look to the state for an avenue of response. Thus, tort law empowers the victims of legal wrongs, through a civil action, to seek and obtain suitable redress from their wrongdoers upon proof of their claim.[102] If the victim (plaintiff) prevails in the tort lawsuit, she obtains a damages award from the court that generates a legal obligation for the wrongdoer (defendant) to pay the amount of damages specified in the judgment.

Since the outset, the main attraction of civil recourse theory has been its capacity to accommodate the variety of remedies offered by tort law (and in particular, punitive damages), only some of which are oriented to making the plaintiff whole.[103] Civil recourse aligns with corrective justice in maintaining a normative structure for tort law that draws on a variety of first-order duties, which, in turn, yield norms of conduct. However, according to civil recourse, the proper legal response to a first-order breach is not a second-order duty to repair. Rather, the breach of a first-order duty affords the victim a right of action: a legal power to seek private redress from her injurer if she chooses to exercise it.[104] Under this reconstruction, the plaintiff's tort remedy (i.e., her private redress) is mediated by the decision to exercise her right of action and the merit of her lawsuit.

By distinguishing matters of liability (i.e., the right of action) from matters of remedy (i.e., the actual private redress sought by the victim who chooses to exercise

99 See Sharkey, "Punitive Damages Transformed into Societal Damages," p. 163. For a retributive rationale of punitive damages in the product liability context, see Chapter 7.

100 Note that Sharkey herself acknowledges that "the empirical validity [of societal deterrence] in the real world is indeterminate." Ibid 146.

101 See Goldberg and Zipursky, Recognizing Wrongs, p. 138 ("Torts are relational wrongs").

102 Ibid 37–38 (the state merely "empowers victims to seek redress if they choose").

103 Ibid 173 (claiming the superiority of civil recourse over corrective justice theorists who ahistorically regard punitive damages as alien to tort law). For certain skepticism in this regard, see Weinrib, "Civil Recourse and Corrective Justice," 289–93 ("aside from nomenclature, the difference between the aggravated damages of corrective justice and the punitive damages of civil recourse is hard to discern.").

104 See Goldberg and Zipursky, Recognizing Wrongs, p. 291.

her right of action), civil recourse endorses the idea that tort law should embrace all responses, whether compensatory or noncompensatory, deemed appropriate redress for victims of the tortious events whose lawsuits are successful. This nuance is important. Tort law thus does not represent a mechanism to "restore" something taken from the victim but rather a law for the redress of private relational wrongs (i.e., redress for what has been done to the victim). Civil recourse extends an invitation to rethink the actual content of tort law's remedial dimension. Under civil recourse, the focus moves from the classic compensatory/noncompensatory remedies divide to the private redress most appropriate for the victim available through the operation of the law of torts. Civil recourse theory offers little guidance, however, as to the sort of private redress that would be appropriate according to the circumstance.

According to civil recourse theory, a central feature of tort law is the special way in which it empowers "private citizens to harness the power of the state to take action against other private citizens."[105] The idea is that the state, in search for civilized coexistence, forbids citizens from taking justice into their own hands, but, in return, it must offer them some legitimate avenue for recourse against their wrongdoers.[106] Following this power-allocation logic, civil recourse theory has explicitly acknowledged the punitive component of tort law by refashioning the victims' right to demand punishment as a legal power for private redress – what Zipursky originally called the "right to be punitive."[107] Under civil recourse, the punitiveness in punitive damages is understood as formal recognition of a legal power that the victim may voluntarily exercise to demand judicial imposition of a monetary award that goes beyond self-restoration when the defendant's conduct has been willful or wanton (i.e., in light of what the defendant did to her and how it was done).[108] In Goldberg and Zipursky's words, "the law allows the tort plaintiff *to be punitive toward a person who has very badly mistreated her.*"[109] However, the civil recourse account of punitive damages says little about the content of the victim's power to be punitive and how it relates to (or differs from) punishment (or retribution), apart from the distinction made between who brings the lawsuit (a private party rather than the state). In fact, by offering a structural power-allocation approach to tort law, these authors end up conceptually detaching the tort victim from the meaningful role of her attitude in exercising her legal power to seek private redress. The power to be punitive is understood as formal recognition of a standing to a private remedy (that can only take the form of an additional monetary payment) in light of

[105] Ibid 165.
[106] Ibid 117.
[107] See B. C. Zipursky, "A Theory of Punitive Damages" (2005) 84 *Texas Law Review* 105, 106–7 (arguing that "it is the plaintiff's right to be punitive, not the system's need to punish the defendant, that explains the special status of punitive damages within American tort law.").
[108] Ibid 151–52. Similarly, Goldberg and Zipursky, Recognizing Wrongs, p. 168 ("Punitive damages are by definition extra-compensatory.")
[109] See Goldberg and Zipursky, Recognizing Wrongs, p. 171 (emphasis in original).

the defendant's action that does not capture the substantive content of the victim's retributive response to reprehensible wrongdoing.[110] Thus, even though civil recourse openly recognizes the "private punitiveness" of punitive damages,[111] it does not offer a substantive account of what the appropriate private redress warranted by the plaintiff's power to be punitive (or to be vindictive) actually entails.[112] Rather, the approach is one of pragmatism: By distinguishing the state's function of punishing offenders for systemic reasons (i.e., the quasi-criminal or regulatory aspect) from the plaintiff's power to demand the punishment of a person who has very badly mistreated her (i.e., the civil aspect), civil recourse proposes a distinction between punitive damages as an "authentic" private tort remedy obtained by the plaintiff by virtue of what the defendant did to her (i.e., the highly culpable wrongdoing) and punitive damages understood as a sort of fine imposed by the state (i.e., regulatory in spirit and thus alien to tort law).[113] The former corresponds to damages that genuinely amount to private redress and does not merit heightened constitutional scrutiny, while the latter do, in as much as they amount to regulation in the guise of redress.[114] This pragmatic approach becomes even more evident in their revealed preoccupation for a defensible explanation (on procedural due process grounds) to the punitive damages constitutional doctrine developed by the Supreme Court of the United States in *BMW* v. *Gore* and *Philip Morris* v. *Williams*.[115]

Zipursky certainly attempted, in his earlier work on punitive damages, to account for the "civil aspect" of punitive damages more substantively.[116] In this work, Zipursky argued that the "civil aspect" (or "subjective punitiveness") focuses on the nature of the wrong that the defendant required the victim to undergo and embodies "a subjective desire and intention to be punitive – to exact a penalty for the purpose of being the one who requires the defendant to endure a hardship."[117] However, his attempt to account more fully for the substantive role and attitude

110 Ibid 171–74.

111 Ibid 171 ("punitive damages are available only in cases of egregious wrongdoing, and never as of right.").

112 I have raised this point in M. G. Martínez Alles, "Tort Remedies as Meaningful Responses to Wrongdoing," in J. Oberdiek and P. Miller (eds.), *Civil Wrongs and Justice in Private Law* (Oxford University Press, 2020), pp. 231–51. Recently, a similar point has been raised by L. Radzik, "Book Review: Recognizing Wrongs" (2021) 131(3) *Ethics* 610. Similarly, see O. Herstein, "How Tort Law Empowers" (2015) 65 *University of Toronto Law Journal* 99, 103 ("Goldberg and Zipursky's conception of tort law as empowering victims is more concerned with the structural and logical features of the legal power that tort law vests in tort victims [...] than with the realities of exercising that power.").

113 See Goldberg and Zipursky, Recognizing Wrongs, p. 170–71.

114 Ibid 171.

115 Ibid 174. For a similarly pragmatic approach from the law and economics camp, see Sharkey, "Punitive Damages Transformed into Societal Damages," p. 185 (arguing that punitive damages framed as societal damages awarded for general deterrence purposes should not be subject to the United States Supreme Court's constitutional excessiveness review whose main object is the need to constrain punishment in civil contexts).

116 See generally Zipursky, "A Theory of Punitive Damages."

117 Ibid 154 (noting that there is a "quality of vengefulness to punitive damages").

of the victim in exercising her legal power to be punitive backfired when other tort scholars started to associate his reconstruction of punitive damages and, more generally, civil recourse theory with revenge.[118] An example of an association of civil recourse with revenge in the context of punitive damages is Antony Sebok's account of punitive damages as a form of state-sanctioned revenge.[119] Inspired by civil recourse theory, Sebok argues that the victim is doing more than delivering the wrongdoer to the court for punishment (i.e., more than exercising her power to be punitive); she is personally presenting reasons to the court for the punishment of the wrongdoer.[120] Those reasons are, according to Sebok, why the defendant deserves to be punished. Following this reasoning, Sebok understands that the best reconstruction of the reasons invoked within the practice is that it "is designed to allow people to seek revenge for a narrow set of wrongs in tort."[121] Since then, Goldberg and Zipursky have determinedly, constantly, and explicitly distanced civil recourse theory from revenge, vengeance, or retribution.[122] This preoccupation emanates from their latest treatment of punitive damages. In it, they succinctly assert that punitive damages take the form "of an additional payment – a payment of money that vindicates the plaintiff and castigates the defendant" without really accounting for what "vindication" or "punishment" really entail in tort law.[123] As a result, the twofold preoccupation in civil recourse theory with demonstrating on one side how the principle of civil recourse can provide guidance for (American) courts thinking through constitutional punitive damages doctrine, and, on the other, the anxiety of dissociating it from vengeance or retribution have taken priority over fully exploring the substantive elements (vindication, retribution, moral outrage) of the responsive aspect of their understanding of punitive damages (i.e., the tort victim's legal power to be punitive against her egregious wrongdoer if she chooses to exercise it) and how it differs from revenge or vengeance.

[118] For a discussion on civil recourse theory and revenge that informs this point, see G. S. Mendlow, "Is Tort Law a Form of Institutionalized Revenge?" (2011) 39 *Florida State University Law Review* 129, 133 (arguing that tort plaintiffs' desire to inflict harm is exceptionally seen when seeking punitive damages, as the only tort remedy the very purpose of which is to harm defendants); Sherwin, "Interpreting Tort Law," 231–36 (arguing that the most plausible answer to why there should be an entitlement to civil recourse is the desire of victims for revenge and that the legal system must accommodate this desire); A. J. Sebok, "Punitive Damages: From Myth to Theory" (2007) 92 *Iowa Law Review* 957 (describing recourse in terms of revenge in punitive damages settings). Recently, see E. Encarnacion, "Resilience, Retribution, and Punitive Damages" (2022) 100 *Texas Law Review* 1025, 1044–50 (treating civil recourse as a revenge-based (or revenge-adjacent) rationale of punitive damages).

[119] See Sebok, "Punitive Damages: From Myth to Theory," 961. Similarly, see Colby, "Clearing the Smoke from Philip Morris v. Williams," 434 (arguing that "punitive damages are legally sanctioned private revenge.").

[120] See Sebok, "Punitive Damages: From Myth to Theory," 1029.

[121] Ibid 1031.

[122] See Goldberg and Zipursky, Recognizing Wrongs, p. 65 (denying that the idea of civil recourse is a way of referring to retribution or vengeance).

[123] Ibid 174.

From a distinct (but related) perspective, Stephen Smith, who focuses on the forms of remedies rather than the role of plaintiffs who bring lawsuits, understands wrong-based damages as "creative orders" in the sense that "they impose new duties on defendants, different from the duties already required by the substantive law."[124] According to Smith, punitive damages are wrong-based damages, which are "roughly the private law equivalent of criminal punishment."[125] He does, to be fair, make clear that he is not suggesting that wrong-based damages are a form of criminal punishment or that they have the same aim as criminal punishment, only that they are "structurally similar to criminal punishment."[126] Punitive damages are not the only damages, though, that Smith includes in his provisional list of wrong-based damages (which include nominal, vindicatory, gain-based, pain and suffering damages, among others), which, in his view, share structural similarity to criminal punishment.

Under Smith's framework, punitive, aggravated, and pain and suffering damages essentially do the same work: They are awarded because the defendant committed a private wrong or, in other words, in order to make clear that the monetary payment represents redress for a wrong suffered by a particular individual. Smith's ambition to find common structural ground for all these court-ordered damages as "responses to private wrongs" has, in my view, an important downside: Treating them all as functionally fungible diminishes the relevance of understanding, identifying, or even justifying the distinctive features and rationales behind each institution. Indeed, Smith asserts that the categories of damages such as punitive, aggravated, and pain and suffering are poorly defined, an assertion that, according to Smith, should not be seen as either significant or surprising since "these awards are all variations on a single theme."[127] He further reaffirms his fluid understanding of these categories of damages when claiming that, when punitive damages fall outside the English historical categories test, the courts can substitute a functionally similar award of aggravated damages.[128] Smith's focus on the form of wrong-based remedies is certainly helpful to understand how the structure of remedial law goes beyond rectification, but at the cost of sacrificing any plausible understanding of the substantive content of tort responses to egregious or humiliating wrongdoing. Even if formally understood as "responses to private wrongs," the claim that there is no relevant distinction between a court-ordered punitive award to condemn the egregiousness of the defendant's conduct and a court-ordered pain and suffering award to account for the impact of the defendant's wrongful conduct on the victim remains unpersuasive. Even though Smith is right in pointing out the deficient treatment, both by commentators and courts, of punitive and aggravated damages,

[124] See S. A. Smith, *Rights, Wrongs, and Injustices* (Oxford University Press, 2020), p. 207.
[125] Ibid 202.
[126] Ibid.
[127] Ibid 208.
[128] Ibid 210.

it does not directly follow that they are somehow identical. To reach that conclusion, we would first need to engage in the more substantive discussions on the proper place and justification for punishment in private law. As I understand it, Smith's structural approach to wrong-based remedies is ill-suited for that aim. This is because his approach treats the justifications for wrong-based damages as structurally similar to criminal punishment by suggesting that wrong-based damages are the private law analogue of retributive justice (in that they aim to restore a balance between wrongdoers and their victims while criminal punishment aims to restore a balance between wrongdoers and society). Smith's argument does not incorporate, however, a retributivist theory of punishment.[129]

G PUNISHMENT AS RETRIBUTION

Marc Galanter and David Luban's *Poetic Justice* offers an early retributivist account of punitive damages.[130] Borrowing from the late Jean Hampton's theory of retributive punishment, they argued that punitive damages punish serious wrongdoing that manifests degrading or demeaning attitudes toward their victims by inflicting "expressive defeat" on the wrongdoer.[131] They asserted that the purpose of punishment is "to reassert the truth about the relative value of the wrongdoer and victim by inflicting a publicly visible defeat on the wrongdoer."[132] Punitive damages would thus aim to refute the message that the wrongdoer is superior to the victim by empowering the plaintiff to defeat the defendant, sending a counter-message of equality.[133] They emphasized that "punitive damages help ensure that economically formidable offenders do not enjoy the benefits of wrongdoing beyond the reach of the law."[134] Consequently, their main focus was on the scaling problem: a retributivist scales punishment to the heinousness of the offense, not to the magnitude of the harm.[135] Even though certain notions of moral condemnation[136] and equalizing moral value between the parties surface in their retributive reconstruction, they end up focusing almost unilaterally on the imposition of punishment on the wrongdoer (particularly on the proportionality of the expressive defeat), overlooking altogether the victim's perspective.[137] In fact, victims are, in their account, somehow

129 Ibid 204 (n63).

130 M. Galanter and D. Luban, "Poetic Justice: Punitive Damages and Legal Pluralism" (1993) 42(4) *American University Law Review* 1393.

131 Ibid 1432.

132 Ibid 1432.

133 Ibid 1432.

134 Ibid 1461.

135 Ibid 1432.

136 Ibid 1428 (punitive damages are "the most important instrument in the legal repertoire for pronouncing moral disapproval of economically formidable offenders.")

137 Ibid 1436–37. For instance, in their analysis of the well-known Ford Pinto case, they note the "poetic justice" of using Ford's cost–benefit calculations regarding human life as a measure of the punitive

disconnected from their role in bringing about the "expressive defeat" in that they are conceived for the most part instrumentally as private enforcers.[138] Regulating the wrongdoer thus becomes the focus with the idea that punitive damages correct undesirable social behaviors. Consequently, largely absent are justifications that victims specially situated might provide for demanding their wrongdoers' punishment or for why they should receive the punitive award directly from their wrongdoers, making this early retributivist formulation vulnerable to the familiar criticism that punitive damages amount to unjustified plaintiff windfalls.

From a different standpoint, Dan Markel offers an understanding of punitive damages as an intermediate civil sanction designed to vindicate the public's interest in retribution in the same way as the criminal law does.[139] Seeking to distinguish punitive damages from revenge, poetic justice, or victim vindication, Markel argues that retributive damages (i.e., punitive damages) empower private parties to act on behalf of the state to seek the imposition of a civil fine determined by the reprehensibility of the defendant's misconduct.[140] Under Markel's framework, punitive damages are conceived as "a scheme of retributive justice committed to condemning misconduct in the public's name, rather than the victim's."[141] Rather than focusing on a private plaintiff's vindicatory interest, punitive damages serve instead "the *public's* interest in retributive justice."[142] Among the main implications of Markel's wrongdoer-centric approach are that the state should (1) receive the bulk of retributive damages and (2) reward plaintiffs' for their efforts (with a fixed award for bringing the matter to the public's attention).[143] In this account, punitive damages function like the criminal law does, mostly focusing unilaterally on the imposition of punishment on the wrongdoer, and are mainly conceived as an outsourcing mechanism in which tort victims represent contingent participants in the practice who demand the imposition of a punitive award on behalf of the state.[144] Markel's account takes the focus away from the victim and places it squarely on regulating punishment for wrongdoers.

More recently, Erik Encarnacion, seeking to debunk the classic contention that punitive awards boil down to unjustified plaintiff pay-outs, has argued that

award the company should pay: There is no better way to counteract the "false view of the wrongdoer's value relative to that of the victim" than by inflicting an economic punishment in the same amount as the company's cost–benefit calculation.

138 Ibid 1451 ("A crucial function of punitive damages is to provide financial incentives for private parties to enforce the law – the bounty system.").

139 D. Markel, "Retributive Damages: A Theory of Punitive Damages as Intermediate Sanction" (2009) 94 *Cornell Law Review* 239.

140 Ibid 239.

141 Ibid 303; and 247 (recognizing that "non-victims should be able to bring actions for retributive damages under certain conditions").

142 Ibid 246 (emphasis in original).

143 Ibid 307 n224 ("the civil system would […] mak[e] a bounty available for plaintiffs as part of the retributive damages structure.").

144 Ibid 307 (emphasizing that "the government could still bring a retributive damage claim against a defendant even without the victim's cooperation").

punitive damages should be understood "as empowering victims to act retributively against their wrongdoers when they act with ill will, and [...] to make the wrongdoers pay, literally, to satisfy the victims' interests in realizing the ideal of resilience."[145] Encarnacion's normative ideal of "retributive resilience" seeks to restore victims to a better state than the one they were in before they were wronged: by acting punitively against their wrongdoers in order to give expression to their resilience interests and emerging financially better off than they were before the wrongdoing.[146] One advantage of his reconstruction (over Galanter and Luban's or Markel's) is its attempt to link defendants and victims in some meaningful way – correctly responding to the deficit of existing wrongdoer-centric reconstructions.[147] However, the exclusive association of the content of victims' resilience interests with their financial situation (i.e., on victims emerging better off financially) presents a challenge for the envisioned theoretical enterprise. The emphasis on justifying the transfer of extra-compensatory relief (the punitive award) from the defendant to the successful plaintiff (i.e., the emphasis on the normative allocation of costs as between defendants and victims) ends up taking attention away from the relevant question of why victims' resilience interests (i.e., to emerge better off financially than before serious setbacks) justify the imposition of harsh treatment on the defendant. One possible answer to the latter is of course that the defendants deserve it. However, Encarnacion explicitly distances himself from "just desert" accounts of retribution.[148] He instead understands the victims' reasons to act punitively toward their wrongdoers through "expressive defeat" reconstructions (inspired by Galanter, Luban, and Hampton), but he does not fully flesh out the connection with the victims' reasons to act resiliently – that is, their interest in emerging better off financially. To that end, Encarnacion resorts to fairness rather than retributive arguments, stating that "it is simply fair to require that wrongdoers finance [victims'] resilience [interests]"[149]; and that "wrongdoers are more fairly *required* to pay, upon demand."[150] A manifestation of this appeal to basic fairness might be seen in Encarnacion's suggestion that the victims' wealth should be a relevant criterion in assessing the punitive award when the defendant

[145] See Encarnacion, "Resilience, Retribution, and Punitive Damages," 1028.

[146] Ibid 1051–72.

[147] For my early argument that leading theories of punitive damages focused unilaterally on the wrongdoer, rendering tort victims a contingent participant in the practice, see M. G. Martínez Alles, "Moral Outrage and Betrayal Aversion: The Psychology of Punitive Damages" (2018) 11(2) *Journal of Tort Law* 245, 246–47.

[148] See Encarnacion, "Resilience, Retribution, and Punitive Damages," 1038 n70 (stating that his account of punitive damages "will be 'retributive' in the broad sense that it tries to explain and justify the permissibility of empowering plaintiffs, in certain cases, to punish [...] in the form of extracting extra compensatory relief without regard to deterrence. But it might not be retributive in the precise sense of seeing the suffering of wrongdoers as intrinsically good.").

[149] Ibid 1055.

[150] Ibid 1064 (emphasis in original).

is relatively moneyless.[151] This suggests that emerging better off financially might not be constitutive of the "expressive defeat" after all – something other than money seems to be doing some work here. It also reveals a disconnect between the focus on victims' emerging better off financially and a retributive rationale of punishment, which dictates the monetary sanction be proportional to the seriousness of the offense, not to the victim's wealth. Encarnacion's reconstruction, as I understand it, might correspond better to a broad reading of the "better position constraint" embedded in classic rectificatory accounts of tort law than in contemporary retributive theory. After all, Encarnacion himself recognizes that "merely getting back to the place where the victim started before the wrongdoing occurred seems, at best, a partial and inadequate response to egregious wrongdoing involving ill will"[152] and that retributive resilience "also counts as a form of corrective justice, broadly construed, which concerns empowering victims to force wrongdoers to rectify their wrongdoings."[153] Regardless of its persuasiveness, Encarnacion's retributive resilience makes a valuable step away from wrongdoer-centric approaches to punishment in torts. More importantly, it makes a step forward in what I believe is the right direction by attempting to account for the victim's perspective in some meaningful way. As will be thoroughly explored in Part II, the reconstruction I submit, *Relational Retribution*, shares the very same preoccupations.

◊ ◊ ◊

CONCLUDING REMARKS

Although the common law of torts has for centuries combined compensatory and punitive responses, punitive damages being the paradigmatic example of a tort institution with salient retributive elements, scant scholarly attention has been devoted to justifying its retributive dimension. In relatively recent history, civil law jurisdictions have introduced (or are considering introducing) punitive damages into their legal systems as well, yet legal scholars in those jurisdictions also remain reluctant to delve deeply into the retributive roots of the institution. Chapter 1 provided an overview of a shared tendency among commentators across jurisdictions to frame the debate on punitive damages such that, in one way or another, directly addressing the fundamental retributive facet of the institution is circumvented. In tort theory, a field currently polarized between variants of rights-based theories (broadly understood) and law and economics accounts, the prevailing approach has sought to promote or perfect the rectificatory and deterrence dimensions of tort law, sometimes by rejecting the institution's retributive facet outright or, more often, by remaining

151 Ibid 1077.
152 Ibid 1063–64.
153 Ibid 1066.

candidly indifferent to it. Tort theorists have also attempted to reduce retribution to compensation, refashion retributive punishment as "something else" so it fits classic rectificatory frameworks, and diminish the relevance of a proper distinction between rectificatory and retributive rationales of tort remedies. It is significant that the few recent attempts to delve into the retributive dimension of punitive damages have yet to yield any full-fleshed retributive rationale for the institution; so far they have either fashioned punitive damages as an instrument to regulate the wrongdoer, diverting attention away from the tort victim who initiates the tort process and demands the imposition of a punitive award for the wrong done to her, or advanced reconstructions that can be, in one way or another, subsumed under broader rectificatory frameworks. These larger trends in tort theory are indicative of a general academic reluctance to search for a plausible theoretical grounding for a genuine place for retribution in torts, which is precisely the aim of Part II.

PART II

The Retributive Rationale

OVERVIEW

Despite the widely accepted understanding of punitive damages as "retribution and deterrence" combined, the large body of sophisticated scholarship on the deterrent aspect of the institution has not been matched by similar efforts to account for its dominant retributive dimension. The as yet unsuccessful search for a convincing account of punitive damages has led me to start by conceptualizing retribution in the context of torts and acknowledging the possibility that this legal mechanism may serve a purpose independent from deterrence. Part II sets about doing just that: taking retribution in torts seriously by articulating the sorely missing justificatory account of the retributive rationale of tort law embedded in punitive damages.

Chapter 3 advances the argument that an approach to punitive damages based on empirical accounts of human behavior may lend itself to a convincing, coherent legal account of the retributive dimension of the institution. Drawing from promising findings in the fields of cognitive and social psychology along with studies from the social sciences on human behavior and decision-making, Chapter 3 charts out an approach to punitive damages based on empirical research that reveals the lay intuitions behind the actual motivations that drive people to punish certain behaviors. Taking the behavior and decision-making literatures as the starting point for inquiry, the chapter demonstrates that the retributive aspect of punitive damages aligns more closely with individuals' moral intuitions regarding punishment than with deterrence. The deterrent function appears less prominent in regular human behavior than tort theory widely maintains. In tort theory's utilitarian variant, for instance, punitive damages are to be calibrated to achieve optimal deterrence, yet research shows that deterring future wrongdoing simply does not figure significantly among the motivations that drive punitive responses when individuals are confronted with specific instances of reprehensible behavior. Chapter 3 demonstrates the failure of legal scholars to give intuitive retributive responses the attention they deserve when attempting to account for the practice of punitive damages.

In an attempt to understand the retributive motivations behind punitive damages, Chapter 3 continues by highlighting the predominant tendency to approach punishment in torts from a one-sided perspective focusing on the wrongdoer. The role of the tort victim in bringing the punitive lawsuit has often been curtly characterized either as some sort of private attorney general moved by a desire to deter undesirable behavior or as an agent exercising her legal power to exact a punitive sanction by virtue of the wrong done to her by the defendant formally conceived in terms of just deserts. Chapter 3 argues, conversely, that the victim's intrinsic response to deliberate wrongdoing involves much more than imposing punishment: It involves her self-identity, that is, the larger meaning she construes from the circumstances of wrongdoing seen as deliberately threatening her individual autonomy, dignity, physical integrity, or even life. Ultimately, the chapter argues that the rich value-laden lay intuitions that drive people to punish certain behaviors through tort law offer a more meaningful understanding of punitive damages. The literature from social psychology and social cognition on human actors' motivations for punishment as well as the "reactive attitudes" distinctively involved in holding others morally accountable that are discussed in moral philosophy offer valuable insight into two particularly powerful cognitive motivations, moral outrage and betrayal aversion, behind the reaction to punish those who wrong us reprehensibly. Together, these rich retributive motivations comprise a significant and as yet missing element in the predominant understanding of punitive damages, one we ought not overlook.

Many tort theorists resist the empirical findings because the research into retributive motivations shows that people rely on their emotions and intuitions for punitive judgments, sentiments that are usually seen not only as impediments to the exercise of reason but also as an affront to legal rationality, logic, and predictability. To tackle these understandable concerns, Chapter 3 ends by addressing the criticism against retributivism as irrational and directly engages the debate over the "rationality" of lay notions of retribution. It argues that moral outrage and betrayal aversion represent contextual retributive motivations that do obey a rationale. Moreover, their "alternate" or "rival" rationality captures the rich moral insight of those intuitions into the proper treatment that members of a community believe are owed in specific circumstances of reprehensible wrongdoing.

Inspired by these powerful insights, Chapter 4 drills down into the most compelling reconstruction of the widely accepted double "punish and deter" function of punitive damages, the aphorism that equates the purpose of the institution with "retribution and deterrence." The chapter articulates a justificatory account of the retributive character of punitive damage awards in a manner that responds to both the relational significance of the victim's role in expressing condemnation and the importance of maintaining institutional modes of moral communication for value affirmation between the private parties involved in a reprehensible tortious situation. A much richer, complex understanding of tort victims provides the foundation on which my reconstruction is built. This understanding is sensitive to the tort victims' values that impinge on their own sense of self-worth as well as the other-regarding norms they believe should be enforced in their community. It is responsive to the moral significance of the wrongdoing for the victim and to the importance that is attributed to the dignitary interests that the defendant's reprehensible behavior encroached or invaded. The main argument that can be induced from it is that retribution in torts is relational. *Relational Retribution* offers a more holistic account of retribution in torts that recognizes the necessary interconnection between the reprehensible character of the defendant's conduct as deserving of punishment and the rich correlative retributive motivations of the victim of seriously disrespectful actions seeking the imposition of the monetary sanction (the punitive award). This relational approach transcends the nearly exclusive and unilateral focus on either the reprehensibility of the defendant's behavior or the notion of deservedness or "just deserts" for the imposition of a monetary sanction. Alternative motives for retribution such as "denunciation" and "value affirmation" often more accurately explain the victim's resolve. Because of the centrality of proportionality in any retributive theory of punishment, the chapter ends by sketching out the qualitative and quantitative aspects of the principle of sanction proportionality under the framework of *Relational Retribution*.

Chapter 5 concludes Part II of this work by addressing the scholarly trends that account for punishment in torts by expanding compensation. It confronts the argument that traditional, compensatory categories of remedies, such as non-pecuniary damages and aggravated damages, perform the function of vindicating the victim's dignitary interests without appealing to notions of punishment and retribution. It shows that despite the initial attractiveness of the proposed solution, reducing punishment to compensation not only overlooks the significance of the victim's perspective but also fundamentally impairs both the expressive dimension of sanctions and the necessary proportionality. It goes on to explain the importance of delineating punishment and compensation as independent and distinctive responses to wrongdoing and why the distinctions demand differentiated treatment.

3

The Punitive Puzzle

Shifting Away from Deterrence

A standard deontological justification for punishment is (broadly associated with) the retributive (or just deserts) rationale according to which punishment should be meted out in proportion to the seriousness of the wrong committed.[1] This justification of punishment involves the role of punishment in righting wrongs already committed, not in any future benefit or desired outcome. Under this rationale, punishment is a morally justifiable end in itself. A corollary principle of retribution is moral proportionality. This principle holds that punishment should reflect the degree of moral offense caused. More serious crimes, hence, deserve more serious punishments. Punishment represents the means to address the moral outrage that reprehensible wrongful conduct provokes. Indeed, a classic theory of retributive justice will concern itself above all with the factors that increase or decrease the moral outrage that the wrongful action produces. The offenders' intentions (i.e., the reprehensibility of their conduct) and the magnitude of the harm are therefore two key components of this rationale.

Another competing justification is built on the consequentialist theory (broadly associated with welfare-maximizing utilitarianism) that society is composed of rational, self-interested individuals. This is the deterrence rationale, according to which the aim of punishment is reducing the frequency and likelihood of future offenses.[2] It holds that the punishment of an offender should not exceed what is sufficient to prevent future instances of the offense. This deterrence rationale is grounded on the assumption that potential offenders act rationally by weighing the extent and likelihood of the benefits and risks of wrongdoing prior to such acts and that the prospect

1 This deservingness approach is often associated with Immanuel Kant who argued that punishment can never be administered merely as a means for promoting another good and should be pronounced over all criminals proportionate to their internal wickedness. See generally I. Kant, *The Science of Right* (W. Hastie Trans., 2010).

2 This utilitarian or consequentialist approach is often associated with Jeremy Bentham who argued that "general prevention ought to be the chief end of punishment, as it is its real justification." See J. Bentham, "Principles of Penal Law," in J. Bowring (ed.), *The Works of Jeremy Bentham* (Russell & Russell, 1962), p. 396.

of punishment changes the result of the cost and benefit analysis of the situation, ideally making the criminal activity pondered unattractive, or, to put it slightly differently, punishment induces people to perform ex ante cost–benefit analyses that, if the punishment is severe enough to outweigh the potential gain, will inhibit them from doing future harm.[3] The most relevant factors under this rationale are the frequency with which the specific wrongdoing occurs and the detection rates (e.g., when it can be deduced that a certain type of wrongdoing is rarely detected, it should be punished more severely).

As the relevant factors in one of these rationales are completely irrelevant for the other, these two justifications for punishment (i.e., retribution and deterrence) seem difficult to reconcile or integrate. For instance, the key elements of retribution (i.e., the reprehensibility of the offender's conduct, the severity of the offense, etc.) are entirely beside the point in deterrence theory. As a matter of fact, a pure utilitarian would always limit the punishment to "just sufficient" to deter future instances of wrongdoing regardless of any consideration of deservingness. Conversely, a pure retributivist would not look any further than the moral culpability of the offender's action in determining the proper punishment.

The fact that there are factors that are uniquely relevant to each of them does not mean that retributive and deterrence rationales never overlap. Indeed, most people probably find both deterring future wrongdoing and fairly punishing offenders to be desirable objectives. While there is nothing wrong with desiring these two aims at the same time, when faced with a specific instance in which punishment for wrongdoing must be decided, we will have to choose: either we care more about the reprehensibility of the defendant's conduct and the magnitude of the harm done or we care more about the frequency of the offense and the probability that it escapes detection.[4] According to Kevin Carlsmith and John Darley, this conflict reaches deep within many individuals: It appears that we are drawn, at an abstract level, to a notion of punishment that serves utilitarian goals, but when faced with a particular case, we consistently choose punishments that more accurately reflect retributive goals.[5]

Carlsmith and Darley conducted a series of experiments to determine which philosophical perspective (i.e., retribution or deterrence) is most relevant to the punitive urge. Despite stated preferences for deterrence as the driving goal of punishment at an abstract level (i.e., at a macro or societal level of consideration for a type of offense in general), their studies suggest that people's reactions to wrongdoing actually reflect a completely different logic in that they fail to assign punishment in

3 Ibid ("If the apparent magnitude, or rather value of [the] pain be greater than the apparent magnitude or value of the pleasure or good he expects to be the consequence of the act, he will be absolutely prevented from performing it.").

4 On this point, see K. M. Carlsmith and J. M. Darley, "Psychological Aspects of Retributive Justice" (2008) 40 *Advances in Experimental Social Psychology* 193, 202.

5 Ibid 207.

a way that is consistent with deterrence aims.[6] Rather than considering the probability that punishment will deter future cases, their studies of intuitive punishment in the criminal context provide evidence that decision-makers punish reprehensible behavior predominantly on the basis of retribution. In sum, people want punishment to deter, but some deep-seated sense of justice requires sentences proportional to the moral severity of the offense.[7]

In that respect, the research of Carlsmith et al. examines whether just deserts or deterrence justifications better describe the motivation of ordinary citizens when they are asked to sanction someone.[8] Their studies explore the relationship between lay intuition, deservingness (i.e., the retributive perspective), and utilitarian objectives (i.e., the deterrence perspective). Through a series of three experiments, they found that, when deciding the proper punishment for prototypical wrongdoing, participants were highly sensitive to factors uniquely associated with the just desert perspective (e.g., the seriousness of the offense). Moreover, even when participants were told to focus on deterrence (e.g., to consider factors such as the frequency with which the offense is committed and the probability of its detection), the participants' sentencing decisions were still primarily driven by their concern for just deserts (again, the reprehensibility of the offender's conduct).[9] "Punishment assignments," they found, "were instead consistent with a theory of punishment based on the moral deservingness of the perpetrator."[10]

Other studies that focus on the factors behind attribution of responsibility also suggest that the motivation for punishment is rooted in nonutilitarian motives. For instance, Alan Fiske and Phillip Tetlock homed in on moral outrage as a critical component in the determination of punishment.[11] They argue that empirical measures of moral outrage predict both punitiveness and punitive intent. Similarly, another study by Jennifer Lerner et al. focusing on the process that unfolds when a person forms a generalized punitive intent found that factors associated with just deserts and moral outrage contribute substantially to attributions of responsibility

6 Ibid 194. Also see J. Baron and I. Ritov, "Intuitions About Penalties and Compensation in the Context of Tort Law" (1993) 7 *Journal of Risk and Uncertainty* 17 (finding that the penalties people impose are "generally uninfluenced by their deterrent effect on future behavior.").

7 On this point, see D. T. Miller and N. Vidmar, "The Social Psychology of Punishment Reactions," in M. Lerner and S. Lerner (eds.), *The Justice Motive in Social Behavior* (Springer, 1981), pp. 145–72 (suggesting that a utilitarian mindset corresponds to an orientation toward macrojustice, whereas a deservingness or retributive mindset is triggered when the orientation is toward microjustice).

8 K. M. Carlsmith, J. M. Darley and P. H. Robinson, "Why Do We Punish? Deterrence and Just Deserts as Motives for Punishment" (2002) 83 *Journal of Personality and Social Psychology* 284.

9 Ibid 299. Also see Carlsmith and Darley, "Psychological Aspects of Retributive Justice," 204–5; K. M. Carlsmith, "The Roles of Retribution and Utility in Determining Punishment" (2006) 42 *Journal of Experimental Social Psychology* 437, 451.

10 See Carlsmith, Darley and Robinson, "Why Do We Punish?," 295.

11 See generally A. P. Fiske and P. E. Tetlock, "Taboo Trade-Offs: Reactions to Transactions that Transgress the Spheres of Justice" (1997) 18 *Political Psychology* 255.

and to punitive behavior.[12] This phenomenon has been termed the "outrage heuristic," by which it is meant that punishment decisions are rooted in the common sense understanding that a sanction's severity should correspond to the outrageousness of the conduct in question.[13]

This dynamic appears to have an analog in the tort context, where there is evidence that the awards of punitive damages by decision-makers tend to map more closely to punitive intuitions than they do to optimal deterrence. For instance, research studies have found that punitive damages decisions do not primarily dwell either on the defendant's ability to escape detection (the likelihood of detection being a crucial factor in the optimal deterrence calculus) or on the link between the award and the defendant's future behavior.[14] When asked to characterize the goals of their punitive damages awards, people tend to emphasize retribution over deterrence.[15] Perhaps the kind of cost–benefit analysis that is required by the standard economic models of deterrence is too sophisticated for most people, or perhaps that analysis, based as it is on rational agent models, does not reflect the fundamental concerns of most people. In either case, recent psychological research on tort law shows that people have difficulty carrying it out in practice. The research indicates that ordinary people do not spontaneously think in terms of optimal deterrence when asked questions about appropriate punishment.[16] Retributive intuitions show that individuals frequently process information and make decisions in intuitive ways that depart from rationalistic modes of judgment or wealth maximization. They suggest that we do not regularly weigh risks, costs, and benefits in the ways anticipated by economic models.[17] These findings, it should be noted, generally follow the conclusions drawn from Daniel Kahneman and Amos Tversky's well-known

[12] See generally J. S. Lerner, J. H. Goldberg and P. E. Tetlock, "Sober Second Thought: The Effects of Accountability, Anger, and Authoritarianism on Attributions of Responsibility" (1998) 24 *Personality and Social Psychology* 563.

[13] On the outrage heuristic, see C. R. Sunstein, "Moral Heuristics" (2005) 28 *Behavioral and Brain Sciences* 531, 538; D. Kahneman and S. Frederick, "Representativeness Revisited: Attribute Substitution in Intuitive Judgment," in T. Gilovich, D. Griffin and D. Kahneman (eds.), *Heuristics and Biases: The Psychology of Intuitive Judgment* (Cambridge University Press, 2002), pp. 49, 65; and D. Kahneman, O. Sibony and C. R. Sunstein, *Noise. A Flaw in Human Judgment* (William Collins, 2021), p. 191 ("outrage hypothesis: the emotion of outrage is the primary determinant of punitive intent").

[14] On this point, see C. R. Sunstein, D. Kahneman and D. Schkade, "Assessing Punitive Damages (with Notes on Cognition and Valuation in Law)" (1998) 107 *Yale Law Journal* 2071, 2126.

[15] See C. R. Sunstein, D. Schakade and D. Kahneman, "Do People Want Optimal Deterrence?" (2000) 29 *Journal of Legal Studies* 237, 250.

[16] See Sunstein, Kahneman and Schkade, "Assessing Punitive Damages," 2111. Also see generally D. W. Shuman, "The Psychology of Compensation in Tort Law" (1994) 43 *Kansas Law Review* 39 (arguing that deterrence is questionable as an aim of tort law if we analyze it from the psychological perspective of human behavior).

[17] See J. W. van Prooijen, *The Moral Punishment Instinct* (Oxford University Press, 2018), p. 37 (arguing that punitive judgments are substantially shaped by the intuitive mental system). Also see generally J. K. Robbennolt and V. P. Hans, *The Psychology of Tort Law* (New York University Press, 2016).

research on judgment and decision-making, which revealed that individuals consistently deviate from the utilitarian economic models.[18] Similarly, Jan-Willen van Prooijen argues that retributive urges to punish are an automatic gut-level response to offenders, which is more suggestive of a predisposition toward instinctive punishment than of fundamentally utilitarian motives.[19]

Moreover, in the particular context of punitive damages, direct evidence that juries are not "able to think well about optimal deterrence" has been documented in empirical studies in the United States.[20] Daniel Kahneman, David Schkade, and Cass Sunstein's studies showed that juries demonstrated substantial agreement on judgments regarding the outrageousness of the defendant's behavior and the appropriateness of punitive damages to punish in individual cases.[21] The perceived outrage and the intent to punish correlated very highly with each other: The degree of outrage at a given act of wrongdoing guides decisions regarding the proper degree of severity of the punishment.[22] The authors thus conclude that outrage is a strong predictor of the intent to punish via punitive damages.[23] Furthermore, there are no conclusive empirical studies showing that punitive damages actually achieve the optimal deterrence supposedly aimed for.[24] Surprisingly, this skepticism over the effectiveness of optimal deterrence is widespread even within the law and economics camp. For instance, Catherine Sharkey not only observes the failure of the economic deterrence rationale to gain predominance in doctrine but also that even the United States Supreme Court has implicitly rejected economic deterrence, placing emphasis on competing retributive rationales of punitive damages.[25]

18 See generally D. Kahneman and A. Tversky, "Prospect Theory: An Analysis of Decision Under Risk" (1979) 47 *Econometrica* 263; A. Tversky and D. Kahneman, "The Framing of Decisions and Psychology of Choice" (1981) 211 *Science* 453; D. Kahneman, *Thinking Fast and Slow* (Penguin, 2011).

19 See van Prooijen, *The Moral Punishment Instinct*, p. 36.

20 See Sunstein, Kahneman and Schkade, "Assessing Punitive Damages," 2126.

21 See D. Khaneman, D. Schkade and C. R. Sunstein, "Shared Outrage and Erratic Awards: The Psychology of Punitive Damages" (1998) 16 *Journal of Risk Uncertainty* 49, 49.

22 On this point, see Sunstein, "Moral Heuristics," 538.

23 See Sunstein, Kahneman and Schkade, "Assessing Punitive Damages," 2085 (arguing that societal outrage at certain behaviors may be expressed through retributive punishment).

24 For empirical work on deterrence in torts more generally, see, for example, G. T. Schwartz, "Reality in the Economic Analysis of Tort Law: Does Tort Law Really Deter?" (1994) 42 *UCLA Law Review* 377, 381 ("[t]he economists' efforts to fine-tune liability rules [...] to achieve near-perfect deterrence. [...] can be sized up as stimulating intellectual exercises that are often lacking in real-world relevance."); W. J. Cardi, R. D. Penfield and A. H. Yoon, "Does Tort Law Deter Individuals? A Behavioral Science Study" (2012) 9 *Journal of Empirical Legal Studies* 567; T. Eisenberg and C. Engel, "Assuring Civil Damages Adequately Deter: A Public Good Experiment" (2014) 11 *Journal of Empirical Legal Studies* 301.

25 See C. M. Sharkey, "Economic Analysis of Punitive Damages: Theory, Empirics, and Doctrine," in J. Arlen (ed.), *Research Handbook on the Economics of Torts* (Edward Elgar Publishing, 2013), pp. 488–89 ("optimal deterrence may be internally coherent [i.e., may explain the normative attractiveness of punitive damages properly conceived], but its fundamental premise fits poorly with the prevailing historical and popular understanding of punitive damages as punishment."). Similarly, see A. J. Sebok, "Normative Theories of Punitive Damages: The Case of Deterrence," in J. Oberdiek (ed.),

The dominance of the retributive rationale is patent in the judicial rhetoric or narrative that courts (and juries where available) employ when issuing punitive damages judgments and, moreover, in the lay understandings of the very aim of punitive awards.[26] The above-mentioned psychological research studies demonstrate that ordinary people assign punishment based on the moral outrage that is generated when someone intentionally wrongs another; that is, in other words, people are intuitive retributivists.[27] All this suggests that stripping punitive damages of their retributivist content would deprive them of a fundamental element.[28] Indeed, from a behavioral perspective, it appears that retribution is even the predominant element of the institution and plays a larger role than is generally recognized. It does not necessarily follow, of course, that deterrence plays absolutely no role – it only follows that people's punitive reactions are not primarily motivated by deterrence. In fact, the studies cited show that people desire some sort of deterrence as well. Retribution and deterrence are to some extent interconnected. Thus, the question becomes, now that the retributive aim has been shown to represent the most dominant element behind the motivation and determination of punishment, identifying the kinds of deterrence that are compatible with the main retributive rationale.

To start, we could understand deterrence as an ancillary effect of the imposition of punishment. In the sense that assigning just punishment means handing down a judgment that may deter the offender (and others) from committing the same wrong in the future, the deterrent effect would merely be understood as a byproduct of a just desert orientation – deterrence as an effect of doing retributive justice. I will refer to such a deterrent effect as *derived deterrence*. Or we could understand deterrence as independent from the imposition of punishment in the sense that

Philosophical Foundations of the Law of Torts (Oxford University Press, 2014), p. 317 ("the most important rationale that the US Supreme Court excludes under its common law theory of punitive damages is the view that punitive damages should be designed to promote deterrence.").

26 See, for example, *Cooper Industries Inc.* v. *Leatherman Tool Group Inc.*, 532 US 424, 432 (2001) (noting that punitive damages "serve the function of deterrence and retribution"); *Pacific Mut. Life Ins. Co.* v. *Haslip*, 499 US 1, 19 (1991) ("[P]unitive damages are imposed for purposes of retribution and deterrence"); and *Exxon Shipping Co* v. *Baker* 554 US 471, 492 (2008) ("[T]he consensus today is that [punitive damages] are aimed not at compensation but principally at retribution and deterring harmful conduct.").

27 See van Prooijen, *The Moral Punishment Instinct*, p. 36 (expressing that "[i]n most situations, deontological motives should trump utilitarian motives when people seek punishment for offenders.").

28 Similarly, see R. Perry, "The Role of Retributive Justice in the Common Law of Torts: A Descriptive Theory" (2006) 73 *Tennessee Law Review* 177 (arguing that retribution is the dominant goal and the better explanation for punitive damages); J. W. Lens, "Justice Holme's Bad Man and the Depleted Purposes of Punitive Damages" (2013) 101 *Kentucky Law Journal* 789, 805 (pointing out that morality-based punishment purpose for punitive damages is prominent in the Court's constitutional analysis, while "deterrence plays second fiddle."). For the opposite view, see G. Calabresi, "Civil Recourse Theory's Reductionism" (2013) 88 *Indiana Law Journal* 449, 467 (criticizing the United States Supreme Court for reducing punitive damages to retributory punishment: "[i]n fact, the Court's single-minded way of looking at punitive damages causes it to miss many other important and economics-based functions that extra-compensatory damages perform in our legal system.").

"punishment" would be one among other available tools for achieving the goal of deterrence. This is in line with the utilitarian account of deterrence already mentioned, deterrence as an aim. I will refer to this conception of deterrence as *autonomous deterrence*. Whereas the former version of deterrence (i.e., derived deterrence) can easily be accommodated within the retributive accounts of punishment that have been described, there is clearly no room for the latter version (i.e., autonomous deterrence). As the referenced literature suggests, decisions regarding punishment and the drive to be punitive are usually primarily motivated by the moral outrage that arouses when confronted with reprehensible wrongdoing regardless of the deterrent effects of the punishment.[29] The utilitarian version of deterrence (autonomous deterrence), however, is clearly inconsistent with lay intuitions regarding punishment, for it provides no satisfactory explanation of why we seek to punish outrageous behavior in the first place.

Considering all this, it seems proper to conclude that any genuine attempt to understand and fully capture the practice of imposing punishment through tort law and the tort process must not only avoid overlooking the predominance of its retributive aim but must also directly delve into the particularities of how those retributive motivations play out in that particular context. In that respect, social psychology has much to say about the motivation behind punishment in the first place. As will be seen in what follows, promising findings are emerging from the fields of cognitive and social psychology and other social science research on human behavior and decision-making with regards to the manner in which ordinary individuals react to conduct deserving of punishment. These findings lead to a new constructive space for rethinking retribution and deterrence in a way that better matches public intuitions of justice, thus making a valuable contribution to enriching the debates surrounding the retributive dimension of tort law.[30]

The underlying proposal is that looking at the motivations of ordinary people regarding punishment could help us to better understand the place of retribution in the tort context. From that perspective, the aim is to explore the reasons why ordinary people often want to punish reprehensible behavior. Referring to human psychology will help us to identify and deepen our understanding of important cognitive and behavioral phenomena regarding what really motivates people to demand that certain reprehensible behavior be judicially sanctioned by, for example, punitive awards. With these insights in mind, I purport to offer a more fundamental retributive reconstruction of punishment in torts, one that is sensitive to the victims' motivations for seeking punitive responses through the articulation of tort law and the

[29] On this point, see Baron and Ritov, "Intuitions about Penalties," 20 ("People [...] tend to ignore the deterrent effect of their [punitive] judgments.").

[30] On this point, see Carlsmith, Darley and Robinson, "Why Do We Punish?," 297 (as a policy implication of the psychological findings, they claim that if what we want to do is to reduce future wrongdoing, then "[t]he most effective means to this end may entail, ironically, a rejection of the utilitarian basis of punishment in favor of a just deserts system that aligns with people's everyday sense of justice.").

tort process. I undertake this challenge in the following sections by disentangling two interrelated but nonetheless distinct aspects that warrant separate evaluation: (1) the victim's retributive motivations for punishment; and (2) the rationality of lay approaches to retribution. It is my belief that there is much to be gained from this approach that has not been sufficiently explored in tort scholarship.

A THE VICTIM'S RETRIBUTIVE MOTIVATIONS FOR PUNISHMENT

Punitive awards in torts have been predominantly studied in the last decades from the one-sided perspective of the wrongdoer.[31] As much of the scholarship reviewed up to now has shown, most representative works on the topic, both in common law and civil law jurisdictions, center on the array of questions raised by the imposition of sanctions on defendants in classical tort lawsuits involving particularly egregious wrongdoing. As a result, much more attention has been paid to the wrongdoers' behavior than to the victims who pursue the imposition of the punitive award in the first place. For instance, in the United States, scholarly debates have focused on whether stricter evidentiary standards should be implemented, whether a cap or ratio for punitive award amounts would be appropriate, or whether split-recovery statutes should be enacted, all of which show concern not only for the constitutional safeguards and proportionality of the punishment imposed on the wrongdoer but also for restricting its availability and limiting its amounts to avoid plaintiff windfalls and exorbitant awards.[32] In the English tradition, where the availability of punitive damages has always been restricted to specific tortious behavior by the "categories test," the nearly exclusive focus on the wrongdoer is even more patent. Scholars have emphasized the importance of the focus of punitive awards upon the outrageousness of the wrong rather than on the plaintiff's right since these scholars appear "more concerned to 'denounce' the wrongdoer, [...], than to 'announce' the right."[33] Similarly, it has been argued that exemplary damages "respond to the defendant's conduct in perpetrating the tort, as opposed to the extent of the interference with the

[31] I have introduced this claim earlier in M. G. Martínez Alles, "Moral Outrage and Betrayal Aversion: The Psychology of Punitive Damages" (2018) 11(2) *Journal of Tort Law* 245.

[32] For examples of scholarly work along these lines, see, for example, M. A. Geistfeld, "Punitive Damages, Retribution, and Due Process" (2008) 81 *Southern California Law Review* 263; C. M. Sharkey, "Punitive Damages as Societal Damages" (2003) 113 *Yale Law Journal* 347; B. C. Zipursky, "*Palsgraf*, Punitive Damages, and Preemption" (2012) 125 *Harvard Law Review* 1757; T. Colby, "Clearing the Smoke from Philip Morris v. Williams: The Past, Present and Future of Punitive Damages" (2008) 118 *Yale Law Journal* 392; D. Markel, "How Should Punitive Damages Work?" (2009) 157 *University of Pennsylvania Law Review* 1383; W. K. Viscusi, "Why There is No Defense of Punitive Damages" (1998) 87 *Georgetown Law Journal* 381, 394–95 (who has long argued that limits on punitive awards are socially desirable in that they protect [corporate] defendants from capricious and potentially devastating judgments).

[33] See, for instance, K. Barker, "Private and Public: The Mixed Conception of Vindication in Torts and Private Law," in S. G. A. Pitel, J. W. Neyers and E. Chamberlain (eds.), *Tort Law: Challenging Orthodoxy* (Hart Publishing, 2013), p. 78.

underlying interests."[34] In Continental Europe and Latin America, where the local discussions (on whether and how to introduce punitive damages) have been predominantly influenced by the scholarly debates and practice of awarding punitive damages in the United States, a similar emphasis on the wrongdoers' perspective is also apparent.[35] For their part, most tort theorists have mainly focused on the wrongdoer as well. Indeed, as illustrated in Chapter 2 of Part I, a one-sided perspective on the wrongdoer has, for a great many scholars, provided the fundamental grounding for rejecting punitive damages in torts, while the greater part of the remaining scholars focuses on the deterrent effect of punitive awards, which similarly emphasizes the behavior of the wrongdoer.[36]

As a result, the role of the tort victim in bringing the punitive lawsuit has often been described either *instrumentally* as some sort of private attorney general moved by a desire to deter misbehavior by the prospect of a monetary gain, which ultimately opens the practice to the criticism that depicts punitive awards as unjustified plaintiff windfalls; or *formally* as an agent exercising her legal power to exact a punitive sanction by virtue of what the defendant did to her and how it was done, which obscures the substantive content of the victim's punitive responses. Consequently, scarce attention has been directed toward an in-depth inquiry examining the retributive motivations of the tort victims who pursue the judicial imposition of punitive awards in the first place. Both in practice and in theory, tort victims' intrinsic motivations to punish reprehensible wrongdoing (i.e., what captures the essence of the victim's punitive responses) have been largely neglected. However, under the bipolar structure of tort litigation, where victims have a central role in exercising their right of action against their wrongdoers, what ultimately motivates them to seek punitive responses through tort law and the tort process becomes particularly relevant.

In fact, if retribution plays a significant role in the laypersons' understanding of punishment, why not explore it more deeply? The focus here is on the motives for punishment of ordinary people, on what drives people to inflict punishment on others. Punishment has often been the object of study not only by moral and legal philosophers but also by social psychologists because it is such a common and essential aspect of our social life.[37] The perceived need to punish instances of rule-breaking is taken as fundamental for the maintenance of social order and is found in all established societies.[38] Van Prooijen argues that punishment "is intentionally providing another person with negative or unwanted outcomes, as a motivated response to the

[34] See J. N. E. Varuhas, "The Concept of 'Vindication' in the Law of Torts: Rights, Interests and Damages" (2014) 34 *Oxford Journal of Legal Studies* 253, 290.

[35] See the scholarly works cited in Section B of Chapter 1.

[36] See generally Chapter 2.

[37] For the argument that notwithstanding cultural differences, "the drive to punish is culturally universal," see van Prooijen, *The Moral Punishment Instinct*, p. 15.

[38] See generally N. Vidmar and D. T. Miller, "Social Psychological Processes Underlying Attitudes toward Legal Punishment" (1980) 14 *Law & Society Review* 565.

perception that this person has violated widely shared norms, values, or rules."[39] Underlying this idea are the questions of why people punish and what motivates them to seek punishment of those who commit egregious actions that they know (or should have known) are wrong. These questions have moral and psychological answers and may lead to paths that not only explore the sources or ultimate motivations for punishment but also what people hope to achieve by demanding punishment.

An approach to understanding retribution in tort law that is based on realistic accounts of human behavior (i.e., lay intuitions regarding motivations for punishment) may provide invaluable insights to enrich our understanding of the institution and figure out constructive ways of dealing with punishment in the tort context.[40] Exploring why victims would choose to actively pursue, through tort litigation, the imposition of punishment (e.g., through punitive damages) for having suffered reprehensible wrongs will direct our attention toward the rich value-laden lay intuitions that drive people to punish certain behaviors under certain circumstances of wrongdoing. A more meaningful understanding of punishment in tort law can be drawn by looking more closely at who we are and how we make sense of reprehensible wrongdoing that threatens our individual autonomy, dignity, physical integrity, or even life.

In the last decade, Cass Sunstein, Daniel Kahneman, and David Schkade have applied insights from the cognitive sciences in an effort to understand how juries actually make decisions involving punitive damages. The authors offer findings of a wide range of systematic biases in jury judgment and decision-making and how they correlate to erratic, unpredictable punitive damage awards.[41] Moreover, Jennifer Robbennolt and Valerie Hans recently published the first comprehensive analysis of tort law that applies modern cognitive and social psychology, offering a psychological approach to the determination of the amount of punitive damages awards.[42] They all call for an incorporation of these insights into punitive damages but have so far limited their analysis to a narrow set of practical implementation issues that mostly involve the retributive intuitions of the decision-makers (i.e., juries and judges), overlooking the retributive motivations of the victims who pursue the punitive response in the first place. The attention paid to the psychological literature,

39 See van Prooijen, *The Moral Punishment Instinct*, p. 10.

40 Arguing for a psychologically realistic approach to offer a more satisfactory account of blame, see V. McGeer, "Civilizing Blame," in D. J. Coates and N. A. Tognazzini (eds.), *Blame. Its Nature and Norms* (Oxford University Press, 2013), p. 188 ("No normative theory worth its salt can afford to ignore the real empirical nature of the sort of beings to which it is meant to apply").

41 For studies showing that jurors are primarily motivated, when evaluating punitive damages, by a sense of moral outrage at reprehensible conduct, see, for example, D. Khaneman, D. Schkade and C. R. Sunstein, "Shared Outrage and Erratic Awards: The Psychology of Punitive Damages" (1998) 16 *Journal of Risk Uncertainty* 49; C. R. Sunstein, "On the Psychology of Punishment" (2004) 11 *Supreme Court Economic Review* 171. More recently, see D. Kahneman, O. Sibony and C. R. Sunstein, *Noise. A Flaw in Human Judgment* (William Collins, 2021), pp. 187–99.

42 See Robbennolt and Hans, The Psychology of Tort Law, pp. 133–41.

however, suggests that the time is ripe for a more thorough application of these insights. I undertake this more comprehensive enterprise in what follows. By drawing from cognitive and social psychology, I seek to understand the motivations of victims of reprehensible wrongdoing to seek some sort of redress through the imposition of a punitive award. I argue that these retributive motivations have received insufficient attention from scholars in their efforts to make sense of the practice of exacting punishment in torts.

The starting point is the psychological observation of the retributivist responses to particularly egregious wrongdoing that many of us intuitively manifest. These intuitive responses prove we either consciously or unconsciously believe some degree of retribution is just. It is commonly accepted that retributive motives are primarily driven by an intuitive desire for justice and just deserts. That retribution for particularly egregious wrongdoing is almost universally sought poses basic moral questions that emotional-intuitive responses can illuminate. Intuitive reactions constitute part of our moral experience, which in turn conforms part of our fundamental human nature.[43] One good reason for turning our attention to victims' retributive concerns can be found in the "moral sentiments" present in the victim's response to egregious wrongdoing. Adam Smith has argued that the object of the anger is not as much causing its targets to "feel pain in his turn … as to make him sensible, that the person whom he injured did not deserve to be treated in that manner."[44] Peter Strawson's seminal discussion of "reactive attitudes" further illuminates and reinforces this point.[45] According to Strawson, "reactive attitudes" refer to the mental states that are distinctively involved in holding others morally accountable. Strawson argues that resentment and related emotions are constitutive of the way that we relate to one another as moral agents. According to Strawson, someone who does not experience the "reactive attitude" of resentment when others violate her rights conveys to others that either she does not believe she has the right or does not put much credence in her rights.[46] It matters to us very much whether the actions of other people convey goodwill, affection, or esteem or, on the contrary, contempt, indifference, or malevolence. As human beings, we make moral demands of others for a modicum of goodwill and regard. Punishment is one social practice to which we resort to express our reaction when the demand is not met. When reprehensible wrongs befall us, a range of moral emotions (which are part of our emotional make-up as human beings) trigger a retributive motive. Resentment and indignation are examples of "reactive attitudes" we assume when someone wrongs us in a morally objectionable

43 See generally van Prooijen, *The Moral Punishment Instinct*.

44 See D. D. Raphael and A. L. Macfie (eds.), *The Glasgow Edition of the Works and Correspondence of Adam Smith: The Theory of Moral Sentiments* (Oxford University Press, 1976), vol. 1, pp. 95–96.

45 See P. F. Strawson, "Freedom and Resentment," in G. Watson (ed.), *Free Will* (Oxford University Press, 1982), pp. 59–80.

46 Ibid 72, 77–80.

way that shows disrespect for our individual moral worth.[47] Strawson argues that the practice of punishment expresses, rather than merely exploits, our moral attitudes.[48] Certainly, resentment and indignation could be considered as negative emotions toward the wrongdoer, but that does not make them morally wrong emotions. They should instead be understood as appropriate responses toward value-demeaning attitudes made manifest in wrongdoers' treatment of the victim. In as much as "reactive attitudes" mediate relations of mutual respect and accountability, they differ from desires for retaliation or revenge. As Stephen Darwall describes, "[reactive attitudes] call for recognition of the legitimacy of our demand and the authority that its address presupposes. They come with an RSVP."[49] The idea is that reactive attitudes do not purport to force or overpower the other but to command her attention by virtue of one person's individual authority to lodge a legitimate claim for recognition from another. In that sense, Darwall argues that Strawson's "reactive attitudes" are not essentially retaliatory but rather "express reciprocal respect and so mediate relations of mutual accountability."[50] For instance, the object of resentment as a "reactive attitude," the argument goes, "is not to retaliate against someone who has injured one, but to hold him responsible in a way that expresses respect for him as a member of a mutually accountable moral community."[51] According to Darwall, reactive attitudes do "not seek to diminish, humiliate, insult, or damage their objects. The acknowledgement they seek is of a reciprocal standing."[52] Darwall acknowledges that "what resentment [as a reactive attitude] seeks is not getting back, but the other's acknowledgement of having wrongfully injured one and the other's taking responsibility for what he has done, for example, through compensation, and, perhaps, punitive damages."[53] Under this light, victims' retributive motivations are better read in terms of accountability – as an "accountability-seeking sentiment" – than as retaliatory emotions.[54] My reconstruction of the content of tort victims' retributive responses to reprehensible wrongdoing finds inspiration in this powerful insight.

In the tort context, we can identify at least two retributive motivations that involve the victim's intuitive reactions provoked by reprehensible wrongdoing: moral outrage and betrayal aversion. Moral outrage is an emotion related to anger

47 Ibid 77. Strawson distinguishes the reaction of resentment (if personally involved) from moral indignation (if indirectly involved). I do not take this distinction up since my intent is only to point out the most basic points of his theory to reinforce the psychological findings.

48 Ibid 80.

49 See S. Darwall, "Justice and Retaliation," in *Honor, History and Relationship. Essays in Second-Personal Ethics II* (Oxford University Press, 2013), p. 60.

50 Ibid 50.

51 Ibid 52.

52 See S. Darwall, "Ressentiment and Second-Personal Resentment," in *Honor, History, and Relationship: Essays in Second-Personal Ethics II* (Oxford University Press, 2013), p. 88.

53 See Darwall, "Justice and Retaliation," p. 52.

54 Ibid 66.

that describes our intuitive tendency to punish reprehensible violations of moral norms. Carlsmith and Darley argue that "[the] 'feeling' of moral outrage is the conscious registration of the intuitive reaction to instances of moral wrongdoing."[55] The retributive urge behind punishment carried out in response to deliberate, reckless, or egregious violations of moral norms is thus primarily motivated by the sense of outrage which the wrongdoer's conduct evokes; that is, they stem from the victim's sense that the offender has broken other-regarding moral norms that represent an affront to her value as a moral equal and that something needs to be done in response (i.e., the sense that justice must be restored).[56] Upon experiencing moral outrage, the tort victim is moved to punish the wrongdoer, to take action by filing a punitive lawsuit against the wrongdoer in order to hold her accountable, to denounce the reprehensible behavior, and to affirm her moral worth.[57] In that sense, the victim's urge to punish such instances of morally objectionable wrongdoing (i.e., the filing of a lawsuit seeking a punitive award) is directly tied to the particular offender: The victim is outraged by the morally objectionable action of the wrongdoer toward her. The victim understands the punitive lawsuit as a relational condemnatory response to affirm her moral worth in relation to the wrongdoer and to reinforce the importance of other-regarding values for the maintenance of the moral fabric of society.[58] The victim's punitive and recognitive aims are thus intertwined in the retributive response. Examples where moral outrage is clearly operative are tortious cases (for instance, those involving defamation, privacy invasion, wrongful eviction, dignitary torts, harassment, among others) where the wrongdoer's reprehensible behavior demonstrates a direct affront to the individual victim's moral worth in the sense that it expresses that the victim is of less value or less worthy of respect or that it is simply allowed to pursue her needs and interests ahead of those of the victim.

Betrayal aversion describes our intuitive tendency to punish betrayals of trust. As Jonathan Koehler and Andrew Gershoff demonstrate in a series of studies, people are averse to betrayal, both real and perceived.[59] For instance, their studies demonstrate that people would assign more punishment to a robbery committed by a security guard than by a burglar. Similarly, people experience greater outrage when faulty wiring in a smoke alarm causes a factory fire than when the same faulty wiring in a refrigerator causes a fire.[60] When safety products fail to

55 See Carlsmith and Darley, "Psychological Aspects of Retributive Justice," 212.

56 See generally van Prooijen, *The Moral Punishment Instinct*.

57 See generally J. M. Darley and T. S. Pittman, "The Psychology of Compensatory and Retributive Justice" (2003) 7 *Personality and Social Psychology Review* 324.

58 For the argument that the desire for recognition, as opposed to retribution, is central to anger, see L. Silva, "Is Anger a Hostile Emotion?" (2024) 15 *Review of Philosophy and Psychology* 383.

59 See J. J. Koehler and A. D. Gershoff, "Betrayal Aversion: When Agents of Protection Become Agents of Harm" (2002) 90 *Organizational Behavior and Human Decision Processes* 244.

60 Ibid.

protect us against the very thing they are designed to prevent, they betray us in a fundamental way.[61] Curiously, aversion to betrayal leads people to react more negatively to betrayal than to injury caused to them without betrayal. Thus, when people believe they have been "betrayed," they treat the offender with more intense moral condemnation than they would for similar acts committed without betrayal: People punish others not only for injury caused but also for trust betrayed. Betrayal aversion is clearly operative, though not exclusively, in the product liability context where corporations are felt to have abused consumers' trust by, for instance, the deliberate imposition of risk of substantial harm by knowingly introducing defective products in the marketplace – Dalkon Shield, Cooper-7 Intrauterine Device, Johnson & Johnson talc, silicone, and breast implant litigations are all examples of punitive awards based in part on the fact that manufacturers concealed adverse information to consumers or directly avoided further testing or recalling their products when confronted with mounting evidence of significant hazards of regular use of the product that consumers could not reasonably anticipate.[62] Risks of serious injury (or even death) involuntarily imposed on consumers by manufacturers who have (or should have) considered the danger are perceived as a breach of trust. Such breaches elicit the betrayal aversion intuition that calls for some concrete response to the callous corporation's action (i.e., to be punitive against the corporate defendant for the trust betrayed). The proper response should hold the corporation accountable, condemn the corporate misbehavior, and affirm the consumer's moral worth. When trust is breached in this manner, those who are betrayed by the morally objectionable behavior of the corporate defendant not only endure the substantial harm deliberately imposed on them (cancer, in the Johnson & Johnson case) but also lose their confidence in the trust-based relationships that are central to a functioning civil society. Following this logic, the betrayed victim understands the punitive lawsuit as a relational condemnatory response that affirms her moral worth vis-à-vis the morally objectionable action of the wrongdoer and reinforces the importance of trust and social cooperation. Once again, the victim's punitive and recognitive aims are intertwined in the retributive response.

As will become clearer in what follows, moral outrage and betrayal aversion represent textured relational motivations for seeking punitive responses (through the articulation of tort law and the tort process), which are authenticated by the situated meaning and significance of the impact of serious tortious wrongdoing (i.e., reprehensible, deliberate, reckless, wanton, egregious) that represents a morally objectionable affront to the victim's self-worth.

[61] On this point, see Robbennolt and Hans, The Psychology of Tort Law, p. 171.

[62] For a survey of punitive damages cases along these lines in the United States, see T. Koening and M. Rustad, "His and Her Tort Reform: Gender Injustice in Disguise" (1995) 70 *Washington Law Review* 1, 39–46.

B THE RATIONALITY OF LAY APPROACHES TO RETRIBUTION

Because retributive motivations show that people rely on their emotions and intuitions for punitive judgments, they depart markedly from a fully rational model for reasoning.[63] From this perspective, retributive motivations are seen not only as impediments to the use of reason but also as an affront to legal rationality, logic, and predictability.[64] Perhaps the reason why so much effort has been made to exclude emotions and intuitions from valid justifications for legal institutions lies in the perception that, in the search for sensible solutions, the law needs to "rise above" such subjective, shifting, and unrationalized inclinations. Put another way, emotions and intuitions have been excluded because the law depends wholly on the rationality underlying and interconnecting its foundations for its legitimacy as a fair and just institution.[65] The question that immediately arises is thus whether tort law (through, for example, punitive awards) ought to explicitly acknowledge and reflect those retributive intuitions.

The alleged emotive-intuitive basis for retributive judgments seems, at least on the surface, to preclude retributive motivations as a valid ground for legal rules and norms. The discomfort of tort scholars with retributive motivations as the justification for punishment in torts arises from two main concerns. On one side is the controversy over the weight of or compatibility of emotions and intuitions considered irrational within legal institutions that are designed to be rational exactly for the purpose of minimizing the room for subjective, individualized judgments. The underlying claim is that tort victims' private motivations to be punitive (or any other) should not be reflected in the design of the legal institution. On the other side is the trend in tort scholarship to associate retribution negatively with notions of "vengeance," "revenge," "private retaliation," or "getting even." For instance, Kit Barker has argued against understanding modern private law as endorsing retributive aims simply because "vengeance is a morally bankrupt practice and therefore

63 Even those who accept retribution have expressed concern about the emotions that drive it. See, for example, M. S. Moore, *Placing Blame: A Theory of the Criminal Law* (Oxford University Press, 1997), pp. 115–27 (discussing the dangers of retributive emotions); J. G. Murphy, "Two Cheers for Vindictiveness" (2000) 2 *Punishment & Society* 131, 137–39 (discussing the dangers of vindictiveness).

64 On this point, see R. C. Solomon, "From Emotions and Choice," in R. C. Solomon (ed.), *What Is an Emotion? Classic and Contemporary Readings* (Oxford University Press, 2003), p. 224 (describing the general view of emotions as "irrational and disruptive," and the widespread belief that "[c]ontrolling one's emotion is [...] like the caging and taming of a wild beast.").

65 See, however, M. C. Nussbaum, *Hiding from Humanity: Disgust, Shame and the Law* (Princeton University Press, 2006), p. 5, 13 ("law without appeals to emotion is virtually unthinkable."); A. M. Lerner, "From Socrates to Damasio, from Langdell to Kandel: The Role of Emotion in Modern Legal Education," in P. Maharg and C. Maughan (eds.), *Affect and Legal Education. Emotion in Learning and Teaching the Law* (Routledge, 2011), p. 152 (arguing for the importance of integrating emotional and value-based considerations in legal education). Also see K. Abrams and H. Keren, "Who's Afraid of Law and the Emotions?" (2010) 94 *Minnesota Law Review* 1997, 2003–11 (describing the rise of the field of law and emotion).

a poor normative platform on which to build [...] a case for punitive damages."[66] Similarly, James Penner has argued that punitive damages "privatise punishment, and that alone brings them worryingly close to a form of private retaliation"; and "as close as can be to state-backed private retaliation for personal gain."[67] John Goldberg and Benjamin Zipursky, for their part, expressly acknowledge that redress through law is not vengeance but worry about the resemblance enough to claim emphatically that their central aspiration is to demonstrate "that the particular notion of wrongdoing at work in tort law is attractive in part because it is not tied to notions of retribution or vengeance."[68] At work is the underlying concern that legitimizing punitive impulses that society has properly delegitimized and suppressed might be seen as an obsolete approach to tort law because it cuts against modern sensibilities.[69] These close associations of retribution with private revenge immediately evoke the perceived importance of protecting the classic legal order. I am referring again to the classic order established by the private–public distinction that justifies the state's monopoly over coercive power (i.e., the right to punish) that is embodied by the criminal law and procedure. The idea behind conferring such right to the state is keeping the power to punish out of the hands of individual victims since that would deform the equilibrium of the legal system. The displacement of private retaliation is not solely regarded as a mature historical development of the law but, in fact, is often described as one of the "central pillars" of the criminal law.[70] Likewise, it has lately been argued that the explanation of significant parts of our modern systems of private law lies in the grant to victims by the state of powers of civil recourse as an alternative path to redress. This grant comes, the theory goes, in exchange for the surrender of their right to seek revenge upon their offenders (or resort to self-help).[71]

[66] See K. Barker, "Punishment in Private Law – No Such Thing Anymore," in E. Bant, W. Courtney, J. Goudkamp and J. M. Paterson (eds.), *Punishment and Private Law* (Hart Publishing, 2021), p. 46.

[67] See J. Penner, "Punishments and Penalties in Private Law, with Particular Reference to the Law Governing Fiduciaries," in E. Bant, W. Courtney, J. Goudkamp and J. M. Paterson (eds.), *Punishment and Private Law* (Hart Publishing, 2021), pp. 117–18.

[68] See J. C. P. Goldberg and B. C. Zipursky, *Recognizing Wrongs* (Harvard University Press, 2020), p. 65 ("being serious about wrongs need not lead to the valorization of vengeance").

[69] See G. S. Mendlow, "Is Tort Law a Form of Institutionalized Revenge?" (2011) 39 *Florida State University Law Review* 129, 129 ("Most would agree that institutions of revenge have no place in a just society").

[70] On this point, see J. Gardner, "Crime: In Proportion and Perspective," in A. Ashworth and M. Wasik (eds.), *Fundamentals of Sentencing Theory* (Oxford University Press, 1998), p. 32 (arguing that the function of the criminal law is to displace revenge by satisfying the retaliatory desires of victims when consistent with its other aims).

[71] See generally Goldberg and Zipursky, Recognizing Wrongs. Similarly, see S. Hershovitz, "Tort as a Substitute for Revenge," in J. Oberdiek (ed.), *Philosophical Foundations of the Law of Torts* (Oxford University Press, 2014), p. 88. For a critique of civil recourse understanding of tort law as placating anger or the inclination or urge to get even as one that generates an unstable amalgam of conceptual and empirical factors, see A. Ripstein, "Civil Recourse and Separation of Wrongs and Remedies" (2011) 39 *Florida State University Law Review* 163, 186.

Understandably, these are widely shared concerns. There is long-standing consensus in our societies that private vengeance, revenge, or retaliation represent an inappropriate normative basis for legal action and that the law should counter them by serving the healthy social function of cooling, rationalizing, channeling, and responding to those powerful emotions.[72] However, it does not seem to follow directly from there that retributive motivations themselves represent a normatively questionable basis upon which no case for punishment (e.g., punitive damages) can be built in tort law. This pervasive tendency of tort scholars to rapidly equate "retribution" to "vengeance" certainly oversimplifies the matter at hand. To start, it has been long argued that retribution differs from vengeance in that the former is institutionalized and must respect limits (for instance, deservedness and proportionality), whereas the latter is an unregulated response, without principled limitations, by which victims seek satisfaction directly and by the means of their choice.[73] Others have pointed out that retribution attaches the punishment directly to the offender, whereas revenge may target an offender's friends or relatives.[74] Others have argued that retribution differs from vengeance because its denunciation of misbehavior is institutionally backed up by the state's coercive power – retribution as condemnation.[75] Regardless of the definition of retribution ultimately embraced, for now my modest point is that, considering the extent to which retributive motivations are embedded in tort law, it appears too simplistic to reject retribution outright as if it were vengeance without further inquiry into the particularities of the institutionalized context in which it is manifest. Instead, the proper question to ask would be whether those retributive motivations institutionalized through courts by means of a legal process that is initiated and substantially controlled by private litigants but overseen by an impartial public authority have a proper place in tort law. In other words, we should be asking the more vexing questions of whether and to what extent we can make sense of those embedded retributive motivations as a normatively appropriate basis for legal action in the tort context without fearing the charge that we are claiming legitimacy for some scheme of state-backed vengeance, revenge, or retaliation for private gain.

72 See R. C. Solomon, "Justice v. Vengeance: On Law and the Satisfaction of Emotion," in S. A. Bandes (ed.), *The Passions of Law* (New York University Press, 2000), pp. 123, 131.

73 On this point, see T. Brooks, *Punishment: A Critical Introduction* (Routledge, 2021); J. Hampton, "Correcting Harms versus Righting Wrongs: The Goal of Retribution" (1992) 39 *UCLA Law Review* 1659; M. M. Gerber and J. Jackson, "Retribution as Revenge and Retribution as Just Deserts" (2013) 26(1) *Social Justice Research* 61 (distinguishing between retribution as revenge and retribution as just deserts); van Prooijen, *The Moral Punishment Instinct*, p. 232 (arguing that revenge and third-party punishment are driven by similar underlying emotions [e.g., anger] but differ in their legitimacy, intensity, and constructive consequences).

74 See D. Markel, "Retributive Damages: A Theory of Punitive Damages as Intermediate Sanction" (2009) 94 *Cornell Law Review* 239, 270–71 (building up from Nozick's distinctions between retribution and revenge).

75 See the scholarly works on expressive theories of retribution cited later in Chapter 4.

Following this thread of thought, I argue that this charge against retributivism in torts not only renders "reason insensitive" and "emotions devoid of sense" but also reveals a misunderstanding of the actual meaning of our retributive intuitions in the sense that it fails to capture the moral insights that retributive motivations express with regards to the proper treatment that members of a community owe to each other in particular circumstances.[76] As Jon Hanson and David Yosifon argue, the understanding of law as a purely cognitive exercise wholly separate from the values of those involved in its construction is misleading.[77] Importantly, however, I do not argue that tort law should maintain an unreflexively responsive posture to the retributive motivations of victims of wrongful behavior. To argue that would be simplistic as well. The mere phenomenon of retributive motivations exhibited by people in response to outrageous wrongdoing is not in itself a prima facie reason for tort law to respond to those intuitions (i.e., the phenomenon does not per se require rules in tort law that are consistent with those intuitions).[78] A legal system does not exist merely to track people's intuitions about appropriate conduct. The legal system is also meant to mold intuitions and behaviors.[79] While sometimes it may be appropriate for the law to operate in a manner consistent with the intuitive beliefs and reactions of the members of the community, other times it is not.[80] That is exactly the point here: We should collectively determine which mismatches matter and which ones do not. However, to be able to do that, we must first acknowledge and evaluate the retributive motivations that shape our punitive reactions.[81]

The point is that the interplay between our intuitive emotions and the law is much more complex, subtle, and highly contextual than legal actors are generally willing to admit.[82] Since emotion and values pervade the law, it appears impossible (and undesirable) to exclude these variables completely from our legal reasoning processes.[83] In fact, studies have shown that reason and emotion are inseparable

[76] See Solomon, "Justice v. Vengeance," p. 129.

[77] See generally J. D. Hanson and D. Yosifon, "The Situational Character: A Critical Realist Perspective on the Human Animal" (2004) 93 *Georgetown Law Journal* 1.

[78] For a discussion on the relationship between moral intuitions and legal rules, see generally M. Kelman, "Moral Realism and the Heuristics Debate" (2013) 5 *Journal of Legal Analysis* 339; and *The Heuristic Debate* (Oxford University Press, 2011).

[79] See R. H. Thaler and C. R. Sunstein, *Nudge: Improving Decisions About Health, Wealth and Happiness* (Penguin, 2008), p. 3 (suggesting that the law should engage in "choice architecture," implementing legal measures that correct for human deviations from rationality).

[80] On whether the effect of cognitive biases on a given legal norm justifies changing that norm, see G. C. Persad, "When, and How, Should Cognitive Bias Matter to Law" (2014) 32 *Law and Inequality* 31.

[81] See Abrams and Keren, "Who's Afraid of Law and the Emotions?," 2003–11 (suggesting that law and emotions seek primarily to (1) illuminate the roles emotions play in legal problems, (2) investigate these roles through interdisciplinary analysis, and if proper, (3) integrate these findings into normative recommendations for the law).

[82] On this point, see generally S. A. Bandes, "Feeling and Thinking like a Lawyer: Cognition, Emotion and the Practice and Progress of Law" (2021) 89 *Fordham Law Review* 1.

[83] On tort law's ability to recognize the value of lay intuitions, see G. C. Persad, "Risk, Everyday Intuitions, and the Institutional Value of Tort Law" (2010) 62 *Stanford Law Review* 1445.

components of a complex, integrative process of considering alternatives and making choices.[84] Before deciding to ignore, denigrate, or reject outright retributive motivations as a matter of across-the-board-policy to directly avoid the stigma of embracing private revenge (or deforming the equilibrium of the legal system), we should first seriously evaluate whether, to what extent, and under which circumstances it would be proper to integrate retributive motivations into tort law. By making sense of retributive motivations in a way that enables a systematic understanding of their place in tort law, I intend to demonstrate in what follows that tort victims' retributive motivations for punishment have, in certain contextual tortious settings, a logic and structure that not just distinguishes them from "vengeance" but rather one that, most importantly, makes them appropriate responses to instances of reprehensible wrongdoing, and that tort law and the tort process play a fundamental role in capturing, channeling, responding, and controlling them.

One way of doing this is to begin by distinguishing the emotions-intuitions that are elicited from the emotive-intuitive reactions, which represent proper responses to certain instances of morally objectionable wrongdoing. Doing so provides a way of identifying the emotive-intuitive responses that properly pertain to which contexts of wrongdoing.

a *Moral Outrage: The Role of Emotions*

The influence of moral outrage in lay judgment has been severely questioned because of the emotive influence that operates within both victims' retributive motivations for punishment and decision-makers' actual punitive judgments. It has been argued that moral outrage is an anger-based automatic response to wrongdoing that is too tightly wrapped up in emotive-intuitive reactions, and thus that it represents an irrational motivation for punitive judgments that should be corrected or overridden by the law. Often, rationality (reasoned responses) and emotionality (emotional responses) are presented as opposing, irreconcilable poles.[85] In Susan Bandes' words, both "the demarcation between reason and emotion, and the possibility of keeping reasoning processes free of emotional variables" have been overstated in mainstream accounts of the rule of law.[86] Although it is true that emotions, such as anger, often blind us to reason, that does not mean that all decisions influenced by anger are morally questionable. Anger is often justified and has moral substance, just as many other emotions. It is possible to feel "moral outrage" at

84 See K. W. Fischer and J. P. Tangney, "Self-Conscious Emotions and the Affect Revolution: Framework and Overview," in J. P. Tangney and K. W. Fischer (eds.), *Self-Conscious Emotions: The Psychology of Shame, Guilt, Embarrassment, and Pride* (Guilford, 1995), pp. 3, 6.

85 See S. H. Pillsbury, "Emotional Justice: Moralizing the Passions of Criminal Punishment" (1989) 74 *Cornell Law Review* 655, 655.

86 See S. A. Bandes, "Introduction," in S. A. Bandes (ed.), *The Passions of Law* (New York University Press, 2000), p. 6.

reprehensible wrongdoing done to us without losing sight of reason.[87] Although emotional reactions can compound to the point of overcoming the capacity to reason clearly or objectively, that this occurs on occasion is not sufficient grounds for disregarding out-of-hand moral judgments reached through less volatile emotional responses.[88] The insistence on the notion that all emotions and intuitions are irrational requires closer examination than the law has generally undertaken. This section sets about doing just that: Taking emotion in tort law seriously.

The depiction of emotions as irrational occurrences, as mysteries that simply happen to us beyond our individual control, impeding rational decision-making, represents a misconception of emotion and its influence on retributive judgments. The relationship between emotion and reason is much more intricate.[89] Our emotions are better understood as complex processes that involve highly cognitive features (for instance, highlighting salience, discerning patterns of relevant information, and weighing risks).[90] It has long been argued that "emotion in concert with cognition leads to truer perception and, ultimately, to better (more accurate, more moral, more just) decisions."[91] Leading philosopher Martha Nussbaum has emphasized the cognitive structure of emotions: They embody judgments about the objects to which they respond.[92] Similarly, Samuel Pillsbury understands that our rational faculties play a critical role not only in reasoning but also in forming emotional responses.[93] There is no reason to believe that emotion lies beyond control just because emotive self-control presents certain limitations. In his view, recognizing the rationality of emotions provides the basis for understanding how we often moralize emotions in the particular legal context of retributive judgments.[94]

Here I follow a cognitive theory of emotion that posits cognitive assessment as critical to emotion.[95] Emotion represents a sensory experience arising out of a cognitive assessment of an event, person, or situation, usually accompanied by a desire for particular action (these are two aspects of emotions: the sensational

[87] See Moore, *Placing Blame*, p. 117 (arguing that there is a rich body of faithful depictions of rational and moral people undisturbed by their urge to punish another for a wrong).

[88] Ibid 118.

[89] For the understanding that the relationship between decision-making and intuition is better characterized as interplay than as dependency of one on the other, see Lerner, "From Socrates to Damasio," 171 (arguing that "[o]ur implicitly built, preconscious emotional brain and our cognitive, reasoning brain are in a continuous process of interaction.").

[90] See K. Oatley, D. Keltner, and J. M. Jenkins, *Understanding Emotions* (2nd ed.) (Wiley-Blackwell, 2006), p. 21.

[91] On this point, see Bandes, "Introduction," pp. 6–7.

[92] See M. C. Nussbaum, *Upheavals of Thought: The Intelligence of Emotions* (Cambridge University Press, 2001), p. 334.

[93] See Pillsbury, "Emotional Justice," 674.

[94] Ibid. Also see generally van Prooijen, *The Moral Punishment Instinct*.

[95] See generally R. M. Gordon, *The Structure of Emotions: Investigations in Cognitive Philosophy* (Cambridge University Press, 1987); R. De Sousa, *The Rationality of Emotions* (MIT Press, 1987).

and the behavioral).[96] Emotions therefore have their own cognitive rationality.[97] In Pillsbury's reconstruction, emotions are a way of making sense of the world, of synthesizing reality and giving it personal meaning. He argues that emotions provide the basic means for relating the inner subjective self to the outer objective world.[98] Thus, for example, recognizing that I care about flagrant violations of bodily integrity allows me to recognize the importance I place on the manner in which we treat each other in society: It is the significance of the morality that binds us together as a community. The evaluative function of emotion implies that a failure to react with outrage or indignation to an egregious wrongdoing might imply a rejection of society's moral code.

To be sure, the cognitive assessment upon which emotion is based may be accurate or mistaken, conscious or unconscious, but in any event, it constitutes an attempt to assess a situation by means that reflect an internal rationality. Emotions serve as a guide to rational inquiry in the sense that they provide a pattern of salience that helps order our thoughts and actions: Emotions direct our attention to certain aspects of a situation, suggesting distinct approaches to the situation depending on the circumstances.[99] As Nussbaum illustrates, "[i]n order to have anger, I must have [a] complex set of beliefs: that some damage has occurred to me […]; that the damage is not trivial but significant; that it was done by someone; probably, that is was done willingly."[100] Moreover, emotions provide meaning to us in a way that reason cannot.[101] As Robert Solomon has expressed, "[a]n emotion is a basic judgment about ourselves and our place in our world, the projection of the values and ideals, structures and mythologies, according to which we live and through which we experience life."[102] Without an emotional component, events mean nothing to us. Our emotions constitute reality and provide us with the means of finding importance in our existence.[103]

According to Javela et al., the emotion of anger tends to arise "when values are compromised, promises and expectations are broken, rules violated, or personal freedom and rights are abridged" by behavior perceived as "intentional, preventable

96 On this point, see Pillsbury, "Emotional Justice," 676.

97 See R. De Sousa, "From the Rationality of Emotion," in R. C. Solomon (ed.), *What Is an Emotion? Classic and Contemporary Readings* (Oxford University Press, 2003), p. 249.

98 See Pillsbury, "Emotional Justice," 677.

99 Ibid.

100 See Nussbaum, *Upheavals of Thought*, pp. 28–29.

101 See A. Damasio, *Descartes' Error: Emotion, Reason, and The Human Brain* (Penguin, 2005), p. 221 (making a strong case, by studying cases of people with brain damage that blocks their access to emotional cues, for the notion that without input from the emotions there can be no true rationality).

102 See R. C. Solomon, *The Passions: Emotions and the Meaning of Life* (2nd ed.) (Hackett Publishing, 1993), pp. 125–26.

103 See C. Calhoun, "Cognitive Emotions?," in C. Calhoun and R. C. Solomon, *What Is an Emotion? Classic and Contemporary Readings* (Oxford University Press, 2003), p. 339.

or unjustified."[104] To say that one is angry about something implies an evaluation of the situation that provokes it. That means that the denomination of a sensation as a particular emotion entails rational analysis. The fact that the rationality of emotions operates at a different level than ordinary deliberative thought processes does not mean that emotions are irrational. Indeed, because emotions stem from cognitive assessments, they are subject to rational control: If a mistake is made in the cognitive assessment that elicits an angry response because of an incorrect evaluation of the situation (e.g., unbeknown to the victim, what the offender did was beyond her control), errors can be subjected to control and change. The implication of this argument is that we have a non-negligible degree of capacity to reason intuitively. It means our intuitive system, which is dominated by heuristics and emotions, is one mode of reasoning that cannot simply be deemed irrational and therefore reflexively disregarded by the law. Following these insights, emotions that are based on cognitive assessments may operate as a substitute for more conventional forms of reasoning.

Another objection that has been raised against acknowledging the rationality of moral outrage is that it cannot cause any intelligible good because the emotions that give rise to retributive judgments are necessarily pathological in moral nature.[105] In this line of thinking, retributive intuitions (e.g., resentment, indignation, anger, outrage) are deemed questionable because they morally worsen our competence to make retributive judgments (due to the negative emotions that give rise to such judgments). These critics argue that the retributive urge is fundamentally bad; that it prevents us from being fully developed virtuous human beings in contrast to the sort of person who acts on such negative emotions.[106] However persuasive this might be, as Michael Moore argues, this supposed lack of virtue on

[104] See J. J. Javela, R. E. Mercadillo and J. M. Ramírez, "Anger and Associated Experiences of Sadness, Fear, Valence, Arousal, and Dominance Evoked by Visual Scenes" (2008) 103 *Psychological Review* 663, 665.

[105] See, for example, M. C. Nussbaum, *Anger and Forgiveness: Resentment, Generosity, Justice* (Oxford University Press, 2016) (who recently suggested that anger too often short-circuits grief ultimately harming those who harbor it); Moore, *Placing Blame*, pp. 119–20 (following Nietzsche in associating retribution with "resentment, fear, anger, cowardice, hostility, aggression, cruelty, sadism, envy, jealousy, guilt, self-loathing, hypocrisy and self-deception.").

[106] For the view that anger is morally problematic because it conceptually involves the desire for payback, see Nussbaum, *Anger and Forgiveness*, p. 46 (distinguishing the counter-productive desire for payback from transitive anger as a constructive desire to move forward). But see, however, V. L. Spring, C. D. Cameron and M. Cikara, "The Upside of Outrage" (2018) 22(12) *Trends in Cognitive Sciences* 1067, 1067–69 (criticizing that the negative characterization of outrage as a corrosive emotion makes us to overlook and under investigate its potential positive effects). For a collection of essays contesting the idea that anger is necessarily concerned with payback, see M. Cherry and O. Flanagan (eds.), *The Moral Psychology of Anger* (Rowan and Littlefield International, 2017) (advancing the idea that anger might instead aim for recognition of shared norms and values). Similarly, see A. Srinivasan, "The Aptness of Anger" (2018) 26(2) *Journal of Political Philosophy* 123, 123–44 (arguing that the claim that anger essentially involves the desire for revenge is misguided).

the part of those who make retributive judgments seems irrelevant in the assessment of whether retributive judgments are accurate.[107] Our moral retributive beliefs reflect our moral beliefs.

One plausible response to this objection comes from the close connection between emotions and morality (i.e., the emotional base of moral judgment). The fact that certain emotions (e.g., resentment, indignation, outrage) are considered to some extent "negative" emotions toward the offender does not necessarily mean that they are "morally wrong" emotions. Moore argues that our emotions constitute our heuristic guide to determining what is morally right.[108] The idea is that we need emotions to ascertain the unfairness of, for example, deliberate deprivation of another's bodily integrity or dignity. Thus, according to Moore, we do a disservice to morality when we accept the opposition of emotions to rationality.[109] He asserts a rationality of the emotions that can make them trustworthy guides to moral insight.[110] Moreover, if we accept the connection between our legal institutions and personal morals, we cannot condemn an institution solely because it responds to or channels "emotions." Indeed, some emotions generate moral insights that our legal system could hardly do without, such as the insight that it is outrageously unfair to deliberately expose others to the risk of severe injury. In fact, we often judge the moral worth of an emotion as a virtue or learn what the correct moral judgments about others are from emotional experiences. In such cases, the emotional experience, for example, of "moral outrage" may generate a firm moral conviction that reprehensible violations of others' physical integrity is not an appropriate manner for people to treat each other in society.

Whether "moral outrage" is virtuous or not seems a different question altogether. Everyone becomes angry or outraged when their bodily integrity or other important protected interests are deliberately violated or openly disregarded by someone else. It is human to feel outraged at a wrongful violation. Moreover, in many cases, lack of outrage can be a symptom of lack of self-respect.[111] And yet, how is it that we grow angry or outraged with someone who has deliberately and without justification caused suffering to a third party? These emotions seem to be the appropriate response of someone who cares about the moral code that binds us together. And to the extent that outrage motivates the particular retributive response (i.e., the punitive award), its virtue evidences the truth of those judgments.[112] Jeffrey Murphy has argued that what he calls "retributive hatred" is a virtuous emotion felt

[107] See Moore, *Placing Blame*, p. 126.

[108] Ibid 116.

[109] Ibid.

[110] Ibid. According to Moore's reconstruction, "[e]motions are rational when they are intelligibly proportionate in their intensity to their objects, when they are not inherently conflicted, when they are coherently orderable, and instantiate over time an intelligible character."

[111] See J. G. Murphy, "Forgiveness and Resentment" (1982) 7 *Midwest Studies in Philosophy* 503, 505.

[112] See Moore, *Placing Blame*, p. 145.

in response to serious wrongdoing.[113] According to Murphy, moral outrage against our offenders can be virtuous when we are the victims of wrongdoing since it can be understood as an expression of self-respect, an affirmation that we do not tolerate such violations of our own rights.[114] Similarly, Jean Hampton has asserted that it is virtuous to feel "moral hatred" at wrongdoing to oneself by others.[115] Likewise, Pillsbury considers the emotion of "moral outrage" to be a perfectly appropriate response to wrongdoing, so long as it is clearly distinguished from vengeance.[116]

Another classical reaction against "moral outrage" as a valid retributive motivation for punitive judgments holds that, because emotion-intuition opposes reason, it also opposes justice in the sense that the emotion impairs both neutral judging and a system of administering justice based on cognition.[117] Accordingly, the more "moral outrage" a legal issue provokes, the harder the courts must work to insulate the legal decision from emotive-intuitive influence. This is precisely the purpose of formalistic rules and depersonalized procedures.[118] An illustration of this attempt to suppress emotional influence in the punitive damages context in the United States is Kip Viscusi's proposal for the protection of corporations from juror retribution when the former engage in explicit cost–benefit analysis.[119] Viscusi's worry is what Sunstein named "the cold-heart heuristic: punish those who adopt a calculating approach to human life."[120] Viscusi proposes giving greater legal protection to corporations for risk analyses by providing a "safe harbor": If a safety precaution fails a cost–benefit test, meaning not adopting the safety measure is the more efficient course of action, then the company cannot be considered negligent, so the plaintiff would be prohibited from introducing evidence that the corporation had performed the cost–benefit analysis.[121] Plaintiffs would thus be unable to introduce evidence regarding the manufacturer's egregious conduct unless the conduct was related to a deficient cost–benefit analysis. The purpose of this insulating strategy is to circumvent the jurors' retributive intuitions to unfeeling

[113] See J. G. Murphy, "Retributive Hatred: An Essay On Criminal Liability and the Emotions," in R. G. Frey and C. W. Morris (eds.), *Liability and Responsibility* (Cambridge University Press, 1991), p. 351.

[114] See generally J. G. Murphy, *Getting Even: Forgiveness and its Limits* (Oxford University Press, 2005).

[115] See generally J. Hampton, "The Retributive Idea," in J. G. Murphy and J. Hampton (eds.), *Forgiveness and Mercy* (Cambridge University Press, 1988), pp. 111–61.

[116] See Pillsbury, "Emotional Justice," 689–90. From a different angle, see Spring, Cameron, and Cikara, "The Upside of Outrage," 1067–69 (suggesting that outrage is a critical force for cohesive collective action).

[117] For a critique of these assertions, see Bandes, "Introduction," p. 6 (arguing that "judges can recruit their emotions to discern patterns and features they may otherwise miss, empathize with different parties, understand different points of view, and in doing so, perceive other legal frameworks.").

[118] Alluding to the popular view that "the judicial decision is the paragon of all rational decisions," see O. Fiss, "Reason in All Its Splendor" (1990) 56 *Brooklyn Law Review* 789, 790.

[119] See W. K. Viscusi, "Pricing Lives for Corporate and Governmental Risk Decisions" (2015) 6(2) *Journal of Benefit-Cost Analysis* 227, 242.

[120] See C. R. Sunstein, "Moral Heuristics" (2005) 28 *Behavioral and Brain Sciences* 531, 536.

[121] See Viscusi, "Pricing Lives," 242.

monetary valuations of life – together with the awareness of the risk that the companies nonetheless introduce into the market – that usually comprise cost–benefit calculations, thus preventing juries from imposing "blockbuster" punitive damages awards for defective products.[122] The cost–benefit test is understood as focusing on objective factors without regard to the manner in which lay individuals conceive serious violations to the individual autonomy, dignity, physical integrity, or even life of others.[123] Likewise, the "moral outrage" motivation cannot be introduced because it is understood as the subjective (emotional), unpredictable impressions of victims and jurors.[124] Jurors are depicted as erratic, reaching decisions on the basis of moral factors rather than according to the rational dictates of optimal deterrence.[125] The underlying implications of Viscusi's proposal seem to be that laypersons should become cost–benefit calculators, meaning they should disregard their moral judgments (i.e., the idea that the law should correct legal actors' flawed decision-making in favor of rationality).[126] If this strategy fails, as is often the case,[127] the solution Viscusi advocates is removing decision-making authority from lay individuals (e.g., jurors) who are more likely to employ an alternative mode of reasoning (i.e., emotions, intuitions) than the rationalistic approach of the cost–benefit test.[128] Contrary to the vast evidence that indicates otherwise, Viscusi seems

122 See W. K. Viscusi, "Corporate Risk Analysis: A Reckless Act?" (2000) 52 *Stanford Law Review* 547, 552–59 (presenting experimental evidence that jurors award higher punitive damages in fact settings in which corporate actors perform explicit, monetized cost–benefit balancing of human safety and product costs).

123 For an example of this point, see G. T. Schwartz, "The Myth of the Ford Pinto Case" (1991) 43 *Rutgers Law Review* 1013, 1014 (noting that the public's reaction to the Ford Pinto case showed "an apparent mismatch between public opinion and the assumptions underlying the risk-benefit test for design liability.").

124 See R. Hastie and W. K. Viscusi, "What Juries Can't Do Well: The Jury's Performance as a Risk Manager" (1998) 40 *Arizona Law Review* 901, 913 (according to which jurors seem to have an "ingrained hostility toward rational, mathematical analyses of benefits and costs in the domain of risk.").

125 See W. K. Viscusi, "The Challenge of Punitive Damages Mathematics" (2001) 30 *Journal of Legal Studies* 313, 314–15 (reporting evidence that the punitive damages mock jurors imposed were based on their sense of appropriate punishment rather than the level calculated to achieve "optimal deterrence" according to the economic model of punitive damages).

126 See S. G. Gilles, "On Determining Negligence: Hand Formula Balancing, the Reasonable Person Standard, and the Jury" (2001) 45 *Vanderbilt Law Review* 813, 860–61 (advocating the use of "jury-friendly Hand Formula instructions," that is, jury instructions that emphasize cost–benefit balancing only "as a gloss on how reasonable people make decisions about accident avoidance.").

127 See D. A. Hoffman and M. P. O'Shea, "Can Law and Economics Be Both Practical and Principled?" (2002) 53 *Alabama Law Review* 335, 394–407 (reviewing evidence that lay citizens refuse to engage in utilitarian balancing in hypothetical tort decision-making contexts). Similarly, see D. Kahneman, I. Ritov and D. Schkade, "Economic Preferences of Attitude Expressions? An Analysis of Dollar Responses to Public Issues" (1999) 19 *Journal of Risk and Uncertainty* 203 (arguing that jurors setting punitive damages awards in civil trials denominated in dollars are answers that are better understood as expressions of attitudes than as indications of economic preferences).

128 On this point, see D. A. Kysar, "The Expectations of Consumers" (2003) 103 *Columbia Law Review* 1700, 1787 n369.

to suggest that judges differ from jurors in their ability to "rationally" engage with cost–benefit analysis.[129]

In a similar line of thinking, Cass Sunstein argues that basing punishment judgments on outrage "tends to produce punishments that are both unpredictable and incoherent, and to result in systems that fall far short of rationality."[130] To be sure, the kind of "irrationality" Sunstein has in mind is once again the inconsistency of people's moral intuitions, which are grounded in outrage, with the economic theory of deterrence (i.e., optimal deterrence). From this viewpoint, those using outrage to guide their punitive judgments seem insensitive to the consequences of punishment generally as their decisions about appropriate punishment mostly bear on the outrageousness of the underlying conduct and fail to take sufficient account of the probability of detection – recall that people are intuitive retributivists who do not necessarily want to increase punitive awards when the likelihood of detection is low or to decrease such awards when the likelihood of detection is high. In sum, these reconstructions depict moral outrage as a detour from rational reasoning that should be corrected.

This rationalistic approach to retributive judgments is inadequate when dealing with the moral outrage involved in the imposition of punishment (i.e., punitive awards) in the tort context. The cost–benefit test and the probability of detection place too much focus on formalistic factors at the expense of the rich, contextual manner in which lay individuals conceive serious acts of disrespect for others. They ignore the epistemic value of moral outrage. As Susan Bandes describes, "anger is a species of information, a signal that a transgression may have occurred, a way to help understand and frame that information, and an impetus to respond to injustice."[131] We ought to feel angered by the deliberate choice of an offender to commit an act of serious disrespect or to knowingly engage in acts that will result in substantial harm or death. Such emotions help us decide what is important and worthy of attention, they demonstrate our commitment to preserving moral order and to a society that promotes respect and regard for others. Moral outrage represents caring for the morality of persons by denouncing the gravity of attitudes of demonstrated disrespect for others. Morally rich meaning would be lost if emotions and intuitions were ignored out of hand for the sake of a more rationalistic approach to

[129] For a similar faith on the "rationality" of decisionmakers, see R. A. Posner, "Emotion Versus Emotionalism in Law," in S. A. Bandes (ed.), *The Passions of Law* (New York University Press, 2000), pp. 310–12 (observing that, unlike jurors, judges discipline themselves to respond to the problems before them with a careful, linear rationality). For the opposite view, see W. J. Brennan (Jr), "Reason, Passion, and 'The Progress of the Law'" (1988) 10 *Cardozo Law Review* 3 (noting that for Justice Cardozo judging involves an interplay of a complex array of forces – rational, emotional, conscious, and unconscious – by which no judge could remain unaffected, which is central to the vitality of the judicial process).

[130] See C. R. Sunstein, "On the Psychology of Punishment" (2004) 11 *Supreme Court Economic Review* 171, 188.

[131] See Bandes, "Feeling and Thinking Like a Lawyer," 12–13.

retributive judgments in tort law. The crucial point is that legal decision-making would be enriched and refined by the consideration of moral outrage in the tort context because it allows the victim to convey the moral significance of the wrongdoing in a way that directs attention to the particular dimensions of wrongfulness that the defendant's morally objectionable behavior conveys, facilitating decision-makers (i.e., judges, jurors) ability to better grasp its significance for the parties involved and for society as a whole and to assess the relevance of the tortious situation from the viewpoint of justice.

Moral outrage is an intuitive-emotive reaction to certain instances of reprehensible wrongdoing that possesses its own rationality based upon a cognitive assessment that has moral content: Being angry at reprehensible acts of disrespect from others implies moral caring and as such constitutes a powerful form of communication for tort victims.

b *Betrayal Aversion: The Role of Lay Judgments of Risk*

Similar objections to the ones raised against the influence of moral outrage on lay judgment have been articulated against betrayal aversion. The difference is that under betrayal aversion, the stark opposition is not presented in terms of emotion versus reason but instead in the language of lay judgments versus expert assessments of risk.

Psychologists showed long ago that mental habits affect how people assess risk.[132] Experts and laypeople assess risk differently, which leads them to disagree over what represents significant risk.[133] Laypeople, so the argument goes, allow their intuition, rather than statistics, to guide their concerns about risk, while experts assess risk in formal terms of probabilistic harm generally conducting expert-driven models of reasoning (such as cost–benefit analysis).[134] More broadly, Daniel Kahneman has recently argued that people generally rely on two systems of reasoning in making decisions – an intuitive system that is dominated by heuristics and emotion (System I) and a rational system that produces judgments that are consistent with rational choice (System II).[135] Evidence suggests that ordinary people assess risk through intuitive, rapid, and automatic cognitive operations (Kahneman's System I thinking), whose reasoning they are often unable to lay out explicitly. Experts,

132 See P. Slovic, "Perception of Risk," in P. Slovic (ed.), *The Perception of Risk* (Taylor & Francis, 2000) (arguing that when it comes to risk perception, ordinary people and experts use "rival rationalities").

133 On this point, see W. Boyd, D. A. Kysar and J. J. Rachlinski, "Law, Environment, and the 'Nondismal' Social Sciences" (2012) 8 *Annual Review of Law and Social Science* 183, 185.

134 By probabilistic, I mean the (objective) standard rendering of risk as the chance or the probability of some loss or harm. For a hybrid interpretation of risk which combines subjective and objective accounts of probability, see J. Oberdiek, *Imposing Risk: A Normative Framework* (Oxford University Press, 2017), p. 34.

135 See generally D. Kahneman, *Thinking, Fast and Slow* (Penguin, 2011).

by contrast, are in a different position: They have the resources and time to do far better than solely rely on heuristics.[136] Evidence suggests that experts' assessment of risk is reflective, slower, self-aware, calculative, and deductive (Kahneman's System II). Under this framework, experts rely on deliberative reasoning, whereas lay judgment is mostly the product of intuitive reactions, which generally lead to errors.[137] Thus, experts take lay judgment about risk to be irrational.

Experts argue that lay concerns about risk arise from simplistic or misleading thought processes that often lead to mistakes in judgment.[138] They argue that ignoring experts could lead laypersons to disregard actual risks that could be addressed in cost-effective fashion, or to take excessive precautions against risks that are not likely to cause much harm. In this context, some argue that expert judgment should dominate risk decisions.[139] Those who distrust lay judgments contend that, when analyzing moral issues, people rely on simple habits of the mind (often called heuristics or cognitive shortcuts) to the detriment of deductive logic in their approach to statistical and probabilistic reasoning.[140] This account holds that nonexperts sometimes resist optimization strategies, such as cost–benefit analysis, as a means of addressing hard moral questions in favor of simple rules of thumb – by relying on a limited number of heuristics to reduce the complexity of assessing probabilities, they resort to simpler judgmental operations even when the logic of these operations leads to erroneous conclusions.[141] For example, someone who takes a plane shortly after getting to know about a plane crash might intuitively overestimate the safety risk of taking the flight. As Cass Sunstein explains, the use of the availability heuristic to assess the likelihood of an airplane crash "can lead to serious errors of fact, in the form of excessive fear of small risks and neglect of large ones."[142] Thus, proponents of the heuristics and biases approach assert that people make predictable mistakes.[143]

[136] See C. R. Sunstein, "Moral Heuristics and Risk," in T. Lewens (ed.), *Risk: Philosophical Perspectives* (Routledge, 2007), p. 168. For the view that Sunstein is overly optimistic about expert rationality, see M. Kusch, "Towards a Political Philosophy of Risk: Experts and Publics in Deliberative Democracy," in T. Lewens (ed.), *Risk: Philosophical Perspectives* (Routledge, 2007), pp. 131–51 (questioning whether experts suffer from the same handicaps as laypeople in thinking about risk). Granted, Sunstein recognizes that experts are also susceptible to their own type of bias, but he insists that "when they disagree, experts are generally right, and ordinary people generally wrong," see C. R. Sunstein, *Risk and Reason: Safety, Law, and the Environment* (Cambridge University Press, 2002), p. 55.

[137] For a classic work along these lines, see C. Jolls, C. R. Sunstein and R. Thaler, "A Behavioral Approach to Law and Economics" (1998) 50 *Stanford Law Review* 1471, 1477–78.

[138] See generally Sunstein, "Moral Heuristics and Risk," pp. 155–57.

[139] See generally C. R. Sunstein, "The Law of Fears" (2000) 115 *Harvard Law Review* 1119.

[140] See Sunstein, "Moral Heuristics," 536.

[141] Ibid 542 (arguing that "[i]n particular cases, sensible rules of thumb lead to demonstrable errors.").

[142] See Sunstein, "Moral Heuristic and Risk," p. 157.

[143] See generally A. Tversky and D. Kahneman, "Judgment under Uncertainty: Heuristics and Biases" (1974) 185 *Science* 1124. Similarly, see M. S. Wogalter, D. J. Brems and E. G. Martin, "Risk Perception of Common Consumer Products: Judgments of Accident Frequency and Precautionary Intent" (1993) 24 *Journal of Safety Research* 97, 100; S. Lichtenstein, P. Slovic, B. Fischhoff, M. Layman and B. Combs, "Judged Frequency of Lethal Events" (1978) 4 *Journal of Experimental Psychology:*

Following this logic, risk assessments should be exclusively assigned to "experts." Accordingly, the technical cost–benefit analysis approach employed by experts is taken as the rational response and considered "necessary" to correct those predictable mistakes that laypersons frequently make. While this conclusion may seem sensible, recent research shows that experts are just as likely as laypeople to err in assessing risk.[144]

Others, holding the opposite view, assert that ordinary judgment reflects an underlying wisdom or a deeper rationality that should be followed.[145] They reject the idea that reliance on heuristics leads to errors, arguing instead that heuristics are what make people intelligent.[146] They contend that the heuristics and biases approach to judgment and choice fails to account for the context in which decisions are often made, hence it is not apt to recognize the advantages of relying on heuristics to make decisions.[147] They argue that people might make choices that seem irrational in constructed scenarios but not in ordinary settings of everyday life where the real incidents of social risk arise. Furthermore, these scholars maintain that people do not rely on the same heuristics in all settings without distinction; rather they argue that people learn to employ the appropriate cognitive shortcut for the given setting, which is called "ecological rationality."[148] From this perspective, what seem to be mental shortcuts are in fact manifestations of deeper levels of rationality. The idea behind this theory is that people do not arbitrarily resort to cognitive shortcuts. Moreover, they argue that the expert approach to risk assessment is too narrow and fails to capture important values that are expressed through lay reactions to risk assessments.[149] The point is that people tend to assess risk in nonprobabilistic terms: They think in qualitative terms which are laden with moral views about the sacred

Human Learning and Memory 551 (reporting individuals' systematic tendency to overestimate the frequency with which death results from unlikely events and underestimate the frequency of death from likely causes).

144 For skepticism on the capacities of "expert rationality," see G. Gigerenzer, *Reckoning with Risk: Learning to Live with Uncertainty* (Penguin, 2002) (arguing that "[e]ven when experts have Ph.D.s. in probability and statistics and have been warned previously about the same errors," they are just as likely as laypeople to err in evaluating risk).

145 On this stance, see G. Gigerenzer, "Moral Intuition–Fast and Frugal Heuristics," in W. Sinnott-Armstrong (ed.), *Moral Psychology: Vol. 2. The Cognitive Science of Morality: Intuition and Diversity* (MIT Press, 2008), pp. 1–46.

146 See G. Gigerenzer and P. M. Todd, "Fast and Frugal Heuristics: The Adaptive Toolbox," in S. Stich (ed.), *Simple Heuristics that Make Us Smart* (Oxford University Press, 1999), pp. 3–5. Also see Slovic, "Perception of Risk," p. 231 (noting that "there is wisdom as well as error in public attitudes and perceptions.").

147 See Gigerenzer and Todd, "Fast and Frugal Heuristics," pp. 3, 5. Moreover, see P. H. Huang, "Diverse Conceptions of Emotions in Risk Regulation" (2008) 156 *University of Pennsylvania Law Review PENNumbra* 435, 442 (arguing that risk perceptions are sensitive to context).

148 See generally Gigerenzer and Todd, "Fast and Frugal Heuristics."

149 See Slovic, "Perception of Risk," p. 231 (arguing that laypeople's "basic conceptualization of risk is much richer than that of the experts and reflects legitimate concerns that are typically omitted from expert risk assessments.").

value of human life, the high value placed on individual autonomy, and deeper and denser forms of rationality which are not directly translatable into a formal measure of probability represented by a number generated by a formula.[150] This not only means that people think more deeply about risk than is assumed but also that their risk assessments are appropriately moderated.[151] This approach holds lay risk assessments to be superior in the sense that they incorporate values other than the actual risk of the defined scenario along.[152]

For example, as William Boyd et al. demonstrate, people are far less tolerant of risks that they perceive to arise from involuntary activities (e.g., contracting a deadly disease from unconsented exposure to toxic substances or to defective products) than ones that arise from events they perceive to be within their control (e.g., motorcycling or skiing).[153] This discrepancy may seem irrational, but it actually reflects the high value people place on personal autonomy. When people impose risks on others without their consent, it impairs human agency by foreclosing options that would have otherwise been available to them.[154] Factors that affect the public's tolerance for risk include whether the risk involves a dreaded illness, whether it could lead to widespread harm or whether the perceived source of the risk is commonly understood to be a trustworthy actor.[155] As Gregory Keating points out, determining the gravity and salience of a risk requires evaluative and qualitative judgments (e.g., how much a particular harm should be feared, how much it would impair our capacity to lead a normal life, how to plan or cope with it, etc.), which differ starkly from mere quantitative assessments of statistical probability.[156] Thus, in addition to the severity and likeliness of the potential harm, individuals also care about qualitative attributes. For laypeople, risk means much more than the expected number of fatalities; people care about their quality of life, about how they might die, and who might be responsible for it. These qualitative factors reflect reasonable concerns that are understandable, yet they do not figure in expert-driven modes of reasoning such as cost–benefit analysis. Focusing solely on lives saved would be near-sighted because it inappropriately ignores such fundamental issues. Similarly, as Douglas Kysar argues in the

[150] For the understanding that people assess risks not as rational actors but as individuals with a particular cultural orientation, see D. M. Kahan and D. Braman, "More Statistics, Less Persuasion: A Cultural Theory of Gun-Risk Perceptions" (2003) 151 *University of Pennsylvania Law Review* 1291. Moreover, see J. K. Robbennolt and V. P. Hans, *The Psychology of Tort Law* (New York University Press, 2016), pp. 47–48 (describing the phenomenon of "probability neglect").

[151] See Boyd, Kysar and Rachlinski, "'Nondismal' Social Sciences," 187.

[152] Ibid 188.

[153] Ibid.

[154] On this point, see Oberdiek, *Imposing Risk*, pp. 84–92; G. C. Keating, "Is Cost-Benefit Analysis the Only Game in Town?" (2018) 91 *Southern California Law Review* 195, 228.

[155] See generally B. Fischhoff, P. Slovic and S. Lichtenstein, "Weighting the Risks: Which Risks Are Acceptable?," in P. Slovic (ed.), *The Perception of Risk* (Taylor & Francis, 2000).

[156] See G. C. Keating, "Pressing Precaution Beyond the Point of Cost-Justification" (2003) 56 *Vanderbilt Law Review* 653, 697; and *Reasonableness and Risk* (Oxford University Press, 2022).

context of product liability, those reasonable concerns cannot be dismissed as irrationalities to be ignored in favor of narrow cost–benefit calculations.[157] In his view, "[m]any aspects of consumer beliefs and behavior can be said to represent a 'rival rationality' that is wider in scope and richer in detail than the stark logic of risk-utility analysis."[158]

The experts' response to this might be that they are able to quantify the variety of qualitative factors that affect lay judgment and factor them into their cost–benefit risk calculations.[159] Instead of recognizing lay judgments as an "alternate (or rival) rationality," they thus argue that those qualities and values are to be incorporated into the expert approach to risk appreciation (i.e., cost–benefit analysis).[160] Advocates for lay judgment as alternate rationality would respond that those qualitative factors cannot be reconciled with a pure rationalist approach. Apart from the difficult pragmatic questions that arise from such a reductionist proposal, Kysar argues that lay citizens will be unable to express the strength of their lay values because their beliefs and attitudes will be converted into a willingness-to-pay value for inclusion in the cost–benefit test.[161] According to Kysar, even if the characteristics that guide lay judgment were accommodated, the results will still represent an exercise of quantification that does not respect lay judgments.

Moreover, recent research on cultural cognition suggests that lay risk assessments reflect the cultural and political mindset of the decision-maker in a way that cannot be rendered through neutral expert-based or economic analysis.[162] Under this view, people do not assess risks as rational actors but as individuals who adopt cognitive strategies that reflect their views about what constitutes a just and meaningful society – individuals with a particular cultural orientation, which embodies a specific set of moral values and societal aspirations.[163] This tells us that efforts to avoid the influence of lay judgments through reliance on expert assessments are likely to be futile. According to Dan Kahan, emotions and intuitions

[157] See Kysar, "The Expectations of Consumers," 1779 (arguing that "individual risk processing is richer, thicker, and more value-laden than the cost-benefit balancing of experts. In short, at this juncture, the rival rationality thesis appears to be at least as robust as its rivals.").

[158] Ibid 1767.

[159] See C. R. Sunstein, "Cognition and Cost-Benefit Analysis" (2000) 29 *Journal of Legal Studies* 1059, 1087–88 (advocating adjusted quantitative assessments to account for qualitative risk values that are broadly recognized).

[160] See R. Cooter and S. Sugarman, "A Regulated Market in Unmatured Tort Claims: Tort Reform by Contract," in W. Olson (ed.), *New Directions in Liability Law* (Academy of Political Science, 1988), p. 174 (arguing that we should be able to bargain for greater or lesser risks to life and limb at different costs).

[161] See Kysar, "The Expectations of Consumers," 1776 n320.

[162] See generally D. M. Kahan, "The Cognitive Illiberal State" (2007) 60 *Stanford Law Review* 115.

[163] See D. M. Kahan, "Two Conceptions of Emotion in Risk Regulation" (2008) 156 *University of Pennsylvania Law Review* 741, 744 (arguing for a "cultural evaluator theory" of risk perception that sees "risk perceptions as embodying individuals' cultural evaluations of the meanings expressed by society's decision to tolerate or abate particular risks.").

are not the impetus that fuels departures from rational decision-making; rather they are "judgments of value" that help us perceive a larger worldview that orients us toward risk.[164] As a result, they cannot simply be translated into a "quantifiable factor" in a cost–benefit formula.

Thus, people do not seem to be as misguided or ignorant as the heuristics and biases approach generally presumes. The fact that the rationality of lay risk assessments operates at a different level from ordinary deliberative thought processes does not mean that those judgments are necessarily irrational. Actually, because people do care about qualitative factors quite apart from the actual probability or statistics of harm, their understanding of risk is able to capture many important aspects, such as the indignity and dehumanization of being a calculated risk of loss in a corporate profit quest, in which lay attitudes toward risk differ from the dictates of hardline expert-driven analysis.[165] Once again, the implication of this argument is that we possess a non-negligible capacity to reason intuitively. It means our intuitive system, which is dominated by heuristics, comprises a particular mode of reasoning that cannot be simply deemed irrational and therefore reflexively disregarded by the law.

Betrayal aversion is a good example of why ignoring lay judgments of risk is inappropriate in the tort context – particularly, in the realm of punitive damages. As Jonathan Koehler and Andrew Gershoff demonstrate in a series of studies, people are averse to perceived betrayal.[166] Aversion to betrayal causes people to react more negatively to betrayal (i.e., harm-causing by persons or mechanisms that promise to protect the ultimately injured party from harm) than to injury caused to them without betrayal (i.e., harm-causing by others that causes equivalent harm). Thus, when people understand certain acts as "betrayal," they treat them with greater moral intensity than similar acts not categorized as such. In one of the studies, Koehler and Gershoff tested the aversity of subjects to betrayal by a safety precaution. They asked whether they would prefer to purchase a car in which the chance of dying in a serious traffic accident was 2 percent or one in which the installation of an airbag reduced the risk of fatality in a serious accident but introduced a 1 in 1,000 risk of fatality due to another cause. When researchers indicated that the risk of death in the latter was unrelated to the airbag, most subjects expressed preference for it. But when the researchers indicated that the extra 1 in 1,000 risk was a direct consequence of the safety precaution, the subjects tended to prefer the more dangerous car. The authors conclude that people are more averse to the potential harm from a safety precaution. Although experts would assess such aversion as irrational, it seems

[164] Ibid 750 (quoting Nussbaum, *Upheavals of Thought*, p. 19).

[165] On this point, see L. Bender, "Feminist (Re)Torts: Thoughts on the Liability Crisis, Mass Torts, Power, and Responsibilities" (1990) 4 *Duke Law Journal* 848, 874.

[166] See generally J. J. Koehler and A. D. Gershoff, "Betrayal Aversion: When Agents of Protection Become Agents of Harm" (2002) 90 *Organizational Behavior and Human Decision Processes* 244.

reasonable that the pain and regret one might feel from opting for a safety measure that subsequently caused serious harm might be worth avoiding, even if this meant taking on an increased level of overall risk.[167]

Experts argue that betrayal aversion affects judgment by inducing people to draw conclusions that are inconsistent with logic or rationality.[168] In their understanding, betrayal aversion merely functions as a mental shortcut that interrupts further analysis, one that effectively instructs us: "once encountering betrayal, punish more and do not analyze the situation further" or "punish betrayals of trust."[169] However, this portrayal of betrayal aversion seems too simplistic to be accepted without further examination. Once we start digging into what betrayal aversion involves, we immediately realize that it is indeed richer and more complex than the experts understand it to be. To begin with, it has been argued that the idea of a universally strong reaction to betrayal can be traced to our human ancestors' need to remain highly vigilant against betrayal and may have some advantages in certain social settings, which makes betrayal aversion fit easily with an "ecological rationality" approach.[170] Moreover, even Koehler and Gershoff have argued that betrayal aversion is rational.[171] Furthermore, betrayal aversion is not an all-purpose heuristic that is used uniformly in many different settings (just as the availability and anchoring heuristics).[172] It is instead a reaction to particular settings that involve breach of trust. Betrayal is a particular reaction to a particular situation. Betrayal aversion is very sensitive to context.[173] It identifies behavior patterns in each particular context in a way that allows for variations in how people might perceive the circumstances in which they find themselves. As Boyd et al. argue, these mental strategies are not uniform; rather "[p]eople embrace mental strategies for thinking about risk that suit who they are, what they believe, and how they see themselves and their society."[174]

167 See J. J. Koehler and A. D. Gershoff, "Betrayal Aversion Is Reasonable" (2005) 28 *Behavioral and Brain Sciences* 556, 557.

168 For the argument that awarding greater punitive damages against a manufacturer of a smoke alarm whose defective wiring led to a fire than against a manufacturer of a refrigerator whose wiring led to the same problem is troubling, see Sunstein, "Moral Heuristics," 537–38.

169 Ibid (arguing that uncritical effort to avoid betrayals produces mistakes and induces people to take unnecessary risks).

170 On this point, see L. Cosmides and J. Tooby, "Cognitive Adaptations for Social Exchange," in J. H. Barkow, L. Cosmides and J. Tooby (eds.), *The Adapted Mind: Evolutionary Psychology and the Generation of Culture* (Oxford University Press, 1992), pp. 163, 177.

171 See Koehler and Gershoff, "Betrayal Aversion is Reasonable," 557 ("[W]e are not persuaded that a finding that people are willing to incur *some* additional cost to avoid betrayal provides sufficient evidence of a moral heuristic gone awry.") (emphasis in original).

172 Arguing that, in decision-making, betrayal aversion is affected by individual characteristics and social situational, emotional, and cognitive factors, see Z. W. Weiguo Qu, "Betrayal Aversion in the Source of Risk: Research Methods and Influencing Factors" (2019) 9(4) *Advances in Psychology* 717, 717–25.

173 For the argument that heuristics and biases are not stable and uniform facets of the human mind but instead highly contextual, see J. J. Rachlinski, "Heuristics, Biases, and Philosophy" (2007) 43 *Tulsa Law Review* 865, 879.

174 See Boyd, Kysar and Rachlinski, "'Nondismal' Social Sciences," 192.

Betrayal aversion can account for variations in how individuals assess risk, which suggests that they cannot be simply reduced to a uniform, quantifiable aspect of a cost–benefit test. For instance, betrayal aversion captures the simple but contoured mental strategies that ordinary consumers employ to understand risk in the mass-market context: Consumers' adverse reaction (i.e., punitive impulse) to manufacturers' risk decision-making is perfectly appropriate when manufacturers deliberately or showing conscious disregard impose involuntary risk of a dreaded form of death or illness for profit by introducing a defective product into the market knowing that it will affect the bodily integrity, individual autonomy, or even life of a number of consumers. The punitive reaction is also appropriate when, for instance, an insurer callously betrays the insured's expectation of peace of mind by implementing a national, company-wide scheme capping payouts on claims in order to meet corporate balance sheet goals.[175] It captures not only the high value people place on life and physical integrity as nontradable goods but also the value of individual autonomy as expressed by the ability to pursue their life plan without unexpected interruption.[176] Lay understandings of risk generate moral insights that our legal system could hardly do without, such as the insight that it is outrageously unfair to deliberately expose others to the risk of severe and devastating injury for corporate profit.

Moreover, and perhaps more importantly, risks of serious illness or death that are perceived as betrayals because they are involuntarily imposed on consumers by powerful manufacturers after deliberation undermine public trust, which forces society to answer certain important questions. The tort victim who demands the imposition of a monetary sanction (e.g., punitive award) understands that unless something is done to acknowledge and condemn the reprehensible wrong done to her, she (and others) cannot longer trust the system. In turn, neglecting these concerns only because they do not directly correspond to the actual quantifiable measures of risk that comprise the expert's rationalistic approach (i.e., cost–benefit analysis) undermines democratic values. Indeed, what rationalistic approaches conceal is that people embrace ways of thinking about risk in the marketplace that are meaningful to them and that reflect how they believe society ought to behave.

All this suggests that understanding punishment in the tort context requires awareness of how laypeople think about risk; we must address the meaning that ordinary people attach to threats rather than treating them as misplaced heuristics that deviate from rationality or rules of thumb that lead us to error in judgments. The purely rationalistic approach, which values above all the opinions of experts

[175] For a punitive award involving similar facts, see *State Farm Mut Auto Ins Co* v. *Campbell*, 538 US 408, 416 (2003).

[176] See Oberdiek, *Imposing Risk*, p. 97 (arguing that "[M]anufacturers who create products that are defective […] diminish [by limiting the safe options of others] the autonomy of people.").

trained in statistical or probabilistic methods and thus deemed better positioned than laypeople to assess the risk of harm, cannot capture the simple but nuanced mental strategies that people adopt for understanding risks. It cannot capture the significance and the meaning that people assign to deliberate exposure to significant risks that threaten life and limb. It cannot capture the evaluative power of laypeople's judgments about risk, trust, and truth.

4

Relational Retribution

Punitive damages are the paradigmatic example of a tort institution with salient retributive elements that have been recognized as such since the very beginnings of the law of torts. Retribution has not only been referred to as the long-standing aim of punitive awards in the case law[1] but also widely acknowledged by most commentators – even by those endorsing purely economic deterrence accounts of the institution.[2] Furthermore, as covered in Chapter 3, retributive intuitions play a significant role in victims' textured motivations for seeking punitive responses

1 Courts have widely acknowledged a retributive function of punitive damages in several common law jurisdictions; see, for example, *Cooper Industries Inc* v. *Leatherman Tool Group Inc*, 532 US 424, 432 (2001) (noting that punitive damages "serve the function of deterrence and retribution"); *Exxon Shipping Co* v. *Baker*, 554 US 471, 492 (2008) ("[T]he consensus today is that [punitive damages] are aimed not at compensation but principally at retribution and deterring harmful conduct."); *Philip Morris USA* v. *Williams*, 549 US 346, 359 (2007) ("[A] punitive damages award, instead of serving a compensatory purpose, serves the entirely different purposes of retribution and deterrence that underlie every criminal sanction."); *State Farm Mut Auto Ins Co* v. *Campbell*, 538 US 408, 416 (2003) (deterrence and retribution); *Pacific Mut Life Ins Co* v. *Haslip*, 499 US 1, 19 (1991) ("[P]unitive damages are imposed for purposes of retribution and deterrence"); *Payton* v. *Abbott Labs*, 437 NE 2d 176 (noting that tort liability has a retributive function); *Uren* v. *John Fairfax & Sons Pty Ltd* [1966] 117 CLR 118, 149 [HCA] (Windeyer J) (moral retribution or deterrence). The Supreme Court of Canada has insisted that exemplary damages "address the purposes of retribution, deterrence and denunciation." See *Fidler* v. *Sun Life Assurance Co of Canada* [2006] SCC 30; [2006] 2 SCR 3, 61; *Whiten* v. *Pilot Insurance Co* [2002] SCC 18, 43, 68, 74, 94; [2002] 1 SCR 595.

2 For example, see M. Galanter and D. Luban, "Poetic Justice: Punitive Damages and Legal Pluralism" (1993) 42(4) *American University Law Review* 1393, 1428–29 (emphasizing that "[D]iscussions of punitive damages should focus on deterrence and retributivist theories."); D. Ellis, "Fairness and Efficiency in the Law of Punitive Damages" (1982) 56 *Southern California Law Review* 1, 76 (finding that "only two [of the objectives potentially served by punitive damages] survive scrutiny: retribution and deterrence."); J. Goudkamp and E. Katsampouka, "Punitive Damages and the Place of Punishment in Private Law" (2021) 84 *Modern Law Review* 1257, 1258 (arguing that in English law, "the characterisation of punitive damages as aberrant on account of their retributive agenda has been endorsed virtually without dissent ever since *Rookes* was decided."); C. M. Sharkey, "Punitive Damages Transformed into Societal Damages," in E. Bant, W. Courtney, J. Goudkamp and J. M. Paterson (eds.), *Punishment and Private Law* (Hart Publishing, 2021), p. 156 (recognizing that courts typically use the language of retributive punishment when awarding punitive damages), among many others.

through tort law and the tort process as well as in the evaluative judgments of decision-makers (jurors and judges). Moreover, it has also been demonstrated that punitive aims are sometimes pursued via other remedies in torts, particularly in jurisdictions where punitive damages are restricted[3] or directly unavailable.[4] The fact is that retributive responses to reprehensible wrongdoing, whether overt or disguised, have undeniably developed over time in the law of torts across jurisdictions without reference to a deeper underlying theory.

In Part I we saw that scant theoretical attention has been devoted to a thorough exploration to provide meaningful justifications of the retributive dimension of tort law.[5] Granted, we can identify authors who have argued that, to some extent, the development of tort doctrine has been influenced or inspired by the notion of retributive justice,[6] and others who have attempted to account for the retributive character of punitive damages in particular.[7] However, such reconstructions represent an isolated minority that have not received full consideration in the debates, perhaps because they have yet to provide a fleshed-out retributive rationale. Instead, the prevailing scholarly approach to retribution in tort law has largely taken three related but different forms, which, in my view, have represented an obstacle to meaningfully address its retributive justifications: (1) retribution as vengeance: Scholars have directly correlated retribution to vengeance and, as a consequence, denounced retribution as a morally bankrupt practice and a poor normative grounding for punishment (punitive awards) in torts; (2) retribution as just deserts: Others have directly correlated retribution to just deserts and, as a consequence, denounced retribution as a one-sided aim which is alien to the interpersonal structure of tort law, depicting punitive awards in torts as an unjustified gain (or windfall) for the victim; and (3) retribution as expressive defeat: Scholars following this line have focused on the condemnatory message conveyed by the imposition of the punitive award on the wrongdoer and, as a consequence, have been asked what gives victims the right to inflict punishment on their wrongdoers instead of the state or another third party.

3 For the argument that in the English legal system "judges not infrequently circumvent the restrictions on the jurisdiction to award punitive damages by imposing punishment via other remedies," see Goudkamp and Katsampouka, "Punitive Damages and the Place of Punishment in Private Law," 1259.

4 I have pointed out this phenomenon in many civil law jurisdictions in Section B of Chapter 1.

5 See Chapters 1 and 2.

6 See, for example, P. Cane, "Retribution, Proportionality, and Moral Luck in Tort Law," in P. Cane and J. Stapleton (eds.), *The Law of Obligations: Essays in Celebration of John Fleming* (Oxford University Press, 1998), p. 170 (arguing that fault-based liability rests on ideas of retributive justice and that there is "no *a priori* reason why tort law should not have punishment as one of its aims."); R. Perry, "The Role of Retributive Justice in the Common Law of Torts: A Descriptive Theory" (2006) 73 *Tennessee Law Review* 163, 179 (arguing that "[retributive justice] plays a limited, but noteworthy, role in tort jurisprudence."); M. A. Kotler, "Utility, Autonomy and Motive: A Descriptive Model of the Development of Tort Doctrine" (1990) 58 *University of Cincinnati Law Review* 1231 (who goes even further by arguing that tort law is a retributive mechanism).

7 I have explored these retributive reconstructions in Section G of Chapter 2.

The critics also ask why condemnation must take the form of harsh punishment instead of, for example, some public or formal declaration or other symbolic punishment.[8]

These correlations are wanting. As I have already argued in Chapter 3, equating retribution to revenge is as unwarranted as equating retribution to irrationality.[9] As for the correlation between retribution and just desert, it accurately reflects the dominant understanding of retributive accounts of the criminal law and tort scholars are certainly right to point out the problems that such a reconstruction poses for tort law.[10] What is not clear is why tort scholars hold on to this correlation as if it were the universal, given truth about retributivism. Can we conceive of an alternative retributive reconstruction of punishment in tort law that is not necessarily limited to the one-sided just desert form of state punishment that dominates criminal law theory? I think we can and we should. After all, criminal law theorists have acknowledged countless modes of retribution, which give the central desert-based reasons for punishment not only distinctive meaning but also differentiated weight, signaling that the desert's "centrality" does not necessarily entail "exclusivity."[11] Other criminal law theorists have offered variants of retributive accounts that do not focus on punishment as just deserts, but instead on the expressive function of punishment as conveying moral condemnation of an offender's acts – retribution as denunciation.[12] Certainly, some tort scholars have suggested that the victim's punitive response to reprehensible wrongdoing involves much more than the mere imposition of a punishment for the defendant's conduct on purely "just deserts" terms; however, they have not as yet offered an in-depth inquiry on what this "much more" involves. These scholars instead have argued that the imposition of the punitive award on the

8 For a critical discussion in the realm of criminal law on why we should choose such methods of communication rather than methods that do not involve hard treatment, see, for example, N. Hanna, "Say What? A Critique of Expressive Retributivism" (2008) 27 *Law and Philosophy* 123; P. Königs, "The Expressivist Account of Punishment, Retribution, and the Emotions" (2013) 16 *Ethical Theory and Moral Practice* 1029; V. Tadros, *The Ends of Harm: The Moral Foundations of Criminal Law* (Oxford University Press, 2011), p. 103, among others.

9 For this argument, see Section B of Chapter 3.

10 For references to the extensive criminal law literature on retributive punishment, see A. Walen, "Retributive Justice," in E. N. Zalta and U. Nodelman (eds.), *The Stanford Encyclopedia of Philosophy* (Winter Edition, 2023).

11 On this point, see D. Husak, "Retributivism and Over-Punishment" (2022) 41 *Law and Philosophy* 169, 174. Additionally, see J. Kleinig, "What Does Wrongdoing Deserve?," in M. Tonry (ed.), *Retributivism Has a Past: Has It a Future?* (Oxford University Press, 2011), pp. 46–62 (rethinking the implications of desert theory).

12 On the expressive dimension of punishment, see generally J. Feinberg, "The Expressive Function of Punishment," in J. Feinberg, *Doing and Deserving: Essays in the Theory of Responsibility* (Princeton University Press, 1970), p. 98 (a punishment is "a conventional device for the expression of attitudes of resentment and indignation, and of judgments of disapproval and reprobation."). For other examples of communicative accounts, see especially A. Von Hirsch, *Censure and Sanctions* (Oxford University Press, 1996); R. A. Duff, *Punishment, Communication, and Community* (Oxford University Press, 2001).

defendant involves expressive defeat but have struggled to offer persuasive reasons to justify empowering victims to exact expressive defeat on the wrongdoer through harsh treatment (i.e., the imposition of a punitive sanction) or why victims should keep the monetary award.[13]

Unless we want to keep acting as if retribution is not playing any role in tort law, the time seems ripe to overcome these deficiencies in tort theory and scholarship. After all, any tort system that imposes retributive sanctions without providing a genuine justification for it should a priori be considered questionable.

A THE WRONGDOER–VICTIM PERSPECTIVE

Retribution as just desert is not concerned with the rectification of harm; rather, it is mainly concerned with the imposition of a sanction because punishment is deserved.[14] The problem of accommodating retribution as just desert into tort law seems to stem from the assumption that punishing the blameworthy party is warranted because and only because of their blame. Retribution is the idea that blameworthy wrongdoers must be punished for their actions because they deserve it. In this logic, most classic retributive theories of punishment take the wrongdoing as their focus, ignoring the difference between the wrongdoing and the wrong that it does to the individual victim and how the wrong itself can be addressed – hence they are inclined to overlook the victim's perspective.[15] Following that logic, criminal theorists tend to approach the question of retribution from the perspective of the person who is being punished and the role of the state in imposing punishment.

13 I have explored this criticism in Section G of Chapter 2.

14 For the classic understanding of retribution, see M. S. Moore, *Placing Blame: A Theory of the Criminal Law* (Oxford University Press, 1997), p. 88 ("the distinctive aspect of retributivism is that the moral desert of an offender is a sufficient reason to punish him or her."). For general treatment of the theory of retributive punishment as the deliberate infliction of pain on the offender based on an assessment of the offender's moral responsibility for committing the offense, see H. L. A. Hart, "Prolegomenon to the Principles of Punishment," in *Punishment and Responsibility: Essays in the Philosophy of Law* (2nd ed.) (Oxford University Press, 2008), pp. 1–27.

15 For recent versions of retributivist challenges to precisely this aspect, see Duff, Punishment, Communication, and Community (arguing that punishment is a mode of moral communication, in that it communicates to offenders the censure or condemnation their crimes deserve); J. G. Murphy and J. Hampton (eds.), *Forgiveness and Mercy* (Cambridge University Press, 1988) (putting the emotional responses to crime as the starting point, they argue that crimes deserve the punishment that makes appropriate certain emotions (resentment, retributive hatred) which are satisfied by or expressed through punishment). Significantly, Jean Hampton's account departs from the traditional retributivist line in that she includes the victims' concerns – an account that will be explored in more detail in what follows. See J. Hampton, "A New Theory of Retribution," in R. G. Frey and C. W. Morris (eds.), *Liability and Responsibility* (Cambridge University Press, 1991), pp. 377–414. Additionally, George Fletcher's victim-vindication theory of punishment points out that what most theories of punishment share is their failure to attend to the victims of crimes. See G. P. Fletcher, "The Place of Victims in the Theory of Retribution" (1999) 3 *Buffalo Criminal Law Review* 51, 54 (arguing that punishment restores the balance between victim and perpetrator by terminating the coercive dominance of one over the other).

This is to some extent reflected in the limited role that victims usually play in the criminal justice context where neither the victim nor the offender plays in principle a formal active role.[16] Indeed, the criminal procedure in its structure and actual operations tends to preclude any meaningful participation by either victims or offenders.[17] One might think that theories of punishment that understood the practice in terms of an expressive and communicative endeavor would give meaningful consideration to victims' concerns (for instance, to their need to express condemnation or reaffirmation of their equal value toward their offenders). However, ultimately, those reconstructions do not necessarily deal with the concerns of victims better than just desert theories. On one side, they are still caught up in the traditional backward-looking justificatory framework for punishment whose focus is still overwhelmingly on the offense: The main criterion is ensuring the offender is made to suffer expressive defeat. On the other side, they struggle with the component of the victim's punitive reaction to the wrong done to her that relates specifically to how she was and should be treated by the offender: They overlook the powerful moral perspective afforded by the victim who also witnesses her responsive behavior toward the wrongdoer. Expressivist accounts mostly concern themselves with the messages sent to the offender and, more generally, to the broader community (to which the victim of course belongs), but not the message's direct bearing to the individual victim herself.[18]

This unilateral focus on the wrongdoer clearly clashes with the bilateral structure of tort law, which is concerned with the interpersonal justice between the parties involved – mutual accountability between claimant and defendant. The unilateral focus is problematic for tort law because it treats punishment as a deserved imposition of a suffering or as an expressive defeat of the wrongdoer without attributing a significant role to the victim, even though it is up to the victim to seek legal redress against the wrongdoer in tort law.[19] Tort law enables the victim to call the wrongdoer to account for her behavior through a public legal process. The victim

16 Advocates of restorative justice theories of criminal law acknowledge this problem of the retributivist accounts highlighting the question of what offenders owe to those whom they have wronged. Note that the main preoccupation of these theories is the restoration of the fractured interpersonal relationship between the offender and the victim (mostly through reconciliation and apologies) and within the community as an alternative to retribution. On the relationship between restorative and traditional models of criminal justice, see A. Von Hirsch, J. V. Roberts, A. E. Bottoms, K. Roach and M. Schiff (eds.), *Restorative Justice and Criminal Justice: Competing or Reconcilable Paradigms?* (Hart Publishing, 2003).

17 To clarify, some jurisdictions allow for victims' impact statements and other procedural measures for fostering victims' participation, but they are certainly exceptional. For more on this point, see Section A of Chapter 9.

18 See, for example, R. A. Duff, *Trials and Punishments* (Cambridge University Press, 1991) (arguing that punishment expresses condemnation toward the criminal).

19 The one-sided focus on the defendant is the classic criticism raised by corrective justice scholars arguing that retribution is inconsistent with the bilateral structure of tort law. I have explored this point in Section A of Chapter 2.

herself must decide whether to bring, or not to bring, a civil lawsuit against the person who wronged her.[20] The case is between the claimant and the defendant. As a consequence, one-sided retribution understood as merely the infliction of warranted suffering (or hardship) on the wrongdoer purely in terms of just desert or expressive defeat does not and cannot satisfactorily convey (or represent) every purpose served by retribution in the law of torts. In other words, the victim's prerogative to be punitive in tort law cannot be justified only in terms of just desert or expressive defeat (i.e., taking the form of the mere imposition of a hardship on the wrongdoer) without invoking any substantive connection between the reprehensibility of the defendant's conduct toward the victim and the significance of the wrongdoing for the victim who claims the imposition of the sanction in the first place (wherein lies its moral wrong: How the manner of the defendant's interference with the victim's protected interests is connected to the inherent value attributed to them in the particular circumstances of the wrongdoing). Retribution in torts cannot be persuasively justified if solely understood in terms of the deservedness or defeating of the wrongdoer (i.e., as exclusively and unilaterally responding to the wrongdoer's action or a desire to discipline the wrongdoer's behavior) without assigning any meaning to the victim's retributive response itself.

Jean Hampton's expressive theory of retribution provides interesting components for a retributive rationale of punitive damages that shows concern for victims.[21] Even though Hampton's retributive reconstruction is concerned with punishment in a broad sense not specifically related to tort law, her project to elaborate a retributive theory that works within both public and private law contexts extends an invitation for further reflection on the retributive rationale of punitive damages in torts.[22] Hampton argues that a theory of retribution should link "punishment to *that which makes the wrongful action wrong*."[23] The issue is thus the criterion that makes the

[20] For the argument that exercising the legal power to hold the defendant accountable lies at the victim's discretion, see J. C. P. Goldberg and B. C. Zipursky, *Recognizing Wrongs* (Harvard University Press, 2020), p. 291 (tort law is a system that, in principle, "empowers victims to seek and obtain redress […] insofar as they seek it"). Similarly, see S. Darwall, "Bipolar Obligation," in R. Shafer-Landau (ed.), *Oxford Studies in Metaethics* (Oxford University Press, 2012), pp. 346–47 (arguing that the exercise of the individual authority of the victim to hold the wrongdoer personally accountable to her solely depends on the will of the victim herself).

[21] See J. Hampton, "An Expressive Theory of Retribution," in W. Cragg (ed.), *Retributivism and its Critics* 1 (Franz Steiner Verlag Wiesbaden GmbH, 1992) (developing an expressive theory of retribution to explain and justify retributive practice); and "Correcting Harms versus Righting Wrongs: The Goal of Retribution" (1992) 39 *UCLA Law Review* 1659, 1686 ("[R]etribution is a response to a wrong that is intended to vindicate the value of the victim denied by the wrongdoer's action through the construction of an event that not only repudiates the action's message of superiority over the victim but does so in a way that confirms them as equal by virtue of their humanity.").

[22] Note that others, such as Galanter and Luban, have built on the work of Jean Hampton too. As described in Section G of Chapter 2, their idea of "expressive defeat" and their notion of expressive defeat's "proportionality" have been influenced by Hampton's retributive reconstruction.

[23] See Hampton, "Correcting Harms versus Righting Wrongs," 1661 (emphasis in original).

wrongdoer's conduct wrong. Her valuable insight is that not every wrongful conduct merits a retributive response. According to Hampton, a retributive response is justified when an act causes moral injury.[24] Hampton distinguishes moral injury from wrongful loss, the former being an affront to the victim's value (which I will refer to as dignitary interest); the latter involving material or psychological damage to that which over a person has a right – her possessions, her body, her psychological well-being – that comes about because of wrongful action. According to Hampton, moral injury is an objective injury to the person's value[25] and has no regard for the peculiarities of the wrongdoer's psychology that led her to commit the wrong.[26] A person is thus morally injured when "she is the target of behavior whose meaning, appropriately understood by members of the cultural community in which the behavior occurs, represents her value as less than the value she should be accorded."[27] Moreover, for Hampton, in order to count as a moral injury, the meaning of the wrong should also involve the wrongdoer's misrepresentation of her value relative to the victim: Her behavior must express her perceived superiority relative to the victim.[28] Clearly, Hampton's account assumes both (1) a certain conception of value (i.e., a conception of human worth) and (2) a certain understanding of how actions can affect that value. As regards (1), Hampton relies on Kant's conception of value, according to which we have worth simply by virtue of being human (i.e., each of us is an "end-in-himself"), to define the kind of moral respect a person deserves.[29] The underlying idea is that "we are obliged to respect our fellow human beings *equally*, no matter the state of their moral character, insofar as each human being is an autonomous, rational being."[30] For Hampton, this Kantian conception of value has played a role in setting the normative standards for acceptable treatment of people in our society.

What makes moral injury wrong is the message conveyed by the wrongdoer's conduct that the victim has less relative value than the wrongdoer – it objectively demeans the victim. The wrongdoer fails to treat the victim in a sufficiently respectful manner. Consequently, the retributive response must express not only that the victim has value but also that the implicit value judgment behind the wrongdoer's behavior was wrong. Punishment, understood as "the experience of defeat at the hands of the victim," is the appropriate response because no one can better reaffirm the

[24] Ibid 1666.

[25] See J. Hampton, "Forgiveness, Resentment and Hatred," in J. G. Murphy and J. Hampton (eds.), *Forgiveness and Mercy* (Cambridge University Press, 1988), p. 45 ("But this objective injury … is usually – although it need not be – associated with a subjective injury. If the person who has been wrongly treated *knows* this, then he will not only *be* but *feel* insulted.") (emphasis in original).

[26] See Hampton, "Correcting Harms versus Righting Wrongs," 1679, 1684–87, 1697.

[27] Ibid 1670–71.

[28] Ibid 1677.

[29] Ibid.

[30] Ibid 1668 (emphasis in original).

truth of the victim's value than the wrongdoer who denied it and nothing can better reassert the victim's truth than the wrongdoer's defeat by the victim.[31] Punishment, then, is justified because of its role in reaffirming the equal value of wrongdoer and victim that entitles them to equal respect. The punishment "lower[s] the wrongdoer, elevate[s] the victim, and annul[s] the act of diminishment."[32] In Hampton's words, "[i]t is a symbol that is conceptually required to reaffirm a victim's equal worth in the face of a challenge to it."[33] Following this line of thinking, Hampton concludes that "retribution is actually a form of compensation to the victim,"[34] for the victim's worth can only be reasserted if it is "repaired" through a loss suffered by the wrongdoer that proves that the victim's value is equal to the wrongdoer's.[35]

Hampton's retributive reconstruction is not exempt from criticism. One important issue is an apparent disconnect in Hampton's reconstruction. Her focus on the transmission of the message correcting the offender's victim-demeaning attitude (i.e., the expressive defeat of the wrongdoer that the imposition of the punishment conveys) does not fully connect to the reaffirmation of the victim's equal value. The sanction, which is not directed at the victim, seems to convey the message that everyone in society as a whole (of which the victim is a member) has as much value as the wrongdoer. That message is not the same as the message that the victim, individually, is the wrongdoer's equal.[36] The punishment, then, seems better understood as defeat at society's hands rather than the victim's, and it can therefore hardly be interpreted as confirming the victim's personal equality vis-à-vis the wrongdoer. This fundamental disconnection obstructs an explanation or justification of punitive damages in terms of bilateral accountability between claimant and defendant. Even if it might suffice as a justification for empowering victims to act punitively against their wrongdoers, it does not sufficiently explain why the victim is specially situated to demand the imposition of a punishment on the wrongdoer (instead of the state or a third party) or why the court should order the defendant to pay the punitive award directly to the plaintiff (instead of to the state or a fund). Notwithstanding, Hampton's concern with the meaning communicated by value-demeaning wrongdoing about the individual victim's worth is an essential component in a retributive rationale of punitive damages. The *Relational Retribution* account that I offer builds on this key insight, albeit with significant twists and adjustments.

31 See J. Hampton, "The Retributive Idea," in J. G. Murphy and J. Hampton (eds.), *Forgiveness and Mercy* (Cambridge University Press, 1988), p. 126.

32 See Hampton, "Correcting Harms versus Righting Wrongs," 1687.

33 See Hampton, "The Retributive Idea," pp. 125–26.

34 See Hampton, "Correcting Harms versus Righting Wrongs," 1698 ("Corrective justice compensates victims for harms, whereas retributive justice compensates victims for moral injuries.").

35 Ibid 1686–87.

36 On this point, I take inspiration from David Dolinko's criticism of Hampton's reconstruction in D. Dolinko, "Some Thoughts about Retributivism" (1991) 101(3) *Ethics* 537, 553.

I argue that retribution in tort law is actually relational. This way of conceiving retribution in tort law basically proposes retribution in relational terms similar to those that we employ when conceiving compensation as a two-party transaction in which the claimant calls upon the defendant to pay for the harm done: In a way that links defendant and claimant – the wrongdoer–victim perspective. I will refer to this as *Relational Retribution*. *Relational Retribution* means not only focusing on the characteristics of the defendant's wrongful conduct as deserving of punishment but also on the correlative retributive motivations of the victim who seeks the imposition of a sanction (e.g., the punitive award).[37] These two elements are necessarily interconnected. The victim's retributive motivations for punishment (moral outrage, betrayal aversion) are linked both to the reprehensibility of the defendant's conduct (i.e., the level of disrespect or disregard for the victim's worth) and to the value attributed to the inherent disparagement of the victim's moral worth conveyed by the defendant's reprehensible behavior. The focus is thus not only on the reprehensible character of the wrongdoer's behavior as warranting some sort of retribution (i.e., just deserts) but also on the manner in which that particular conduct constituted an affront to the victim's self-worth. The underlying idea is that a value-driven approach that is sensitive to victims' retributive motivations offers more promise for understanding and justifying punishment in tort law than one that ignores retributive motivations altogether.

The distinctive retributive response is hence motivated by the victim's "reactive attitudes" (moral outrage, betrayal aversion) in *relation* to the wrongdoer's value-diminishing treatment.[38] *Relational Retribution* focuses not only on the punishment as the imposition of a deserved sanction on the wrongdoer but also on the significance of the wrongdoing for the victim (i.e., what it means to be wronged in a value-diminishing fashion, how it has affronted her moral worth, and what is needed in order to reaffirm it),[39] constructively capturing the authentic meaning of the retributive responses that serious acts of disrespect elicit from victims. The meaning is constructively incorporated by properly acknowledging both the retributive and the recognitive elements at play.[40] As a result, the conflict

[37] For the opposite view, see A. Ripstein, *Private Wrongs* (Harvard University Press, 2016), p. 268 (arguing that the plaintiff's degree of anger or resentment is nonrelational). Similarly, see E. J. Weinrib, *The Idea of Private Law* (Harvard University Press, 1995), p. 82 (arguing for the irrelevance of "the particular features – desires, endowments, circumstances, and so on – that might distinguish one agent from another").

[38] See, for example, Hampton, "The Retributive Idea," pp. 143–61 (arguing that it is right to desire retribution against wrongdoers, because retribution counteracts the demeaning implications of the wrong).

[39] For a related but clearly different approach, see L. Radzik, "Tort Processes and Relational Repair," in J. Oberdiek (ed.), *Philosophical Foundations of the Law of Torts* (Oxford University Press, 2014), p. 235 (Radzik's reconciliation theory of tort law focuses on the significance of wrongdoing for the parties involved but with the aim of reconciling their moral relationship).

[40] For the retributive and recognitive components of retributive motivations, see Section A of Chapter 3.

stemming from the egregious tort comprehends all those properly involved: the wrongdoer and the victim. The victim understands the retributive response both as a vehicle for the communication of the moral condemnation stemming from the distinct reprehensible manner in which the defendant disparaged her self-worth (to mark the defendant's reprehensibility) and as a mechanism to affirm her value as a moral equal vis-à-vis the wrongdoer, reinforcing the significance of the other-regarding values at stake in those wrongful interactions.[41] The underlying idea is that victims have authentic claims by virtue of being specially situated in relation to their wrongdoers to cause the state (i.e., the court) to impose a condemnatory sanction on the particular defendant who wronged them in a manner that diminished their value. In that sense, the actual imposition of the punitive sanction at the hands of the victim (indirectly, through the court) creates a "new debt" owed by the defendant to the victim for the value-diminishing treatment. The punitive sanction conveys condemnation for the purpose of the victim's self-assertion. This notion of retribution understands the imposition of a monetary sanction (a punitive burden on defendants) as a mode of moral communication between the victim and the wrongdoer (as a communicative process enabling victims to call to account the person who wronged them in a reprehensible fashion) and ultimately the wider society.[42] The condemnatory message conveyed by the imposition of the monetary sanction reaffirms the victim's equal worth relative to the wrongdoer if it is punitive: If it is understood as a burdensome imposition on the defendant (i.e., it demands something from the defendant) initiated by the victim (mediated by the court) that purports to give material force to the condemnatory message for the value-diminishing manner in which the defendant's reprehensible conduct affronted the victim's self-worth.[43] The punitive element makes it harder for the defendant to ignore the condemnatory message by imposing a substantial cost (i.e., a new debt). At the same time, by paying off the "new debt" owed to the victim, the defendant formally communicates recognition of the wrong she committed against the victim, reaffirming the victim's relative equal worth as a result. In that sense, formal declarations or purely symbolic

41 On the communicative aspect of punishment, see Duff, Punishment, Communication, and Community, pp. 79–80 ("[w]e should rather talk of [punishment's] communicative purpose: for communication involves, as expression need not, a reciprocal and rational engagement.").

42 I take inspiration here from Antony Duff's understanding of the criminal process as a "communicative process of calling alleged criminal wrongdoers to account." See R. A. Duff, "Torts, Crimes and Vindication: Whose Wrong Is It?," in M. Dyson (ed.), *Unravelling Tort and Crime* (Cambridge University Press, 2014), p. 149. Moreover, he also understands the tort process (as a mode of civil recourse) in a similar communicative fashion.

43 On this point, see Antony Duff's work on the punitive sense of damages as remedies for wrongs in "Repairing Harms and Answering for Wrongs," J. Oberdiek (ed.), *Philosophical Foundations of Tort Law* (Oxford University Press, 2014), p. 227 ("Damages as remedies for wrongs should also consist in something designedly burdensome, authoritatively imposed on a wrongdoer as a proportionate response to his wrong: they should be punitive.").

punishments (even if directed at the victim) are likely to prove inadequate since they are not burdensome enough to reaffirm the victim's worth. The underlying idea is that the reaffirmation of the victim's value requires the recognition that punishment for what the wrongdoer has done to her is deserved and that something burdensome from the wrongdoer is required in return to account for the wrong done. Accordingly, *Relational Retribution* acknowledges not only that reprehensible wrongdoing deserves punishment but also that victims are specially situated vis-à-vis their wrongdoers (1) to seek value affirmation by demanding the judicial imposition of the punishment on the wrongdoer (i.e., punitive damages) and (2) to receive the monetary sanction directly from the wrongdoer.

Certainly, not all wrongful conducts merit a relational retributive response of the kind described here. Rather, the wrongful conducts that are retributively relevant share a common component of moral reprehensibility that is attached to the particular value-diminishing manner in which the defendant carries out that conduct toward the victim. The victim perceives the defendant's wrongdoing as demonstrating a morally significant measure of disregard or disrespect toward her self-worth; this I refer to as dignitary interest. It is related to what the defendant's conduct demonstrates about the victim – to the disregarding or disrespectful message that the conduct conveys regarding the treatment of the victim, which triggers the retributive response. For instance, the wrongful conducts in question are those whose meaning expresses that the victim is of less value than the wrongdoer (i.e., that the victim is less worthy of respect), in the sense that the wrongdoer is allowed to put her needs and interests ahead of those of the victim. The underlying idea is that certain behavior can be particularly wrongful because it carries meaning with regard to human value: It is insulting to us and attempts to degrade us.[44]

To be sure, the dignitary interest is not something that varies among individuals but rather is absolute.[45] When a person is subject to conduct that explicitly or implicitly treats her in a value-diminishing way (i.e., as though they were somehow worth less than oneself, or simply worthless), failing to show the minimum equal measure of respect due to all persons, that person can be said to have suffered an affront to her dignitary interest. Thus, to discover if a victim's dignitary interest was invaded, we cannot merely consider her injury; we must also examine the particular characteristics of the wrongdoer's behavior (i.e., at how the defendant acted toward the victim). The invasion of the victim's dignitary interest is thus observable through such an examination

[44] See J. G. Murphy, "Forgiveness and Resentment," in J. G. Murphy and J. Hampton (eds.), *Forgiveness and Mercy* (Cambridge University Press, 1988), p. 25 (explaining that we deeply resent moral injuries because they are messages – symbolic communications – that say to us that we do not count for the wrongdoer).

[45] In John Murphy's words, individual dignity entails "the irreducible, intrinsic worth of each human being simply by virtue of their personhood." See J. Murphy, "The Nature and Domain of Aggravated Damages" (2010) 69 *Cambridge Law Journal* 353, 361.

of the expressive content of the defendant's conduct.[46] This means paying particular attention to the manner of the defendant's conduct and the meaning of her action, in the objective sense. Indeed, what ultimately matters most is that the defendant's conduct objectively communicates an attitude of disrespect toward the victim, independently of whether the defendant subjectively assumes that attitude – though intentionality or wantonness will likely be present in most cases.[47] The focus is thus on the expressive content of the defendant's action, not on the subjective reasons why she performed it, even though the circumstances and motives might at times be relevant in determining the expressive content of the action and vice versa – elements of reprehensibility, such as that the defendant has been grossly careless, reckless, self-seeking, malicious, or something alike, will usually be involved in the description of the conduct. To be clear, the dignitary interest protected is of an objective nature, meaning that the imposition of the sanction (e.g., the punitive award) comes in response to an objective affront to the victim's dignitary interest in itself, rather than in response to its impact on the victim (e.g., emotional distress, pain and suffering, etc.). The victim's emotional distress is usually associated with the loss of dignity that is connected to individual accomplishments, social positions, or individual talents – a subjective dignitary interest that is generally protected through a compensatory remedy.[48] Hence, the relevant dignitary interest at the core of the relational retributive response is conceptually different from the emotional distress the plaintiff could have experienced as a consequence of the wrongful conduct. The classic response to the subjective emotional distress experienced by the victim is the compensatory one (subject to their availability in the specific jurisdiction), while the appropriate response to the invasion of the victim's dignitary interest that the offender's wrongful conduct objectively expresses is better conceived as a retributive one.

Once we begin to understand the victim's retributive response as relational (i.e., as going far beyond a purely retributive "just desert" rationale of punishment), we become aware of the morally rich expressive dimension that the *Relational Retribution* approach brings into view.[49] As can be inferred, there is something in

46 In the words of Holmes, "even a dog distinguishes between being stumbled over and being kicked." See O. W. Holmes, *The Common Law* (Little Brown, 1923), p. 3.

47 On this point, see A. J. Sebok, "Punitive Damages: From Myth to Theory" (2007) 92 *Iowa Law Review* 957, 1014 n254 ("all that matters [...] is that the defendant's conduct can be said to instantiate the attitude of disrespect for which punitive damages are awarded.").

48 For a distinction between objective and subjective injury to dignity in the context of compensatory aggravated damages in English law, see Murphy, "The Nature and Domain of Aggravated Damages," 362–65. For a distinction between fundamental dignity ("which is held by all of humanity") and prosaic dignity ("attained as the result of individual talents, accomplishments, and social position") in the context of aggravated damages in Canadian law, see J. Berryman, "Reconceptualizing Aggravated Damages: Recognizing the Dignitary Interest and Referential Loss" (2004) 41 *San Diego Law Review* 1521, 1522; 1535–41.

49 *Relational Retribution* builds on expressivist insights in that it recognizes that value-diminishing wrongdoing and punishment carry expressive meaning and that understanding their communicative capacity is important to grasp retributive condemnation for the victim's value affirmation.

the nature of the wrong that the defendant required the victim to endure that can divulge a certain attitude toward her that elicits a desire to be punitive (i.e., to file a punitive lawsuit) that far exceeds the private interest in rectification for the harm done. Indeed, when one person offends another person's self-worth, far more than physical, material, or emotional harm is involved. On one hand, the offender is perceived as expressing contempt for the person harmed, as asserting power over her, or as attempting to assert superiority over her. On the other hand, the victim understands the offense as a direct affront to her value as a moral equal.[50] The victim of such an invasion to her dignitary interests intuits that compensation does not sufficiently capture either the reprehensibility of the wrongdoer's conduct or the meaning that the content of that conduct conveys regarding her moral worth. She intuits that compensation cannot comprehensively capture the moral wrong of the act in question such that her value as a moral equal is reaffirmed.[51] The retributive response is thus grounded on the substantive content of the relationship between the nature of the wrong that the defendant's reprehensible conduct required the victim to endure, which authenticates the motivation to be punitive, and the victim's need for value affirmation that goes beyond the plain logic of just deserts as the sole imposition of a hardship (or suffering) on the defendant. Indeed, the retributive response (i.e., the imposition of the punitive sanction) is meant to address the relational need of the victim to affirm her moral worth vis-à-vis the wrongdoer by communicating disapproval of the value-diminishing treatment that she received from the wrongdoer through her demand for the judicial imposition of a punitive burden on the wrongdoer. In that sense, the retributive response involves much more than the imposition of a punishment for the defendant's conduct on purely "just deserts" terms.[52] It involves instead a relational form of retributivism that incorporates the victim's value-affirming elements in the equation. Indeed, a retributive rationale focusing exclusively on the offender and the punishment deserved does not begin to capture the significance of this set of victims' value judgments. The retributive response is thus primarily motivated by the victim's need to reclaim her self-worth. Through the imposition of punishment (e.g., by extracting a punitive damage award), the victim seeks to reaffirm that she is as worthy as the wrongdoer.[53] In other words, through *Relational Retribution*,

[50] For a discussion of such consequences in the context of interpersonal relations, see F. Heider, *The Psychology of Interpersonal Relations* (Martino Fine Books, 2015).

[51] For the idea that compensation addresses the consequences of the wrongdoing but not what was morally objectionable about it, see R. Kumar, "Why Reparations?," in J. Oberdiek (ed.), *Philosophical Foundations of the Law of Torts* (Oxford University Press, 2014), p. 198.

[52] For the claim that there is no evidence that the motive of most tort plaintiffs is to make the defendant suffer, see J. M. Solomon, "Equal Accountability through Tort Law" (2009) 103 *Northwestern University Law Review* 1765, 1813.

[53] Note that Hampton claims that the offender must be treated in such a way as to annul the appearance of her superiority over her victim, whereas *Relational Retribution* focuses instead on victims' affirmation of their own moral worth. See Hampton, "Correcting Harms versus Righting Wrongs," 1686–87.

the victim reestablishes the moral balance between the parties.[54] In this logic, the payment of the monetary sanction from the defendant to the victim is understood as a proper response to the wrong done to her, which neutralizes the widely shared objection that punitive damages awards represent an undeserved windfall to plaintiffs.[55] For their part, psychological studies demonstrate that punishment helps the victim-reactor to reestablish her psychological equilibrium by redressing the sense of diminishment created by the wrongful act.[56] Moreover, that psychological research also indicates that restoring equal moral standing in a relationship leads to satisfaction on the part of the wronged person.[57] Other experimental studies have shown that both victims and third parties perceive punishment as raising the victim's social standing, whereas failure to punish lowers it.[58]

The underlying idea is that we should devote attention to how the judicial imposition of a sanction assists us, as a community, to convey our values and beliefs on the proper treatment of people in our society – and what our rejection of egregious wrongful conducts says about the worth and value of the members of our society as embodied in the victim and how seriously we take them.[59] The proposal that we channel our reprobation (i.e., condemnation) through compensation, on the other hand, implicitly conveys the message that there is nothing qualitatively different between common damage awards for accidental harm and damage awards for outrageous, wanton, humiliating, reckless, or distressing behavior.[60] This is because, under a compensatory logic, the expression of the particular value-diminishing

54 George Fletcher's victim-vindication theory of punishment, which rejects traditional retributive theories in that they do not accord victims a central role within the structure of desert, similarly argues that punishment is meant "to overcome [the dominance gained by the offender] and reestablish the equality of victim and offender." See Fletcher, "The Place of Victims in the Theory of Retribution," 58 (retributive justice demands "seeking equality between offender and victim by subjecting the offender to punishment."). This attempt to fit victim-based justifications of punishment into a retributive framework has been met with skepticism from retributivists who conclude that Fletcher's program "doesn't look retributive; it looks compensatory to the victims." See M. Moore, "Victims and Retribution: A Reply to Professor Fletcher" (1999) 3 *Buffalo Criminal Law Review* 65, 76.

55 This objection resonates, both in the literature and in the case law, since the very beginning. On this point, see Section A of Chapter 2.

56 On this point, see D. W. Shuman, "The Psychology of Compensation in Tort Law" (1994) 43 *Kansas Law Review* 39, 57.

57 Ibid.

58 See, for example, K. Bilz, "Testing the Expressive Theory of Punishment" (2016) 13(2) *Journal of Empirical Legal Studies* 358.

59 See Murphy, "Forgiveness and Resentment," p. 20 (arguing that "we all have a duty to support the moral order, and order represented by clear understandings of what constitutes unacceptable treatment of one human being by another.").

60 For an explanation of the social and personal need to express condemnation when confronted with certain transgressions, see S. Lamb, "The Psychology of Condemnation: Underlying Emotions and Their Symbolic Expression in Condemning and Shaming" (2003) 68 *Brooklyn Law Review* 929, 931–34. For a detailed study on how people respond differently to carelessly inflicted harm, intentionally inflicted harm, and reckless conduct, see J. M. Darley and T. S. Pittman, "The Psychology of Compensatory and Retributive Justice" (2003) 7 *Personality and Social Psychology Review* 324, 336.

manner in which the victim was treated is mainly limited to require the defendant to pay more through higher compensatory pain and suffering awards or aggravated awards (depending on the particular jurisdiction). Certainly, steeper awards send the message that egregious wrongdoing leads to higher compensatory awards (i.e., quantitative difference), but they do not necessarily convey the specific motives for the greater award (i.e., what was morally objectionable about the defendant's behavior) in a way that is respectful of the significance of the wrongdoing for the victim (i.e., what it means to be treated in a value-diminishing way, how it has affected her self-worth) and the correlative retributive motivations elicited in those particularly egregious circumstances of wrongdoing. Compensating the victim in that way would not only imply a lack of concern for the value-diminishing manner in which she was treated and regarded by the defendant but also convey a devaluation of the significance and richness of the victim's retributive motivations that authenticate the condemnatory response that is in order for the wrongdoer's serious act of disrespect. As a consequence, the relational needs of the victim (i.e., the need to communicate the interpersonal message of condemnation for self-assertiveness) would not be realized by such a compensatory response as she will still be disrespected and undervalued as an equal member of society.[61] Furthermore, by not explicitly acknowledging the retributive purpose, we risk giving the impression that those damages awards are no more than a "price" whose payment makes up for reprehensible behavior (as a misdeed that may be licensed at a cost) rather than representing genuine "sanction" for particularly egregious acts (as a misdeed that will not be tolerated by the community).[62] In other words, while compensatory awards frame the wrongdoing in terms of a price that can be raised if conduct is egregious, they do not convey the moral significance of the wrongdoing for the victim in value-driven relevant terms – the morally objectionable component of the value-diminishing behavior that calls for condemnation in order to affirm the victim's moral worth.[63] The compensatory response lacks condemnatory quality in that it fails to meaningfully account for the victim's perspective. Moreover, as it will become clearer in the following section, this lack of condemnatory quality also impairs the deterrent effect (i.e., derived deterrence) of the retributive response in that it does not send an accurate message either to the wrongdoer or the wider community – recall that victims also expect that the punishment will change the wrongdoer's behavior going forward.[64] Accordingly, the imposition of a punitive sanction results from a

[61] On this point, see T. G. Okimoto and T. R. Tyler, "Is Compensation Enough? Relational Concerns in Responding to Unintended Inequity" (2007) 10(3) *Group Processes and Intergroup Relations* 399.

[62] Similarly, J. Feinberg distinguishes punishments, which express condemnation, from penalties, which do not.

[63] This points out to a distinction between payments of money as a price or a cost (compensatory awards) and payments of money as a punishment or sanction (punitive awards). For an analysis on the differences between "sanctions" and "prices," see Section B of Chapter 7.

[64] On "derived deterrence," see Chapter 3.

two-way juridically controlled and condoned process that carries messages about the offender, about the victim, and about society's other-regarding values.[65] Indeed, punishment is understood by the victim as a vehicle for communicating (1) to the wrongdoer, that she is worthy of respect; and (2) to the wider community, that the wrongdoer's conduct is disapproved and subject to moral condemnation because it violates the basic standards of mutual treatment in our society.

The relational retributive response is comprised of two interrelated aspects: (1) the victim's legal power to be punitive against the wrongdoer (i.e., standing to file the punitive lawsuit) which is triggered by the retributive motivations authenticated by the distinct value-diminishing manner in which the defendant invaded her dignitary interest; and (2) the court's power to punish the wrongdoer for the affront to the victim's dignitary interest that the wrongdoer's behavior objectively conveys (i.e., in the sense that contemptuous, contumelious, or diminishing treatment of others is per se objectionable and widely perceived as such), which is the legal basis for determining which particular circumstances of wrongdoing properly call for retributive sanction. In this way, *Relational Retribution* overcomes the myopic focus on the characteristics of the defendant's conduct as deserving of punishment in favor of a more holistic and inclusive approach that also captures the rich, value-laden retributive motivations of victims actively pursuing the imposition of the sanction (e.g., the punitive award). Recognition of the victim's (legal) power to be punitive (i.e., the distinctive standing to judicially claim the imposition of a sanction) is at the core of the relational retributive dimension.[66] This not only helps to understand the appropriateness of victims' retributive reactions to specific instances of reprehensible wrongdoing but also supports recognizing a meaningful reactive role to victims, whose specially situated relation to their wrongdoers affords them a unique opportunity to convey the moral significance of the wrongdoing and seek value-affirmation through a punitive lawsuit. Most importantly, it undoubtedly dissipates the widely shared concern regarding the negative effects associated with admitting retribution as an appropriate normative basis for punishment in torts because of its similarity to private revenge (i.e., the concern with legitimizing victims' desire to punish offenders by making them suffer). By rejecting an exclusively backward-looking deservedness dominance and focusing instead on an inclusive wrongdoer–victim and value self-assertiveness rationale for the actual imposition of punishment, a process that takes place in a court of law respecting the structures of the legal system and the legal procedure, *Relational Retribution* leaves no room for the sort of private revenge envisaged by tort scholars. As is explored further in Part IV, the imposition of a punitive award through tort law understood in this retributively relational fashion becomes an appropriate

65 For this point, see G. Binder, "Victims and the Significance of Causing Harm" (2008) 28 *Pace Law Review* 713, 715.
66 On the tort victims' legal power to be punitive, see Section A of Chapter 9.

avenue for people to treat and respond to each other, and tort litigation a legitimate institutional channel to meaningfully address those relational concerns.[67]

B THE PRINCIPLE OF SANCTION PROPORTIONALITY

Proportionality is a central element in any retributive theory of punishment.[68] However, criminal law theorists have repeatedly claimed that, despite the frequency with which it is invoked, the concept of proportionality "remains poorly understood."[69] As leading philosopher Douglas Husak put it, the principle of proportionality is "notoriously difficult to apply and is hard to formulate precisely."[70] Most criminal law scholars agree that punishment should fit the crime but most struggle to explain why some crimes are more serious than others and why some punishments are more severe than others.[71] The fact is that we lack any widely agreed measure of what makes a particular crime more or less serious than another and a particular punishment more or less severe than another.[72]

Criminal theorists' reluctance to consider the victim's perspective on the seriousness of the offense in the criminal law context is understandable: Once the offense takes place, the conflict ceases to be abstract and becomes specific to the victim's reality. The seriousness of the offense for the victim is measured by what happened to her and the consequences entailed (e.g., texting-while-driving is more serious for the victim if the consequence of the accident is permanent disfigurement than it

[67] On why the tort process is a legitimate avenue for punitive responses to reprehensible wrongdoing, see Part IV.

[68] See generally A. Von Hirsch and A. Shworth, *Proportionate Sentencing* (Oxford University Press, 2005) (proportionality requires that the severity of the punishment should be a function of the seriousness of the crime). See also T. Honoré, *Responsibility and Fault* (Hart Publishing, 1999), pp. 13, 83–84, 92, 123, 138 (recognizing that retribution requires proportionality between the severity of the sanction and the moral gravity of the offence); A. Von Hirsch, "Proportionality in the Philosophy of Punishment" (1992) 16 *Crime & Justice* 55, 56 (asserting that "[s]anctioning rationales differ from one another largely in the emphasis they give the principle of proportionality."); D. Husak, "Strict Liability, Justice, and Proportionality," in A. P. Simester (ed.), *Appraising Strict Liability* (Oxford University Press, 2005), pp. 95–97 (arguing that "[each of the components (censuring, hard treatment) of a definition of punishment] gives rise to its own distinctive principle of proportionality.").

[69] On this point, see M. Tonry, "Preface," in M. Tonry (ed.), *Of One-Eyed and Toothless Miscreants: Making the Punishment Fit the Crime* (Oxford University Press, 2019), p. vii.

[70] See Husak, "Retributivism and Over-Punishment," 175. Similarly, see G. Yaffe, *The Age of Culpability: Children and the Nature of Criminal Responsibility* (Oxford University Press, 2018), p. 61 (proportionality remains "one of the most elusive of the central concepts in the theory of punishment.").

[71] For this point, see M. Tonry, "Is Proportionality in Punishment Possible, and Achievable?," in M. Tonry (ed.), *Of One-Eyed and Toothless Miscreants: Making the Punishment Fit the Crime?* (Oxford University Press, 2019), p. 6. For the argument that proportionality is a relational concept and that there is substantial divergence of views among criminal law theorists regarding what should be proportional to what, see M. N. Berman, "Proportionality, Constraint, and Culpability" (2021) 15 *Criminal Law and Philosophy* 373.

[72] See generally D. M. Kahan, "Punishment Incommensurability" (1998) 1 *Buffalo Criminal Law Review* 691.

would be if only minor physical injury results), while the seriousness of the offense for the offender is measured by the wrongfulness of her behavior in the abstract (e.g., texting-while-driving is a wrongful conduct that consciously disregards the safety of others regardless whether the result is permanent disfigurement or minor injury). The offender deserves to be punished fairly on account of her wrongful behavior, regardless of the victim's experience with the actual consequences of the wrongdoing.[73]

Ex post consideration of the victim's perspective, however, seems to work differently in the tort context. Under a relational framework of retribution, the perspective of the victim who seeks the imposition of the monetary sanction for a particular instance of reprehensible wrongdoing done to her is equally important as the perspective of the defendant who is being sanctioned. Both perspectives should be carefully considered. When the victim seeks a punitive response, the tort process must be reoriented toward the identification of the seriousness of the defendant's conduct in relation to the particular situation of the victim (again, the wrongdoer–victim perspective). The moral significance of the wrongdoing that the victim's punitive reaction conveys is directly linked to the defendant's degree of reprehensibility toward her – the more reprehensible the conduct, the greater the affront to the dignitary interest, the greater the victim's relational need to communicate the wrongness of the defendant's conduct and affirm her moral worth. In this regard, empirical studies have shown that people tend to rank and rate diverse cases in essentially the same way. The studies reveal that citizen judgments show an extraordinary degree of correlation between judgments of outrageousness and judgments about appropriate punishment.[74] Similarly, in the tort context, it has been argued that people have a remarkable high degree of moral consensus on the degree of outrage and punitive intent that are appropriate for punitive damages cases, which cuts across differences in gender, race, income, age, and education.[75]

As should be clear by now, not all misconduct merits a retributive response. This represents the qualitative dimension of retribution. Since the standard of conduct in tort law is generally categorized in vague, indeterminate terms (such as "reprehensible," "high-handed," "outrageous," "egregious," "insulting," "cynical," "flagrant," and "contumclious"), if compared to the advanced and highly typified categorization of penal offenses which is typical of the criminal law, civil courts have the task to assess on a case-by-case basis whether the particular conduct denounced

73 On this point, see Moore, "Victims and Retribution: A Reply to Professor Fletcher," 65 (who rejects giving any special voice to crime victims because it would entail assigning different punishments to equally culpable offenders – thus, violating the principle of ordinal proportionality).

74 See generally C. R. Sunstein, D. Kahneman and D. Schkade, "Assessing Punitive Damages (with Notes on Cognition and Valuation in Law)" (1998) 107 *Yale Law Journal* 2071.

75 Pointing out to this phenomenon in the context of sexual harassment cases, see C. R. Sunstein and J. M. Shih, "Damages in Sexual Harassment Cases," in C. A. MacKinnon and R. B. Siegel (eds.), *Directions in Sexual Harassment Law* (Yale University Press, 2004).

by the victim in the individual trial before them is one that merits a retributive response. Factors relevant to this assessment generally include the defendant's state of mind, the nature of the wrong and the extent of the harm caused, the defendant's efforts to mitigate the harm caused, and the victim's vulnerability,[76] among others. Ultimately, what "reprehensibility" entails depends on the particular legal system in question: some jurisdictions require intentionality; others also include gross negligence and reckless behavior; still others even expand it to include behavior that shows failure to take reasonable precautions to avoid significant harm, among other possibilities. For instance, common law courts have recognized an interest in punishing tortfeasors who behave in one of several reprehensible manners. These circumstances include: acting "in reckless disregard of the consequences"[77]; when the wrongdoer "likely knew or ought to have known … that his conduct would naturally or probably result in injury"[78]; by showing, for example, that the wrongdoer acted "in an outrageous manner or with fraud, malice, wantonness or oppression"[79]; with a "willful and conscious disregard of the rights or safety of others"[80]; with a "conscious wrongdoing in contumelious disregard of another's rights"[81] or "conscious disregard for … a great probability of causing substantial harm"[82]; with "ill will" toward the victim; or behavior "so outrageous that malice toward a person injured as a result of that conduct can be implied."[83] Moreover, punitive damages statutes enacted in some jurisdictions also codify the standard of punitive conduct in broad terms, such as when the defendant "intentionally harmed the plaintiff without just cause or acted with a deliberate and flagrant disregard for the safety of others"[84] or when the "conduct has shown a deliberate or reckless disregard of an outrageous nature for the claimant's rights."[85] For their part, and following these trends, the English Law Commission has recommended that punitive damages be available in exceptional cases of "deliberate and outrageous disregard of the plaintiff's rights"[86]; while the American Restatement (Second) of Torts has stated that "punitive damages may be awarded for conduct that is outrageous, because of the defendant's evil

76 Examples of victims' vulnerabilities as a factor that heightens the degree of reprehensibility have been discussed in punitive damages cases involving schemes put forward by powerful corporations (e.g., insurance companies) that directly target elderly, disabled, or uneducated consumers. More timely examples include privacy cases involving digital platforms exploitative targeting of minors.

77 *Hoy* v. *Angelone*, 554 Pa 134 (Pa 1998).

78 *Union Pac R R* v. *Barber*, 149 SW 3d 325, 343 (Ark 2004).

79 *Wackenhut Corp* v. *Canty*, 359 So 2d 430, 435–36 (Fla 1978).

80 *Simon* v. *San Paolo US Holding Co*, 113 P 3d 63, 76 (Cal 2005).

81 *Uren* v. *John Fairfax & Sons Pty Ltd* [1966] 117 CLR 118, 138 [HCA] (Taylor J) and *Gray* v. *Motor Accident Commission* [1998] 196 CLR 1, 16 [HCA].

82 *Calmes* v. *Goodyear Tire & Rubber Co*, 575 NE 2d 416, 419 (Ohio 1991).

83 *Tuttle* v. *Raymond*, 494 A 2d 1353, 1361 (Me 1985).

84 Punitive Damages Missouri Bill 2020.

85 Crime and Courts Act 2013, s34(6)(a) (which permits punitive damages for publication of news-related material by someone who is not a member of an approved regulator).

86 Law Commission, *Aggravated, Exemplary and Restitutionary Damages*, Law Com 247 [1997] 1.20.

motive or his reckless indifference to the rights of others."[87] As discussed in Part I, punitive damages are generally available in the United States whenever the defendant's conduct reaches a certain degree of "reprehensibility," but the availability of England's exemplary damage awards has been instead restricted from the very outset to specific categories of torts – recall the "categories test."[88]

As can be observed, a defendant's behavior might be considered "reprehensible," which would make it a candidate for a retributive response, depending on their motivations (e.g., intent, maliciousness, wantonness), on the representation of the consequences of their actions (e.g., conscious or reckless indifference to the other's rights), and on the attitudes toward those who were wronged (e.g., insulting, deceitful, self-seeking, oppressive, abusive, exploitative). However, the fact that most of these elements sometimes overlap and are usually present in cases where punitive damages are awarded does not mean that they necessarily do. Indeed, under *Relational Retribution*, the plaintiff has to make the case that the particular reprehensible manner in which the defendant carried out the conduct toward her represents a value-diminishing affront to her dignitary interest that merits condemnation and demands value affirmation regardless of the particular subjective state of mind of the defendant at the time.[89] To clarify, the defendant's state of mind (i.e., intention, malice) is usually present and represents an important (and challenging) epistemic element for plaintiffs to invoke in making their punitive claims, but it is ultimately not required for the imposition of a punitive response since reprehensible wrongdoing that represents a value-diminishing affront to victims' dignitary interest is perfectly possible without direct intention. Tortious cases involving reckless behavior for which punitive damages are usually awarded are good examples of the latter. In certain cases, moreover, intention can be inferred either through presumptions informed by the reprehensible schemes of conduct put forward by the defendant or assumed in the case of offences that can only be committed with intent, such as certain forms of profit-seeking economic torts.[90] The bottom line is that the focus is instead on the more holistic description of the reprehensible value-diminishing pattern of behavior that warrants a punitive response.

[87] Restatement (Second) of Torts §908(2) (1979).

[88] On the English and Anglo-American approach to punitive damages, see Section A of Chapter 1.

[89] For an insightful work on the minor role of mens rea in torts, see P. Cane, "Mens Rea in Tort Law" (2000) 20 *Oxford Journal of Legal Studies* 533, 543.

[90] Similarly, see E. Bant and J. M. Paterson, "Systems of Misconduct: Corporate Culpability and Statutory Unconscionability" (2021) 15 *Journal of Equity* 63, 76–91 (proposing a system-based approach for attributing corporate blame on the basis of the argument that corporations' "mental states" can be discerned through their adopted and implemented "systems of conduct, policies and practices" – for instance, certain objective patterns of behavior may evidence a predatory intention to produce a harmful outcome while others may reveal callous disregard for patent risks of harmful consequences). Moreover, see E. Bant, "Culpable Corporate Minds" (2021) 48 *University of Western Australia Law Review* 352, 358 ("[H]uman-centric mode[s] fail [] to address the complexities of dealing with modern corporate defendants, where the corporation has no natural 'mind' and the knowledge of its human agents is often dissipated through complex, decentralized structures.").

The relational rationale of retribution I advance acknowledges these idiosyncratic aspects of the logic of tort law (i.e., general standards of conduct categorization followed by case-by-case evaluations of conduct reprehensibility) and, more importantly, offers novel insights to assist courts in their task of identifying sanctionable conduct. In fact, the underlying idea of the relational framework is that understanding the moral significance of the wrongdoing by examining the victim's retributive motivations for punishment, which are authenticated by the value attributed to the invaded dignitary interest, will better instruct legal actors regarding the kind of value-diminishing behavior (and the degree of reprehensibility) that merits a punitive response in the tort context. This level of indeterminacy of the standard of conduct facilitates a richer contextual evaluation of what counts as reprehensible behavior under the circumstances of the wrongdoing, allowing community input on wrongfulness within the boundaries of tort liability. The idea is that defendants' wrongful conducts are qualified as meritorious of a retributive response by their invasion of the victim's dignitary interest. The wrongful conducts that thus warrant retribution share a common component of moral reprehensibility that is attached to the value-diminishing manner in which the defendant carries out that conduct toward the victim. It is related to what the defendant's conduct expresses about the victim's dignitary interest – to the message that the conduct conveys regarding the treatment of the victim. As shown earlier, a retributive claim is elicited in response to wrongful conducts that violate victims' dignitary interests by signifying diminished respect for the other party's value, by disregarding the other party's individual autonomy, and by oppressively or exploitatively abusing power over the other party, among other value-diminishing behaviors. All these factors understood in a holistic manner integrate the relevant elements for a proper evaluative judgment on conduct reprehensibility, which is sensitive to the value of the victim's perspective.

If the defendant's conduct merits sanction, the court must determine the amount of the award in direct proportion to the seriousness of the offense (i.e., to respect the principle that no one be punished more severely than she deserves).[91] This is the quantitative aspect of retribution. The metric of punishment severity is a contested matter that poses a challenge to the principle of proportionality.[92] Criminal law theorists disagree on whether severity of punishments should be understood objectively focusing on acts, culpability, and desert without attending to the different effects of punishment on different people (e.g., objective durations of imprisonment, fixed monetary sanctions) or in subjective terms of their individualized effects

[91] See J. Feinberg, "The Classic Debate," in J. Feinberg and J. Coleman (eds.), *Philosophy of Law* (6th ed.) (Wadsworth Publishing, 1999), pp. 727–28 ("The proper amount of punishment to be inflicted […] is that amount which fits, matches, or is proportionate to the moral gravity of the offense.").

[92] For this point, see M. Matravers, "The Place of Proportionality in Penal Theory: Or Rethinking Thinking about Punishment," in M. Tonry (ed.), *Of One-Eyed and Toothless Miscreants: Making the Punishment Fit the Crime* (Oxford University Press, 2019), p. 93.

by assessing the amount of suffering or distress experienced by particular offenders so they endure the right amount of it. The idea is that offenders may experience sanctions differently (i.e., some may suffer more or less than deserved because of their experience and preferences), and that their punishment should reflect these experiential differences to achieve proportionality between the seriousness of the offense and the severity of the sanction.[93]

This way of conceptualizing the problem of punishment severity, no matter whether the objectivists or subjectivists prevail, overlooks the victim's perspective. In the tort context, under a relational retributive rationale where desert plays an important but not exclusive role, sanction proportionality would be served when the amount of punishment reflects both *just desert* for the defendant and *value affirmation* for the victim whose dignitary interest was affronted by the value-diminishing reprehensible wrongdoing. The imposition of the monetary sanction is understood as an expression of disapproval for purposes of value affirmation in the sense that the defendant is ultimately being coerced by the victim's punitive claim to endure a monetary sanction (the punitive award) that would not otherwise be imposed on wrongdoing that lacks reprehensibility. In order to be genuinely retributive, the proper amount of the monetary sanction (i.e., the severity of the punitive award) should thus consider not only the seriousness of the offense (i.e., the degree of reprehensibility)[94] but also its impact on the defendant's welfare as a proper means of communication between the victim and the offender and, ultimately, the broader society. The idea is that the victim's relational need of value affirmation is addressed if the amount of the monetary sanction communicates a condemnatory message reaffirming the victim's worth. For instance, if a rich defendant is ordered to pay to the victim an insignificant monetary sanction, the victim often perceives the sanction as insufficient (and even as insulting or disrespectful), because a sanction that is not onerous represents an inadequate affirmation of her equal moral worth vis-à-vis

93 On this debate in the criminal law realm, see generally A. J. Kolber, "The Subjective Experience of Punishment" (2009) 109 *Columbia Law Review* 182 (arguing that a successful justification of punishment must take account of offenders' subjective experience when assessing punishment severity); J. Masur, J. Bronsteen and C. Buccafusco, "Retribution and the Experience of Punishment" (2010) 98 *California Law Review* 1463, 1469 ("[T]he decisions about which punishments to impose and the decisions associated with proportionality must depend on knowledge about how those punishments are typically experienced by offenders."); J. Bronsteen, C. Buccafusco and J. Masur, "Happiness and Punishment" (2009) 76 *University of Chicago Law Review* 1037, 1037 ("When the state punishes a criminal, it inflicts suffering."). For the opposite view, see D. Gray, "Punishment as Suffering" (2010) 63 *Vanderbilt Law Review* 1617 (arguing that punishment is neither justified nor measured by its capacity to produce pain and suffering); D. Markel and C. Flanders, "Bentham on Stilts: The Bare Relevance of Subjectivity to Retributive Justice" (2010) 98 *California Law Review* 907, 915–16 (arguing not only that retributivists need not take subjectivism too seriously but also that they must reject it); and K. W. Simons, "Response, Retributivists Need Not and Should Not Endorse the Subjectivist Account of Punishment" (2009) 109 *Columbia Law Review* 1.

94 This is one of the three guideposts introduced by the United States Supreme Court in *BMW v. Gore* for courts to consider when reviewing whether punitive damages awarded are grossly excessive under the Due Process Clause.

the wrongdoer. This means that the actual imposition of the monetary sanction sends different messages depending on the financial situation of the defendant. The underlying idea is that punitive awards framed as percentages of the defendant's income or wealth likely provide a better approximation of the experiential severity of monetary sanctions than flat sums. This understanding, drawn from generalizations informed by human psychology, is that the experienced severity of monetary sanctions hinges on the defendant's wealth.[95]

This implies that the metric of punishment severity should be tailored to the defendant's financial situation for monetary sanctions to be understood as a form of genuine retributive punishment as opposed to a tax or pricing mechanism for incentivizing efficient behavior.[96] However, the relevance of the defendant's wealth in the calibration does not necessarily mean that we should endorse subjectivity since, for the sanction to be retributive, there is no need to tailor it to the individual defendant's psychological experience of suffering (e.g., distress for economic hardship) or to inquire into her uniquely subjective utility curve regarding the value of money to ensure the defendant's suffering is proportionate to the offense. Tailoring the amount of the sanction to the psychological profile of the individual defendant (i.e., to the subjective reaction of hardship or distress experienced by the deprivation of means that the monetary sanction entails) might be proper under a revenge-focused account of retribution where the victim seeks the imposition of the sanction to impose a level of suffering on the offender (i.e., the victim desires the defendant's suffering). Conversely, under a value affirmation account, which the *Relational Retribution* rationale endorses, the victim seeks the imposition of the monetary sanction not to impose subjective suffering on the defendant but instead to communicate moral condemnation of the defendant's wrongful conduct for purposes of self-assertion. The purpose of the condemnation is reasserting the victim's worth. Therefore, to assess the condemnatory impact of monetary sanctions, we only need to know how wealthy defendants are without inquiring into their subjective psychological experience of suffering. In that sense, a wealthy defendant who engages in the same reprehensible wrongdoing should be required to pay a larger monetary sanction than a poorer defendant because it is reasonable to assume that the experiential severity of the defendant with the lower income is greater than that of the defendant with the higher income. The severity of the monetary sanction depends on what proportion of the defendant's means it takes – not on its absolute amount. This is explained by the general principle of the diminishing marginal utility of wealth – any addition to a person's wealth is used to satisfy less important and less urgent needs.

Most importantly, this approach not only dilutes the usual objection raised by those who argue that juridical persons, such as corporations, cannot be punished

95 On this point, see Masur, Bronsteen and Buccafusco, "Retribution and the Experience of Punishment," 1464.

96 For an analysis on the differences between "sanctions" and "prices," see Section B of Chapter 7.

on retributive grounds because they cannot experience pain, suffering, or deprivations[97] but also reinforces the undesirability of allowing tort insurance since the financial impact on the defendant would be reduced if monetary sanctions (i.e., punitive awards) were insurable.[98] The point is that the defendant should bear the punitive burden; otherwise, the defendant would not be punished and the victim's worth would not be reaffirmed if an insurance company pays the imposed monetary sanction. Moreover, it offers a response to why a mere formal declaration (e.g., mere words, a letter of apology) or a purely symbolic punishment would not serve the purpose of the retributive sanction either. Once again, the punitive sanction serves its condemnatory purpose reasserting the victim's worth if it truly burdens the defendant: It must be conceived as a burdensome imposition on the defendant meant to provide tangible force to the wrongdoer's condemnation for the reprehensible wrong done to the victim. As Stephen Smith points out "[f]or the law's condemnation to be taken seriously it is important that it be conveyed at least in part in a tangible form […]. [which reflects] the nature of the wrong."[99]

Following this logic, to avoid the disproportionate punitive impact of monetary sanctions on rich and poor defendants, we should look to methods that allow systematic tailoring of the sanction amount to the defendant's ability to pay.[100] Fixed amounts, for example, are ill-advised since fixing the amount of the sanction to the offense affords no consideration to differences in defendants' wealth, which would in turn burden the poor more than the rich.[101] In other words, because a fixed

97 For the argument that "corporations cannot be *retributively* punished because they cannot be harmed or set back in ways that could satisfy the requirement to answer a wrong against persons with an equivalent or fitting deprivation against the wrongdoer," see S. W. Buell, "Retiring Corporate Retribution" (2020) 83 *Law and Contemporary Problems* 25, 26 (emphasis in original).

98 For those concerned with nonpayment, note that, because the monetary sanction is tailored to the defendant's ability to pay, they may be paid more often and more fully.

99 See S. A. Smith, *Rights, Wrongs, and Injustices* (Oxford University Press, 2020), p. 205. For skepticism on expressivist theories of damages, see generally S. Steel, "On the Moral Necessity of Tort Law: The Fairness Argument" (2021) 41 *Oxford Journal of Legal Studies* 192; and "Damages without Loss" (2023) 139 *Law Quarterly Review* 219.

100 In the context of punitive damages, the majority of United States courts and legislatures have recognized the relevance of the defendant's wealth in determining the extent of the punitive award and it is also often reflected in jury instructions. Under the English law, its importance has been originally emphasized by Lord Devlin in *Rookes* ("the means of the parties … are material in the assessment of exemplary damages," *Rookes* 1228). Furthermore, the recently proposed provision to introduce civil penalties in France considers, in order to quantify the monetary penalty, the defendant's ability to pay and, in the case of legal persons, their revenue. See Project de Réforme du Droit de la Responsabilité Civile 2017, subs. 5, art. 1266–61 ("[T]he penalty is proportionate to the seriousness of the fault, the financial means of the wrongdoer, and the profit gained from the wrongful conduct. The penalty cannot be more than tenfold the amount of the profit gained. If the wrongdoer is a corporation, the penalty can be up to 5 percent of the amount of the highest turnover before tax made in France in the tax years since the year preceding that when the fault was committed.").

101 For instance, in *BMW v. Gore*, 517 US 559, 591 (1996), the United States Supreme Court observed that "a fixed dollar award will punish a poor person more than a wealthy one."

amount for a particular offense has a different impact on defendants with different incomes, the severity of the sanction imposed on the defendant does not correlate with their ability to pay. If two defendants perceive the monetary sanction imposed differently due to a difference in personal wealth, then for at least one of them the sanction is not truly proportional. Upper limits that cap the amount of sanctions, for their part, would also be problematic, particularly when the wrongdoer is especially wealthy, since the appropriate monetary sanction would probably exceed the cap limit. In these cases, the monetary sanction would benefit the wealthy defendants by directly impeding the imposition of the proportionate sanction in the particular case. Conversely, a system of sanctions called *day fines*,[102] which is administered by several European and Latin American countries, overcomes these shortcomings by providing more precise calibration of the monetary sanction both to the seriousness of the offense and to the defendant's wealth.[103] Day fines establish the metric for punishment severity in reference to its impact on the welfare of the particular offender instead of resorting to statistical averages or typical cases. Its operation involves two steps. First, a day-fine unit (e.g., 15, 50, or 110 units) is determined for the misconduct only on the basis of the seriousness of the offense without regard to the offender's means (this is the objective element). The more serious the offense, the greater the number of units (i.e., reprehensibility is expressed by the number of units). The number of units appropriate for each offense is determined by a unit-rate system (benchmark numbers). Hence, the same number of day-fine units is applied for each instance of the same offense. Second, the value of the day-fine unit is identified for the particular defendant (the subjective element). This calculation considers the defendant's personal income or wealth (e.g., the average or a fraction of the defendant's daily income after taxes and deductions for basic needs).[104] Hence, the translation of the punishment units into monetary terms depends on the

[102] I have been inspired here by the work of Douglas Husak who points out to the potential advantages of adopting such a system in the criminal law context. See D. Husak, "Kinds of Punishment," in H. M. Hurd (ed.), *Moral Perplexities and Legal Puzzles: The Work of Larry Alexander* (Cambridge University Press, 2018), pp. 22–38. For an alternative adaptation of the system of day fines to tort law, see R. Perry, "Income-Dependent Punitive Damages" (2018) 95 *Washington University Law Review* 835 (putting forward and defending a method for incorporating the defendant's wealth factor into the punitive damages calculation).

[103] Initially developed in Scandinavia in 1920 and 1930, and then introduced to Germany in the late 1960s and early 1970s, to France and Portugal in the early 1980s, to Spain and Poland in the mid 1990s, and to Switzerland in 2007. It was also adopted in the early twentieth century by many Latin American systems, such as Argentina, Colombia, Ecuador, Guatemala, Honduras, Nicaragua, Paraguay, and Uruguay. Several jurisdictions in the United States experimented with day-fines (such as Staten Island [New York], Milwaukee [Wisconsin], Maricopa County [Arizona], Polk County [Iowa], and Bridgeport [Connecticut]) but the American experience with day-fines has been limited and sporadic if compared with the European experience.

[104] For example, in Finland, "[o]ne sixtieth of the average monthly income of the person fined, less the taxes and fees defined by a Decree and a fixed deduction for basic consumption, is deemed to be a reasonable amount of a day fine." Crim. Code ch.2 (a), 2(2) (Fin.)

defendant's ability to pay.[105] For example, one way of making such a translation is to consider one unit of punishment to equal one day's pay, or some fraction of a day's pay. The total amount is then calculated by multiplying the number of day-fine units (which depend on the severity of the offense) by the value of the unit (which depends on the financial situation of the defendant). As a result, day fines involve a combination of the objective and subjective elements, which are necessary for relational proportionality.

Proportionality understood in relational terms is thus not committed to the horizontal requirement that equally reprehensible wrongdoing be sanctioned equally severely since the proper amount of the punishment will depend not only on the seriousness of the offense but also on the relative wealth of the defendant.[106] The point is that imposing two defendants a different monetary sanction for the same (or similar) reprehensible behavior is not treating them unequally but rather acknowledging the fact that the amount of the sanction is likely to be greater for one than for the other (e.g., a monetary sanction of six days' pay will represent a larger sum of money for high-income offenders than for poorer ones). Moreover, proportionality thus understood makes it possible to factor whether the defendant has already been sanctioned (namely, by a fine) since this will be reflected in the defendant's ability to pay.

Since condemning the wrongdoer and reaffirming the worth of the victim is central to *Relational Retribution*, a possible objection would be that systems of sanctions like day fines could be perceived as inadequately condemnatory in cases involving low-income defendants who engage in highly outrageous behavior because the nominal amount of the sanction would be quantitatively scant. This objection seems to point to an apparent gap between the experienced severity imposed by the monetary sanction on the wrongdoer and the meaning that the monetary sanction has for the victim and for society more generally. However, this objection overlooks that a monetary sanction that is calibrated by the seriousness of the offense and the defendant's ability to pay has a punitive impact on the offender, which sends an unambiguously condemnatory message: The imposition of such a monetary sanction expresses disapproval by signaling to the defendant (and others) that on top of the compensation for the harm caused to the victim she has a *new debt* that is sufficiently burdensome

105 For example, in Germany, one unit is valued as an offender's average daily income, after taxes. In Sweden, the unit is calculated as 1/1,000th of the offender's average discretionary income – that which the offender could afford to give up if she adopted a "strict economy" – with adjustments for taxes, debts, and assets. See generally D. C. McDonald, J. Greene and C. Worzella, *Day Fines in American Courts: The Staten Island and Milwaukee Experiments* (Washington, DC: National Institute of Justice, Department of Justice, 1992).

106 On this point, see D. Husak, "Why Legal Philosophers (Including Retributivists) Should be Less Resistant to Risk-Based Sentencing," in J. W. de Keijser, J. V. Roberts and J. Ryberg (eds.), *Predictive Sentencing: Normative and Empirical Perspectives* (Hart Publishing, 2019), pp. 44–45 ("Retributivists should preserve the role of desert while weakening its strength […]. If we have good reason to inflict different amounts of punishment on two offenders who have committed equally serious crimes, we should not be worried that our decision does not preserve proportionality.").

for her whether or not the total amount could be considered low in objective terms. Besides, there is no clear correlation between low monetary sanctions and lack of condemnation, since low-level punitive awards could generate high levels of condemnation for a defendant who understands the imposition of the sanction as an expression of disapproval. In any case, the expressive power of the punitive sanction in the tort context hinges on the circumstance that the victim herself can call upon the court to impose a new obligation for the defendant to pay more than she would normally be required under the rectificatory principle when her behavior is deemed reprehensible. The monetary sanction thus expresses authoritative moral condemnation and gives voice to the victim to reaffirm her moral value vis-á-vis the offender. The social meaning of a punitive sanction in torts is thus clearly condemnatory, for the additional amount imposed on the defendant sends the message that the monetary sanction is not a "price" for misbehaving but a "genuine sanction" for engaging in reprehensible behavior.[107] This ties into the psychological studies that explore more deeply the expressive and emotive qualities of money beyond its narrow classic depiction as an economic tool for incentivizing desired behavior, a better understanding of which could more accurately predict and guide behavior.[108] Moreover, since the expression of the degree of reprehensibility under the day-fines system is done by the number of units assigned (e.g., 15, 50, 110 units) rather than by the final amount of the award, courts may very well serve the expressive condemnatory dimension of the imposed sanction by emphasizing in their decisions the number of units reflecting the gravity of the offense.[109] Most importantly, the imposition of a proportional monetary sanction in a fair procedure that exhibits sensitivity to the relational concerns of the parties communicates respect for both the defendant and the victim. It also expresses the latter's need to reaffirm her equal value vis-à-vis the wrongdoer and, ultimately, her status as an equal member of the broader community. Ultimately, relational proportionality mainly concerns determining the appropriate quantity that the defendant should pay to the victim (in relation to the seriousness of the wrongdoing and the amount that represents a significant burden), rather than the amount the plaintiff should receive. As can be inferred, proportionate punishment, understood in relational retributive terms, achieves the aim of retribution and its derived deterrence effect – which might be reinforced by other complementary measures, such as profit-stripping in pertinent cases of profit-seeking wrongs.

[107] For the claim that the social meaning of money cannot be reduced to simple "commodification," see J. Steele, "Satisfying Claims? Money, Tort, and 'Consumer Society'" (2011) 20 *Social & Legal Studies* 516, 519. Also see F. Stark, "Tort Law, Expression, and Duplicative Wrongs," in J. Oberdiek and P. B. Miller (eds.), *Civil Wrongs and Justice in Private Law* (Oxford University Press, 2020), pp. 441–62 (identifying the potential clash of expressive messages in cases of wrongs that can form the basis of both civil and criminal liability).

[108] For this point, see J. Y. Lee, "Money Norms" (2017) 49(1) *Loyola University Chicago Law Journal* 57.

[109] This could require predetermining an appropriate range of units for each category of wrongful conduct.

A *day fines* system of monetary sanctions is certainly an attractive one for a relational understanding of retribution, which requires an ex post, individualized, and dynamic tailoring of punishment proportionality such that the contextual situation of the wrongdoer and the victim are equally respected.[110] It would also dissipate the widespread objection that, even when judgments of outrage and punitive intent are widely shared, monetary sanctions in torts (i.e., punitive awards) are unpredictable (in that people drastically disagree about the appropriate amount) and incoherent (in that people who are similarly situated may not be treated similarly) because decision-makers lack a "modulus" (a reference wrong to which a specific dollar amount is attached that people can use as a standard for comparison with other wrongs) to translate those moral judgments into dollar amounts – what is called "magnitude scaling without a modulus."[111] However, I do not intend to claim here that the *day fines* system is necessarily superior – there could very well be other competing proposals worth exploring and comparing. Moreover, I do not intend to offer a concrete proposal for better design and implementation of a workable system of *day fines* either. Determining how many punishment units to assign to each type of offense[112] and how to turn punishment units into monetary amounts that capture offenders' differing abilities to pay[113] certainly involves a complex process that would require normative commitments that vary in function with the past practices and culture of a given political community. What I do intend, however, is to establish what factors we should consider when discussing the relational proportionality of monetary sanctions in the tort context.

110 As should be evident by now, the single-digit ratio between punitive and compensatory damages held by the United States Supreme Court in *State Farm* v. *Campbell* to determine what constitutes a (dis)proportionate punitive damages award would not respect relational proportionality. On the fundamental distinction between punishment and compensation that is at the core of *Relational Retribution*, see Chapter 5.

111 On this objection, see C. R. Sunstein, "On the Psychology of Punishment" (2004) 11 *Supreme Court Economic Review* 171, 172. On how rankings of dollar awards can be used to reduce noise in punitive damages awards, see D. Kahneman, O. Sibony and C. R. Sunstein, *Noise. A Flaw in Human Judgment* (William Collins, 2021), pp. 194–99.

112 For instance, questions to be considered are whether to prescribe a range of punishment units or a "presumptive" number of units to be imposed; whether to prescribe the variations in punishment units prescribed for aggravating and mitigating factors; and whether to permit the punishment units to reflect considerations such as the defendant's prior history of wrongful behavior. See McDonald, Greene, and Worzella, "Day Fines in American Courts," 4.

113 Ibid 5. For example, questions on how to factor in offenders' wealth as well as their income in figuring their ability to pay, or whether to adjust valuation formulae for offenders' poverty and lack of income, as well as for "off the records" income; the fraction used to calculate the daily unit; whether to set upper and lower nominal limits on a daily unit; whether to establish minimum and maximum number of days, etc. Also, the development of procedures and policies for obtaining information about offenders' means and for the use of that information by other parties would be required.

5

Overcoming Compensatory Reductionism

It could be argued that answers to the problems addressed by the relational retributive rationale are already found in traditional compensatory responses, such as nonpecuniary damages for pain and suffering and aggravated damages for mental distress or dignitary harm. The claim suggests that traditionally compensatory categories of remedies could play the role of upholding the victim's dignitary interest without appealing to notions of punishment and retribution. In short, these accounts contend that compensatory remedies can achieve the same objective in at least the two following alternatives: (1) through higher nonpecuniary awards, or (2) through the imposition of aggravated damages. In what follows, I deal with each separately.

A SANCTIONING UNDER THE LABEL OF NONPECUNIARY DAMAGES

Tort scholars and courts, both in common law and civil law jurisdictions, have acknowledged the routine practice of smuggling punitive elements into compensatory damages.[1] It has been argued that the notion of dignitary harm resulting from defendants' reprehensible wrongdoing affirms the presence of punishment in the law of torts, albeit in a covert or concealed fashion, for the practice of awarding greater compensation for pain and suffering maintains the primary focus on repairing the victim. Because of the inherently blurry line between compensation

[1] For examples across jurisdictions where this practice has been observed, see Chapter 1. Also see M. Rustad and T. Koenig, "The Historical Continuity of Punitive Damages" (1993) 42 *American University Law Review* 1269, 1322 ("[American] states that do not allow punitive damages sometimes assess damages in excess of actual damages to compensate for an act's maliciousness."); V. E. Schwartz and L. Lorber, "Twisting the Purpose of Pain and Suffering Awards: Turning Compensation into 'Punishment'" (2002) 54 *South Carolina Law Review* 47 (examining the trend of using pain and suffering damages to "punish" in the United States). Moreover, for empirical studies suggesting that decision-makers who are blocked from expressing their punitive intent through punitive damages find other mechanisms through which to achieve the same goals, see E. Green, D. Coon and B. Bornstein, "The Effects of Limiting Punitive Damages Awards" (2001) 25 *Law & Human Behavior* 217, 226–28.

and punishment in the case of injuries that result from insult, emotional anguish, or humiliation, awards for emotional harm are especially likely to include punitive elements concealed under ostentatiously compensatory grounds.[2] By consequence, because the consideration of compensatory remedies for such harms often includes punitive aspects, introducing punitive damages becomes both redundant and creates a double-counting problem. To put it differently, similarly as when punitive damages are awarded, the defendant's conduct and motives – factors eschewed in classic tort theory – become relevant for the assessment of the appropriate compensation for the pain and suffering of the victim on the understanding that the more morally outrageous the wrongdoing, the more distress and pain are suffered by the plaintiff, and the greater the compensatory award should be.[3]

Accordingly, commentators and courts have recognized a risk of overlap between emotional distress and punitive damages generated by consideration of the reprehensibility of the defendant's conduct, since "the jury's conclusion about the plaintiff's level of emotional trauma might well reflect its view concerning the reprehensibility of the defendant's conduct."[4] Furthermore, the Restatement (Second) of Torts acknowledged this phenomenon, pointing out that "[i]n many cases in which compensatory damages include an amount for emotional distress, such as humiliation or indignation aroused by the defendant's act, there is no clear line of demarcation between punishment and compensation and a verdict for a specified amount frequently includes elements of both."[5] Precisely on this issue, empirical studies have reported that "[a]lthough pain-and-suffering awards are essentially compensatory, there can be little doubt that such awards sometimes reflect jury judgments about the egregiousness of the defendant's behavior. Hence, such judgments are likely to have a punitive component."[6] The Supreme Court of the United States has referred to the same issue in *State Farm*, a resonant case concerning punitive damages, expressing that

2 See, for example, *Diet Drugs (Phentermine/Fenfluramine/Dexfenfluramine) Prods. Liab. Litig.*, 369 F 3d 292, 310 (3d Cir. 2004) (acknowledging that "mental anguish, pain, or loss of consortium [could serve as] vehicles for sub rosa punitive damages"). For an empirical analysis of the so-called crossover phenomenon, see C. M. Sharkey, "Crossing the Punitive-Compensatory Divide," in B. H. Bornstein, R. L. Wiener, R. Schopp and S. L. Willborn (eds.), *Civil Juries and Civil Justice: Psychological & Legal Perspectives* (Springer, 2008), p. 101 (acknowledging that in many cases in which compensatory damages include an amount for emotional distress, there is no clear line of demarcation between punishment and compensation and a verdict for a specified amount frequently includes elements of both).

3 See D. B. Dobbs, *Dobbs Law of Remedies: Damage-Equity-Restitution* (2nd ed.) (West Publishing, 1993), p. 310.

4 *McDonough* v. *City of Quincy*, 452 F 3d 8, 24, 25 (1st Cir. 2006) (adding that "the high award may partly reflect punishment for what the jury may have concluded was the degree of reprehensibility of the conduct.").

5 Restatement (Second) of Torts §908 (1979).

6 See C. R. Sunstein, D. Kahneman and D. Schkade, "Assessing Punitive Damages (with Notes on Cognition and Valuation in Law)" (1998) 107 *Yale Law Journal* 2071, 2133.

> [t]he compensatory damages for the injury suffered [...] [were likely] based on a component which was duplicated in the punitive award. Much of the distress was caused by the outrage and humiliation [...] suffered at the actions of [the wrongdoer]; and it is a major role of punitive damages to condemn such conduct. Compensatory damages, however, already contain this punitive element.[7]

To conclude, there is solid ground for the assertion that nonpecuniary damages, such as those for pain and suffering, cannot avoid making some assessment of the reprehensibility of the defendant's conduct, explicitly or otherwise, when determining the proper award. The reason for this is that the amount of emotional damages suffered by the plaintiff is measured, to a significant extent, in function with the defendant's motive – the more reprehensible the conduct, the greater the impact on the victim and the greater the award.[8] If valid, additional awards for punitive damages based on the same criteria of reprehensibility would lead to a double-counting problem.[9] Furthermore, to the degree that nonpecuniary damages are affected by the wantonness of the defendant's conduct, an argument can be made that awards of pain and suffering already – though covertly – contain an element of sanction. Hence, this reasoning goes, it is highly likely that higher awards for nonpecuniary damages in cases of reprehensible behavior already include a significant punitive component that would not be present in the event of wrongdoing that lacked comparable dimensions of wantonness.

B AGGRAVATED DAMAGES

Continuing, the deliberateness of the wrongdoing plays an important role in so-called aggravated damages, which regard "the [wanton] manner in which the wrong is committed as having a relational significance that properly entitles the victim to claim a higher level of damages from the tortfeasor."[10] Aggravated damages allow damage awards to be augmented where a tort is committed under particularly humiliating or distressing circumstances. They are an added compensation to a plaintiff for injury to her feelings and dignity caused by the manner in which the defendant acted.[11] Indeed, aggravated damage awards have generally been held to

[7] *State Farm Mut Auto Ins Co* v. *Campbell*, 538 US 408, 426 (2003).

[8] Theodore Sedgwick first raised this problem observing that sometimes the amount of pain and suffering experienced by the plaintiff was a function of the defendant's motive. See T. Sedgwick, A *Treatise on the Measure of Damages* (7th ed.) (Baker, Voorhis & Co., 1880).

[9] For instance, Justice Foster's opposition to punitive damages stemmed from the fact that they were an impermissible form of "double counting," see *Fay* v. *Parker* [1873] 53 NH 342, 361–62.

[10] See E. J. Weinrib, "Civil Recourse and Corrective Justice" (2011) 39 *Florida State University Law Review* 273, 293.

[11] On this point, see A. Ripstein, *Equality, Responsibility and the Law* (Cambridge University Press, 2012), p. 150 (referring that "aggravating circumstances surrounding a tort may lead to aggravated damages because they can be seen as aggravating the plaintiff's injury."). Similarly, see Weinrib, "Civil Recourse and Corrective Justice," 292.

be compensatory in nature and are usually accorded when plaintiff's harm involves injury to the plaintiff's feelings caused by insult, humiliation, shame, degradation, or dishonor, particularly in actions involving intentional torts.[12]

Aggravated damages are a common feature in England[13]; however, they have largely been overlooked in the United States,[14] with the exception of a few American scholars who have recently started to study them.[15] The idea of aggravated damages was first articulated in the English precedent *Rookes* v. *Barnard*, where Lord Devlin restricted punitive damages to exceptional categories of torts while introducing the distinction between punitive damages stricto sensu and aggravated damages. According to Lord Devlin, "in cases where the damages are at large the jury [...] can take into account the motives and conduct of the defendant where they aggravate the injury done to the plaintiff. [...] These [malevolence or spite or the manner of committing the wrong] are matters which the jury can take into account in assessing the appropriate compensation."[16]

Since then, aggravated damages have raised strong disagreement among scholars and commentators, mainly because drawing a clear line between them and punitive damages is extremely difficult.[17] Even Lord Devlin acknowledged in *Rookes* that the line between the compensatory and the punitive aim of these remedies was not easy to draw.[18] Lord Devlin thought that restricting the availability of exemplary damages would "remove from the law a source of confusion between aggravated and exemplary damages which has troubled the learned commentators on the subject."[19] However, according to Lord Devlin's description of the cases in which damages

12 See generally A. Tettenborn, "Punitive Damages – A View from England" (2004) 41 *San Diego Law Review* 1551; J. Murphy, "The Nature and Domain of Aggravated Damages" (2010) 69 *Cambridge Law Journal* 353; M. Tilbury, "Aggravated Damages" (2018) 71 *Current Legal Problems* 215.

13 The use of the "aggravated damages" label and the distinction between the latter and punitive damages is more frequent in common law jurisdictions such as England, New Zealand, Australia, and Canada.

14 Describing some American scholars as "prisoners of their preoccupation with American tort law [...] not follow[ing] through on what [their reference to aggravated damages in other jurisdictions] implies," see Weinrib, "Civil Recourse and Corrective Justice," 292.

15 See, for example, J. C. P. Goldberg and B. C. Zipursky, "Civil Recourse Revisited" (2011) 39 *Florida State University Law Review* 273, 359–62; D. Markel, "How Should Punitive Damages Work?" (2009) 157 *University of Pennsylvania Law Review* 1383, 1387–97; D. G. Owen, "Aggravating Punitive Damages" (2010) 158 *University of Pennsylvania Law Review PENNumbra* 181, 192.

16 *Rookes* v. *Barnard* [1964] AC 1129, 1221.

17 For a description of the disagreement over aggravated damages generated in England by *Rookes* v. *Barnard*, see generally Murphy, "The Nature and Domain of Aggravated Damages." For an explanation on the judicial disagreement over punitive damages generated in England by *Rookes* v. *Barnard*, see J. Morgan, "Reforming Punitive Damages in English Law," in L. Meurkens and E. Nordin (eds.), *The Power of Punitive Damages. Is Europe Missing Out?* (Intersentia, 2012), pp. 184–89.

18 See *Rookes* 1221 ("when one examines the cases in which large damages have been awarded for conduct of this sort, it is not at all easy to say whether the idea of compensation or the idea of punishment has prevailed.").

19 Ibid 1230.

have been increased as a consequence of the defendant's wanton manner of causing the injury, the increased awards can "more easily be justified on that ground [of aggravated damages] than on the ground that they were exemplary."[20] Furthermore, he added that "[a]ggravated damages in this type of case can do most, if not all, of the work that could be done by exemplary damages."[21] This clearly shows that Lord Devlin was not necessarily regarding aggravated damages as strictly compensatory but rather emphasizing the exceptional nature of exemplary damages, since most cases can be treated as aggravated damages. To be sure, this approach does not necessarily rule out a punitive component for aggravated damages – quite the contrary, it seems to recognize it (even if punishment occurs accidentally).[22] However, only a few scholars have argued that aggravated damages are indistinguishable from punitive damages (or "punitive damages in disguise") since they both focus on the defendant's behavior and are triggered by the same threshold of reprehensible conduct.[23] Rather, most legal scholars and commentators have strived to show that aggravated damages are clearly compensatory in that they are awarded when the wantonness of the defendant's conduct aggravates the plaintiff's injury.[24]

According to Alan Beever, aggravated damages "compensate for violations of dignitary interests," which justifies the focus on the defendant's behavior as necessary to discover the injury to dignity given that "our sole epistemological access to the

[20] Ibid 1229.

[21] Ibid 1230.

[22] Similarly, see J. Goudkamp and E. Katsampouka, "Punitive Damages: Ten Misconceptions," in E. Bant, W. Courtney, J. Goudkamp and J. M. Paterson (eds.), *Punishment and Private Law* (Hart Publishing, 2021), p. 204. But see J. Murphy, "Anomalies in Tort Law: A Cause for Concern?" (2023) 86 *Modern Law Review* 872, 888 (questioning that "punishment *by accident* can hardly be taken as evidence of the courts pursuing [a] retributive agenda.") (emphasis in the original).

[23] Advocating for this view, see, for example, P. Cane, *The Anatomy of Tort Law* (Hart Publishing, 1997), p. 114 (arguing that "aggravated damages are effectively indistinguishable from punitive damages, and in [his] view, they should be abolished."); J. Goudkamp and E. Katsampouka, "Punitive Damages and the Place of Punishment in Private Law" (2021) 84 *Modern Law Review* 1257, 1277–79 (showing ample examples on how English courts sometimes award aggravated damages in order to punish the defendant and on how they consider, in deciding whether to award and quantifying them, the same factors that they bear in mind when awarding punitive damages); B. Feldthusen, "Punitive Damages: Hard Choices and Hight Stakes" (1998) *New Zealand Law Review* 714, 750 (arguing that even when a theoretical distinction can be drawn, there is probably no practical difference between aggravated and exemplary damages).

[24] For scholarly work emphasizing the compensatory angle, see, for example, Murphy, "The Nature and Domain of Aggravated Damages," 359 ("the aggravated damages due are to compensate the injury to dignity, not to punish the tortfeasor"); A. Beever, "The Structure of Aggravated and Exemplary Damages" (2003) 23 *Oxford Journal of Legal Studies* 87, 92–93 ("it is plausible to regard aggravated damages as genuinely compensatory"); Tilbury, "Aggravated Damages," 243 (arguing that aggravated damages are justified in the need to avoid the risk of under-compensation of claimants who have suffered injuries that have no objective monetary value, but that have been exacerbated by the egregious manner in which the wrong occurred). Moreover, see Law Commission, *Aggravated, Exemplary and Restitutionary Damages*, Law Com 247 [1997] 2.1 ("[aggravated damages] are damages awarded for a tort as compensation for the plaintiff's mental distress.").

claimant's injury is through the examination of the defendant's actions."[25] In his view, the focus on the defendant's conduct is thus not problematic since it is only concerned with vindicating the plaintiff's rights and not with expressing condemnation of the defendant. Similarly, John Murphy has argued that aggravated damages compensate injuries to the claimant's dignity in some objectively verifiable way.[26] Ernest Weinrib, for his part, argues that aggravated damages "compensate [...] for the injury that high-handed wrongdoing does to the plaintiff's dignity"; they are "a [compensatory] response to the dignitary aggravation of a wrong."[27] He conceives the wrong as an injury to the right-holder's dignity in the subjective sense (an intangible loss)[28]; therefore, he regards the awarding of aggravated damages as reparation for injury.[29] Similarly, other scholars have argued that "where there is already injury in place that the law recognizes as damages, this added 'insult' to injury would count more accurately as 'aggravated,' than as punitive, damages."[30]

Following the same logic, Dan Markel has emphasized that "the utilization of enhanced awards to repair the injury that the defendant's misconduct caused to the plaintiff's dignity, [...] are more precisely labeled 'aggravated' damages, as they are called in various common law jurisdictions."[31] Indeed, according to Markel's pluralistic structure, punitive damages are also meant to advance nonretributive goals such as compensation of the injury to the dignity of the victim – what he calls "aggravated damages" or "victim vindication."[32] Under his framework, aggravated damages are nonretributive, serve a compensatory role, and are available only if dignitary harms are not already covered under classic compensatory damages awards.[33] While Markel distinguishes himself from punitive damage scholars who articulate victim vindication in terms of punishment and retribution, his main purpose in doing so is to make the argument that, even though other scholars present themselves as refining the relationship between punitive damages and retributive justice, their conceptions are better understood as more consistent with his conception of compensatory aggravated damages. Thus, Markel argues that these "retributive"

25 See Beever, "The Structure of Aggravated and Exemplary Damages," 90.

26 See Murphy, "The Nature and Domain of Aggravated Damages," 376.

27 See Weinrib, "Civil Recourse and Corrective Justice," 292.

28 See E. J. Weinrib, "Punishment and Disgorgement as Contract Remedies" (2003) 78 *Chicago-Kent Law Review* 55, 91.

29 See Weinrib, "Civil Recourse and Corrective Justice," 289.

30 See B. Chapman and M. Trebilcock, "Punitive Damages: Divergence in Search of a Rationale" (1989) 40 *Alabama Law Review* 741, 763 (discussing aggravated damages for compensation of dignity harms). In a similar line of thinking, see Owen, "Aggravating Punitive Damages," 192.

31 See Markel, "How Should Punitive Damages Work?," 1395.

32 Ibid 1387 n4 (arguing that aggravated damages "are meant to account for, and thereby vindicate, that part of a victim's injury, not already compensated in all jurisdictions, for insults to one's personal dignity.").

33 Ibid 1416–17, and 1420. However, Markel displays certain inconsistencies when dealing with the nature of aggravated damages: While in some sections of his work he refers to them as compensatory in nature; in others, he includes them under the umbrella of extra-compensatory damages.

accounts of victim vindication should be translated into a compensatory rationale.[34] Similarly, David Owen has recently offered a reparative (or restorative) account of punitive damages. It is his understanding that, contrary to the usual interpretation of their declared goals of punishment and deterrence, punitive damages are normally imposed by juries and courts to provide additional compensation to victims of aggravated wrongs by awarding them the "aggravated" damages to which they are entitled.[35]

The underlying claim that can be inferred from these accounts of aggravated damages is that compensatory remedies already play in tort law the role that is ascribed to punitive-damages-as-victim-vindication. More precisely, these scholars do not see a distinction worth drawing between "vindicating" the plaintiff's dignitary interest and "compensating" the plaintiff for such injury since both are ultimately a compensatory response.[36] As a result, these authors oppose punitive damages because they do not see the sense of introducing an additional institution rooted in punishment and retribution to vindicate the victim's dignitary interests. In their view, "vindication" and "condemnation" are dichotomous,[37] even though the claim that the plaintiff's rights are vindicated through condemnation of the defendant's conduct is perfectly plausible – as I argued earlier when discussing *Relational Retribution*. Instead, they argue that aggravated damages awards can handle the task just as well in the same kinds of cases by according higher compensatory damages awards to the plaintiff. Consequently, they conclude that the distinction between punitive damages (for victim vindication) and aggravated damages is largely redundant and therefore not worth the effort to introduce because, at the end of the day, they believe all these awards boil down to increased compensation.

C DISTINGUISHING PUNISHMENT FROM COMPENSATION

The two critical accounts I have just summarized raise important questions to consider: Are these "compensatory" responses satisfactory or do compensatory approaches to punishment miss something? After examining the redundancy critique of punitive awards (namely, the double-counting issue), are there good reasons

34 Ibid 1396 n40, and 1416.

35 See Owen, "Aggravating Punitive Damages," 192.

36 For a different take on this, see Ripstein, "Equality, Responsibility and the Law," p. 151 (when referring to the early case of *Wooden-Ware Co.* v. *United States*, 106 US 432 [1882], he expresses that "although the victim suffered an additional dignitary loss, and the punitive damages serve to address that loss, their purpose is not to compensate for it. Indeed, their point is precisely that the dignitary loss is not compensable. They serve instead to vindicate the right."); and Goldberg and Zipursky, "Civil Recourse Revisited," 361 (arguing that the concept of "aggravated damages" does not capture the notion that "there is little plausibility in the claim that a monetary damages award actually serves to repair a rupture in dignity.").

37 Similarly, see J. N. E. Varuhas, "The Concept of 'Vindication' in the Law of Torts: Rights, Interests and Damages" (2014) 34 *Oxford Journal of Legal Studies* 253, 268.

to distinguish punishment from compensation? One possible reply is that those reduction-to-compensation accounts overlook the potential value of the role of punishment in tort law. One problem with those reconstructions that prevents them from fully appreciating the importance of the retributive aspect of the equation is the disproportionate attention on the quantitative dimension of the issue. Indeed, their focus is on the double-counting aspect common to both these critiques of punitive damages: They argue that the "punitive element" is already covered in either higher pain and suffering awards or complementary aggravated damages awards. In other words, these critiques overlook an important qualitative aspect, namely, the relevance and significance of explicitly distinguishing compensation for the dignitary harm suffered by the victim from punishment for the reprehensibility of the wrongdoer's conduct invoked to uphold the victim's dignitary interest.

For instance, Anthony Sebok distinguishes among different orders of rights violations in an attempt to draw a line between compensatory and punitive remedies.[38] According to Sebok, when a defendant's wrongful treatment violates a private right possessed by the plaintiff without any regard for the plaintiff's possession of that right, the defendant has violated at least two rights: the primary right (to physical security, property, etc.) and the right to be treated as someone deserving respect for those primary rights.[39] The idea is that the defendant's intentional invasion of the plaintiff's primary rights instantiated a certain attitude toward the plaintiff's primary rights, namely the attitude that she is free to violate them. Thus, for Sebok, "this attitude – that the plaintiff's primary rights are not worthy of respect – maps the borderline between claims for compensatory damages and claims for punitive damages."[40]

Indeed, when victims are confronted with egregious or humiliating wrongdoing, they seek vindication for the invasion of their dignitary interest through the imposition of a punishment (punitive award) as a means of value affirmation that is independent and apart from their claims for compensation for the factual consequences of the wrong (e.g., the emotional and mental distress). As I have already argued, compensation and punishment are distinct relational responses to instances of wrongdoing that has befallen us, and, as such, it makes sense to inquire whether these qualitatively different responses warrant separate treatment. This point is

38 See A. J. Sebok, "Normative Theories of Punitive Damages: The Case of Deterrence," in J. Oberdiek (ed.), *Philosophical Foundations of the Law of Torts* (Oxford University Press, 2014), p. 327 (pointing out that "[c]onflating the reasons for punishment and compensation mischaracterizes what occurs when common law courts turn to the question of punishment in torts cases."). Also see Sedgwick, A Treatise on the Measure of Damages, 357 (Sedgwick insisted that the fact that the wrongdoer's motive might determine both compensatory damages for pain and suffering and exemplary damages did not mean that they should produce identical damage awards because they were not grounded on the same wrong).

39 See generally A. J. Sebok, "Punitive Damages: From Myth to Theory" (2007) 92 *Iowa Law Review* 957.

40 Ibid 1014.

reinforced by the uncertainty over the just and proportionate amount of punishment that should be imposed that is generated when the punitive component is meted covertly under the label of compensatory remedies – we should call punishment for what it is in order to question it as such.

Even in those jurisdictions (such as Mexico) where effort is made to conceptually demarcate the punitive and compensatory facets of nonpecuniary damages by providing each with a differentiated treatment, the problem persists because the availability and recognition of punitive awards hinge on the availability and recognition of the nonpecuniary damages.[41] By consequence, the availability of punishment might be excluded in wrongful situations that involve particularly reprehensible behavior deserving of sanction but in which, for some reason, the claim for nonpecuniary damages is not successful or directly not legally recognized as such under that particular legal system. Timely examples are found in reprehensible tortious cases involving value-diminishing invasions of privacy and various types of harassment (online or otherwise), which mostly involve intangible harms (e.g., addiction, depression, diminished self-esteem, among others) that are extremely difficult to establish as legally protected in the current practice of most tort systems across jurisdictions. These examples certainly reinforce the need to disentangle punishment from compensation. In sum, linking the punitive claim to the compensatory claim for nonpecuniary damages not only ignores the relevance of the conceptual distinction between punishment and compensation, but it also undermines the attention punishment deserves in its own right from the availability and recognition of other types of damages.

This qualitative distinction between punishment and compensation is important for at least two main reasons: the expressive dimension of sanctions and their proportionality. Both are briefly explored in what follows.

a *The Expressive Dimension of Sanctions*

The main argument against compensatory reductionism is that, in superimposing punishment upon compensation, it dilutes the expressive function of the punitive sanction to a vanishing point. This occurs both when the defendant's wrongful conduct is covertly sanctioned through higher compensatory awards (mostly under the label of nonpecuniary damages) and when wrongs are discreetly compensated under the label of aggravated damages for pain suffered by the victim rather than as punishment for egregious behavior. Even though it could still be argued that augmented compensatory remedies for pain and suffering and aggravated damages already contain some measurement of punishment because they do indeed take into account the reprehensible character of the defendant's conduct, they do so in a narrower,

[41] I have explored this point in Section C of Chapter 2.

short-sighted sense. They focus only on the immediate transactional consequences of the wrong in that, as explained earlier, the reprehensible manner of the commission of the wrong is likely to have increased the loss suffered (i.e., the emotional harm caused by the reprehensible conduct is greater). However, as Joel Feinberg has expressed, punishment loses much of its meaning if it is not made known.[42] It is important to transmit the message that the action in question is one that calls for punishment specifically due to its reprehensibility. As Scott Hershovitz asserts in the specific context of tort law, "punitive damages help mark the gravity of the wrong" and "[t]hey do justice through the message that they send about the victim's standing and the wrongdoer's responsibility."[43] Recall that under Hershovitz's expressive account of tort law, the concept of tort addresses the wrong in that the tort remedy intends to recognize and address the fact that a wrong has been committed against another.[44]

If we do not intelligibly differentiate punishment from compensation, clearly distinguishing wrongful conducts that merit a retributive response from those that demand a solely compensatory one is not always possible. This is highly problematic for at least two reasons: (1) lumping them together prevents us from clearly conveying moral condemnation of wrongful conducts that are not to be tolerated because they violate the basic standards on how we should treat one another in our society; and (2) it closes a legitimate avenue for the victim to achieve value affirmation by expressing her condemnatory sense of the effect that the reprehensible, undeserved wrongdoing had on her life (her experience of injury), and, in this way, it closes an avenue for her to reassert her true value vis-à-vis the offender.

Indeed, those reductionist responses do not and cannot comprehensively capture either the moral wrong of the act in question or the moral significance of the wrongdoing for the victim involved in that they lack condemnatory quality. In other words, they end up once again overlooking the victim's perspective: the connection between the distinct manner in which the defendant invaded the victim's dignitary interest and the victim's correlative retributive motivations, which are elicited by the inherent value attributed to the invaded interest and the victim's need for valuation affirmation through condemnation. Indeed, underlying the retributive rationale is value affirmation as a means to acknowledge the meaning of the invasion to the victim's dignitary interest. All this lies behind the retributive motivations (moral outrage and betrayal aversion) that serious acts of disrespect elicit, provoking the victim's call for a distinctive retributive response that reflects and is understood to reflect the moral significance of the wrongdoing by conveying a clear condemnatory message that aptly captures the meaning of the dignitary invasion and the need for value affirmation.

42 See J. Feinberg, "The Expressive Function of Punishment," in J. Feinberg, *Doing and Deserving: Essays in the Theory of Responsibility* (Princeton University Press, 1970), pp. 95–118.

43 See S. Hershovitz, "Tort as a Substitute for Revenge," in J. Oberdiek (ed.), *Philosophical Foundations of the Law of Torts* (Oxford University Press, 2014), p. 97.

44 On Hershovitz's account, see Section D of Chapter 2.

The idea is that unexcused moral wrongs demand expression of the other-regarding values affected in those situations.[45] Sanctioning the defendant is justified not only in order to vindicate the plaintiff's dignitary interest following reprehensible wrongful conduct whose content expresses lack of respect for her but also in order to condemn conduct that offends the moral and legal standards of the society in which we are immersed.[46] Furthermore, an important element of the expressive function of sanctions is identifying the conducts that are seen as an affront to our common understanding of standards for mutual treatment among members of society. The imposition of the sanction (i.e., punitive damages) expresses to the wider society that the defendant's treatment of the victim and the diminished status the defendant's action implicitly attributed to the victim are inappropriate (i.e., it conveys a moral judgment regarding the inappropriateness of the defendant's behavior).[47]

Once again, the proposal that we channel reprobation through compensation, on the other hand, implicitly conveys the message that there is nothing qualitatively different between common damage awards for accidental harm and damage awards for outrageous, wanton, humiliating, or distressing behavior that violates dignitary interests. This is because the expression of the particular manner in which the plaintiff's dignitary interest was violated is mainly limited to require the defendant to pay more through higher compensatory pain and suffering awards or aggravated damages awards. Certainly, these steeper awards send the message that egregious wrongdoing leads to higher compensatory awards (i.e., quantitative difference) but they do not necessarily convey the specific motives for the greater compensation (regarding the nature of the egregiousness of the behavior) that is respectful of the significance of the retributive motivations elicited in those particularly egregious circumstances of wrongdoing, which add an extra condemnatory dimension to the wrong. By treating punishment and compensation as interchangeable, we risk giving the impression that those damages are no more than a "price" whose payment makes up for reprehensible conduct rather than representing a genuine "sanction" for the reprehensible behavior. It is in the latter sense that the distinction has intrinsic importance.

45 Similarly, see P. Hieronymi, "Articulating an Uncompromising Forgiveness" (2001) 62 *Philosophy and Phenomenological Research* 529, 546 (asserting that "[a] past wrong against you, standing in your history without apology, atonement, retribution, punishment, restitution, condemnation, or anything else that might recognize it as a wrong, makes a claim. It says, in effect, that you can be treated this way, and that such treatment is acceptable.").

46 On this point, see J. G. Murphy, "Forgiveness and Resentment," in J. G. Murphy and J. Hampton (eds.), *Forgiveness and Mercy* (Cambridge University Press, 1988), p. 25 (arguing that the decision not to punish is also expressive: It communicates to the victim and to the wider society the idea that such treatment, and the status it attributes the victim, are appropriate); Hershovitz, "Tort as a Substitute for Revenge," 102 (arguing that courts do not render justice by moving money around in response to wrongdoing but rather through the messages they send about our relations with one another).

47 Similarly, M. Chamallas and J. Wriggins, *The Measure of Injury: Race, Gender, and Tort Law* (New York University Press, 2010) (underscoring the expressive importance of tort damages as a signal of the plaintiffs' social worth).

It becomes extremely relevant to make explicit both the specific conduct we are sanctioning when we impose punitive damages and the reasons why we pursue a punitive response. In this sense, the distinction between punishment and compensation becomes essential if we are really committed to sending the right messages. The point is that different damages awards (pain and suffering, punitive, aggravated) have distinctive meanings and communicate discrete messages beyond the general communicative feature of tort remedies – which conveys that the fact that the defendant has to pay damages to the plaintiff communicates that the former has committed a wrong that was a wrong to the latter.

b *The Proportionality of Sanctions*

Because compensatory damages awards are rectificatory, their focus is by definition on the impact of the defendant's conduct on the individual victim (i.e., the harm inflicted) and attempt to restore the victim to her rightful position. On the basis of that impact (i.e., the effect on the victim's tangible and intangible protected interests), the judge in the tort process determines the proper amount of damages to be awarded to the plaintiff, which acquires a subjective tinge and varies according to the particular circumstances of the victim in question. Conversely, when the individual victim seeks punishment (i.e., the imposition of a punitive award), the tort process must be reoriented toward the identification of the seriousness of the defendant's conduct with relation to the plaintiff who demands the imposition of the retributive response. The conduct displayed by the defendant is objectively reprehensible and its sanction must necessarily be evaluated by the judge separately from the subjective characteristics of the victim (which should only be relevant to decide on the parallel claim for nonpecuniary damages). In that sense, the conduct of someone who injures a pedestrian while driving drunk is objectively reprehensible, regardless of whether the victim (the pedestrian) is a successful pianist, a law professor, or a beggar, because all of them have equal moral worth and deserve to be treated with equal consideration and respect by the wrongdoer. This example brings out the importance of properly identifying the specific conduct to be sanctioned and delineating it from the consequential impact of that conduct on the individual victim. In order to respond proportionally to the seriousness of the defendant's behavior in a qualitative sense, we require assurance that only reprehensible conduct that merits a retributive response will be sanctioned.

Assuming the defendant's conduct merits sanction, the judge must then determine the amount of the award in direct proportion to the seriousness of the offence in a quantitative sense. Since reductionist practices of awarding damages do not explicitly distinguish between compensation and punishment, they are inconsistent with the proportionality requirements for the imposition of a sanction. They fail to respond qualitatively and quantitatively in proportion to the seriousness of the offence. Rather, they respond exclusively to the impact of sanctionable conduct on the victim, impairing any possibility of control over the just and proportionate punishment that should be imposed for the reprehensible conduct. Ultimately, any sanction imposed by the state, whether through criminal law or tort law, should be called, treated, and controlled as such to make sure that it is proportional to the gravity of the sanctioned conduct.[48] Admittedly, the classic tort process would generally require redesigning to adequately channel demands for punishment and properly guide the procedural activity of the parties and the courts.[49] For instance, relevant questions include how to tackle multiple punishments, whether to introduce distinctive rules for shifting the burden of proof, and whether punitive claims require stricter standards of proofs (such as "clear and convincing evidence") than the typical "preponderance of evidence" standard for compensatory claims. After all, defendants should be afforded a form of respect through the tort process as well – I discuss some of these aspects in Part IV.

Ultimately, the bottom line is that the conceptual distinction between punishment and compensation and the practical implications for differentiated treatment that derive from it are far from trivial and demand a thorough and more refined debate not only on the general question of the proper place for punishment in tort law but also, in particular, on the level of relative autonomy between compensatory and punitive responses to wrongdoing. Continuing the widely acknowledged practice of punishing in covert fashion as if it were legitimate or justified does not seem acceptable. The time has come to recognize that we do sometimes punish under the framework of tort law and to give punishment the space and specific treatment that it requires in the context of the different legal systems.

◊ ◊ ◊

CONCLUDING REMARKS

In accounting for the ongoing existence of punitive damages, scholars have (over) emphasized the wrongdoer's behavior and, as a consequence, failed to give victims' retributive responses the attention they deserve. This focus has devoted too much attention to the deterrent aspect of punitive damages (i.e., the argument that they ought to be calibrated to achieve deterrence). Deterrence may well be the value most cited in legalist accounts, although accredited research in the social sciences has clearly shown that deterring future wrongdoing simply does not figure significantly among the motivations that drive punitive responses when individuals are confronted with specific instances of reprehensible behavior and that calculating

48 Similarly, see L. Zedner, "Reparation and Retribution: Are They Reconcilable?" (1994) 57 *Modern Law Review* 228, 248.

49 Whether procedural redesign would be needed (or the extent of the needed revision) ultimately depends on the features of each jurisdiction.

the precise degree of punishment that deters the conduct in question factors very little. Conversely, the available empirical findings demonstrate that the retributive dimension of punitive damages aligns more closely with moral intuitions than the deterrent objective.

The study of moral outrage and betrayal aversion brings to light the underlying values at the core of the retributive motivations that are triggered when people confront certain types of reprehensible misbehavior, in particular those that undermine their autonomy of action or cause serious harm. It suggests that a more meaningful understanding of punitive damages can thus be found in the rich value-laden lay intuitions that drive people to punish certain behaviors through tort law. Moral outrage and betrayal aversion possess, in certain tortious settings, a logic and structure that makes them appropriate responses to instances of reprehensible wrongdoing. Studies demonstrate that moral outrage and betrayal aversion are two powerful retributive motivations behind "reactive attitudes" to punish those who wrong us in a reprehensible fashion that obey their own rationality. It turns out that tort victims' retributive responses to reprehensible wrongdoing involve much more than the mere imposition of punishment: They involve affirmation of self-worth through recognition of self-identity and equal moral status in the community and the meaning they construe from the circumstances of reprehensible wrongdoing that threatens their individual autonomy, dignity, physical integrity, or even life.

These retributive motivations hold meaning; they express other-regarding values and comprise a significant, as yet missing element in the predominant understanding of punitive damages. To integrate the insights retributive motivations hold, purely rationalistic approaches to punitive damages might well be complemented with a more expansive approach that leaves room for the respectful consideration of emotive-intuitive responses. According to this expanded logic, punitive damages should be reelaborated so that the denser, deeper, and richer retributive motivations of individual tort victims to certain serious acts of disrespect are properly addressed. This is not to say that tort law should categorically look for legitimacy in retributive motivations. It means that following the unreflective path of plainly denying, suppressing, or directly ignoring the widely acknowledged emotional component that our retributive responses express as powerful forms of moral communication leaves a crucial factor out of the equation. The challenge undertaken is just this, completing the equation by better capturing the constructive features of retributive motivations and mapping them out against the social practices and institutional frameworks that might give them meaningful expression and proper constraint. Only with a full picture of the retributive motivations, social practices, and institutional frameworks will it be possible to determine whether punitive damages work as a valuable, normatively fitting response to reprehensible wrongdoing. The time is ripe to integrate into tort responses considerations that more accurately reflect the significance and meaning of the particular circumstances of the wrongdoing for both the private parties involved and society as a whole.

Importantly, Part II adds a new, fundamental dimension to the current narrative by developing the missing retributive components of a robust alternative to the dominant deterrence theories of punitive damages. Following a cross-disciplinary approach that enriches tort law with insights from the literature on social cognition regarding victims' retributive motivations, from moral philosophy on "reactive attitudes" and from the criminal law debates over the retributive justifications for the imposition of punishment, Part II devises the novel notion of *Relational Retribution*. This notion not only offers an analytical framework to think about punitive damages across jurisdictions but also, most importantly, unchains the classic approach to punishment in torts from the exclusive and unilateral perspective of the defendant (wrongdoer perspective), taking a novel tack that purports to fully integrate the long-overlooked perspective of the victim of value-diminishing reprehensible wrongdoing who seeks the imposition of a punitive award through tort law (wrongdoer-victim perspective). *Relational Retribution* comfortably suits both the bilateral structure of tort law and the proactive role traditionally allocated to the victim in tort litigation. By recognizing the necessary interconnection between defendant and claimant, *Relational Retribution* not only implies proportional punishment for the imposition of a deserved monetary sanction for reprehensible behavior but also highlights the significance of the wrongdoing for victims – the correlative retributive motivations of tort victims of seriously disrespectful actions who seek the imposition of the punitive award – and their authentic demand for denunciation and value affirmation. Importantly, devising a relational retributive account of punitive damages that links wrongdoers and their victims poses a challenge to the long-standing criticism from corrective justice accounts of tort law, which argue that punitive damages are exclusively concerned with communitarian interests that lie outside the interests of the private parties involved. Moreover, it poses a challenge to the few normative reconstructions of punitive damages, particularly those from the law and economics camp, which have overemphasized the utilitarian consequences of punitive awards by anchoring their justification in their usefulness as a tool to internalize costs and achieve optimal deterrence (which, ultimately, reduce punishment to deterrence). Last, while attempts to reduce punishment to compensation compete for dominance, none of them clarifies, as *Relational Retribution* does, its justifications such that the retributive, compensatory, and deterrent dimensions of the law of torts are properly identified and distinguished.

PART III

Retribution in the Mass-Market Setting

OVERVIEW

Assessing retribution in the mass-market setting is particularly relevant to the enterprise of understanding the ultimate justification for punitive responses in the product liability context, one in which punitive damages are regularly imposed (in the United States at least) on callous corporations for marketing defective products in wanton disregard for consumer safety. For this enterprise, Chapter 6 differentiates among the various manners through which individuals and collective entities typically engage in reprehensible value-diminishing tortious behavior and, on that basis, identifies two distinct contexts of wrongdoing: (1) the one-on-one context associated with the classic interpersonal tortious situations where one individual directs her conduct toward another individual (e.g., personal insult, defamation, or the more contemporary dignitary torts such as cyberbullying or online harassment), and (2) the collective context involving tortious situations arising from impersonal market transactions between consumers and corporations (most notoriously, the deliberate sale of unsafe products for private gain). Chapter 6 makes the case that a sufficiently informed conversation on the place of punishment and retribution in the mass-market context (particularly, the place of punitive awards in product liability litigation) requires an improved understanding of both the relevant markers for reprehensible corporate behavior in that particular context and the correlative retributive motivations of consumers that are elicited in those particularly value-diminishing reprehensible wrongful situations.

In order to make evident the particular power dynamics that frame the consumer-manufacturer relationship in the mass-market context, Chapter 6 insists on the importance of taking into account the influence of the contextual dynamics in the mass-market setting of productive activities – particularly the pervasive asymmetry, between manufacturers and consumers, of information pertaining to the product's safety – in any attempt to understand punitive awards against modern corporate wrongdoing. The aim of Chapter 6 is twofold: it seeks (1) to identify the significance of mechanisms in product liability regimes meant to restore balance in the consumer-manufacturer relationship; and (2) to set the stage for further examination of the place and role of punitive damages in product liability litigation as an institution that not only empowers consumers to obtain private redress but also provides a legitimate channel to communicate self-regard through the courts by denouncing the open violations of societal trust that manufacturers' wrongful behaviors convey when they fail to fulfil consumers' safety expectations by prioritizing their own private gain over the risk of significant harm to consumers.

Building on this line of thinking, Chapter 7 advances an understanding of punitive damages in the product liability context centered on consumers' betrayal aversion as the relational retributive motivation that responds to violations of societal trust in the marketplace. By contrasting two different approaches to "societal trust," *Expert* versus *Layperson*, Chapter 7 argues that punitive damages should be understood as relational retributive sanctions that communicate disapproval for purposes of the victims' self-assertion, not as prices solely meant to fine-tune cost-benefit formulas to attain optimal deterrence. Ultimately, Chapter 7 develops an expressive dimension of punitive awards as yet unexplored but worth maintaining. This is the dimension that becomes clear when we distinguish retribution from deterrence in open violations of societal trust by corporations in the mass-market context. Last, Chapter 8 shows how this novel angle of the discussion on the place of punitive damages in product liability litigation further illuminates the debate over the consequential impact of the distinctive design defect liability tests (Consumer Expectations; Risk-Utility), which are operative in the product liability context of various legal systems. This is particularly relevant in the context of current global discussions over adopting or revising product liability laws to address the evolving risks to consumer safety posed by artificial intelligence. Moreover, the extent to which product liability lawsuits and direct risk regulation interact as complementary legitimate avenues for fostering consumer safety is briefly discussed, with an eye to provoking fresh deliberation over product liability regimes that are responsive to the safety challenges posed by artificial intelligence and other new technologies in the marketplace.

6

Understanding the Collective Context of Wrongdoing

The distinctive feature of the classic torts setting is the interpersonal interaction between the defendant and the individual victim. This basically means that the defendant's wrongful conduct is directed toward an individualized person, representing one-on-one interactions that are characteristic of the classic torts setting. In this individual setting, the offender's wrongful conduct directed toward the victim is understood as a violation of the particular norms for proper treatment of the individual victim by the defendant (i.e., it alludes to norms for interaction and engagement with one another). Historically, this interpersonal aspect has been a predominant feature in most English and American punitive damages awards during the nineteenth century, which involved the behavior of an individual defendant that was particularly humiliating to a specific plaintiff.[1] A paradigmatic example is the 1872 Illinois case of *Alcorn* v. *Mitchell* in which a jury awarded punitive damages to a plaintiff who was spat upon.[2] In those days, punitive damages were only awarded for a relatively small number of torts involving conscious and intentional harm inflicted by one person to another.[3] The list of intentional torts included assault and battery, libel and slander, and intentional interference with property.[4] As some commentators have described, punitive damages were used for personal vindication in those cases. They allowed the plaintiff to actively

[1] On this point, see A. J. Sebok, "Punitive Damages: From Myth to Theory" (2007) 92 *Iowa Law Review* 957, 1009 (reporting that the common thread in early English and American cases focused on the insulting and humiliating character of the defendant's act).

[2] For more details on this case, see S. Hershovitz, "Tort as a Substitute for Revenge," in J. Oberdiek (ed.), *Philosophical Foundations of the Law of Torts* (Oxford University Press, 2014), p. 86.

[3] For an explanation of England's law of punitive damages, see P. Cane, *The Anatomy of Tort Law* (Hart Publishing, 1997), p. 115. Also, for the historical roots of punitive damages, see A. Calnan, "Ending the Punitive Damage Debate" (1995) 45 *DePaul Law Review* 101.

[4] For examples of early punitive damages in the United States, see R. W. Hammesfahr and L. S. Nugent, *Punitive Damages: A State-by-State Guide to Law and Practice* (West Publishing, 2012–13), p. 6. For examples regarding early punitive damages cases in England, see A. Tettenborn, "Punitive Damages – A View from England" (2004) 41 *San Diego Law Review* 1551, 1552–53.

address the defendant and rescue her honor.[5] Similarly, the American Restatement (Second) of Torts stated that "[f]or certain types of dignitary torts, the law serves the purpose of vindicating the injured party. Thus, in suits for defamation, invasion of privacy or interference with civil rights, the major purpose of the suit may be to obtain a public declaration that the plaintiff is right and was improperly treated."[6] Nowadays, those traditional versions of dignitary harms are being revised to redress contemporary harms involving the use of new technologies such as revenge porn, cyberbullying, AI-generated defamation, and online harassment, among others.[7]

I now shift the focus from the classic individual tort setting to a mass-market setting dominated by large-scale impersonal market transactions of consumers with corporations. In the mass-market setting, it is not unusual to encounter manufacturers who engage in reprehensible practices (or schemes of systemic mistreatment) that show conscious or reckless disregard for the interests of others; practices that potentially and simultaneously affect an enormous number of people. Moreover, courts regularly hear lawsuits initiated by a plaintiff who denounces a flagrant practice that also affects a broader group of people who are not before the court (e.g., other consumers of the same dangerous product marketed as safe by the manufacturer). The physiognomy of the defendant-plaintiff equation in this context is very different from the original one-on-one tort setting: The defendant is generally a manufacturer engaging in fraudulent-type conduct for private gain that has the potential to cause widespread harm to a large number of consumers, and the plaintiff is usually just one of the many affected.[8]

Certainly, a person injured by a defective product does not necessarily experience the personal humiliation and embarrassment provoked by the invasions of dignity, such as being spat in the face, that originally gave rise to punitive damage awards in the eighteenth and nineteenth centuries. Nor is the experience necessarily similar to more contemporary dignitary harms, such as personal insult, defamation, or harassment, where the reprehensible conduct is still directed by one specific individual to another. Different contextual factors qualify our relationships with others that in turn shape the substantive content of our punitive reactions in distinctive ways. For instance, a distinctive qualitative difference is introduced by the lack of interpersonal interaction between the parties: The punitive response provoked by

5 Identifying personal vindication as one of the rationales of punitive damages according to the leading judicial opinions in the mid-nineteenth century, see A. Sebok, "What Did Punitive Damages Do? Why Misunderstanding the History of Punitive Damages Matters Today" (2003) 78 *Chicago-Kent Law Review* 163, 200. For historical background on punitive damages and the emphasis on honor and vindication, see D. Ellis, "Fairness and Efficiency in the Law of Punitive Damages" (1982) 56 *Southern California Law Review* 1, 12–20.

6 Restatement (Second) of Torts §903 (1979).

7 For example, the Cyber-Safety Act 2013 (Nova Scotia) created the tort of cyberbullying (s 21).

8 Asbestos-related diseases are a good example of widespread harm. The many deaths that resulted from asbestos were the outcome of asbestos manufacturers' active concealment of the danger of unprotected exposure.

the deliberate or reckless exposure of the consumer to risks that threaten individual autonomy, life, or limb by manufacturers who introduce the defective product in the market for private gain differs from the victim's punitive response to the reprehensible wrongdoing of a particular individual who acts in a humiliating, value-diminishing, or disrespectful way against her in particular. In the latter, the victim understands the direct affront to her dignitary interest as *personal*, while in the former, the affront is mediated and understood by the victim as *impersonal* in that it could also involve others who are similarly situated in relation to the wrongdoer.

In the mass-market setting, the wrongdoer's conduct is simple (or general) in the sense that it is not acting in a certain way against a particular individual person nameable in advance but against the public as a whole – it does not directly involve personal treatment. It involves actions against almost anyone who happens to be in a position to be affected (e.g., consumers of a knowingly defective product or of a certain fraudulent scheme). The focus of attention is on the carefulness that manufacturers owe consumers (e.g., the duty not to market defective products). The manufacturer who knowingly or recklessly sends to market a cancer-producing product breaches a duty owed to society at large (i.e., the duty of noninterference or the duty of noninjuriousness), not only a duty owed uniquely to an individual plaintiff who happened to develop the cancer as a result of taking the drug and subsequently bring a tort lawsuit.[9] For instance, marketing a defective automobile may not cause injury to everyone who purchases or rides in one, but it nevertheless causes a common danger of injury to all, and very likely results in actual injury to a number of people who cannot be identified in advance. The approach developed generally treats consumers as a collective body. Therefore, those interpersonal interactions that were at the core of the individual torts setting are absent, and in their place in the mass-market setting are, predominantly, impersonal market transactions.

Importantly, this impersonal feature of market transactions, however helpful for understanding the particularities and the typical dynamics of the mass-market context and the victim's punitive reactions to those instances of reprehensible corporate wrongdoing, does not necessarily do away with the relational character of the retributive rationale. This is because, even if a general duty of noninterference may be owed to the "public at large" or to "an indefinite class of persons" (e.g., potential consumers of a defective product), the particular duty of noninjury owed uniquely to the individual victim whose dignitary interest has been invaded by the reprehensibility of the defendant's conduct is always *relational* in the sense that only the victim herself is specially situated in relation to the wrongdoer to demand a punitive response – the victim's legal power to be punitive derives precisely from the violation of her dignitary interest affected by the reprehensibility

9 See A. Ripstein and B. C. Zipursky, "Corrective Justice in an Age of Mass Torts," in G. J. Postema (ed.), *Philosophy and the Law of Torts* (Cambridge University Press, 2001), pp. 218–19 (introducing the distinction between relational and nonrelational duties and noninjury and noninjuriousness duties).

of the defendant's conduct to her.[10] The victim is therefore the only party (not the state nor any third parties) who has the power to demand the imposition of a punitive award against the defendant.[11] In other words, the defendant is only vulnerable to the particular victim's demand for a punitive response. This encapsulates the structure of what Stephen Darwall and Julia Darwall call "relational or bipolar obligations," according to which "injured victims of violated bipolar obligations owed to them have a distinctive standing to hold their injurers responsible that neither third parties nor the community at large have."[12] In the authors' framework, the form of authority and accountability that underpins private law is a distinctive individual authority to whom the victim must bring claims, at her discretion, against the offender and hold her personally accountable.[13] The point is that "there is a special individual authority an obligee has to hold the obligor personally answerable that can [...] be exercised only by the right-holding obligee herself at her discretion."[14] In a similar line of thought, John Goldberg and Benjamin Zipursky hold that the vulnerability of the defendant does not only turn on whether the defendant committed a wrong; it also turns on who brings the lawsuit.[15] The plaintiff is seen as having a private power to exact remedies from those who have committed wrongs against her. An individual is only afforded a private power in light of her right to redress the wrong done to her. Once again, the condemnatory response (i.e., the punitive award) aims to encompass the specific situation of the wrongdoer and the individual victim as a means of recognizing the victim's dignitary interest not to be treated in the value-diminishing manner that the particular defendant demonstrated and to obtain appropriate recognition of her equal value vis-à-vis the wrongdoer.

A PUNISHMENT IN THE MASS-MARKET CONTEXT: AN OVERVIEW ACROSS JURISDICTIONS

We have thus witnessed a transition from remedies designed to punish one-on-one torts to remedies designed to deal with reckless corporate conduct performed with indifference toward the consequences for the health and safety of others that has

[10] Similarly, see J. C. P. Goldberg and B. C. Zipursky, "The Fraud-on-the-Market Tort" (2013) 66 *Vanderbilt Law Review* 1755, 1761. For the opposite view, see A. Beever, "The Structure of Aggravated and Exemplary Damages" (2003) 23 *Oxford Journal of Legal Studies* 87, 107 (claiming that "[l]iability for exemplary damages, is not a 'term of relation' between the parties, it results from 'a wrong to the public at large.' Exemplary damages do not operate in personam.").

[11] On the tort victims' legal power to be punitive, see Section A of Chapter 9.

[12] See S. Darwall and J. Darwall, "Civil Recourse as Mutual Accountability" (2011) 39 *Florida State University Law Review* 17, 19.

[13] Ibid 20, 24.

[14] Ibid 26.

[15] See generally J. C. P. Goldberg and B. C. Zipursky, *Recognizing Wrongs* (Harvard University Press, 2020).

widespread impact on the public as a whole. This transition helps to understand why the modern focus on American punitive damages shifted from intentional behavior directed at specific individuals to reckless behavior entailing widespread danger for the public. In most of the cases, the main motivations of corporate decisions are perceived as profit seeking rather than direct animus toward consumers – manufacturers do not desire to cause substantial harm but calculate that it is too costly to take steps that would reduce the risks that their conduct will indeed impose substantial and unjustified injury on consumers.[16] This transformation of punitive damages from its original focus on personal wrongs to its new focus on large-scale impersonal wrongs, one particularly patent in the United States, is closely connected to industrialization and its systematized mechanisms for large-scale production and commerce.[17] Before we address that connection, however, it is important to look more closely at the transition itself.

Classic American tort law originally grew out of one-on-one interactions.[18] We have already noted that, historically, punitive damages cases involved the behavior of an individual defendant that was particularly humiliating to a specific plaintiff. Admittedly, the number of punitive damages claims against corporate defendants – as opposed to individuals – only began to increase in the late nineteenth century and beginning of the twentieth century.[19] However, the rise of punitive damages complaints against corporations did not necessarily trigger the transition that I explore here. At that point in time, the type of defendant, individual versus corporation, did not constitute the most relevant factor. Quite the contrary, it is important to remark that, at around the end of the nineteenth century, most punitive damages awards against corporations – most often involving railroads – still stemmed from interpersonal interactions and were directed toward a specific individual.[20] For instance, there were cases that dealt with wanton or oppressive acts of a corporation's agents (e.g., the train conductor) toward a specific individual (e.g., a passenger).[21]

[16] For this point, see M. Rustad and T. Koenig, "The Historical Continuity of Punitive Damages" (1993) 42 *American University Law Review* 1269, 1310–11; and D. G. Owen, "Punitive Damages in Products Liability Litigation" (1976) 74 *Michigan Law Review* 1257, 1304.

[17] See G. E. White, "The Emergence and Development of a Law of Torts: 1870–1930" (2014) 11 *University of St. Thomas Law Journal* 463, 502 (explaining the profound effects of mass-market distribution of products on tort law); R. A. Nagareda, *Mass Torts in a World of Settlement* (Chicago University Press, 2007) (arguing mass torts are by-products of industrialization).

[18] See J. F. Witt, *The Accidental Republic: Crippled Workingmen, Destitute Widows, and the Remaking of American Law* (Harvard University Press, 2006), p. 7 (noting that "[f]or Holmes – or at least for the Holmes who wrote *The Common Law* in 1881 – the case of Brown v. Kendall, in which one man accidentally struck another with a stick while separating two fighting dogs, became the paradigm case for his theory of tort law.").

[19] Distinguishing between "American punitive damages for personal torts (1793–1870)" and "corporate punitive damages (1870-present)," see M. Rustad, "Happy No More: Federalism Derailed by the Court that would be King of Punitive Damages" (2005) 64 *Maryland Law Review* 461, 472–85.

[20] Ibid 487–88 (discussing punitive damages awards against the railroad in the late nineteenth century).

[21] See, for example, *Lake Shore & Mich S Ry Co v. Prentice*, 147 US 101, 104 (1893).

The standard at that time for corporate punitive liability was thus functionally equivalent to the standard for individual punitive liability. To be sure, the main legal concern at the time was whether a corporation could be held liable for punitive damages based on the wrongful acts of their agents. The focus was thus on identifying the circumstances under which punitive damages may be awarded against a corporation when, for instance, the injurious act of the individual agent was authorized or ratified by the board of directors or other governing body of the corporation, in which case the act is deemed an act of the corporation.[22] The academic debate therefore mainly focused on the dubious fairness or utility of assessing punitive damages against corporations for the misbehavior of their employees.[23] It is important to point out that the scholarly dispute over vicarious liability for punitive damages is ongoing in common law jurisdictions, particularly in England, where the master's tort theory of vicarious liability has been rejected[24] and punitive damages have mostly maintained the focus on the wrongful act of the individual agent.[25]

In a parallel fashion, the punitive damages cases in the consumer context that started to arise around the mid-twentieth century in the United States were also grounded on personal interactions with an individual consumer – particularly involving creditor collection practices such as the harassment of debtors, wrongful

[22] On this point, see S. D. Thompson, "Liability of Corporations for Exemplary Damages" (1895) 41 *Central Law Journal* 308, 309.

[23] The logic and fairness of assessing punitive damages against a corporation for the misbehavior of its employees has been questioned from the start by courts and commentators, see, for example, *Roginsky* v. *Richard-son-Merrell Inc*, 378 F 2d 832 (2d Cir. 1967); C. McCormick, *Handbook on the Law of Damages* (West Publishing, 1935) Ch. 10 §80; T. Sedgwick, A *Treatise on the Measure of Damages* (7th ed.) (Baker, Voorhis & Co., 1880); C. Morris, "Punitive Damages in Tort Cases" (1931) 44 *Harvard Law Review* 1173; Note, "The Assessment of Punitive Damages Against An Entrepreneur for the Malicious Torts of His Employees" (1961) 70 *Yale Law Journal* 1296; Note, "Exemplary Damages in the Law of Torts" (1957) 70 *Harvard Law Review* 517; Note, "Exemplary Damages Against Corporations" (1942) 30 *Georgetown Law Journal* 294. In English law, see, for example, *Rowlands* v. *Chief Constable of Merseyside Police* [2006] EWCA Civ 1773; [2007] 1 WLR 1065 [42, 46] (Moore-Bick LJ reflected that although "it is contrary to principle to punish a person whose behaviour is not in any way blameworthy," awarding punitive damages would express the Court's disapproval of both the conduct of the individual and the corresponding institution).

[24] Meaning that a defendant whose liability is vicarious cannot be considered a wrongdoer.

[25] For scholarly treatment of punitive vicarious liability in English law, see P. Gilliker, *Vicarious Liability in Tort: A Comparative Perspective* (Cambridge University Press, 2010) (questioning the imposition of liability on the faultless employer in *Rowlands v Chief Constable of Merseyside Police*); Beever, "The Structure of Aggravated and Exemplary Damages," 96 (referring to vicarious liability for punitive damages as an "injustice of the first order"); Tettenborn, "Punitive Damages," 1567–68 (arguing that it is not consistent with a punitive rationale to impose punitive damages on a defendant independently of its blameworthiness); P. Morgan, "Vicarious Punishment: Vicarious Liability for Exemplary Damages?," in E. Bant, W. Courtney, J. Goudkamp and J. M. Paterson (eds.), *Punishment and Private Law* (Hart Publishing, 2021) pp. 287–318 (arguing that punitive vicarious liability is only justified in cases involving oppressive, arbitrary or unconstitutional action by the servants of the government – i.e., the *Rookes* first category). This debate, however important, is not essential to the argument defended in this section.

repossession, and wrongful attachment and garnishment.[26] The radical change toward a more collective understanding of the institution of punitive damages only came about when corporate behavior started to be channeled through schemes of mass production and aggregation that involved widespread threats to the public.[27] Corporate behavior inasmuch as "isolated incidents" directed to individual plaintiffs was no longer the central issue, but rather patterns of fraudulent-type conduct that occurred at the implementation level in response to executive policy decisions on how mass-market business was to be conducted, fraudulent practices that had widespread impact on the public at large. The changing dynamics were thus rooted not only in the massive scale of the fraudulent-type behavior but also in its impersonal nature. For instance, one of the features of mass markets is precisely the relevance of the scale of the wrongdoing (i.e., how widespread it is), mainly because of its expanded impact on a large number of broadly dispersed people. Mass markets have the potential to spread harms across a large number of people who do not have any preexisting relationships with either the manufacturer or with one another (for example, smokers of Philip Morris cigarettes, women with adulterated Poly Implant Prothèses, owners of defective Ford Pintos, patients treated with cancer-producing Actos medicine, or addictive opioids). Moreover, these widespread harms are very often either difficult to detect or, if detected, difficult to link to defendant conduct, generally because of acts of concealment and manipulation of information. The law has therefore been forced to adapt to the modern reality of large-scale impersonal wrongs. Accordingly, the evolution from the original one-on-one tort to the modern mass tort phenomenon is reflected in the institutional transformation of the tort system as a whole, punitive damages being no exception to this process.

The relevance of these evolving factors eventually became evident through the availability of punitive damages in product liability litigation in the United States. Before 1970, there was only one reported decision upholding an award of punitive damages in a product liability case, one involving the fraudulent marketing of a dangerous drug that had caused serious injury to thousands of people.[28] From the 1970s onward, the frequency of punitive damages awards in product liability litigation grew, generally involving the attempts of manufacturers to conceal known defects from consumers (e.g., litigation against manufacturers of products containing asbestos,

[26] For a review of the common law and statutory availability of exemplary damages in consumer litigation, see D. A. Rice, "Exemplary Damages in Private Consumer Actions" (1969) 55 *Iowa Law Review* 307.

[27] For one of the earliest discussions on the desirability of extending the punitive damages doctrine to product liability litigation to punish and deter the marketing of defective products in flagrant disregard of the public safety, see Owen, "Punitive Damages in Products Liability Litigation"; M. E. Wheeler, "A Proposal for Further Common Law Development of the Use of Punitive Damages in Modern Product Liability Litigation" (1989) 40 *Alabama Law Review* 919.

[28] *Fleet* v. *Hollenkamp*, 52 Ky 175, 13 B Mon 219 (1852).

Diethylstilbestrol, Bendectin, Dalkon Shield birth control devices, among others).[29] Moreover, as the consumer protection movement gained strength in the United States (starting in the late 1950s and early 1960s), the pattern of punitive damages also began to change. From charges of outrageous acts of libel, slander, defamation, and acts of assault, the complaints predominantly shifted to demands for punitive awards because of unsafe or defective products or failure to warn of or disclose known or inherent risks.[30] The recurrent patterns of behavior described as fraudulent-type misconduct thus became: knowing violations of safety standards; inadequate testing and manufacturing procedures; failures to warn of known dangers before marketing; and post-marketing failures to remedy known dangers.[31] By then, a certain understanding had spread regarding the evolution of punitive damages from the paradigmatic individual tort to a means of social control against reckless corporate actions that endanger the greater public.[32] Judiciable complaints were no longer limited only to injuries of individual plaintiffs but also now included threats to public safety.[33] These claims for punitive damages are understood as claims for public or regulatory wrongs, not as classic torts or private wrongs.[34]

As a result, the modern understanding of American punitive damages in the mass-market context has thus veered from its original private-law roots focusing on the wrongful act of the individual agent to a more regulatory reading focusing on the collective behavior of corporate agents.[35] These debates were influenced to a certain extent by the law and economics approach to American tort law that flourished in the 1970s and persists to the present day.[36] The expansion of punitive

[29] MER/29 cases launched the era of punitive damages awards in modern product liability litigation in the United States. See, for example, *Toole* v. *Richardson-Merrell Inc.*, 251 Cal App 2d 689, 60 Cal Rptr 398 (1967).

[30] On this point, see M. Peterson, S. Sarma, and M. Shanley, *Punitive Damages: Empirical Findings* (Institute for Civil Justice, Rand 1987). Moreover, see Rustad and Koenig, "The Historical Continuity of Punitive Damages," 1303 (pointing out to the expanded role of punitive damages in consumer protection during the initial decades of the twentieth century).

[31] For an analysis of these trends of manufacturer's behavior, see Owen, "Punitive Damages in Products Liability Litigation," 1329.

[32] On this point, see Rustad, "Happy No More," 485–86.

[33] For the evolution of products liability law in the United States, see generally D. G. Owen, "The Evolution of Products Liability Law" (2007) 26 *Review of Litigation* 955.

[34] See M. L. Rustad, "Torts As Public Wrongs" (2011) 38 *Pepperdine Law Review* 433, 439.

[35] For instance, Sharkey refers to a study in the United States showing that individuals sought punitive damages in 10 percent of cases against individuals as compared to 16 percent against businesses. See C. M. Sharkey, "Punitive Damages Transformed into Societal Damages," in E. Bant, W. Courtney, J. Goudkamp and J. M. Paterson (eds.), *Punishment and Private Law* (Hart Publishing, 2021), p. 162. For their part, Goudkamp and Katsampouka's empirical work on punitive damages shows the reverse situation in the United Kingdom: Punitive damages are sought more often against individuals than against corporations. See J. Goudkamp and E. Katsampouka, "An Empirical Study of Punitive Damages" (2018) 38 *Oxford Journal of Legal Studies* 90, 106.

[36] For influential works arguing that product warranties allocate product risks efficiently, see G. Priest, "A Theory of the Consumer Product Warranty" (1981) 90 *Yale Law Journal* 1297; "The Best Evidence of the Effect of Products Liability Law on the Accident Rate: Reply" (1982) 91 *Yale Law Journal*

damages to cases involving corporate reckless indifference leading to widespread harms facilitated the introduction of economic deterrence rationales of the punitive institution, starting in the 1980s and intensifying from the 1990s onward to the present day.[37] This expansion partly explains the dominance of deterrence rationales of punitive damages in the United States.[38] Behind the deterrence rationales grounded on economic incentives is the theory that because corporations seek above all to maximize value and profit, economic incentives that affect the corporation's bottom line are more efficient and proper than retributive sanctions that would, in principle, require that a corporation experiences pain, suffering, or deprivation.[39] However, as I argued in Part II and will refine further in what follows, the undisputable retributive foundations of the punitive institution, coupled with the lack of empirical evidence supporting the claim that imposing punitive damages in those cases genuinely achieves the expected efficient behavior, have presented major obstacles for the acceptance of loss internalization rationales in the courts.[40]

The situation is quite different in England. The factual transition from the individual tort to the modern mass tort phenomenon did not prompt an institutional transformation of punitive damages under English law. Historically, in its origins in English law, punitive damages played a role in protecting ordinary citizens from oppression by powerful interests.[41] The underlying logic of the punitive remedy was focused on protecting the king's subjects from royal agents in order to

1386; and "The Invention of Enterprise Liability: A Critical History of the Intellectual Foundations of Modern Tort Law" (1985) 14 *Journal of Legal Studies* 461; A. Schwartz, "The Case Against Strict Liability" (1992) 60 *Fordham Law Review* 819; and "Proposals for Products Liability Reform: A Theoretical Synthesis" (1988) 97 *Yale Law Journal* 353. For the opposing view, see S. P. Croley and J. D. Hanson, "Rescuing the Revolution: The Revived Case for Enterprise Liability" (1993) 91 *Michigan Law Review* 683 (arguing for expanding product liability law). On the evolution of the current rationale for strict product liability in the United States, see M. A. Geistfeld, "Strict Products Liability 2.0: The Triumph of Judicial Reasoning Over Mainstream Tort Theory" (2021) 14(2) *Journal of Tort Law* 403.

37 On this point, see Sharkey, "Punitive Damages Transformed into Societal Damages," 164.

38 I explore deterrence rationales of punitive damages further in Section A of Chapter 7.

39 For instance, some have argued that corporations cannot be retributively punished. See, for example, S. W. Buell, "Retiring Corporate Retribution" (2020) 83 *Law and Contemporary Problems* 25, 45 ("Because corporations cannot experience such pain, suffering, or deprivations, they cannot be punished *on retributive grounds*.") (emphasis in original). For a different view, see Section B of Chapter 4.

40 The fact that the optimal deterrence rationale for imposing punitive damages in cases of corporate wrongdoing in the United States was applied once (to the best of my knowledge) and by Judge Posner is revealing, see *Mathias* v. *Accor Economy Lodging Inc.*, 347 F 3d 672 (7th Cir. 2003). For an insightful comment on this case, see E. M. Bublick, "Mathias v Accor Economy Lodging, Inc (2003): Judge Richard A. Posner's Message and Method on Punitive Damages," in J. Goudkamp and E. Katsampouka (eds.), *Landmark Cases in the Law of Punitive Damages* (Hart Publishing, 2023), pp. 281–302.

41 For an evolution of punitive damages in English law, see J. Edelman, "In Defence of Exemplary Damages," in C. E. F. Rickett (ed.), *Justifying Private Law Remedies* (Hart Publishing, 2008), pp. 228–29.

minimize abuse of executive power.[42] In essence, it involved protecting individuals with limited resources against individuals or agents who enjoyed asymmetrically greater power that could otherwise be wielded to unjustly overpower them. The well-known cases *Wilkes* v. *Wood* and *Huckle* v. *Money* are two paradigmatic examples where punitive damages were imposed against government agents for taking the unjustified action of entering and searching the homes of two private citizens without a valid warrant.[43] The availability of punitive damages in these situations involving "[o]ppressive, arbitrary or unconstitutional actions by servants of government" is recognized under the categories identified by Lord Devlin in *Rookes* v. *Barnard*.[44] Nowadays, the mass tort phenomenon might call for a similar protective logic of the punitive institution but one focusing on abuse of power by private corporations instead of government officials: It may reveal the need to offer protections to consumers against powerful economically motivated private corporations.[45] However, despite the frequency with which it has been repeatedly pointed out that punitive damages in English law "have a part to play in discouraging abuses of power in a democratic society,"[46] to date they have not been made available (to the best of my knowledge) in the consumer context where similar power dynamics are replicated and parallel arguments for the need of protection mechanisms might resonate persuasively – especially as regards the challenges imposed by artificial intelligence (AI) and other new technologies on consumer safety in the marketplace.[47]

Why this is the case in England might be explained by many overlapping factors that certainly exceed my reach. For instance, it could be explained by the anomaly stigma, the original limited availability of punitive damages, and the predominant approach to tort law in England as interpersonal justice, all of which have already been noted in Part I. It could also be connected to the influence exercised by the original EU Products Liability Directive, which, fueled by the ambition to harmonize legislation across the European Union for the sake of a well-functioning internal market, led most Member States to address these questions in a way that

[42] See D. Nolan, "Tort and Public Law: Overlapping Categories?" (2019) 135 *Law Quarterly Review* 272, 282 (pointing out the "abuse of power" rhetoric employed in the imposition of exemplary damages against public defendants in the case law – particularly in *Kuddus* and *Rookes*).

[43] *Wilkes* v. *Wood* [1763] 98 ER 489 and *Huckle* v. *Money* [1763] 95 ER 768.

[44] *Rookes* v. *Barnard* [1964] AC 1129, 1221.

[45] For the view that there is something distinctive about the misuse of public power that suggests that the exemplary damages doctrine should not be extended to private defendants exercising corporate power, see Nolan, "Tort and Public Law," 291.

[46] See, for example, *Watkins* v. *Home Office* [2006] UKHL 17; [2006] 2 AC 395 [75] (Lord Walker).

[47] Noting that punitive damages are not available under the United Kingdom Consumer Protection Act 1987, see J. Goudkamp and E. Katsampouka, "Punitive Damages: Ten Misconceptions," in E. Bant, W. Courtney, J. Goudkamp and J. M. Paterson (eds.), *Punishment and Private Law* (Hart Publishing, 2021), p. 192. Similarly, on the unavailability of exemplary damages in Australian consumer law, see E. Bant and J. M. Paterson, "Should Specifically Deterrent or Punitive Remedies Be Made Available to Victims of Misleading Conduct Under the Australian Consumer Law?" (2019) 25 *Torts Law Journal* 99, 109.

purports to disentangle product liability from torts and contracts – mostly considered to be idiosyncratic in each national jurisdiction.[48] As a consequence, implementing the directive did not necessarily require national jurisdictions to embark on a thorough discussion of whether punitive damages available in torts (as is the case in England) should be extended to the product liability realm. Clearly, these are just partial, tentative explanations.[49] Besides, following the United Kingdom's withdrawal from the European Union, product liability litigation and consumer protection law in England could very well take a divergent direction in the decades to come. While the European Union has recently revised the 1985 Product Liability Directive to ensure that it remains relevant in the digital age,[50] for instance, some English scholars have already distanced themselves from the approach the European Union is ready to follow.[51]

In most European jurisdictions, the EU Product Liability Directive's ambition of full harmonization (and, again, disentanglement from torts and contracts) dominated the discussion on product liability and has mainly focused over the years on questions of attribution (e.g., strict liability), available exceptions (e.g., developments of risk), delineation of the concept of defective product, and limits to the scope of recovery (e.g., caps, limits on nonpecuniary damages). While the EU Product Liability Directive was influenced (and to some extent inspired) by the United States experience of product liability, punitive damages did not enter the conversation in Europe. As detailed in Part I, this is hardly surprising considering the historical attitude of resistance both to introducing punitive damages in the national laws of EU Member States and enforcing foreign punitive damages judgments (mostly those imposed in product liability litigation in the United States) in these jurisdictions. However, given the dynamic, evolving character of the current discussion on the place of punishment in private law in most jurisdictions where a trend toward attempting to better understand punitive damages is currently observable,[52] the conversation could very well take a different direction in Europe

48 Products liability directive declaration: "products liability is not tort, not contract."

49 For instance, among other aspects, they do not account for the particular relationship between risk regulation and torts, which certainly takes different forms depending on the jurisdictions. For more on this point, see Section B of Chapter 8.

50 Briefly, the new Directive maintains the strict liability standard; extends the scope of application to software and digital manufacturing files as well as certain defects that arise after manufacture; expands categories of liable persons to include software producers, digital service providers, and online platforms; expands categories of harm to loss or corruption of data; and assists claimants to establish liability by recognizing their rights of access to information in the defendant's control and by reversing the burden of proof for defectiveness and causation in certain circumstances [Directive (EU) 2024/2853 of the European Parliament and of the Council of 23 October 2024 on liability for defective products and repealing Council Directive 85/374/EEC].

51 See generally D. Nolan, "Against Strict Product Liability," in D. Nolan, *Questions of Liability. Essays on the Law of Tort* (Hart Publishing, 2023), pp. 392–426 (arguing for abandoning strict liability and reverting to a fault standard).

52 On this point, see Chapter 1.

in the years to come – particularly in the context of the current discussions on how to design a better product liability regime that is more responsive to the challenges posed by the rapid development of new technologies.

The narrower point I want to make in this section is that the scholarly discussion over the place of punitive damages in product liability litigation has been largely absent (also probably due to a lack of any practice to account for) under both English and European laws. Conversely, it has been vast, rich, and extensively dealt with under American tort law, where the availability of punitive damages in product liability litigation has historically played a salient role. As regards the situation in those civil law jurisdictions in Latin America (Argentina, Chile, and to a certain extent Mexico) where punitive damages are available in the consumer context, the practice of imposing punitive awards in product liability litigation is not only too recent to yield a reliable account but also, more importantly, it has been, as described in Part I, predominantly influenced by the American experience and scholarly debates on the subject.[53] This combination of factors explains the predominance of references to American practice in this and Chapter 7. However, the emphasis on United States jurisprudence and scholarship should not lead the reader to believe that the following discussion is only relevant for an American audience. Quite to the contrary, the ambition of Part III is to prompt a global conversation on the proper place of punitive damages in the product liability context and its retributive justifications beyond the borders of the United States. After all, since tort liability for harm caused by defective products originated in the United States before influencing the European discussion on the topic, the importance of understanding punitive damages in product liability litigation in the United States cannot be overstated. It arguably represents a pertinent source of experience often overlooked (or plainly misunderstood) by legal scholars exclusively trained in the European product liability debate and practice.[54] Moreover, making the American experience accessible beyond those civil law jurisdictions where punitive damages are already operative in product liability litigation[55] may comprise a valuable source of guidance and awareness for local discussions on how they might best be implemented. Besides, in the current global economy, reprehensible corporate behavior manifesting reckless indifference for the rights and well-being of consumers is so commonplace that no one can afford to ignore it wherever they are. Egregious corporate misbehavior that ought to be punished and deterred may take place in every jurisdiction. Moreover, the rapid development of AI technologies is exacerbating

[53] On this point, see Section B of Chapter 1.

[54] For an insightful description of these dynamics, see J. Stapleton, "Products Liability in the United Kingdom: The Myth of Reform" (1999) 34 *Texas International Law Journal* 45, 47.

[55] Note that punitive damages are also available in product liability litigation in China (Tort Law of the People's Republic of China 2009, art. 47). For a recent comment on this, see Z. Wang and J. Gong, "The Punitive Compensation Liability for Defective Products in China – Centered on the Article 1207 of Tort Liability in Civil Code" (2021) 244(1) *Journal of Shandong University* 119.

the need to address the adequacy of existing product liability regimes worldwide to ensure not only that they are fit for the digital age but also that they provide sufficient protection for consumers of AI-enabled products. Two proposals have recently been advanced by the European Commission laying out the European approach to AI liability. While one proposal introduces extra-contractual civil liability rules for AI systems,[56] the other revises the original Product Liability Directive of 1985.[57] In fact, the recently revised Product Liability Directive adapted the existent strict product liability regime to the digital age by, among other measures, extending the scope of application to software and digital manufacturing files as well as certain defects that arise after manufacture, and introducing presumptions of defectiveness of the product and of the causal link between the defectiveness of the product and the harm.[58] Regarding recoverable heads of damages, making punitive damages available has not been discussed; however, the possibility of expanding the scope of recovery is in principle largely left to Member States. The implementation of these initiatives remain to be seen. Meanwhile, bringing the relevant debates on punitive damages to bear in the product liability context will contribute to this discussion not only by improving the understanding of the fundamental retributive rationale of the institution but also by helping to identify the relevant markers in a global discussion of the proper place for punishment in the marketplace.

B MASS-MARKET POWER DYNAMICS: WHAT DRIVES PUNITIVE RESPONSES TOWARD CORPORATE WRONGDOING?

Any attempt to understand punitive awards against modern corporate wrongdoing must seriously consider the influence of contextual dynamics in the mass-market setting in which productive activities are carried out. The particular power dynamics that frame the manufacturer-consumer relationship in the mass-market context are in fact well known.[59] These power relationships themselves fall into

56 Proposal for a Directive of the European Parliament and of the Council on adapting noncontractual civil liability rules to artificial intelligence (AI Liability Directive) (COM (2022) 496 final). Note that the EU Commission withdrew the proposal on February 11, 2025.

57 Proposal for a Directive of the European Parliament and of the Council on liability for defective products (COM (2022) 495 final 2022/0302 (COD). Note that the new EU Product Liability Directive has recently been approved. See Directive (EU) 2024/2853 of the European Parliament and of the Council of 23 October 2024 on liability for defective products and repealing Council Directive 85/374/EEC.

58 For a detailed analysis and critical assessment of the proposals, see P. Hacker, "The European AI Liability Directives – Critique of a Half-Hearted Approach and Lessons for the Future" (2023) 51 *Computer Law and Security Review* 105871; G. Wagner, "Liability Rules for the Digital Age – Aiming for the Brussels Effect" (2022) 13(3) *Journal of European Tort Law* 191.

59 For an insightful analysis of the role of power in different tort law contexts, see M. Shapo, *The Duty to Act. Tort Law, Power, and Public Policy* (University of Texas Press, 1978). For the role of power in the context of punitive damages, see D. G. Owen, "Civil Punishment and the Public Good" (1982) 56 *Southern California Law Review* 103, 104.

a variety of types. They take a different form depending on the type of power that the defendant holds and the kind of vulnerability that affects the plaintiff. In our modern society, consumers engage in economic transactions with corporations on a daily basis through take-it-or-leave-it standardized forms, contracts, and sales methods. These well-known contracting practices – which are characterized by the use of fine print, technical jargon, and the deliberate use of unclear, ambiguous clauses – are aspects that reflect an imbalance of negotiating power, which basically means consumers often have almost no say in the terms of their transactions.[60] Manufacturers also enjoy superior knowledge: They are experts with regards to product safety and have the assets, experience, and ability to compile data, carry out tests, conduct experiments, and make changes in the product. While manufacturers enjoy a near monopoly of knowledge regarding their products' development and specific features, consumers' knowledge is often imperfect to the point of making them unable to fully assess the product or service for purchase (e.g., the quality of the product, from its material composition to the assembly procedures of production, and so on).[61] Consumer decisions, therefore, are generally made with minimal information and knowledge of the product.

The content of the manufacturer-consumer relationship is therefore characterized above all by negotiation imbalance and knowledge asymmetry.[62] Both characteristics invoke an idea of the manufacturer as "epistemic authority," who almost exclusively holds information over the terms of the agreements and the design and safety of its products. Clearly, the manufacturer is in the best position to fully comprehend the costs and benefits of the product and has the knowledge to undertake the most relevant decisions regarding the product's safety and design to its advantage. Furthermore, as a practical matter, these decisions are mostly taken within the nearly exclusive sphere of the manufacturer's control without significant external interference, but for some oversight or supervision (to varying degree depending on the type of product and the jurisdiction) by public agencies and (sometimes insufficient or deficient) regulations for the disclosure of information meant to redress the knowledge asymmetry.[63]

60 See F. Kessler, "Contracts of Adhesion. Some Thoughts about Freedom of Contract" (1943) 43 *Columbia Law Review* 629, 632 (famously introducing the concept of contracts of adhesion as "standard contracts [which] are typically used by enterprises with strong bargaining power.").

61 For an early depiction of these dynamics, see, for example, *Henningsen* v. *Bloomfield Motors*, 161 A 2d, 69, 83 (NJ 1960) ("[U]nder modern conditions the ordinary layman [...] has neither the opportunity nor the capacity to inspect or to determine the fitness of an automobile for use; he must rely on the manufacturer who had control of its construction.").

62 On consumers' structural vulnerability, see generally M. G. Martínez Alles, "Reducing Inequality in Consumer Transactions: The Significance of Aggravated Vulnerabilities," in K. E. Davis and M. Pargendler (eds.), *Legal Heterodoxy in the Global South* (Cambridge University Press, 2025), pp. 77–111.

63 See J. W. Lens, "Product Recalls: Why is Tort Law Deferring to Agency Inaction?" (2016) 90 *St John's Law Review* 329 (pointing out the fact that public agencies often have access to much less information than manufacturers on specific safety problems and move much more slowly and with far less flexibility than private manufacturers). For a different perspective, see A. M. Polinsky and S. Shavell,

In what follows, I explore some of the many ways in which manufacturers exploit those asymmetries for gain and how this directly relates to defining the role of punitive damages in the mass-market setting. Exploitative behavior occurs when manufacturers consciously take advantage of their superior position in the market to mislead consumers regarding design defects or potential risks of significant harms from the products they are introducing in the market, which they know beforehand will cause widespread harm to consumers.[64] The problem arises when there is a deliberate or reckless corporate strategy to earn a profit by jeopardizing public safety. To varying degrees of sophistication, judges and product liability scholars have drawn attention to the different ways in which market dynamics influence corporate behavior for some time.[65] Indeed, product liability case law is quite revealing of judges' understanding of how firms actually behave within the market context and the impact of that behavior on the consumer.[66] In all appearance, judges find a strong correlation between the behavior of firms and the relative vulnerability (or uninformed position) of the consumers. Similar ideas were developed to a greater degree of elaboration and theoretical grounding by product liability scholars borrowing from the science of human behavior. These scholars offer evidence – from within the market context – of what they call "manipulation" by firms toward consumers.[67] They argue that the

"The Uneasy Case for Product Liability" (2010) 123 *Harvard Law Review* 1437, 1453 (arguing that agency regulation of mass-marketed products provided enough incentivize for corporations to ensure the safety of their products, thereby rendering further incentives created through product liability law more or less unnecessary).

64 See D. G. Owen, "Punitive Damages in Products Liability Litigation" (1976) 74 *Michigan Law Review* 1257, 1259 (describing that "[o]n occasion, […], manufacturers abuse their control over safety information and market defective products in flagrant disregard of the public safety.").

65 See, for example, *Toole* v. *Richardson-Merrell Inc.*, 251 Cal App 2d 689, 60 Cal. Rptr. 398 (1967) (an early product liability case where a color television manufacturer included a high voltage transformer in each set that it knew was prone to catch fire and, when informed that its sets were causing frequent fires, refused to spend one dollar per unit to eliminate the hazard). For more examples on flagrant corporate behavior in early product liability litigation, see Owen, "Punitive Damages in Products Liability Litigation," 1259–61; F. W. Morgan, "The Evolution of Punitive Damages in Product Liability Litigation for Unprincipled Marketing Behavior" (1989) 8 *Journal of Public Policy & Marketing* 279.

66 For example, see *Ford Motor Co.* v. *Stubblefield*, 319 SE 2d 470, 481 (Ga. Ct. App. 1984) (noting that Ford made "conscious decisions to defer implementation of safety devices in order to protect its profits"); *Ford Motor Co.* v. *Nowak*, 638 SW 2d 582, 593 (Tex. Ct. App. 1982) (emphasizing evidence that Ford ignored several complaints of problems by consumers); *Leichtamer* v. *American Motors Corp.*, 424 NE 2d 568, 578 (Ohio 1981) (allowing punitive damages against a manufacturer who knew of the defect and continued to advertise the product as safe); *Gillham* v. *Admiral Corp.*, 523 F 2d 102, 106 (6th Cir. 1975), cert. denied, 424 US 913 (1976) (noting that the defendant received numerous consumer complaints about television set fires and failed to remedy the problem; that the managers were aware of the fire hazard and its precise cause; and that the company failed to warn consumers).

67 The main scholarly works along these lines are: J. D. Hanson and D. A. Kysar, "Taking Behavioralism Seriously: The Problem of Market Manipulation" (1999) 74 *New York University Law Review* 630; "Taking Behavioralism Seriously: Some Evidence of Market Manipulation" (1999) 112 *Harvard Law Review* 1420; and "Taking Behavioralism Seriously: A Response to Market Manipulation" (2000) 6 *Roger Williams University Law Review* 259.

demands of mass marketing create incentives for manufacturers to mislead consumers concerning the risks associated with their products. In fact, they go further by arguing that firms must necessarily "manage," if not outright manipulate, consumers' risk perceptions of their products (either by raising consumer perceptions of product utility or by lowering perceptions of product harmfulness) in order to survive in a competitive market.[68]

With regards to punitive damages, a decision that followed similar expectations regarding exploitative practices on the part of manufacturers, such as minimizing perceptions of product harmfulness, is found in the United States Supreme Court smoking case, *Philip Morris USA* v. *Williams*.[69] In *Williams*, the jury found that Philip Morris, the manufacturer of the plaintiff's preferred cigarettes, knowingly and falsely led the plaintiff to believe that smoking was safe. Similar charges are present in Justice Stevens' dissenting opinion: He describes Philip Morris' behavior as "[e]ngaging in a campaign of deceit in distributing a poisonous and addictive substance to thousands of cigarette smokers statewide."[70] Outside the United States, the Superior Court of Quebec issued a historical punitive damage award against three large tobacco companies in Canada.[71] This resonant judgment brought by smokers was decided on the grounds of the exploitative practices of tobacco manufacturers toward consumers. The manufacturers were condemned for knowingly marketing a dependence-creating product without informing the public of this feature, for knowingly failing to inform of the cancer risks of smoking, and for its willful intent to "disinform" smokers.

The well-known Ford Pinto case is another prototypical example of corporate misbehavior that led to a punitive damage award.[72] In this case, Ford Motor Company officials realized that the design of the gas tank in their Pinto cars was defective because its location made it susceptible to exploding in rear-end collisions. The firm considered changing the design but decided not to take any measure because the cost of putting the tank in a safer location was deemed too high in relation to the number of lives that would be saved by doing so.[73] The implementation of the executive

68 See generally Hanson and Kysar, "Some Evidence of Market Manipulation" (focusing on the cigarette industry as a strong example of the power of market manipulation). For a comprehensive account of how markets manipulate, see A. Kuenzler, *Restoring Consumer Sovereignty: How Markets Manipulate Us and What the Law Can Do About It* (Oxford University Press, 2017); and "Competition Law Enforcement on Digital Markets – Lessons from Recent EU Case Law" (2019) 7(2) *Journal of Antitrust Enforcement* 249.

69 549 US 346 (2007).

70 Ibid.

71 *Cécilia Létourneau* v. *Imperial Tobacco, Rothmans Benson & Hedges and JTI MacDonald*, Superior Court of Quebec, Canada, May 27, 2015, 1018 (The Supreme Court of Canada favors granting punitive damages only in exceptional cases for "malicious, oppressive and high-handed" misconduct that "offends the court's sense of decency.").

72 *Grimshaw* v. *Ford Motor Co.*, 174 Cal Rptr 348 (Cal Ct. App. 1981).

73 For a discussion of the Pinto case, see G. T. Schwartz, "The Myth of the Ford Pinto Case" (1991) 43 *Rutgers Law Review* 1013, 1020–22; D. G. Owen, "Problems in Assessing Punitive Damages Against Manufacturers of Defective Products" (1982) 49 *University of Chicago Law Review* 1, 56 n264

decision not to disclose this information meant concealing from Pinto owners (and potential new owners) the risk of death and substantial personal injury to which traveling in a Pinto exposed them. Recently, General Motors (GM) behaved in a similar fashion with regards to a faulty ignition switch problem. Although GM engineers were aware of problems with the ignition switch in early stages of production (as early as 2001), the switch was approved for installation in several vehicle models. The switches, when jostled, caused the cars' motors to stall, leaving drivers unable to maintain speed without functioning air bags. Subsequently, even though GM's management was aware of numerous fatalities and injuries that were caused by the ignition switch defect, the company kept the information secret from car owners and did nothing to fix the problem until 2014, when they finally decided to recall the affected vehicles from the market.[74] A pattern of similar conduct can be observed in these product liability punitive damages cases: first comes a defective product; second, the defect becomes known and yet the manufacturer decides not to correct it because the cost is deemed excessive; and, third, the product is marketed as safe without disclosing the defect.

Another example is the punitive award against drug makers for intentionally hiding the cancer risks of the Actos diabetes medicine.[75] The plaintiff began taking Actos in 2006 to treat type 2 diabetes. In 2011 he was diagnosed with bladder cancer. A few months after his diagnosis, the United States Food and Drug Administration announced that they had found increased risk of bladder cancer in patients taking Actos for more than one year. Drug makers possessed clinical evidence of the increased risk in the early 2000s but did not warn physicians and patients before 2011. Moreover, there was evidence that the drug maker Takeda destroyed documents and emails relevant to the case, supporting the plaintiff's claim that Takeda concealed Actos' health risks for many years. Similar patterns of orchestrated deception to the public are patent in the two separate recent and ongoing cases of product liability litigation in the United States. The one that has received the most attention concerns corporate activity that may have triggered the opioid epidemic and spread of fentanyl use in the United States. Purdue Pharma knowingly engaged, to increase profits, in aggressive marketing tactics encouraging the prescription of the addictive pain medicine OxyContin without publicly disclosing the high risk of addiction and abuse that ultimately caused thousands of deaths due to overdose.[76]

(reproducing the Grush-Saunby Report that mathematically detailed the costs and benefits behind Ford's decision not to correct the fuel tank defect of the Pinto model).

74 Reporting on this, see T. Krisher, "Death Toll from General Motors Ignition Switches Rises to 57," Associated Press, February 23, 2015.

75 *Terrence Allen et al.* v. *Takeda Pharmaceuticals North America Inc. et al.* (US Dist Ct W Dist of Louisiana 2014).

76 On the Purdue Pharma litigation, see A. R. Gluck, E. C. Burch and A. S. Zimmerman, "Against Bankruptcy: Public Litigation Values versus the Endless Quest for Global Peace in Mass Litigation" (2024) 133 *Yale Law Forum* 525.

Attention has also been devoted to the recent punitive lawsuits against Johnson & Johnson (J&J) for knowingly marketing as safe a talc-based baby powder tainted with a toxic substance linked to ovarian cancer (and other types of cancer linked to asbestos exposure). Over decades, thousands of users exposed themselves to significant risks caused by regular use of the J&J talcum powder, risks of which the corporation was aware but declined to disclose.[77]

That is a small sampling of a fraction of the most notorious examples from an endless list of court cases that have brought to light recurrent patterns of conscious misbehavior by corporations toward consumers. In each of the cases described, the misbehavior involved actions taken to mislead the public concerning the product's safety and was manifested through systemic schemes implemented in accordance with the firm's policy decisions on how to conduct the business.[78] The implication of such practices by manufacturers is that consumers cannot possibly be considered fully informed or empowered because they simply lack the capacity to detect the purposively concealed product risks – at least not before they result in serious injury or even death to consumers. Empowering consumers to be punitive through courts could help restore some balance to reduce the current asymmetry of information and power that exists in the mass-market setting. The precise extent to which product liability litigation impacts safety has yet to be determined, but it is undeniable that product liability regimes, as complementary mechanisms (to, for instance, risk regulation), facilitate consumer protection by providing victims with an avenue for private redress and expression of self-regard through the courts that is worth maintaining. As I explore next in Chapter 7, product liability litigation provides a valuable avenue for consumers to communicate both their genuine expectations of safety in the marketplace (i.e., the risks deemed unacceptable for manufacturers to impose on others) and their correlative punitive responses when manufacturers fail to fulfill those expectations by prioritizing private gain over preventing significant harm to consumers. The specific place and role of punitive damages in product liability litigation in responding to those exploitative practices will be examined, and, here again, as extensively argued in Part II, a more meaningful understanding of punitive damages and its retributive underpinnings becomes apparent if we shift from an exclusive focus on the defendant's conduct and toward an approach that holistically integrates the victim's perspective into an inclusive wrongdoer-victim equation. The dominance of deterrence-oriented rationales of punitive damages focusing on the defendant's conduct in the mass-market context (particularly, in the

77 Reporting on the Johnson & Johnson litigation, see C. Cep, "Johnson & Johnson and a New War on Consumer Protection," The New Yorker, September 12, 2022.

78 For examples of lax safety corporate culture, see W. K. Viscusi, "Pricing Lives for Corporate and Governmental Risk Decisions" (2015) 6(2) *Journal of Benefit-Cost Analysis* 227, 242 (describing the clear attempt by General Motors Company to reduce the likelihood of being found out by withholding the information from NHTSA for seven years and entering into confidential settlements with the parties who did and sued).

United States) has led us to overlook for too long not only the undeniable retributive aspect of the institution but also, most importantly, the nuanced meaning behind the victim's demand for the imposition of the punitive award in cases of reprehensible corporate wrongdoing. Following the *Relational Retribution* framework developed in Part II, Chapter 7 offers a retributive reconstruction of punitive damages in the mass-market context that is respectful of the victim's perspective. Chapter 7 presents a novel retributive reading of the institution that is sensitive not only to the substantial role of the consumer in filing the punitive lawsuit but also, significantly, to the substantive content of her punitive response when confronted with instances of reprehensible corporate wrongdoing in the mass-market setting.

7

Punitive Damages as Retributive Sanctions for Violations of Societal Trust

Because of knowledge asymmetry, manufacturers are considered experts – epistemic authorities who occupy a position of control over the relevant information of their products (i.e., no one knows their products better). On the other side of the equation, consumers are generally poorly informed, sometimes moved by necessity, and make many decisions in a nonreflexive manner. Therefore, the argument can be made that expert manufacturers have, as epistemic authorities, a general duty to make fundamental decisions regarding the design and safety of their products in a way that avoids exposing consumers to unknown harm (i.e., the duty of noninterference). Manufacturers must assure consumers that they will not deliberatively abuse the superiority of their knowledge in any way that may cause consumers or the public substantial harm (e.g., that they will not deceive consumers about addictive or unsafe features of their products). Following this logic, consumers have a correlative safety expectation that, when significant harms are at stake, manufacturers will exert their superior knowledge and power fairly.[1] This is what I refer to as "societal trust" – the consumers' positive expectation that manufacturers will not exercise their knowledge superiority in an abusive way that risks their individual autonomy, physical integrity, or lives. The fundamental idea underlying the necessity of this assurance is that consumers rely on the ability and willingness of manufacturers to market safe products (i.e., reliance that the products available in the market will not threaten consumer safety).[2] To be trustworthy, manufacturers must assure consumers that the products they introduce in the market will not put their lives, physical integrity, or individual autonomy in jeopardy.[3]

[1] On this point, see R. Korzec, "Dashing Consumer Hopes: Strict Products Liability and the Demise of the Consumer Expectations Test" (1997) 20 *Boston College International and Comparative Law Review* 227, 236 (arguing that "consumers are entitled to an expectation that manufacturers, as experts in the field, will sell products which are as safe as possible, given technological and scientific feasibility.").

[2] Noting that an individual in industrial society is absolutely dependent on the conscientiousness of corporations and manufacturers, see E. A. Ross, *Sin and Society: An Analysis of Latter-Day Iniquity* (Cornell University Press, 2009), p. 3.

[3] See, for example, *Escola* v. *Coca Cola Bottling Co.*, 150 P 2d 436, 443 (Cal 1944) (Traynor, J., concurring) (consumers no longer approach products warily but accept them on faith, relying on the reputation of the manufacturer or the trade mark).

Reliance on experts is necessary for democratic societies to flourish and develop. Consumers must entrust, day in and day out, their safety to the discretion of expert decision-makers (who work for manufacturers and regulators). Still, the level of trust placed in experts to ensure product safety warrants further examination, for lately we have seen many examples where expert decision-making of product manufacturers has come under scrutiny.[4] For instance, well-known product safety scandals, such as the use of adulterated silicone breast implants in France (Poly Implant Prothèse) or the use of carcinogenic talc in the United States (Johnson & Johnson), reveal a discrepancy between the definition of acceptable risk by experts (manufacturers, regulators, surgeons) and lay people (the physical experience of risk by prosthetic and talc users).[5] This discrepancy has intensified in the context of recent safety scandals involving artificial intelligence (AI). One example is the self-driving Uber cars, which failed to avoid fatal, preventable accidents. Another involves the fear that AI-enabled robotic surgery tools to assist doctors during operations could cause avoidable harm to patients. At a deeper level, the discrepancy between statistical and lay assessments of risk poses a complex question for our society: How firm should the trust placed in experts be? Rapidly evolving technologies present a new challenge for risk regulators, manufacturers, and consumers alike.

This development requires constant vigilance and updating from regulators to keep up with scientific developments, while, for their part, producers must always be attuned to technological advances that require quality and risk management monitoring for post-launch safety and be prepared to take appropriate corrective action (e.g., product recall and software updates) whenever necessary for consumer safety.[6] Consumers are increasingly aware of their limited access to important information and the exponential growth of their vulnerability to significant harm due to new technologies. Certainly, consumers cannot place complete trust in suppliers (manufacturers, producers) for product safety. Nor can they exclusively rely upon the regulatory process (direct risk regulation) to protect them from every potentially adverse effect of the suppliers' safety decision, which begs the question of how to determine

4 For vast examples of product liability litigation uncovering manufacturers' consumer fraud in withholding negative information about the safety of their products, see W. Wagner, "When All Else Fails: Regulatory Risky Products through Tort Litigation" (2007) 95 *Georgetown Law Journal* 693. Also see generally H. W. Micklitz, "Risk, Tort and Liability," in S. Grundmann, H. W. Micklitz, and M. Renner (eds.), *New Private Law Theory: A Pluralistic Approach* (Cambridge University Press, 2021), pp. 272–97.

5 For a discussion of this discrepancy between experts and laymen, see C. Greco, "The Poly Implant Prothèse Breast Prostheses Scandal: Embodied Risk and Social Suffering" (2015) 147 *Social Science & Medicine* 150.

6 See generally D. Fairgrieve, G. Howells, P. Møgelvang-Hansen, G. Straetmans, D. Verhoeven, P. Machnikowski, A. Janssen and R. Schulze, "Product Liability Directive," in P. Machnikowski (ed.), *European Product Liability – An Analysis of the State of the Art in the Era of New Technologies* (Intersentia, 2017); G. Howells, C. Twigg-Flesner and T. Wilhelmsson, *Rethinking EU Consumer Law* (Routledge, 2017).

the desirable level of interaction between administrative agencies, legislatures, and courts to effectively protect consumers from risky products – which is precisely the question to which I turn in Chapter 8. At this moment, the point I would like to make is that in this increasingly complex scenario, creating the conditions for a more trustworthy marketplace in which experts (manufacturers, producers, regulators) better identify with the people they serve (consumers) appears more relevant and urgent than ever before.[7]

Trust plays as central a role in business relationships as it does in personal ones. Here I follow the concept of trust defined in a cross-disciplinary review carried out by Denise M. Rousseau et al.[8] According to the authors, trust is "a psychological state composing the intention to accept vulnerability based on positive expectations of the intentions or behavior of another."[9] Jonathan Koehler and Andrew Gershoff elaborate on this definition, arguing that there are at least three components at the core of a trusting relationship: (1) dependency among the parties, (2) vulnerability of at least one party, and (3) positive expectations or beliefs by at least one party.[10] Moreover, they identify trust relationships that are asymmetric in the sense that the dependency, vulnerability, and positive expectations can be significantly larger for one party than the other. Regarding such asymmetric trust relationships, Koehler and Gershoff argue that the relationship between consumers and manufacturers with regards to product safety constitutes one of these.[11] Again, drawing from the features of trust in Rousseau et al., they inferred that violations of trust take place when there is (1) exploitation of a vulnerable dependent party and/or (2) violation of the vulnerable party's "positive expectations" about the behavior of the other party.[12] The violation of the positive expectations of the vulnerable party can be translated in the consumer context as a violation of the implicit promise not to harm purposively. To be sure, such violations of trust are seen as a threat to the social order that allows consumers to harbor a positive expectation of safety in the first place.[13]

Identifying the meaning of societal trust is fundamental in determining the circumstances under which the violation of the consumer's positive safety

[7] On trust relationships, see T. T. Frankel, *Fiduciary Law* (Oxford University Press, 2010). For the relationship between the technocratic approach to AI and citizens trust, see generally J. Laux, S. Wachter and B. Mittelstadt, "Trustworthy Artificial Intelligence and the European Union AI Act: On the Conflation of Trustworthiness and Acceptability of Risk" (2024) 18 *Regulation & Governance* 3.

[8] D. M. Rousseau, S. B. Sitkin, R. S. Burt and C. Camerer, "Not So Different After All: A Cross-Discipline View of Trust" (1998) 23 *Academy of Management Review* 393.

[9] Ibid 395.

[10] See J. J. Koehler and A. D. Gershoff, "Betrayal Aversion: When Agents of Protection Become Agents of Harm" (2002) 90 *Organizational Behavior and Human Decision Processes* 244.

[11] Ibid 249.

[12] Ibid 247.

[13] On this point, see M. J. Lerner, *The Belief in a Just World: A Fundamental Delusion* (Springer, 1980) (Lerner explores the "just world hypothesis," which indicates that people have a powerful need to believe that the social world is orderly, predictable, and fair).

expectations concerning the behavior of the other party may elicit a punitive response. In undertaking this enterprise, we realize that the actual meaning of societal trust depends on how the content of the consumer's positive expectation of safety is constructed: whether it is set, for example, at one point on the cost-efficiency curve or another. Consumers may simply expect manufacturers to correctly and accurately execute the appropriate cost–benefit analysis in order to make cost-effective safety decisions that meet the recommended minimum standards from a societal standpoint,[14] or they may expect manufacturers to make fundamental safety decisions independently of the recommended cost-justified measures.[15]

In what follows, I explore these two possible reconstructions. I call the first "The Expert Approach to Societal Trust." In this reconstruction, consumers are taken as utterly rational actors who seek to maximize their well-being. Its main focus is on the incentive effects of liability on potential corporate wrongdoing as a mechanism to achieve efficiency (i.e., optimal deterrence). Punitive awards are best understood as a price and consumers as formally performing the function of private enforcers of that expected efficient behavior from corporations. I call the other reconstruction "The Ordinary Person Approach to Societal Trust." Here consumers are treated substantively as imperfectly rational lay individuals who share basic moral intuitions about risk, trust, and equal respect (i.e., on how people should regard and treat one another in society). The main focus in this reconstruction is on identifying and accounting for value-driven reactions of lay individuals to egregious corporate misbehavior that require consideration of a plurality of substantive competing values other than efficiency (and its corollary, expected behavioral outcomes). Among these substantive competing values are the sacred value of human life and the high value we place on individual autonomy. Under this framework, punitive awards are not understood as a price but as a retributive sanction for reprehensible corporate conduct and consumers play the substantive role of communicating well-situated disapproval of that misbehavior in a way that clearly conveys condemnation and value affirmation.

As will be seen in what follows, the different ways in which the positive expectation of safety is constructed under each approach alter not only the way in which corporate behavior is assessed by consumers but also the diverse responses and reactions called for. This is because the particular way in which we understand certain

14 For a description of this approach, see N. Komesar, "Injuries and Institutions: Tort Reform, Tort Theory, and Beyond" (1990) 64 *New York University Law Review* 60, 61 n101 (holding that "the jury's action [in the Ford Pinto case], whatever its intent, served the nonretributive purpose of correcting the future calculations of Ford and other potential injurers by establishing the societally correct parameters.").

15 For a leading proponent of this approach, see generally G. C. Keating, *Reasonableness and Risk. Right and Responsibility in the Law of* Torts (Oxford University Press, 2023). Moreover, see D. G. Owen, "Problems in Assessing Punitive Damages against Manufacturers of Defective Products" (1982) 49 *University of Chicago Law Review* 1, 22 n97 (pointing out to the importance of addressing the tension between the interests of efficiency and autonomy in product liability cases).

behavior necessarily changes our reactions toward it. The underlying idea is that distinguishing the different ways in which corporate behavior can be understood is fundamental in the process of elucidating the true motivations of consumers' punitive responses in the mass-market context.

A THE EXPERT APPROACH TO SOCIETAL TRUST: PUNITIVE DAMAGES AS PRICES

This approach is dominated by the interest in advancing efficiency as the ultimate value.[16] Consumers are assumed to be agents capable of rational calculation who seek aggregate welfare.[17] Accordingly, manufacturers are expected to make the cost-effective investments in product safety recommended by the execution of the cost–benefit analysis that correctly reflects the consumers' estimation of acceptable risk.[18] Violations of societal trust will thus necessarily involve some error in the execution of that cost–benefit test (i.e., when the figures or measurements used in the calculation or the estimation of acceptable risk are mistaken).[19] Underlying the idea of acceptable risk in aggregate terms is the belief that products that are excessively safe do not represent the greatest benefit for society, but rather that society benefits most when an optimal balance between product safety and product cost is achieved.[20] Manufacturers are thus entrusted to execute that technical task correctly and their behavior is to be judged by the care put into their calculations of costs and benefits in addition to the accuracy of those calculations from the standpoint of efficiency. Again, under this view, societal trust could only be considered violated when there is error in the execution of the technical task of balancing costs and benefits.

16 For classic examples of scholars who believe that the point of the common law of torts is to promote an efficient allocation of resources, see generally W. M. Landes and R. A. Posner, *The Economic Structure of Tort Law* (Harvard University Press, 1987); R. A. Posner, "The Economic Approach to Law" (1975) 53 *Texas Law Review* 757, 764 ("the logic of the law is really economics").

17 See Landes and Posner, *The Economic Structure of Tort Law*, p. 6 ("[T]he germ of the [economic analysis of torts] is Bentham's proposition that people maximize utility in all areas of life."). Pointing out that, with the rise of law and economics in modern legal analysis, financial incentives have become the default mechanism for understanding and changing behavior, see J. D. Hanson, "Introduction: Ideology, Psychology, and Law," in J. D. Hanson (ed.), *Ideology, Psychology, and Law* (Oxford University Press, 2012), pp. 3–12.

18 See generally R. A. Posner, "A Theory of Negligence" (1972) 1 *Journal of Legal Studies* 29.

19 On this point, see J. D. Hanson and K. D. Logue, "The Costs of Cigarettes: The Economic Case for Ex Post Incentive-Based Regulation" (1998) 107 *Yale Law Journal* 1163, 1176 n42 (explaining that "'[e]fficiently safe products,' [are] products for which manufacturers have made all cost-justified investments in safety. 'Inefficiently unsafe products' are those for which not all such investments have been made.").

20 For an analysis of the complexity of the relationship between product safety and product liability, see R. C. Ausness, "Danger is My Business: The Right to Manufacture Unsafe Products" (2014) 67 *Arkansas Law Review* 827, 831–34 ("[the] more popular standard is optimal safety. This efficiency-based standard [...] requires manufacturers to make cost-effective investments in product safety.").

The cost–benefit test yields what are taken as the appropriate cost-justified precautions that should be implemented for the safety of the products introduced by manufacturers in the market. It also enables manufacturers to identify precautions that should be rejected because their high cost outweighs the known risk of harm to consumers. The amount that manufacturers are expected to spend on product safety is determined, as a matter of fact, by the point at which the marginal cost of additional safety measures overtakes the expected reduction of product-related accident costs that will ensue. In *United States* v. *Carroll Towing Co.*, Judge Learned Hand introduced the formal expression of that cost–benefit test for negligence law.[21] According to the *Hand Formula*, defendants should be liable for negligence if the burden (B) of taking a precaution is less than the probability (P) of harm resulting if the precaution is not taken, multiplied by the magnitude of the loss (L): $B < P \times L$. Thus, in order to induce defendants to act efficiently, compensatory damages should be equal to the loss, resulting in expected liability equal to the product of $P \times L$.[22]

Under this economic logic, manufacturers are rational self-interested actors who decide whether to conform or not to a given safety standard by balancing the costs of compliance with the expected costs of liability.[23] Actors will have incentives to take reasonable care if they are forced to pay for the harms (no more or less) that taking unreasonable risks causes.[24] As a consequence, they are somehow allowed to knowingly market unsafe products as long as they do it efficiently and are willing to pay for all the product-related accidents introduced in society as a result. It turns out that these actors do not always end up paying for all the harms caused by their decisions because of the deficiencies of the liability system itself: failure to sue, difficulties to detect wrongdoing, inability to prove negligence or causation, among others. Thus, manufacturers speculate on those under-enforcement problems of the liability system, only considering in their analysis the "expected compensatory damages" rather than the "actual compensatory damages." This creates a distortion in their analysis that has to be corrected in order to induce efficient behavior. In theory, manufacturers (i.e., rational actors) who speculate by low-balling the expected compensatory damages that will be successfully claimed against them will have to factor in the additional costs of extra-compensatory damages. If the extra-compensatory damages equal the difference between actual compensatory damages and the low estimate of expected compensatory damages, then the cost–benefit analysis will be properly reweighted for efficiency.

21 159 F 2d 169, 173–74 (2d Cir. 1947).

22 Introducing this economic interpretation of the Learned Hand formula for negligence as an explanation of the inner workings of legal doctrine, see Posner, "A Theory of Negligence," 52 ("the basic formal structure of the negligence system broadly supports an economic theory of negligence").

23 See generally R. D. Cooter, "Punitive Damages, Social Norms, and Economic Analysis" (1997) 60 *Law and Contemporary Problems* 73, 80.

24 See S. Shavell, "Strict Liability versus Negligence" (1980) 9 *Journal of Legal Studies* 1, 25.

In this logic, punitive damages are understood as extra-compensatory damages that play the role of mitigating enforcement errors.[25] According to Robert Cooter, when rational actors engage in violation of the standards of law and morality through intentional wrongdoing motivated by errors in enforcing compensatory damages (e.g., problems of detection or proof of causation, etc.), optimal deterrence requires increasing compensatory damages by the reciprocal of the enforcement error (i.e., attributing additional liability).[26] Understood in this way, punitive damages can offset enforcement errors and restore efficient deterrence to the liability system. Cooter calls this method for computing punitive damages the "rule of the reciprocal," which applies to most "self-seeking by firms."[27] As a consequence, when problems of detection are not present, such as in cases like the unmissable oil spill involving the Exxon Valdez accident, the rule of the reciprocal suggests that courts should not impose punitive damages because the rational actor could not have expected to escape liability when performing its cost–benefit risk analysis. As can be observed, the focus is on the under-enforcement problem of the liability system that results from underdetection of wrongful conduct. It basically holds that when the estimated compensatory damages alone will not induce an actor to take cost-justified safety precautions, then punitive damages are necessary to force the actor to internalize the full scope of harms caused by her actions.

Efficient incentives for injurers thus require setting liability equal to the net harm done to others.[28] Purely compensatory damages will not induce optimal care if the negligent injurer expects to escape liability for some of the harms they cause. In this under-enforcement context, the goal of punitive damages is to address this problem by increasing damages for the harms that are detected by a sufficient amount to ensure that injurers' expected liability equals the social cost of their wrongful conduct. It seeks to ensure that all the costs of harmful acts are placed on the liable actor. Again, the relevant element for punitive damages to be warranted is whether there is an under-enforcement issue, not whether the conduct was flagrant, malicious, or egregious.

As is to be expected, this optimal deterrence (or loss internalization) rationale for punitive damages has been the dominant approach taken by most torts scholars who

[25] See R. Cooter, "Economic Analysis of Punitive Damages" (1982) 56 *Southern California Law Review* 79, 101; and "Punitive Damages for Deterrence: When and How Much?" (1989) 40 *Alabama Law Review* 1143, 1148–53; D. Ellis, "Fairness and Efficiency in the Law of Punitive Damages" (1982) 56 *Southern California Law Review* 1, 25–29.

[26] See Cooter, "Punitive Damages, Social Norms, and Economic Analysis," 74; and "Punitive Damages for Deterrence," 1143 (offering an analysis of this issue that he calls "enforcement error").

[27] Ibid "Punitive Damages for Deterrence," 1148; and "Punitive Damages, Social Norms, and Economic Analysis," 90.

[28] On this point, see R. D. Cooter and A. Porat, *Getting Incentives Right: Improving Torts, Contracts, and Restitution* (Princeton University Press, 2014), p. 12 ("[T]he net harm equals the actual harm minus the benefits to others.").

engage in the economic analysis of law.[29] Mitchell Polinsky and Steven Shavell are two such scholars who offer a specific formula to calculate the amount of punitive damages that are necessary to achieve optimal deterrence, which they called the "punitive damages multiplier."[30] The "multiplier" for the determination of punitive damages is based upon the probability of detection. Thus, in order to make injurers pay for the harms they cause, "the total damages [compensatory plus punitive damages] imposed on an injurer should equal the harm multiplied by the reciprocal of the probability that the injurer would be found liable when he ought to be."[31] The multiplier works in the following way: If the injurer has a chance of escaping liability (i.e., the probability of detection is less than 100 percent), the proper amount of damages in those instances in which the injurer is found liable should be equivalent to the harm done to the victim multiplied by the reciprocal of the probability of being found liable. In this way, on average, the injurer will be paying for the total harm done and this will generate efficient behavior regarding cost-effective precautions. The threat of a monetary sanction (i.e., the punitive award) far beyond what would be required to compensate the plaintiff is thought to induce rational manufacturers to behave efficiently (i.e., it will provide the proper incentives for them to internalize total costs in their ex ante cost–benefit calculations).

An insightful well-known criticism to this economic approach has been articulated by Gregory Keating, who questions whether it might be desirable to demand more than the efficient level of safety investment when life itself is threatened with severe or irreparable injury.[32] Keating acknowledges that from the economic perspective it is irrational to press precaution beyond the efficient point because we all would be richer if we chose not to take the extra precautions demanded by the safety norms.[33] However, he asks whether there are ever good reasons for society to press precaution beyond the point of cost justifications. Keating argues that one possible response lies in considerations of fairness, which is concerned with the distributions of burdens and benefits among distinct persons.[34] He contends that when risks threaten devastating injury (such as premature death or severe injuries whose

[29] For examples of scholarship along these lines of thinking, see Cooter, "Economic Analysis of Punitive Damages"; M. A. Polinsky and S. Shavell, "Punitive Damages: An Economic Analysis" (1998) 111 *Harvard Law Review* 869; C. M. Sharkey, "Punitive Damages as Societal Damages" (2003) 113 *Yale Law Journal* 347; K. N. Hylton, "A Theory of Wealth and Punitive Damages" (2008) 17 *Widener Law Journal* 927, among others.

[30] See Polinsky and Shavell, "Punitive Damages: An Economic Analysis," 889. The multiplier is also discussed in judicial opinions by Judges Richard Posner and Guido Calabresi, see *Mathias* v. *Accor Economy Lodging Inc.*, 347 F 3d 672, 677 (7th Cir. 2003); and *Ciraolo* v. *City of New York*, 216 F 3d 236, 242 (2d Cir. 2000) (Calabresi J., concurring). Also see R. Craswell, "Deterrence and Damages: The Multiplier Principle and Its Alternatives" (1999) 97 *Michigan Law Review* 2185.

[31] See Polinsky and Shavell, "Punitive Damages: An Economic Analysis," 874 n124; 889.

[32] See generally G. C. Keating, "Pressing Precaution beyond the Point of Cost-Justification" (2003) 56 *Vanderbilt Law Review* 653.

[33] Ibid 658.

[34] Ibid 659, 668.

debilitating effects cannot be fully undone), fairness must be exercised at the time that the risk is imposed (i.e., ex ante), not after the injury takes place (i.e., ex post).[35] According to Keating, when devastating injury is risked, "it is unfair to treat the harm being risked as comparable to *any* benefit which might be gained, no matter how trivial that benefit is in the lives of those who reap it."[36] And he adds, "[i]t is only fair to ask some people to bear a significant risk of devastating injury when the burden of eliminating that risk is comparable to the burden of bearing it."[37] In his view, cost–benefit analysis ignores this because it treats all costs and all benefits as interests that are fungible at some ratio of exchange and aggregates costs and benefits across persons. Cost–benefit analysis supposes that loss of life or health by some can always be offset by an increase in wealth to others, independently of how trivial the effect of that increased wealth may be in the lives of those who benefit from it.[38] Keating claims that it is unfair to treat trivial benefits and devastating losses as comparable simply because they are not. His charge against cost–benefit analysis (and cost-justified precaution) is their insensitivity to the demand that death and devastation should only be risked for the sake of a comparable value.[39] The bottom line is that fair treatment of risks of devastating injury requires us to take more than cost-justified precaution against their occurrence.

This expert approach to societal trust has three major implications. The first is a one-sided focus on deterring the defendant's behavior. The one-sidedness follows from the concentration of attention on the relationship between the behavior of the manufacturer and efficient results (i.e., the rationality of manufacturer behavior when executing cost–benefit analysis to decide which precautions to take). The expert approach thus fixates on the incentive effects of liability (i.e., the possible obligation to pay a higher monetary award) on potential corporate wrongdoing as a mechanism to achieve efficient deterrence. A second major implication of the expert approach is relegating the plaintiff to a contingent role. This role is conceptually reduced to an instrumental function in service of the goal of wealth maximization that can be characterized as an enforcement role: The tort victim is seen as a sort of private attorney general legally incentivized to enforce efficient behavior from manufacturers by the prospect of monetary gain (i.e., the punitive award).[40]

35 Ibid 657.

36 Ibid 660 (emphasis in original).

37 Ibid.

38 Ibid 668.

39 Ibid 746. For a similar line of thinking in the environmental law context, see D. A. Kysar, *Regulating From Nowhere: Environmental Law and the Search for Objectivity* (Yale University Press, 2010), p. 196 (arguing that "[t]he logic of optimization embedded within cost-benefit analysis marginalizes and even erases crucial questions of ethics and responsibility that were once at the heart of environmental law.").

40 Describing the enforcement of social norms through the attorney general as one of the functions of punitive damages, see G. Calabresi, "The Complexities of Torts: The Case of Punitive Damages," in M. S. Madden (ed.), *Exploring Tort Law* (Cambridge University Press, 2005), pp. 336–47.

In this construction, the victim–wrongdoer relationship is not essential but rather contingent or derivative.[41] The tort victim thus resorts to tort law to advance an aggregate goal (efficiency and wealth maximization), which is external to her. Tort liability is understood as a systemic and aggregate response to wrongdoing regardless of whether the injured party herself or a third party brings the lawsuit – it approximates a market-driven approach to litigation in which whoever is best positioned or most motivated to sue should do so, since the purpose is to promote the most efficient (or socially desirable) allocation of resources to safety concerns.[42] This implies disconnecting the ultimate goal of efficiency from the actual wrong committed by the manufacturer to the victim. On one side, the primary normative relationship ties the manufacturer to the goal of optimal deterrence, and, on the other, the victim's role is similarly primary related to that very same goal.[43] The relationship between wrongdoer and victim loses its relevance in this perspective that prioritizes the relationship between the behavior of both the defendant and plaintiff with the ultimate goal of efficiency. This fixation places the emphasis on creating incentives that encourage defendants to take the most efficient level of precaution and plaintiffs to correct breaches of efficiency through litigation. Hence, the defendant-plaintiff relationship is "mediated" by the aim of efficiency.

A third major implication of the expert approach relates to the second. The formal and abstract understanding of the tort victim in the expert approach conceptually reduces the plaintiff to a rational actor who can be considered apart from the substantive significance of the reprehensible wrong done to her.[44] This economic reading of lawsuits requires assuming litigant rationality and overlooks not only the reprehensible character of the defendant's conduct (since the relevant element is the rationale of the manufacturer's behavior when executing cost–benefit calculations to decide which precautions to take) but also other value-driven reactions of the victim of the reprehensible corporate wrongdoing that do not have bearing on the "expected" economic behavioral outcome (efficiency, optimal deterrence).[45] From this economic perspective, any other substantive motivation the plaintiff may have for pursuing the punitive lawsuit against egregious corporate wrongdoing,

For a discussion on the origins and applications of the concept of private attorney general, see generally W. B. Rubenstein, "On What A 'Private Attorney General Is – And Why It Matters'" (2004) 57 *Vanderbilt Law Review* 2129.

41 I further explore this claim in Part IV.

42 For proposals favoring third party litigation, see E. Guttel, A. Harel and S. Lavie, "Torts for Nonvictims: The Case for Third-Party Litigation" (2018) 2018 *University of Illinois Law Review* 1049 (they focus on cases in which the victim is not the "cheapest compensation seeker" and identify third parties that are more likely to litigate).

43 For an economic account of the normative structure of tort law, see Landes and Posner, *The Economic Structure of Tort Law*. For a comprehensive review of the early literature on the economics of litigation in the United States, see R. D. Cooter and D. L. Rubinfeld, "Economic Analysis of Legal Disputes and Their Resolution" (1987) 27 *Journal of Economic Literature* 1067.

44 On the significance of the tort victim, see Chapter 9.

45 On tort victims' retributive motivations, see Section A of Chapter 3.

such as desire for justice, vindication of her rights, or condemnation, should be in principle regarded as misguided, or irrational.[46]

In short, the expert approach to societal trust focuses exclusively on producers' technical task of balancing costs and benefits, which mostly follows market-oriented mandates. Those mandates cannot begin to capture the nature and range of ordinary people's responses to reprehensible corporate misbehavior that imposes a significant risk of devastating harm on them. Under this approach, the limited role that is left to consumers is basically reduced to identifying errors made by experts (manufacturers, producers) in the execution of the technical task of balancing costs and benefits when deciding the level of safety precautions to undertake (i.e., when the figures, weights, or measurements used in the calculation are mistaken). The consumer filing a punitive lawsuit is thus formally understood as a mere enforcer of the experts' decision-making that follows market-oriented mandates. Product liability lawsuits involving punitive awards are in this sense conceived as a tool to fine-tune the cost–benefit formula, full stop.

As discussed earlier, the general underlying idea is that tort law (or the liability system) must be supplemented with a punitive damage regime (or any other extra-compensatory arrangement) in order to overcome the system's deficiencies (i.e., the under-enforcement problem) and generate the right incentives to achieve the goal of optimal deterrence. Thus, broadly speaking, punitive damages are understood as a price that plays the gap-filling role.[47] In other words, the strategy is all about pricing behavior in order to force actors to internalize social costs appropriately – be they taxes, fines, subsidies, punishments, tort awards, or contractual liabilities, all are seen as fungible instruments meant to induce desirable behavior.[48] The idea of pricing immediately brings markets to mind. Guido Calabresi has in fact argued that at times we could view the liability rule as a mechanism to mimic the market.[49] Following this logic, punitive damages are conceived as a tool (or mechanism) we can use to attain marketplace-like results (for instance, loss internalization, gain elimination). Accordingly, punitive damages take the form of the multiplier effect when people shirk liability. Calabresi believes this is exactly the idea underlying Polinsky and Shavell's reconstruction that explains the multiplier's efficiency.[50]

46 On why victims sue, see Section B of Chapter 9. Problematizing this point, see Owen, "Problems in Assessing Punitive Damages," 17 (noting that litigants do not go to court to provide the judge with an opportunity to pursue her vision of optimal risk reduction but to have their claims vindicated).

47 For the argument that punitive damages are one way to fill the gap between allowed compensation and perfect compensation, see Cooter, "Punitive Damages, Social Norms, and Economic Analysis," 81.

48 On this point, see, for example, Cooter and Porat, Getting Incentives Right, p. 2 ("[L]iability could be seen […] as a price to internalize the harm caused.").

49 See generally G. Calabresi and A. D. Melamed, "Property Rules, Liability Rules, and Inalienability: One View of the Cathedral" (1972) 85 *Harvard Law Review* 1089 (discussing more generally the use of liability rules to achieve socially optimal resource allocations that might not be reached otherwise).

50 See G. Calabresi, "A Broader View of the Cathedral: The Significance of the Liability Rule, Correcting A Misapprehension" (2014) 77 *Law and Contemporary Problems* 1, 7.

Under this logic, the defendant's conduct is not assessed as "flagrant" or "egregious" or "reprehensible" but as conduct that substantially deviated from the optimal level of care. That is to say, the so-called "punitive" response is not grounded on the reprehensible character of the defendant's conduct but on her failure to take adequate precautions. Thus, the extra-compensatory response is almost completely detached from the moral character of the conduct itself. This is why it makes sense to think of punitive damages as the "price" that manufacturers might have to pay if they seek to profit from the chances of nondetection for careless conduct and therefore the "price" they should factor ex ante into their cost–benefit analysis calculations. A "price" is considered a payment of money that is required in exchange for permission to act in a certain way.[51] Indeed, we commonly think of a "price" amorally as the mere fee whose payment allows us to act as we wish.[52] It is therefore logical that manufacturers might understand the monetary sanction as a "license fee" for profitable business practices regardless of the nature of what is compromised on the other side of the equation. The disconnection from the moral character of the conduct frames nearly all manufacturer behavior as permitted, that is, as a legitimate choice between taking and not taking optimal precautions as long as the manufacturer is willing to pay the "price" of noncompliance (e.g., punitive awards).

To illustrate this phenomenon, I refer to real-world experiments on the psychology of sanctions. A study conducted by Ann E. Tenbrunsel and David M. Messick demonstrated that sanctions sometimes induce people to evaluate and make decisions in business rather than ethical terms.[53] In a simulated setting, participants were given the role of factory manager and asked to determine the extent to which they would employ chimney scrubbers to reduce their factory's toxic emissions. In the absence of sanctions, people viewed this decision as basically an environmental or ethical issue in which running the scrubbers was the "right" thing to do. When a financial sanction was implemented for failure to run the scrubbers, however, attitudes changed. Then, people started thinking of the decision as a business decision fundamentally about profit maximization rather than an ethical or environmental decision. Another interesting study on the "crowding out effect" of monetary sanctions was conducted by Uri Gneezy and Aldo Rustichini.[54] In their study, parents were fined if they failed to pick up their children on time from the daycare center. Contrary to what was expected, the authors showed in their study that the fine actually increased rather than decreased the number of parents who picked up their children late. Their explanation of this effect was that the fine altered the parent's perception of the situation. Once the fine was introduced, the parents began

[51] See generally R. D. Cooter, "Prices and Sanctions" (1984) 84 *Columbia Law Review* 1523.

[52] Ibid 1543–44.

[53] See A. E. Tenbrunsel and D. M. Messick, "Sanctioning Systems, Decision Frames, and Cooperation" (1999) 44 *Administrative Science Quarterly* 684.

[54] U. Gneezy and A. Rustichini, "A Fine is a Price" (2000) 29 *Journal of Legal Studies* 1.

thinking, "the teacher is taking care of the child in much the same way as she did earlier in the day. Since I am paying a price for the additional time (which is called a 'fine'), there is nothing wrong with paying for the additional service whenever needed."[55] Instead of seeing the fine for late pick up as a sign of moral disapproval, the parents regarded it as a reasonable price to pay in exchange for additional after hours of childcare.[56]

These studies suggest that monetary sanctions may actually remove moral considerations from decisions and, as a consequence, displace intrinsic motivations to cooperate.[57] That is to say, they suggest that financial sanctions undermine certain moral behavioral norms, for example, they "may undermine the feeling that it is wrong to put one's own interests first."[58] That means that monetary sanctions could cause people to frame a decision previously considered ethical in nature (i.e., it is acceptable to do this?) in business terms (i.e., it is cost-effective to do this?), which may even lead to lower compliance rates.[59]

Granted, understanding punitive damages as prices aligns well with the rational, self-interested behavior of the manufacturer and the contingent and formal understanding of the tort victim that characterizes this expert approach. In fact, corporations have been seen to manipulate figures, sums of money, and abstract formulas in a way that is completely detached from the real issues at stake: as contrasting "costs with costs" instead of "costs with lives and limbs of the consumers." The inner logic of punitive damages as prices indirectly encourages detached, external product safety assessments.

However, this reconstruction has been strongly criticized from various angles. To begin with, it makes economic deterrence the exclusive function of punitive damages, completely overlooking the patent retributive dimension of the

55 Ibid 14–15.

56 Arguing that sanctions that look more like punishments rather than prices are less likely to induce the crowding-out effect, see Y. Feldman and D. Teichman, "Are All 'Legal Dollars' Created Equal?" (2008) 102 *Northwestern University Law Review* 223, 225.

57 See generally E. L. Deci, R. M. Koestner and R. A. Ryan, "Meta-Analytic Review of Experiments Examining the Effect of Extrinsic Rewards on Intrinsic Motivation" (1999) 125 *Psychological Bulletin* 627.

58 On this point, see E. Van Dijk, L. B. Mulder and E. W. Kwaadsteniet, "For the Common Good? The Use of Sanctions in Social Dilemmas," in P. A. M. Van Lange, B. Rockendbach and T. Yamagishi (eds.), *Reward and Punishment in Social Dilemmas* (Oxford University Press, 2014), pp. 71–72; Feldman and Teichman, "Are All 'Legal Dollars' Created Equal?," 262 (showing that fines induce a perception of the sanction as a price – and this, in turn, may encourage agents to indulge in private risk-benefit analyses).

59 For studies suggesting that intrinsic motivation may be better at achieving desired behavioral outcomes than extrinsic motivation, see Y. Feldman and O. Lobel, "The Incentives Matrix: The Comparative Effectiveness of Rewards, Liabilities, Duties, and Protections for Reporting Illegality" (2010) 88 *Texas Law Review* 1151, 1152 ("[i]n some cases offering monetary rewards to whistle-blowers will lead to less, rather than more, reporting of illegality."); D. M. Kahan, "Trust, Collective Action, and Law" (2001) 81 *Boston University Law Review* 333, 338–39 (arguing that "the advent of incentives will produce […] less, not more, of such [desirable] behavior.").

institution – directly equivocating punishment with deterrence, thus diminishing the former.[60] The focus on behavior as right or wrong according only to an efficiency standard as well as understanding tort litigation's purpose as correcting "defective" behavior in exclusively economic terms fails to factor in features of the normative landscape that have a fundamentally deontic character. For instance, this reconstruction does not account for the historical common law retributive roots of the institution that emphasize the conventional requirement of conduct reprehensibility (originally, real malice or wanton misconduct).[61] Furthermore, it ignores the practice of courts to favor proportionate punishment when determining punitive damages over deterrence-oriented factors, such as probability of detection.[62] Recall the research studies from social sciences discussed in Part II demonstrating that, in practice, people have difficulty performing and conforming to the strict cost–benefit analysis embraced in the standard economic models of deterrence.[63] As discussed in Part II, these studies reveal that the punishment decisions of lay decision-makers tend to map more closely to retributive intuitions than to optimal deterrence objectives. Similarly, this research also demonstrates that jurors frequently reject the Polinsky–Shavell instructions as a useful tool in determining the appropriate civil penalties.[64] Some scholars have even argued that courts are incapable of successfully executing a rigorous cost–benefit negligence analysis.[65] Besides, as has already been pointed out, the lack of any conclusive empirical studies confirming the real-world effectiveness of optimal deterrence also throws its feasibility into question.

Another set of powerful objections to the expert's approach to punitive damages are based on the unilateral focus on the defendant's behavior and the extrinsic character of the goal of efficient deterrence, which not only implausibly depicts wrongdoers and victims as disconnected from the other but also displays indifference to the substantive content of tort victims' motivations to resort to tort litigation for punitive responses to egregious wrongs done to them. As argued in Part II, one of the problems with such a contingent and formal reconstruction of the tort victim is that it lies at odds with people's intuitions regarding punishment: It fails to explain satisfactorily why tort victims would want to punish outrageous behavior in the first

[60] I have explored this in detail in Section E of Chapter 2.

[61] See J. C. P. Goldberg and B. C. Zipursky, *Recognizing Wrongs* (Harvard University Press, 2020), p. 171 (recalling the "traditional and still-prevailing common law rule that punitive damages are available only in cases of egregious wrongdoing").

[62] See, for instance, *BMW* v. *Gore*, 517 US 559, 575 (1996) (where the United States Supreme Court has held that due process requires penalties [punitive damages] to be imposed proportionally).

[63] See Chapter 3.

[64] See N. R. Feigenson, "Can Tort Juries Punish Competently?" (2003) 78 *Chicago-Kent Law Review* 239, 275–76.

[65] See A. Schwartz, "Proposals for Products Liability Reform: A Theoretical Synthesis" (1988) 97 *Yale Law Journal* 353, 386–88 (arguing that courts are simply incapable of applying a negligence rule that will yield efficient outcomes); K. W. Viscusi, *Reforming Products Liability* (Harvard University Press, 1991), p. 212 (conceding that courts are ill-equipped to conduct cost–benefit tests).

place since it is unable to capture the substance and range of ordinary people's punitive reactions to reprehensible wrongdoing.[66] Once again, economic deterrence overlooks any other substantive value-driven motive for people to seek a punitive response through tort litigation in those reprehensible tortious situations apart from the expected behavioral outcome of achieving optimal deterrence. Moreover, as most product liability punitive damages cases involve some sort of concealment of product risks or manipulation of risk perceptions from manufacturers to consumers (recall the pervasive incentives for manufacturers to withhold information in the mass-market context), consumers are less likely to have access to the information needed to act as the fully informed and rational calculators who seek to maximize their welfare that the expert approach assumes. As argued in Part II and further explored in the following section and in Part IV, the motives that lead victims to seek recourse in tort law and the tort process for appropriate responses to wrongdoing are much richer and more textured and meaningful than those captured by the narrow economic logic of the rational actor typically used by expert-based approaches in their models.[67]

B THE ORDINARY PERSON APPROACH TO SOCIETAL TRUST: PUNITIVE DAMAGES AS RETRIBUTIVE SANCTIONS

Is efficiency the ultimate value around which ordinary people construct the meaning of societal trust? Do consumers expect manufacturers to take cost-effective precautions no matter what is at stake? Are consumers at ease with the corporate practices of engaging in instrumentalist assessments of the value of human life that are then weighed against the monetary cost of precautionary measures? All these questions challenge the expert approach assumption that consumers are purely rational calculators seeking to maximize their welfare and suggest that there exist alternative explanations that align better with ordinary people's moral intuitions about risk and trust.[68] For instance, the understanding of ordinary people regarding the

[66] See Chapter 3.

[67] I explore in detail tort victims' motivations to sue in Section B of Chapter 9.

[68] For scholarship along these lines, see, for example, B. Schwartz, "Crowding Out Morality: How the Ideology of Self-Interest Can Be Self-Fulfilling," in J. Hanson (ed.), *Ideology, Psychology, and Law* (Oxford University Press, 2012), p. 179 (arguing that the economists rational self-interest conception of human behavior is not only a flaw but also a reductionist one because it overlooks other aspects of human nature); A. L. Alstott, "A Fine is Not a Price: Insights for Law," in J. Hanson (ed.), *Ideology, Psychology, and Law* (Oxford University Press, 2012), p. 187 (arguing that "[w]e should be aware that people are moved by their situation and by other-regarding motives as much as or more than financial payoffs and self-regarding preferences."). Also see H. Latin, "Activity Levels, Due Care, and Selective Realism in Economic Analysis of Tort Law" (1987) 39 *Rutgers Law Review* 487, 487 (arguing that economic analysis rests on completely "unrealistic assumptions about human and institutional behavior," and hence is not "legally useful"); and "'Good' Warnings, Bad Products, and Cognitive Limitations" (1994) 41 *UCLA Law Review* 1193, 1249–55 (denying that consumers act rationally in the way economic analysis suggests).

imposition of risks of devastating injury aligns well with what Gregory Keating refers to as the "safety-based standard."[69] This safety standard requires risk to be reduced to a point where "no significant risk" of devastating injury remains. Therefore, this safety-based standard does not require any inquiry into the costs of risk reductions; instead it requires a determination of the level at which the risk created by exposure to the product ceases to be "significant."[70] What consumers expect from manufacturers is risk evaluation, not cost assessment. The consumer's expectation is that risks of devastating injury be reduced until they are insignificant, without regard to cost.[71] The bottom line is that fair treatment of risks of devastating injury requires manufacturers to take more than cost-justified precaution against their occurrence – which of course does not necessarily mean absolute safety.[72] The underlying idea is that manufacturers should not assume that the cost-justified level is the default standard to follow in every circumstance without further reflection.[73] Instead, they have to refine what is the "justified" level of precaution in every case by considering the (qualitative) significance of the risk at stake.[74]

To think only in terms of monetary value is to overlook the actual value that people often place on, for example, safety, life, autonomy, or equal respect.[75] In fact, a growing body of empirical research suggests that lay citizens refuse to engage in utilitarian balancing.[76] People actually shy away from any instrumentalist assessment of the value of human life and physical integrity and usually refuse to reduce the human safety risk tradeoff assessment to nothing more than a cost–benefit test. For instance, Guido Calabresi points out that the outrage of the jury that assessed punitive damages in the famous Ford Pinto case "was probably explained by the fact that Ford had justified burning up people by offering cold statistics about the cost of changing the placement of the gas tank."[77] Moreover, if we admit that market dynamics involve moral values, it is also plausible to assert that some societal trust is based on the shared assumption that market practices rest on a culture of honesty, recognized

69 See Keating, "Pressing Precaution Beyond the Point of Cost-Justification," 748 (arguing that the safety-based standard is sensitive to the incommensurabilities of value that define the problem of devastating injury).

70 Ibid 685.

71 Ibid 699.

72 Ibid 746 (arguing that "[t]he criterion of cost justification is appropriate for regulating harm to goods that are fungible and replaceable.").

73 See G. C. Keating, "Is Cost-Benefit Analysis the Only Game in Town?" (2018) 91 *Southern California Law Review* 195, 261 ("cost-benefit analysis is not the only game in town, and cost-justified precaution is not the only plausible standard of precaution.").

74 This does not mean that those determinations are unchallengeable.

75 On this point, see R. H. Pildes and E. S. Anderson, "Slinging Arrows at Democracy: Social Choice Theory, Value Pluralism, and Democratic Politics" (1990) 90 *Columbia Law Review* 2121, 2150–51 (while discussing public culture, they refer that safety is a value that is "hierarchically incommensurable to" economic considerations relating to safety expenditures).

76 See, for example, D. A. Hoffman and M. P. O'Shea, "Can Law and Economics Be Both Practical and Principled?" (2002) 53 *Alabama Law Review* 335, 394–407.

77 See Calabresi, "The Complexities of Torts," p. 341.

limits on self-interest, and fair dealings, whether these lead to greater efficiency or not. As Barry Schwartz's research on judging fairness in market situations demonstrates, most people find applying moral standards in evaluating market transactions perfectly appropriate.[78] His studies show that the marketplace is not understood as "an amoral playing field in which anything that is not illegal is acceptable" or as "a place in which the naked and unrestrained pursuit of self-interest is condoned."[79]

The ordinary consumer expects manufacturers not to speculate with numbers and abstract figures when lives and limbs are at stake. Hence, they generally reject discussions of whether a given manufacturer used the correct figures in its cost–benefit analysis. Ordinary people do not think that manufacturers' expectations of future profits should completely outweigh the moral considerations involved when those manufacturers knowingly engage in behavior that exposes consumers to unreasonable risk of harm.[80] What the ordinary consumers expect from knowledgeable manufacturers is that they refrain from purposely exposing them to the risk of serious harms of which consumers are unaware, openly jeopardizing their physical integrity or individual autonomy for economic profit. In this line of thought, psychological research on taboo trade-offs has shown that people see human life as a sacred value not subject to an instrumentalist assessment against monetary profit. According to Alan P. Fiske and Phillip E. Tetlock, people often become angry when asked to exchange a protected value for money because those exchanges are viewed as morally degrading and threatening to the social order.[81] Underneath this argument is a belief that understanding life as priceless (i.e., as not comparable or quantifiable in terms of other interests) serves an important social purpose, despite the fact that we realize that human life is given a monetary value in tradeoffs every day in explicit and implicit ways.[82] Guido Calabresi writes: "[t]he problem is that although we know at some level that not every safety measure is worth paying for and that some accidents – however horrible – are 'worth having,' yet we are committed to the ideal that life is a pearl beyond price. And we are determined, as a society, to hold to both contradictory views."[83]

78 On this point, see Schwartz, "Crowding Out Morality," p. 177.

79 Ibid.

80 See M. Douglas and A. Wildavsky, *Risk and Culture* (California Press, 1982), p. 73 ("One salient difference between experts and the lay public is that the latter, when assessing risks, do not conceal their moral commitments but put them into the argument, explicitly and prominently.").

81 See A. P. Fiske and P. E. Tetlock, "Taboo Trade-Offs: Reactions to Transactions that Transgress the Spheres of Justice" (1997) 18 *Political Psychology* 255, 256 (their research regarding "taboo trade-offs" shows that people refuse to explicitly compare human life [a "sacred" category] and monetary profit [a "secular" category]).

82 On this tension, see, for example, J. Baron, "Tradeoffs Among Reasons for Action" (1986) 16 *Journal for the Theory of Social Behaviour* 173 (arguing that despite what people say about incommensurability, they all the time make tradeoffs between incommensurables, such as life and property); and G. Calabresi and P. Bobbit, *Tragic Choices* (W. W. Norton & Company, 1978), p. 20 (stating that we can continue on with the naïve belief that our society does not establish an acceptable number of auto deaths, but that this figure results from thousands of independent, atomistic actions).

83 See Calabresi, "The Complexities of Torts," 341.

Distorting reality for private gain is an open breach of societal trust that cannot be ignored. When there are misleading conducts leading consumers to believe something that does not correspond to reality, then we can say that the consumers' freedom to pursue their personal life plan has been taken away. Thus, from the perspective of the ordinary consumer, societal trust is violated when manufacturers knowingly place defective products as safe in the stream of commerce with sufficient knowledge that people are likely to be severely harmed as a consequence. Recent product liability punitive damages cases against corporate misbehavior involving trading life for profit are a good illustration of these lay understandings.[84] In those cases, General Motors and Takeda Pharmaceuticals were respectively aware of the risks of fatal collisions because of an ignition switch defect (General Motors) and the health risks of bladder cancer in patients who took the drug Acto for over a year (Takeda), but both decided to conceal those risks to consumers and only warned people about them nearly a decade later, after many had been severely injured or even died as a result of the defect or of taking the drug for a prolonged period. The consumers' denouncement of that sort of deceptive misbehavior is a manifestation of the lay understanding of life's sacred value, which is nontradeable for profit and of the high value people place on physical integrity and individual autonomy, in that General Motors and Takeda were perceived as imposing significant risks of harm on others that could not possibly be deemed "cost-justified" without weakening the moral fabric of society.

In the eyes of the ordinary consumer, manufacturers' choices are not seen as the abstract choice by a rational agent not to take certain safety precautions that would affect its bottom line but as a concrete, willful decision to harm people. The way we understand conduct is connected to how we attribute responsibility and blame. To clarify, if we see the manufacturer's conduct in terms of a decision to harm people, particularly when the conduct is reprehensible, the deaths or serious injuries that result from the conduct have different significance for us and we would probably seek to express our disapproval of the wrongdoing, whereas when we understand the same conduct as the outcome of a rational calculation to maximize efficiency, then it is plausible to think of punitive damages as merely a price or tool to disincentivize similar calculation errors in the future regardless of the reprehensibility of the defendant's conduct.[85] Our judgments of responsibility and blame thus change depending on the way in which we understand the manufacturer's choice.[86] The famous Ford

[84] For relevant examples see Section B of Chapter 6.

[85] On the cost of dispositionism, see A. Benforado and J. D. Hanson, "The Cost of Dispositionism: The Premature Demise of Situationist Law and Economics" (2005) 64 *Maryland Law Review* 24, 61 (arguing that the problem with a dispositionist view is that "[i]s like a pair of blinders. It is a means of not seeing what might trouble us, a way of believing that everything is all right – that we are safe, that our groups are deserving, and that our systems are fair and safe from collapse.").

[86] See generally J. D. Hanson and D. A. Kysar, "Taking Behavioralism Seriously: Some Evidence of Market Manipulation" (1999) 112 *Harvard Law Review* 1420 (using the example of tobacco litigation to show how the changing perceptions of the tobacco industry over two decades reflect the shift in attributions of causation, responsibility, and blame).

Pinto case offers a good illustration of these dynamics. If we think of the Ford Pinto auto accident fatalities as independent, atomistic accidents that happened in different places, at different times, involving different, perhaps even exculpatory circumstances, then those deaths have a completely different meaning than when we look at them as the consequence of someone's knowing choice to expose others to a significant risk of harm in the hope of reaping greater economic profit.[87] When situations are framed as a consequence of choice, our reaction changes. The understanding of the real choices involved in a more holistic manner changes our perceptions and reactions.[88] Furthermore, a decision not to save a particular individual's life is very different than a decision not to invest in precautions that might reduce the risk of fatality. As Calabresi and Bobbit explain, "the choice is less exposed [in the latter] and therefore less destructive of some of the basic values involved."[89]

From there, it could be argued that the manner in which ordinary consumers assess the safety measure decisions of manufacturers is sensitive to the complexity of the plurality of values (e.g., the sanctity of life, the deep-seated desire to live autonomously) involved in those decisions, departing deeply from the experts' techniques for assessment in purely efficiency terms. Moreover, this different way of assessing corporate behavior will also explain their distinctive reactions toward it.[90] As will be seen, consumers' reactions rest on the expectation of a manifestation of a certain degree of regard from corporations toward them. Their reactions, which are informed by moral values on how we should all regard one another, are natural human reactions to the indifference that others display through attitudes and actions toward us.[91] As Linda Radzik argues, because people hold the same moral-laden attitudes toward collectives as they do toward individuals, they "[e]xpect a certain level of treatment from those institutions. They feel angry, resentful, betrayed, distrustful, insulted or threatened when those expectations are violated."[92]

87 On this vein, showing that people interpret intentional harm as worse than unintentional (but equally damaging) harm, see D. L. Ames and S. T. Fiske, "Intentional Harms Are Worse, Even When They're Not" (2013) 24(9) *Psychological Science* 1755.

88 On situationism, see generally J. Hanson and D. Yosifon, "The Situational Character: A Critical Realist Perspective on the Human Animal" (2004) 93 *Georgetown Law Journal* 1.

89 See Calabresi and Bobbit, Tragic Choices, p. 40.

90 On this point, see D. A. Kysar, "Preferences for Processes: The Process/Product Distinction and the Regulation of Consumer Choice" (2003) 118 *Harvard Law Review* 525, 532 (arguing that "[t]here is reason also to believe that public reactions to health and safety hazards are richer and more value-laden than typical expert assessments.").

91 On tort victims' retributive motivations, see Chapter 3.

92 See L. Radzik, "Tort Processes and Relational Repair," in J. Oberdiek (ed.), *Philosophical Foundations of the Law of Torts* (Oxford University Press, 2014), p. 238. Similarly, see V. P. Hans, *Business on Trial: The Civil Jury and Corporate Responsibility* (Yale University Press, 2000), pp. 112–38 (Hans provides direct evidence that individuals hold corporations to higher standards because they expect corporations to be more competent and knowledgeable: "[m]ore is expected of a reasonable corporation than a reasonable person.").

These reactions are illuminated in the behavioral research study of betrayal aversion conducted by Jonathan Koehler and Andrew Gershoff denoted in Part II.[93] In their study, the authors suggest that a form of consumer betrayal occurs when products cause the very harm they are entrusted to guard against. Their starting premise is the hypothesis that trust and betrayal share a strong connection. From there, they explore what they call "asymmetric trust relationships" (relationships in which one party is supposed to protect the other against certain harms) and how people respond to violations of it (when the protecting party causes the harm they were to protect against).[94] Koehler and Gershoff refer to such violations of trust as "betrayals" when "an agent of protection actively causes the very harm he or she was entrusted to prevent."[95] In their reconstruction, consumers form "asymmetric trusting relationships" with safety products not only because consumers willingly accept the vulnerability to which the products expose them but also because the consumers rely on implicit expectations that the manufacturers will protect them from, not cause, the very harms against which the manufacturers are entrusted to guard. When manufacturers break the implicit promise of protection, they violate the trust consumers have placed in them, threatening the social order that allowed consumers to have a positive expectation of safety in the first place.[96] Koehler and Gershoff assert that increasing evidence indicates that such betrayal generates strong animosity that translates into an intent to punish the agents responsible. According to them, those consumers' desires to punish perceived betrayal and to eliminate betrayal risks where possible reflect both the disruption that betrayals wreak upon our social fabric and the importance of maintaining trust and order in our societies.[97]

Even though this phenomenon is described as "object betrayal" (in the sense that the product itself is betraying the consumer), Koehler and Gershoff predict that people will respond with the same desire to impose punishments on those believed to be responsible (i.e., the manufacturer of the betraying product) as strong as those they would inflict for personal betrayal.[98] Accordingly, in the context of product safety betrayal, the researchers found that people reacted more strongly (in terms of the punishment inflicted and the retributive reactions triggered) to acts considered betrayal than to identical bad acts that did not violate a duty or promise to protect.[99] Koehler and Gershoff's studies support the idea that people react to

93 See Koehler and Gershoff, "Betrayal Aversion," 244.

94 Ibid.

95 Ibid 245.

96 Ibid 249.

97 Ibid 245; 257.

98 Ibid 249.

99 Ibid 257. Similarly see J. Baron, "The Effect of Normative Beliefs on Anticipated Emotions" (1992) 63 *Journal of Personality and Social Psychology* 320 (In a study on anticipated emotions, it was found that most people say they would feel angrier if they were blinded from a vaccine for a disease than if they were blinded from an untreated disease).

consumer betrayal with punitive intent. As a matter of fact, people who imagined being harmed by a malfunctioning safety product were more likely to seek punitive damages.[100] All these predictions are consistent with the research introduced in Part II that finds a strong correlation between reactive attitudes of anger, outrage, or betrayal and acts believed to deserve punishment.[101] In such instances, there is a perception that the community's moral standards have been egregiously violated and that the treacherous behavior represents a significant departure from the substantive values regulating how we should be regarded and treated by others.

As can be inferred, the expert approach to punitive damages has no moral credibility in the eyes of ordinary consumers (i.e., it does not reflect their moral intuitions about risk and trust). The ordinary person approach is much more aligned with people's everyday sense of justice and better suited to integrate their value-driven motivations to punish reprehensible corporate behavior. In fact, when a corporation exposes consumers to unreasonable risk of serious harm by prioritizing the pursuit of its own private ends over the appropriate regard for the interests of others, laypeople's responsive attitudes are rooted in value-driven motivations quite removed from economic deterrence. The realization that a corporation has betrayed the consumer's trust by exposing her to significant safety risks to her life, physical integrity or individual autonomy, a risk of which she was unaware, gives rise to punitive reactions that not only respond to the perceived need to make a forceful statement condemning the corporation's disregard for public standards of safety (in terms of risks that can acceptably be imposed on others in pursuing private economically-oriented interests) but also to the need to reaffirm her own self-worth vis-à-vis the value-diminishing reprehensible behavior of the offending corporation that made a deliberate decision to prioritize private gain over consumer safety.

By now, the idea that punitive responses should be governed by efficiency alone should seem inadequate and unconvincing. The "ordinary person approach to societal trust" is instead able to capture the relevance of those qualitative factors that the expert approach is unable to appreciate, namely the plurality of substantive values (life is a pearl beyond price, the significance of leading an autonomous life) that inform the punitive reactions of ordinary consumers toward deliberate impositions of unreasonable risks of significant harm for private gain by powerful actors in the marketplace. The ordinary person's approach directly expresses commitment to those substantive values: Victims' retributive reactions find their authenticity in shared moral attitudes regarding risk, trust, and the equal respect deserved by every member of the community. Under this approach, the ordinary consumer plays a substantive role in denouncing the moral significance of the corporate wrongdoing that violates her positive expectation of safety in line with the intuitions that laypeople share about risk and trust (i.e., which risks are unacceptable to impose on others

[100] See Koehler and Gershoff, "Betrayal Aversion," 250.
[101] See Chapter 3.

for private gain). The victim herself is specially situated to expose the corporate misbehavior and hold the corporation accountable by judicially demanding the corporate defendant to answer the question of how the wrong came about. The tort victim understands product liability punitive damages litigation as a legitimate avenue for communicating to the egregious manufacturer that it inadequately considered the significance of the risk that should prevail in those circumstances – mainly that lives and limbs are nontradable for profits, making the cost-justified level of precaution objectionable in those situations.

Product liability punitive damages lawsuits are a means for tort victims to communicate to manufacturers the condemnatory message that they should have acted differently in the ex ante scenario of risk-assessment decision-making. These lawsuits also convey the message that expert cost–benefit analysis is ill-equipped to respect or do justice to the complexity of values at stake in risk evaluation. Assessing the complexity is not only about numbers and efficiency and numbers cannot possibly fully represent it. People refuse to accept that the value of autonomy to pursue a personal life plan be dismissed by the callous behavior of a profit-seeking corporation. Punitive lawsuits afford consumers an opportunity to judicially condemn egregious corporate misbehavior by affirming their self-worth vis-à-vis the offending corporation. They provide an opportunity for victims to obtain a condemnatory response that is respectful of the meaning and significance of having been reprehensibly wronged in a value-diminishing fashion by an indifferent corporate defendant that put its interests ahead of theirs, an opportunity that is unavailable for most individuals seeking redress against powerful corporations in other legitimate venues.[102] In this logic, a punitive response pursued through product liability litigation is understood as a communicative act that directly addresses the wrongdoer. It directly expresses disapproval for the reprehensibility of the corporate defendant's violation of societal trust (betrayal of the consumer's safety expectation) and calls for a condemnatory response for the purpose of reasserting the victim's self-worth vis-à-vis the defendant, thus further reinforcing other-regarding values in society and the maintenance of the social order.

Sanctioning reprehensible corporate behavior that exposes consumers to risks of significant harm for private gain represents a proper retributive response to communicate condemnation for consumer betrayal by reasserting the individual consumer's true value vis-à-vis the offending corporation.[103] However, to be able to understand what it means exactly to retributively sanction a certain kind of corporate misbehavior, more attention on the difference between "sanctions" and "prices" is necessary. According to Robert Cooter, it is often difficult to determine whether legal responses to prescribed activities represent prices or sanctions. He identifies distinctive elements that differentiate sanctions from prices with the aim of distinguishing when

[102] On why tort law, see Part IV.
[103] On sanction proportionality, see Section B of Chapter 4.

an activity should be sanctioned and when it should be priced. In his reconstruction, "a price is invariant with respect to the actor's state of mind and variable with respect to the harm caused by his action, while a sanction is variable with respect to states of mind affecting the seriousness of the fault and the need for deterrence."[104] A price depends upon the extent of harm because its purpose is to internalize the cost of an activity and to allow individuals to decide whether to engage in it. By contrast, a sanction is related to the state of mind of the offender because its purpose is to deter and punish. In this line of thinking, he concludes that prices are preferable when clear, reliable information on external costs exists, while sanctions should be preferred when there is a clear community standard and external costs are unclear.[105] He alludes to punitive damages as an example to illustrate factors that enable us to distinguish a sanction from a price: "(a) they are attached to a forbidden action; (b) they depend upon the actor's state of mind; and (c) their purpose is to deter."[106] In parallel fashion, Robert Cooter and Ariel Porat argue that liability can be seen as a sanction to deter wrongdoing or as a price to internalize the harm caused.[107] A price is usually a payment of money required in exchange for permission to do something. A price allows the individual to choose to take a certain action as long as she pays for it. A monetary sanction is a cost imposed for doing something forbidden.[108] In other words, the authors say, "[p]rices nudge and sanctions compel."[109]

Coming from another angle, Guido Calabresi believes that there are times when punitive damages cannot be explained in terms of an effort to mimic the optimalization of market dynamics. Rather, they must sometimes be understood as a collective decision to deal with the sanctioning of certain kinds of undesirable conduct through tort law without necessarily resorting to the criminal law and its principles.[110] Thus, in his view, certain rules for liability and noninsurable punitive damages can be compared instead to mimics of the criminal law. In Calabresi's terms, "mimicking the criminal law" represents the idea that there are certain tortious conducts that are so reprehensible or egregious that they should not be understood as having a "market price" we could choose to pay for permission to engage in. Rather, by mimicking the criminal law, the attempt is made to convey the message that the behavior in question is "inalienable," that is, incapable of being sold or transferred, but without going so far as to make the issue a criminal matter – we do not want the entitlement to be shifted in such contexts, but we do not want to formally forbid its shift either. Of essence is not any willingness to pay a market price (even with multiplier) but sanctioning behavior that is disapproved in our society.

[104] See Cooter, "Prices and Sanctions," 1552.
[105] Ibid.
[106] Ibid 1543.
[107] See Cooter and Porat, Getting Incentives Right, p. 22.
[108] See Cooter, "Prices and Sanctions," 1552.
[109] See Cooter and Porat, Getting Incentives Right, p. 17.
[110] See Calabresi, "A Broader View of the Cathedral," 8.

Thus, in Calabresi's view, if a collective decision to allow punitive damages in certain contexts reflects an attempt to approach the criminal law, the word that would be used to describe it is "sanction."[111]

The relevance of these theoretical reconstructions is that they make a fundamental difference between sanctioning and pricing behavior explicit.[112] They recognize that sanctions play a role when there is something distinctive in the character of the conduct (i.e., the activity is forbidden or particularly egregious and reprehensible) that makes us recoil from the idea of considering the act as permissible in exchange for payment (which motivates the "inalienability" argument). In that respect, it is commonly understood that sanctions are attached to conducts we disapprove of in our society because they violate clear community standards for acceptable behavior. Because of the nature of those standards, society does not wish to price their violation but to sanction it. In fact, as seen earlier, we do not want corporate defendants to be able to justify their reprehensible conducts as allowed for a price but rather force them to recognize them as "disapproved" by society at large through a sanction. The underlying idea is that society objects to corporations that engage in objectionable acts for financial gain. The punitive sanction is thus to be understood as the collective response that reflects society's views of the undesirability of flagrant corporate behavior.

Those reconstructions, however, face a major shortcoming. They reduce sanctions to their deterrent effect, in that they are neither understood as autonomous from deterrence nor as having any intrinsic value in themselves. Rather, they are depicted instrumentally in terms of their deterrent effect on the wrongdoer's behavior. That is to say, in terms of the efficacy of applying sanctions to regulate behavior in socially desirable directions – the wrongdoer perspective. The problem is that focusing on the deterrent effect of sanctions on the wrongdoer misleads us into believing that the only relevant aspect for consideration is the consequences of imposing sanctions (whether or not the desired behavioral outcome is actually achieved), which makes us lose sight, in turn, of the tort victim's moral attitudes (the entire range of value-driven motivations) of which sanctions are, in essence, the expression. In other words, it diverts our attention to the effects of the sanction on the wrongdoer's behavior and away from the richness of the original moral content that is what genuinely gives sanctions their inherent value. Once again, it turns our attention away from the victim's perspective.[113]

All this implies that the question of whether sanctions ultimately achieve their deterrent objective can be separated from the question of what makes the sanction intrinsically valuable as such. Indeed, it has been argued that people are not necessarily moved by the actual deterrent effect of sanctions, for they would still

[111] Ibid.

[112] On this point, arguing that what prevents economists from understanding the normative character of the law is their conceptualization of sanctions as prices, see Cooter, "Prices and Sanctions," 1543.

[113] On the relevance of the victim's perspective, see Part II.

sanction egregious behavior even if they knew that deterrence was very unlikely. For instance, Neil Vidmar and Dale T. Miller have shown that, even when supporters of deterrence theory are provided with incontrovertible evidence of the inefficacy of deterrence, their attitudes regarding capital punishment do not change.[114] All this strongly suggests that the basis for these attitudes in favor of sanctions may be rooted in other value-driven motivations quite apart from deterrence. The research of John M. Darley and Thane S. Pittman on the psychology of retributive justice is helpful here.[115] Their studies suggest the significance of an emotional component (what they called "moral emotions") to the reaction to reprehensible wrongdoing. They have found that deliberate violations that threaten (or undermine) other people's autonomy of action through harms to their person arouse moral emotions (anger, indignation, outrage, disgust) that trigger a retributive reaction.[116] Accordingly, someone who seriously proposes a trade-off that compromises a taboo subject (by accepting loss of human life for increased profit, for example) is seen as violating a fundamental social truth, which elicits one of the moral emotions that triggers a strong retributive response denouncing the effect on our lives of their decision to put their interests ahead of ours. Similarly, Michael Rustad and Thomas Koenig suggest that the reason that we impose punitive damages on non-natural persons (manufacturers of defective products) simply follows from the powerful effect of those entities on our lives.[117] When an enormous corporation causes unjustified injury, we instinctively become very angry and react with punitive intent. This explains the motivation to impose punitive damages on, to take the most famous example, the carmaker Ford after learning that it knew about a design flaw that made one of its models prone to exploding. The motivation to punish is not only related to the egregious behavior but also to the need to communicate our disapproval of their callous decision-making and reaffirm our own value vis-à-vis the offending corporation.

Moreover, other studies have identified the need to express condemnation that stems from fear experienced when someone or some person or entity fails to exhibit due regard for our care.[118] Once more, taking the Ford Pinto case as a paradigmatic example, when corporations put a monetary value on our safety (or our lives) by taking risks that expose us to significant harm for economic reasons based on a cost–benefit analysis, we experience outrage based on the "most primitive fear that we won't be taken care of, that those in charge of our care can put their own needs ahead of ours."[119]

[114] See generally N. Vidmar and D. T. Miller, "Social Psychological Processes Underlying Attitudes toward Legal Punishment" (1980) 14 *Law and Society Review* 565.

[115] See generally J. M. Darley and T. S. Pittman, "The Psychology of Compensatory and Retributive Justice" (2003) 7 *Personality and Social Psychology Review* 324.

[116] Ibid 332–33.

[117] See M. Rustad and T. Koenig, "The Historical Continuity of Punitive Damages" (1993) 42 *American University Law Review* 1269, 1312.

[118] On this point, see S. Lamb, "The Psychology of Condemnation: Underlying Emotions and Their Symbolic Expression in Condemning and Shaming" (2003) 68 *Brooklyn Law Review* 929, 942.

[119] Ibid 943.

In behaving this way, offending corporations deny the right of the consumers to be free from unnecessary harm by detrimentally using them as a means to promote their profit-seeking ends. The knowledge that a corporation has deliberately imposed on consumers safety risks of which they were unaware generates the sensation of impotence and indignation, which elicits the punitive response.[120] This is why, when a jury awards punitive damages, it is understood that "they may be making a symbolic expressive statement of their outrage, but they likely also want to express the more personal injunction that someone should have 'taken care.'"[121] The underlying idea is that punishment should be imposed against reprehensible wrongdoing, for, otherwise, a feeling of incompleteness and a sense of failed justice would remain.[122]

Understanding punitive damages as retributive sanctions enables the institution to retain its intrinsic meaning. Sanctions understood as sanctions communicate moral norms.[123] The substantive role of the ordinary consumer in pursuing punitive damages through tort law differs deeply from the contingent role of the economically motivated rational consumer acting as some sort of attorney general charged with promoting efficient behavior. Punitive damages as sanctions respond and are authenticated by the intrinsic retributive motivations of ordinary consumers to denounce condemnation for violations of societal trust (betrayals of consumers' safety expectations) by reasserting their self-worth vis-à-vis the offending corporate defendant and thus reinforcing the other-regarding standards of society.

Clearly, we have reached a point, in light of the scholarship reviewed, where re-signifying the ordinary consumer as a rich source of morally-laden understandings of risk and trust is required, as is reconceptualizing the attention courts ought to pay to lay understandings when gauging the significance of risk that should prevail under those particular tortious circumstances, aspects that will be the focus of analysis in Chapter 8 and, to some extent, in Part IV.

C DISTINGUISHING RETRIBUTION FROM DETERRENCE: THE EXPRESSIVE DIMENSION

A body of legal scholarship has grown up around the law's expressive function in recent decades.[124] The scholars mainly focus on the importance of the statements

[120] Arguing that a "feeling of individual impotence in the face of massive organizations" is in part "[w]hat fuels the [...] protest against corporate misbehavior," see R. Heilbroner, *In the Name of Profit* (Doubleday, 1972), p. 200.

[121] On this point, see Lamb, "The Psychology of Condemnation," 943.

[122] For more on tort victims' motivations to sue, see Section B of Chapter 9.

[123] Affirming that "[t]he expression of moral condemnation is done in our society via the assignment of punishment," see Darley and Pittman, "The Psychology of Compensatory and Retributive Justice," 326.

[124] See, for example, L. Lessig, "The Regulation of Social Meaning" (1995) 62 *University of Chicago Law Review* 943; C. R. Sunstein, "On the Expressive Function of Law" (1996) 144 *University of Pennsylvania Law Review* 2021; D. M. Kahan, "What Do Alternative Sanctions Mean?" (1996) 63 *University of Chicago Law Review* 591; E. S. Anderson and R. H. Pildes, "Expressive Theories of

made through law that have been obscured by emphasis on a conception of law that prioritizes its role in governing behavior directly. Beyond the law's expressive message, the idea that the imposition of punishment carries a message of condemnation seems to be commonplace among criminal theories.[125] For instance, Dan Kahan has argued that society should understand criminal punishment as a language in the sense that, aside from the concrete consequences for defendants (imprisonment, fines, etc.), the imposition of punishment also expresses meaning and conveys specific messages about society's values and norms.[126] Kahan's scholarship and theories show how the focus on the law and the failure to enlarge the scope of inquiry end up ignoring important aspects of punishment.

As already discussed, when it comes to retributive sanctions, it can be argued that "making statements" has an intrinsic value that goes beyond not only the specific punishment imposed (i.e., the punitive award) but also beyond its deterrent effect. Under the expert approach, society fails to "make a statement" about the reprehensibility of corporate behavior (i.e., it fails to convey a message of moral condemnation) because it folds punitive damages into the (extrinsic) economic incentives that are essentially responsive only to the goal of optimal deterrence. Under this economic approach, the "expressive" aspect of the extra-compensatory award is completely drained from its moral component (i.e., the award does not correlate to disapproval in that it lacks condemnatory quality). Instead, under the ordinary person approach, the punitive sanction is understood as having an intrinsic value, value that is independent of its potential to deter misbehavior, meaning that deterrence plays a secondary role in that it is the *derived effect* of the imposition of a punishment. From this angle of reasoning, it becomes plausible to think of punitive damages as retributive sanctions that "make statements" that convey condemnation and, as such, evoke a particular expressive angle worth exploring.[127]

There are in fact some theoretical reconstructions of punitive damages that do give attention to their expressive aspect. For instance, Anthony Sebok believes that because punitive damages are designed to induce people to conform their behavior

Law: A General Restatement" (2000) 148 *University of Pennsylvania Law Review* 1503; R. D. Cooter, "Expressive Law and Economics" (1998) 27 *Journal of Legal Studies* 585. In the torts' literature, see, for example, E. K. Best, "Atypical Actors and Tort Law's Expressive Function" (2012) 96 *Marquette Law Review* 461; S. Hershovitz, "Treating Wrongs as Wrongs: An Expressive Argument for Tort Law" (2017) 10(2) *Journal of Tort Law* 405 (arguing that tort liability expresses the judgment that the defendant wronged the plaintiff). More recently, also see J. Arlen and L. A. Kornhauser, "Battle for Our Souls: A Psychological Justification for Corporate and Individual Liability for Organizational Misconduct" (2023) 3 *University of Illinois Law Review* 673 (deploying an evidence-based deterrence theory to evaluate the law's ability to deter through expressive channels and sanctions in the context of corporate misconduct).

[125] To make it concise, see references on expressive theories of punishment cited in Chapter 4.

[126] See Kahan, "What Do Alternative Sanctions Mean?," 593 (arguing that "[p]unishment is not just a way to make offenders suffer; it is a special social convention that signifies moral condemnation.").

[127] I thoroughly engage with this argument in Section B of Chapter 4.

to societal norms, they must be interpreted as punishments (and not just as prices) in order to achieve their expressive purpose.[128] Sebok understands punitive damages as a means to ensure that we treat each other's rights as constraints on our behavior rather than as suggestions that can be ignored in exchange for payment. Therefore, when Sebok alludes to the expressive content of the punitive sanction, he is focusing on its ability to communicate a mandatory, not an optional, norm for behavior such that conformity is more likely. Similarly, Marc Galanter and David Luban understand punitive damages as a special form of retribution they call "poetic justice." In their view, punitive damages punish the wrongdoing by inflicting "expressive defeat" on the wrongdoer.[129] They illustrate expressive defeat through the Ford Pinto case, showing how inflicting monetary defeat on Ford (mirroring its own cost–benefit analysis as the appropriate way of determining the scale of punitive damages) actually represented an especially expressive form of punishment.[130] They emphasize that "to deter would-be offenders fully from engaging in morally outrageous behavior, the price tag must be high enough to make the enforcement lottery an unattractive option."[131] Moreover, they argue that only when the punitive damages far exceed potential gains will companies turn their eyes away from the balance sheet and toward the law.[132]

As is now easily inferred, the attractiveness of these expressive accounts of punitive damages is that they are able to capture the relevance of factors that the economic approach is unable to do, in this case the value of expressing moral condemnation. However, one weak point that all these reconstructions have in common is that instead of dealing with the expressive dimension as such, they – similarly to the expert approach – end up also focusing on its deterrent effect – on how a punitive sanction that conveys an unmistakable statement of moral condemnation will affect the choices of future actors by canceling the expected gains. For this reason, it might be said that these expressive accounts are somehow "mediated" by the deterrent consequences so desired (to negate any economic rationale for it).

Once again, the problem with the expressive approaches to punishment that focus on deterrence is that, by reducing sanctions to their deterrent effect and overlooking the victim's perspective, they lead us to depreciate intrinsic motivations

[128] See A. J. Sebok, "Normative Theories of Punitive Damages: The Case of Deterrence," in J. Oberdiek (ed.), *Philosophical Foundations of the Law of Torts* (Oxford University Press, 2014), p. 327.

[129] See M. Galanter and D. Luban, "Poetic Justice: Punitive Damages and Legal Pluralism" (1993) 42(4) *American University Law Review* 1393, 1442–43. I have explored their account of punitive damages in Section G of Chapter 2.

[130] Ibid 1440 (stating that "high punitive damages awards hit *homo economics* where it hurts: an eye for an eye, a tooth for a tooth, and a bottom line for a bottom line. It is poetic justice.") (emphasis in original).

[131] Ibid 1430–31.

[132] Ibid.

inherently worth preserving, namely the complexity of values that inform the statement of moral condemnation together with the victim's need for value affirmation that is conveyed by the relational retributive response. The underlying idea is that the expression of moral condemnation cannot be comprehended as a *moral condemnation* without explicit identification of the range of values that inform and authenticate the retributive response because, really and ultimately, our sanctioning practices are an expression of our moral attitudes. As already referred, the instrumental depiction of punishment in terms of its deterrence outcome diverts our attention to the effects of the sanction and away from the richness of the original substantive content of the victim's retributive motivations that is what actually gives sanctions their inherent value as such. Scott Hershovitz's understanding of punitive damages similarly points out the need to seek genuine retributive responses in some cases, regardless of their deterrent effects. Recall that according to Hershovitz, punitive damages communicate condemnation by marking the gravity of the wrong and correcting the message that wrongdoing sends about the victim's social standing.[133]

As I understand it, then, the expressive content of the punitive sanction can be disentangled in the following way: (1) punitive damages awards express moral condemnation of egregious corporate conduct that openly violates societal trust, in that they convey the message to the offender (and anyone else listening) that such egregious action is fundamentally wrong and strongly disapproved of by the individual victim and by the society at large, and (2) punitive damages awards serve as a vehicle for the expression of the intrinsic retributive reactions of ordinary consumers toward those powerful actors in the marketplace, reactions that find their authenticity in the common moral attitudes regarding the proper treatment deserved by every member of the community, and in the victim's need for value affirmation in *relation* to the offending corporation. The fundamental idea is that both elements are constitutive of the expressive content of the relational retributive response in an inseparable way – the retributive motivations attached to the expression of moral condemnation for purposes of value affirmation authenticate the punitive sanction. It now seems difficult to deny that people seek punitive damages for principled reasons, for punitive damages express their commitment to those shared substantive values.[134] This is why the failure to punish "consumer betrayals" is seen as weakening the "moral fabric" of society.[135]

[133] I have explored Hershovitz's account in Section D of Chapter 2.

[134] For studies along these lines, see D. M. Gromet, "Psychological Perspectives on the Place of Restorative Justice in Criminal Justice Systems," in M. E. Oswald, S. Bieneck and J. Hupfeld-Heinemann (eds.), *Social Psychology of Punishment of Crime* (Wiley-Blackwell, 2009), p. 44 (offering evidence that people may be concerned with the community or society in general when responding to wrongdoing).

[135] Similarly, see J. K. Robbennolt and V. P. Hans, *The Psychology of Tort Law* (New York University Press, 2016), p. 202 ("[T]he imposition of a sanction instructs community members about the boundaries of right and wrong, and clarifies where the line is drawn.").

A more value-driven discourse about the substantive content of the victim's retributive responses to egregious corporate wrongdoing could not only foster deliberation over the nature of our obligations to each other but also have a powerful effect in conveying much more enriched social messages. The bottom line is that too much would be lost if we simply accepted the reductive reconstruction that punitive awards are mostly and ultimately about achieving some sort of deterrence as autonomous from retribution in the mass-market context. The focus should be instead on imposing proportionate punishment from where deterrence ensues (derived deterrence).[136]

[136] I have explored this claim in Section B of Chapter 4.

8

Product Liability, Risk Regulation, and New Technologies

Product liability regimes have predominantly been understood as a protective mechanism enabling consumers to obtain ex post private redress for harm caused by a defective product. By exploring the place of retribution in the mass market context, the preceding chapters offer instead a broader, novel, and interdisciplinary understanding of product liability punitive lawsuits (particularly those involving wanton disregard for consumer safety) as a complementary and legitimate avenue for consumers to participate in the construction of the meaning of (un)acceptable risk in our society, which goes beyond the sole aim of seeking ex post private redress. It offers a reading of product liability that acknowledges the significance and richness of the consumer's perspective and relevant role in bringing the punitive lawsuit. Under this new light, product liability litigation provides a channel for private individuals to express substantive values of great importance in a judicial forum for which few alternative legitimate or effective avenues exist. The underlying idea is that, in order to avoid becoming a society that rejects utter reliance on experts, we should find an official forum for expert and layperson understandings of risk to speak to each other and interact. In this context, it becomes relevant not only to rethink the proper place and scope of punitive damages in product liability litigation but also, and perhaps more importantly, to initiate a fresh discussion about product liability regimes that might influence the behavior of market actors such that societal trust in experts grows stronger. Exploring what lies beyond the dominant deterrence rationale of sanctions in the marketplace is a timely enterprise in the face of the immediate challenges presented by the evolving risks of artificial intelligence to consumer safety and the prospect of improving the capacity of our current regimes to influence the conduct of market actors in ways that are conducive to reinforcing societal trust in experts. In what follows, I briefly explore some of these aspects with the aim to set the stage for future conversations.

A CONSUMER EXPECTATIONS VERSUS RISK-UTILITY

Liability for product design defects (and defective warnings and instructions) has historically followed one of two tests: (1) the consumer expectations test and (2) the risk-utility analysis.[1] Under the former, a product is defective in design "if the plaintiff demonstrates that the product failed to perform as safely as an ordinary consumer would expect when used in an intended or reasonably foreseeable manner."[2] A product is thus deemed defective if it poses a risk that an ordinary consumer would not expect to find in it, and the question of what an ordinary consumer would expect is largely left to the jury (in common law systems that follow the United States model) or to the judge (in most civil law jurisdictions and certain common law jurisdictions such as England). Under the risk-utility analysis, a product is defective if the risks of injury associated with its design are deemed greater than the product's benefits. The risk-utility test comes in different variants, but generally, as compared to the consumer expectation test, it is thought to invite more deference from judges and jurors (when available) to the testimony of design experts and engineers, as opposed to everyday intuitions (i.e., the safety expectations of ordinary consumers). The theory is that only experts and engineers have the necessary technical expertise to evaluate and accurately weigh against each other those risks. The courts and juries, by contrast, are thought to lack the expertise required for sound policy judgments about the social acceptability of the risks that products pose to human safety. The underlying idea is that complex risk tradeoffs exclusively require expert explanation.

Most courts in the United States currently use some form of risk-utility analysis,[3] though some employ the consumer expectations test[4] and others have adopted a hybrid approach under which claims of design defect for relatively simple and familiar design issues are adjudicated under the consumer expectations test, while

1 For the evolution of product liability law in the United States, see generally D. G. Owen, "The Evolution of Products Liability Law" (2007) 26 *Review of Litigation* 955. For an overview of product liability law in the United States, see generally M. A. Geistfeld, *Principles of Products Liability* (3rd ed.) (Foundation Press, 2020). For an overview of product liability law in Europe, see W. H. van Boom, J. S. Borghetti, A. Bloch Ehlers, E. Karner, D. Nolan, K. Oliphant, A. Scarso, V. Ulfbeck and G. Wagner, "Product Liability in Europe," in H. Koziol, M. D. Green, M. Lunney, K. Oliphant and Y. Lixin (eds.), *Product Liability: Fundamental Questions in a Comparative Perspective* (DeGruyter, 2017).

2 See A. D. Twersky and J. A. Henderson (Jr), *Torts: Cases and Materials* (3rd ed.) (Wolters Kluwer, 2011), p. 740.

3 See, for example, *Branham* v. *Ford Motor Co.*, 701 SE 2d 5 (SC 2010) ("[35] of the 46 states [] utilize some form of risk-utility analyses in their approach to determine whether a product is defectively designed.").

4 For instance, in *Aubin* v. *Union Carbide Corp.*, 177 So 3d 489 (Fla 2015) and *Ford Motor Company* v. *Trejo*, 402 P 3d 649 (Nev 2017), the Supreme Court of Florida and Nevada respectively rejected the use of risk-utility analysis as departing deeply from the United States current majority trend for design defect analysis.

more complex claims of design defect are adjudicated under the risk-utility test.[5] Conversely, the EU Product Liability Directive, which provides for a form of the consumer expectations test,[6] has to a certain extent harmonized European jurisdictions[7] and (at least for now) the United Kingdom.[8]

Moreover, the risk-utility test is usually applied in the context of fault-based systems of product liability that focus on whether the manufacturer considered the foreseeable benefits and risks associated with the product design adopted as compared to safer alternatives (i.e., the emphasis is on the manufacturer's ability to achieve optimal levels of safety when designing products).[9] On the other hand, the consumer expectations test is usually applied in the context of strict product liability systems that focus on any product defects that fail to meet the ordinary consumer's

5 Pointing out this phenomenon, see A. D. Twerski and J. A. Henderson (Jr), "Manufacturers' Liability for Defective Product Designs: The Triumph of Risk-Utility" (2009) 74 *Brooklyn Law Review* 1061. For an overview of the risk-utility variants and the hybrid approaches adopted by courts in the United States, see D. G. Owen and M. J. Davis, *Owen & Davis on Products Liability* (4th ed.) (Thomson West, 2014), para. 8:14. For a recent insightful analysis of the confusion between strict product liability and negligence-based liability for defective products in the United States, see M. A. Geistfeld, "Strict Products Liability 2.0: The Triumph of Judicial Reasoning over Mainstream Tort Theory" (2021) 14(2) *Journal of Tort Law* 403 (arguing that scholars' fixation on negligence ignores the implied warranty rationale for strict product liability currently used by the courts in the United States).

6 The test is one of reasonable or legitimate expectations rather than one to determine whether the manufacturer exercised due care: "A product shall be considered defective where it does not provide the safety that a person is entitled to expect." (art. 7.1) [Directive (EU) 2024/2853 of the European Parliament and of the Council of 23 October 2024 on liability for defective products and repealing Council Directive 85/374/EEC].

7 See generally D. Fairgrieve and R. Goldberg, *Product Liability* (3rd ed.) (Oxford University Press, 2020); and G. Howells, "Product Liability. A History of Harmonisation," in D. Fairgrieve (ed.), *Product Liability in Comparative Perspective* (Cambridge University Press, 2005). But see J. S. Borghetti, M. Santos Silva, D. Fairgrieve, P. García, A. Keirse, P. Machnikowski, E. Rajneri, C. Schmon, V. Ulbeck, V. Vallone and H. Zech, "Relevance of Risk-benefit for Assessing Defectiveness of a Product: A Comparative Study of Thirteen European Legal Systems" (2021) 29(1) *European Review of Private Law* 91 (examining how different courts in Europe take account of risk-benefit considerations in determining whether a product is defective and casting doubt on the level and scope of harmonization of product liability law in the EU). Similarly, underscoring the problems created by the drive toward maximum harmonization in the EU, see G. Howells, C. Twigg-Flesner and T. Wilhelmsson, *Rethinking EU Consumer Law* (Routledge, 2017). Moreover, also see J. Goudkamp and D. Nolan, *Winfield & Jolowicz on Tort* (20th ed.) (Sweet & Maxwell, 2020) para. 11–31 (arguing that the risk-utility approach is consistent with the United Kingdom case law).

8 In the United Kingdom, the EU Product Liability Directive of 1985 was implemented by Part I of the Consumer Protection Act 1987. However, as noted before, following the UK's withdrawal from the EU, some English scholars have already distanced themselves from the EU approach. For instance, see D. Nolan, "Against Strict Product Liability," in D. Nolan, *Questions of Liability. Essays on the Law of Tort* (Hart Publishing, 2023), pp. 392–426.

9 In the United States, the Restatement (Third) of Torts (1998) adopted the risk-utility test as the sole standard for determining whether a design defect exists: "(b) [A product] is defective in design when the foreseeable risks of harm posed by the product could have been reduced or avoided by the adoption of a reasonable alternative design by the seller or other distributor, or a predecessor in the commercial chain of distribution, and the omission of the alternative design renders the product not reasonably safe." See Restatement (Third) of Torts: Products Liability §2(b) (1998).

reasonable safety expectations (i.e., the emphasis is on whether the quality of the product meets an acceptable risk standard for the ordinary consumer).[10] As is fairly evident, the latter allows room for courts to consider the qualitative lay understandings of risk expressed as the safety expectations of the ordinary consumer, while the former matter-of-factly precludes such consideration in favor of expert assessments (e.g., designer and engineer testimony) of the existence and availability of safer alternative designs as well as the relevant tradeoffs, which, as shown in Part II and above, do not meaningfully capture lay judgments.[11]

The technical risk-utility test, a form of cost–benefit analysis that functions like the negligence standard of reasonable care,[12] fits very well with the "expert approach" in that it focuses on formalistic factors (i.e., it employs an expert-driven methodology comparing the additional safety that an alternative safer design would provide to the cost of employing such a design) without regard for the nuanced contextual manner in which lay individuals conceive serious acts of disrespect for others. As already discussed in Chapter 3, lay understandings of risk follow a distinct form of rationality based upon cognitive assessment, which has moral content: disapproving acts of disrespect to the life, bodily integrity, or individual autonomy of others expresses moral care. We, as citizens, have a legitimate interest in informing the discussion over the (un)acceptable risks manufacturers are allowed to impose on consumers in the marketplace. It is our duty to communicate our disapproval of the choice of a manufacturer to disregard the life and limb of others for profit. Such expressions demonstrate our commitment to preserving moral order and to a society that promotes respect and regard for others. Morally rich meaning would be lost if lay understandings of risk were ignored out of hand for the sake of an exclusive rationalistic approach to risk as solely cost justification.[13] Moreover, allowing some room for lay assessments of risk to be respectfully considered in the tort process becomes even more important if we wish to improve the quality of manufacturers' responses to the moral challenges posed by risk decision-making in the marketplace. We have

[10] The EU Product Liability Directive holds the manufacturer liable for harm caused by a product defect regardless of the manufacturer's fault: "The claimant is required to prove the defectiveness of the product, the damage suffered and the causal link between that defectiveness and that damage." (art 10.1) [Directive (EU) 2024/2853 of the European Parliament and of the Council of 23 October 2024 on liability for defective products and repealing Council Directive 85/374/EEC]. In the United States, the Restatement (Second) of Torts (1965) originally imposed a system of strict liability to the consumer for "product[s] in a defective condition unreasonably dangerous [to the user or consumer]" even where "the seller has exercised all possible care." See Restatement (Second) of Torts §402(A) (1965).

[11] For the point that "an early [consumer expectations] legal test of defective design, which has now been largely supplanted by and incorporated into the risk-utility test, emphasized the way products violated or betrayed consumer expectations," see J. K. Robbennolt and V. P. Hans, *The Psychology of Tort Law* (New York University Press, 2016), p. 172.

[12] The risk-utility test draws on the well-known *Carroll Towing* formalistic formulation for negligence. *United States* v. *Carroll Towing Co.*, 159 F 2d 169 (2d Cir. 1947).

[13] I have explored this claim in detail in Section B (b) of Chapter 3 and in Chapter 7.

a legitimate interest in encouraging moral market practices that align better with our deep-seated intuitions about other-regarding risk, trust, and truth.

All this suggests that our understanding of product liability punitive damages lawsuits in the mass-market context would benefit from greater awareness of the actual thinking processes lay consumers follow when they think about risk. We must address the meaning that ordinary consumers attach to threats rather than treating them as mere variables or coefficients in technical risk-utility formulas to be enforced.[14] Indeed, looking back at the product liability punitive damages cases mentioned earlier, it becomes evident that it would be wrong to assess the significance of Takeda or General Motors' wrongdoing by simply adding up numbers formulaically or even using risk-utility complex math. Instead, we have to weigh the other value considerations at stake by assessing the safety expectations of the consumers informed by the particular sequence of wrongdoing – that is, the fact that they produced and marketed a substandard product in full knowledge of the defect without regard for any possibility of rectifying it and without warning consumers of the risks for long enough to allow significant harm to take place. Such considerations are only brought to light in the tort process where judgments of rights and responsibility are central. The tort process thus becomes an invaluable institutional framework where laypeople, by making their particular case for ex post compensatory and punitive remedies, can express the meaning they attach to ex ante exposure to risk of significant harm by manufacturers and what they really care about when it comes to the risks deemed (un)acceptable to impose on others.[15] To that end, courts should avoid insulating the legal decision from the influence of the ordinary consumer understanding of risk such that manufacturers are provided a "safe harbor" by allowing them to excuse themselves with a formal demonstration of the "correctness" of their cost-justified precautions.[16]

While experts' assessments are certainly important, the lay understandings of risk, that of ordinary consumers, also matter and often matter equally. Risk decisions are not only probabilistic market-oriented decisions as experts usually claim, they are qualitative life-changing decisions for people too. Once we understand that the differences between expert assessments (which mostly involve a narrow value system based on the economic concept of efficiency) and lay judgments (which reflect

[14] On a similar vein, rejecting exclusive expert "economic thinking" in risk assessments for a more "holistic" approach to risk that restores a "sense of moral urgency to the protection of life, health, and the environment," see F. Ackerman and L. Heinzerling, *Priceless: On Knowing the Price of Everything and the Value of Nothing* (The New Press, 2004), p. 11.

[15] On the meaning-producing dimension of the tort process, see Section A of Chapter 10.

[16] Similarly, see M. S. Shapo, *Products Liability and the Search for Justice* (Carolina Academic Press, 1993), p. 194 (indicating that "[c]ourts hold it proper to announce rules aimed at making sellers behave more safely than they do, even when it might be technically inefficient for them to do so [...] Most economists have one craft-oriented focus, and that is on efficiency. But lawyers [and courts] have a broader aim, and that is to secure justice.").

more pluralistic value systems) are often a matter of different competing values, sustaining that expert judgments of risk should always prevail over lay assessments no matter what becomes challenging. There is no compelling reason to believe that expert opinion should always outweigh layperson understandings, meaning that the assumption that product risk assessments should be exclusively assigned to experts (e.g., manufacturers, producers, regulators, designers and engineers testimony, etc.) is, at least in part, unconvincing.[17] It is not convincing because such an approach overlooks the plurality of other competing values (such as the sacred value of human life or the high value we place on individual autonomy) apart from aggregate welfare, which are worth considering and reconciling when determining which risks it is acceptable for manufacturers to impose on others in the marketplace.[18] The point is that both rationales offer some wisdom and both embrace values (i.e., aggregate welfare, individual autonomy, life as nontradable) worth pursuing in our society. Moreover, the question over the place of expert assessments of risk becomes even more pertinent in the current landscape of emerging technologies where the uncertain nature of AI risks challenges probabilistic understandings of risk and experts themselves are unsure of the potential future risks and ramifications.[19]

The remaining challenge is thus integrating expert and lay people assessments of risk in constructive ways.[20] The bottom line is that the ordinary consumer, through the operation of tort law and the tort process, has a fundamental yet underappreciated role to play in the construction of the meaning of risk in our society – that is, in participating in the increasingly important and complex task of determining which risks are actually (un)acceptable to impose on others in the marketplace. They possess wisdom that can help experts. To perform that role, consumers require legitimate, genuine avenues that convey that wisdom to experts, so the latter better understand and identify with the former, creating a more trustworthy society that values dialogue between experts and ordinary consumers – feeding a virtuous cycle by which trusting creates trustworthiness. Product liability punitive litigation offers a channel for private individuals to express shared values of great importance (for instance, by exposing callous corporate misbehavior and holding corporations

17 For more reasons to be skeptical of this assumption, see R. Epstein, "The Risks of Risk/Utility" (1987) 48 *Ohio State Law Journal* 469, 476 ("[W]hat starts out as a faithful application of the utilitarian calculus ends up as an unprincipled battle of the experts. Everything is admissible; nothing is quantifiable; nothing is dispositive."); D. G. Owen, "Risk-Utility Balancing in Design Defect Cases" (1997) 30 *University of Michigan Journal of Law Reform* 239, 240 ("[F]ew courts or commentators have attempted to unravel the mysteries that lie within the various formulations of the balancing equation.").

18 See H. Dagan, "Pluralism and Perfectionism in Private Law" (2012) 112 *Columbia Law Review* 1409 (arguing that pluralism should be explicitly embraced in legal argumentation).

19 For references on this point, see the literature cited in the following section.

20 On this point, see P. Slovic, "Perception of Risk," in P. Slovic (ed.), *The Perception of Risk* (Taylor & Francis, 2000), p. 231 (arguing that ("[e]ach side, expert and public, has something valid to contribute. Each side must respect the insights and intelligence of the other.").

accountable for misrepresenting or withholding from public view critical information about adverse effects of their products) in a judicial forum for which few alternative legitimate or effective avenues exist.[21] Product liability punitive lawsuits thus represent a legitimate vehicle for voicing and capturing ordinary consumer judgments on the significance of risk, rather than as merely a channel for experts to fine-tune risk-utility formulas.

Tort law's capacity to acknowledge the value of everyday risk intuitions and incorporate them into the decision-making process provides invaluable insights in the product liability context that not only enable us to better comprehend the safety expectations of ordinary consumers in the mass market and their correlative punitive reactions when manufacturers reprehensibly fail to meet those expectations.[22] These insights also enable us to engage more meaningfully in the legal debates over the standards of liability for product design defects adopted by different legal systems. For instance, a standard of product liability that follows the consumer expectations test is better equipped to respect or do justice to the thicker and richer conceptions of risk of lay people that are informed by other-regarding qualitative judgments, conceptions that cannot be reduced to numbers or be adequately represented by them.[23] Such a standard also recognizes the value of providing lay people with a legitimate avenue not only for the expression of the meaning of significant risk (i.e., which risks are acceptable to impose on others) that aligns with their intuitions about risk and trust but also for the communication of the condemnatory message that life and limbs are nontradable for profit and that the affirmation of the victim's value is called for. These are all in and of themselves good reasons for preserving product liability punitive lawsuits as a legitimate condemnatory response to reprehensible corporate wrongdoing, which is sensitive to the complexity of the plurality of competing values involved in the violation of the ordinary consumer expectations of marketplace safety (i.e., that follows the consumer expectations test).

B PRODUCT LIABILITY AND RISK REGULATION AS COMPLEMENTS, WITH AN EYE TO THE AGE OF ARTIFICIAL INTELLIGENCE

The extent to which product liability lawsuits and the implementation and enforcement of risk regulation interact as complementary legitimate avenues

[21] On the significance of the tort process, see Chapter 10.

[22] On tort law's ability to recognize the value of lay intuitions, see G. C. Persad, "Risk, Everyday Intuitions, and the Institutional Value of Tort Law" (2010) 62 *Stanford Law Review* 1445.

[23] Similarly, see M. S. Shapo, *Tort Law and Culture* (Carolina Academic Press, 2003), p. 225 (comparing the consumer expectations test "with a more psychologically oriented view of law [tied] closely to the wellsprings of human behavior."); D. A. Kysar, "The Expectations of Consumers" (2003) 103 *Columbia Law Review* 1700, 1789 (arguing that the consumer expectations test protects consumers' beliefs about the values of product safety, whereas the more narrowly focused risk-utility test "appears to express a preference for the technical expertise of engineers.").

for fostering product safety has been addressed differently in distinct legal systems and cultures.[24] For instance, product liability litigation has evolved in the United States as a regulatory tool for consumer safety protection, whereas in Europe product liability litigation has historically played a much narrower role of ex post private redress to consumers of defective products.[25] The differences over the relative role of product liability litigation are partly explained by the underlying social, political, and cultural attitudes toward the desired extent of regulation by the state in the United States and Europe.[26] If, in the United States, efforts to foster risk regulation and its public enforcement are generally resisted and seen with suspicion,[27] Europe has long embraced regulation and enforcement as the primary mechanisms for effective consumer protection from risky products.[28] However, this depiction, even if accurate, should not be overstated. The fact is that the United States often resorts, admittedly in limited fashion, to safety regulation, and, inversely, Europe is gradually recognizing the limits of safety regulation dominance, as demonstrated by its recent consideration of the potential advantages of a broader role for product liability litigation as a complement to the regulatory state.[29] For instance, the recently enacted European legal framework on Artificial Intelligence (Artificial Intelligence Act),[30] which

24 See generally G. Howells and D. G. Owen, "Products Liability in America and Europe," in G. Howells, I. Ramsay and T. Wilhelmsson (eds.), *Handbook of Research on International Consumer Law* (2nd ed.) (Edward Elgar, 2018).

25 For a description of the different approaches, see M. Reimann, "Liability for Defective Products at the Beginning of the Twenty-First Century: Emergence of a Worldwide Standard?" (2003) 51 *American Journal of Comparative Law* 751, 784.

26 Ibid 816–29 (mentioning several possible factors: widespread availability of public health in Europe, litigation costs and fees, among others). For an analysis of the competing regulatory models in the EU and the USA in the context of the digital economy, see A. Bradford, *Digital Empires, The Global Battle to Regulate Technology* (Oxford University Press, 2023).

27 But see G. C. Keating, *Reasonableness and Risk. Right and Responsibility in the Law of Torts* (Oxford University Press, 2023), p. 228 (arguing that "[d]irect regulation of risk is the best available response to the limitations of the law of torts, and the regulation required must be responsive to the gravity of the harm at issue.").

28 See G. Howells, "The Relationship Between Product Liability and Product Safety. Understanding a Necessary Element in European Product Liability through a Comparison with the U.S. Position" (2000) 39 *Washburn Law Journal* 305 (pointing out to regulation instead of litigation as the European approach to product safety). Also see generally E. T. Schroeder, "Note. A Tort by Any Other Name? In Search of the Distinction between Regulation through Litigation and Conventional Tort Law" (2005) 83 *Texas Law Review* 897, 897–98 (summarizing the positions of many of these critics).

29 See T. T. Arvind and J. Gray, "The Limits of Technocracy: Private Law's Future in the Regulatory State," in K. Barker, K. Fairweather and R. Grantham (eds.), *Private Law in the 21st Century* (Hart Publishing, 2017), pp. 237–56 (describing the trend of displacement of private law by the regulatory state in Europe while exploring a broader role for private law). For an example of recent scholarly work arguing for expansion of product liability in Europe, see C. Busch, "Rethinking Product Liability Rules for Online Marketplaces: A Comparative Perspective" (July 31, 2021), available online at SSRN: https://ssrn.com/abstract=3784466.

30 Artificial Intelligence Act (Regulation (EU) 2024/1689 of the European Parliament and of the Council of June 13, 2024).

approaches artificial intelligence through a set of complementary, proportionate, and flexible rules relating to four different levels of risk: unacceptable risk, high risk, limited risk, and minimal risk, has sparked new discussions over the potential role of product liability litigation for harms resulting from defective AI-enabled products and the correlative need to update the EU Products Liability Directive (PLD) of 1985 to adapt it to the digital age.[31] In this context, the expert group on liability and the new technologies has looked into changing the PLD.[32] While some scholars home in on the fundamental concepts of the directive (including whether the definition of "defect" fits the PLD's purpose), others have taken a broader approach by conceiving a product liability regime focused on the challenges posed by emerging technologies.[33] Indeed, proposals for both an AI Liability Directive[34] and a revised Product Liability Directive[35] were under discussion at the time of writing. All these developments suggest that the time has arrived to rethink the proper place and scope of product liability in European law. Looking even further at the struggle of regulatory agencies across the globe to regulate or provide regulations that meaningfully protect consumer safety from the risks posed by new technologies, it seems more important than ever to rethink the relationship between risk regulation and product liability litigation as complementary instruments to which we might turn for meaningful

[31] For a recent initiative that seeks to spark discussion and to inspire further action on the topic, see C. Twigg-Flesner, *Guiding Principles for Updating the Product Liability Directive for the Digital Age* (ELI Innovation Paper Series, 2021). Moreover, see generally G. Wagner, "Robot, Inc.: Personhood for Autonomous Systems?" (2019) 88 *Fordham Law Review* 591.

[32] See Expert Group on Liability and New Technologies, "Liability for Artificial Intelligence and Other Emerging Digital Technologies" (November 2019); and European Commission, "Report on the Safety and Liability Implications of Artificial Intelligence," The Internet of Things and Robotics COM (2020) 64 final (2020 Report). What was unarguable is that the PLD was nearly 40 years old; its original, intended aim of harmonization has never been fully realized; and the standards of liability focusing on product defectiveness and the consumer's expectations test have recently come under intense scrutiny in the context of autonomous vehicles.

[33] For instance, determining what constitutes a defect of an advanced AI system might require a comprehensive understanding of its functioning for which current definitions of defects are ill-suited. For an analysis of this and other challenges that demand localized attention, see O. Dheu and J. De Bruyne, "Artificial Intelligence and Tort Law: A 'Multi-faceted' Reality" (2023) 2–3 *European Review of Private Law* 261.

[34] Proposal for a Directive of the European Parliament and of the Council on adapting noncontractual civil liability rules to artificial intelligence (AI Liability Directive) (COM [2022] 496 final) (among the key measures considered are instituting a rebuttable presumption of causality establishing the link between the failure of an AI system and the resulting harm and requiring access to the data used in specific high-risk AI systems). Note that the EU Commission withdrew the proposal on February 11, 2025.

[35] Proposal for a Directive of the European Parliament and of the Council on liability for defective products (COM [2022] 495 final 2022/0302 [COD]) (among the key measures are expanding it to cover intangible products, including software and AI systems, and lightening the burden of proof in complex cases). Note that the new EU Product Liability Directive has recently been approved. See Directive (EU) 2024/2853 of the European Parliament and of the Council of 23 October 2024 on liability for defective products and repealing Council Directive 85/374/EEC.

responses to the challenges ahead.[36] We should thus remain open to the possibility that, rather than tweaking the existent regime to accommodate evolving circumstances, devising a specific product liability regime for AI systems might be a preferable response to the problem.[37]

The risk-based approach is thought to offer a compromise between the need for innovation and investment in new technologies and the need to protect consumers from unrecognized risks of new developments.[38] The flexibility and dynamism of this approach introduce troubling uncertainty as to what amounts to "acceptable risk," an assessment that moreover attributes additional responsibility to experts (manufacturers, producers, regulators, among others) and, as a consequence, raises relevant questions on how, when, and who should ultimately participate in the definition of the risks deemed acceptable for imposition on others in our society. This risk-based approach to the problem, which ex ante specifies lists of AI practices and systems falling into the categories of prohibited AI and high-risk AI with an inevitable degree of abstraction, generality, and vagueness, heightens both the urgency of the discussion over ordinary consumers' conceptions of risk and the need for constructive integration and richer dialogue between expert and lay understandings of risk to foster an ecosystem of trustworthy artificial intelligence.[39] If AI harms are constructed as risks, their probabilistic nature poses a challenge to regulators by limiting their capacity to predict with accuracy the possibility of future safety concerns that might emerge, for instance, when general-purpose AI systems are operative. The likelihood of a harmful event and its further ramifications (such as the magnitude of the harm that it can cause) might be almost impossible for regulators (and other experts, such as manufacturers, developers, and operators) to gauge.[40] In this uncertain context, the premises of regulatory control and scientific certitude come under question. At the end of the day, the regulator's focus is limited to the safety risks that have already been detected or anticipated. The regulator is seldom fully

36 On the need to abandon the habit of treating torts in isolation and instead study their integration within a web of institutions that share responsibility for protecting the urgent interests of members of society, see generally Keating, Reasonableness and Risk. From a different angle, see M. L. Lyndon, "Tort Law and Technology" (1995) 12 *Yale Journal on Regulation* 137 (arguing that tort law plays a valuable role in the management of new technologies).

37 Similarly, see J. S. Borghetti, "Taking EU Product Liability Law Seriously: How Can the Product Liability Directive Effectively Contribute to Consumer Protection?" (2023) 1 *French Journal of Legal Policy* 136.

38 On the meaning of risk and how it shapes its regulation, see M. Weimer, "The Origins of 'Risk' as an Idea and the Future of Risk Regulation" (2017) 8(1) *European Journal of Risk Regulation* 10.

39 For the argument that technology causes changes in the sociotechnical landscape that generate a need for constant re-evaluation of regulatory regimes, see L. Bennett Moses, "Regulating in the Face of Sociotechnical Change," in R. Brownsword, E. Scotford and K. Yeung (eds.), *The Oxford Handbook of Law, Regulation and Technology* (Oxford University Press, 2017), pp. 573–96.

40 See M. E. Kaminski, "Regulating the Risks of AI" (2023) 103 *Boston University Law Review* 1347, 1347 (arguing that risk regulation works best on quantifiable problems and struggles with hard-to-quantify harms).

able to grasp new developments or changes, particularly of those AI systems that have the capacity to modify themselves.[41] In light of this uncertainty, product liability litigation might prove a valuable generator of new knowledge and information about safety risks initially considered "limited" or "minimal" by the regulator that should instead be deemed "high" or even "unacceptable."[42] Product liability litigation might thus play a valuable *complementary* role in assisting regulators in their assessments of risk and in their postmarket monitoring and control. Importantly, the ordinary consumer's understanding of risk that transpires in product liability litigation might contribute to improve risk regulation by integrating lay judgments in their expert assessments and even perhaps to help mitigate the latent threat of private-sector capture of regulators – for in general, consumers have proven to be reliable agents in service of the public interest in safety. Indeed, as it will become clearer in Chapter 10, at the intersection of product liability litigation and risk regulation we may find a constructive means to integrate and elicit richer dialogue between expert and lay understandings of risk since both generate relevant knowledge worth considering in the difficult task of determining which risks are (un)acceptable to impose on others.

The desired level of risk regulation and of product liability litigation in a given society is an important question that I do not directly address.[43] My point is that thinking about the relationship between product liability litigation and risk regulation in a more nuanced and intertwined manner might better capture their respective meanings for and correlative roles in protecting consumer safety.[44] Behind this point is the inference, largely supported by empirical studies and reiterated several times already, that they play a complementary, not a substitutive role. This means that legal systems should ideally aim for an interconnected balance between risk regulation and product liability litigation and, most importantly, resignify the role of the ordinary consumer in voicing, through product liability litigation and other available regulatory processes for participation, their understandings of risk, trust, and truth.[45] The resignification should reflect the nature and depth of our interpersonal relationships with one another as a constructive means to close the

[41] For the many challenges that regulators face in assessing AI risks, see generally S. Whittam, "Mind the Compensation Gap: Towards a New European Regime Addressing Civil Liability in the Age of AI" (2022) 30 *International Journal of Law and Information Technology* 249.

[42] On the knowledge-producing role of the tort process, see Section B of Chapter 10.

[43] For the complex interaction between tort litigation and regulation, see N. F. Engstrom and R. L. Rabin, "Pursuing Public Health through Litigation: Lessons from Tobacco and Opioids" (2021) 73 *Stanford Law Review* 285 (following lessons from both tobacco and opioids, they offer insights for how tort litigation complements – and, under certain conditions, can catalyze – broader regulatory strategies). Similarly, see Howells, "The Relationship between Product Liability and Product Safety," 345 (arguing that the question between product safety and product liability is one of balancing rather than choosing between one and the other).

[44] For an influential scholarly work along these lines, see Keating, Reasonableness and Risk.

[45] I engage with this claim in further detail in Section B of Chapter 10.

understanding gap between experts and ordinary consumers while fostering an ecosystem of societal trust and mutual respect.

◊ ◊ ◊

CONCLUDING REMARKS

By exploring the place of retribution in the mass-market context, Part III brings to light a broader, novel, and interdisciplinary understanding of product liability punitive lawsuits (particularly those involving wanton disregard for consumer safety) as a complementary mechanism (within an ecosystem of institutions charged with protecting consumer safety in the marketplace) and a legitimate avenue for ordinary consumers to participate in the definition of (un)acceptable risk in our society, an understanding that goes beyond the sole classic aim of seeking ex post private redress for harm caused by defective products. Fundamentally, this approach acknowledges the significance and richness of the consumer's perspective and her substantive role in bringing the punitive lawsuit. In striving to understand the substantive content of the retributive reactions of victims of violations of societal trust by callous manufacturers in the marketplace, this reconstruction offers a powerful retributive reading of product liability punitive litigation rooted in the betrayals of consumer trust that challenges the purely efficiency-based rationale of the dominant deterrence-oriented accounts of punitive damages as prices that reduces consumers to private enforcers following a self-interest-driven rationale. Seen in this new light, product liability punitive litigation provides a legitimate, substantive channel for private individuals to express deeply held values (that life is a pearl beyond price, for example, or the deep-seated drive to be able to live autonomously) in a judicial forum for which few alternative or effective avenues exist. This approach legitimates product liability litigation as a channel for the institutional communication of the condemnatory message that life and limbs are non-tradable for profit as well as the reaffirmation of the victim's value that the callous behavior of the corporation diminished. Under this relational retributive reading, product liability punitive lawsuits not only provide valuable insights that help to grasp the plurality of values that lie behind the safety expectations of consumers in the marketplace and that authenticate the ordinary consumer's correlative retributive reactions when manufacturers deliberately fail to fulfill those expectations but also represent a powerful mechanism for moral oversight of the market by bringing to light all the dimensions of the reprehensible corporate wrongdoing. These lawsuits are capable of sending clear messages that help corporations align their behavior with people's moral intuitions about risk, trust, and truth. These are all in and of themselves good reasons to maintain product liability punitive lawsuits as a legitimate condemnatory response to reprehensible corporate wrongdoing because of their sensitivity to the plurality of values involved in the violation of the ordinary consumer expectations of safety and recognition of the significance of the victim's need for value affirmation vis-à-vis the powerful corporation in a retributively relational fashion. Exploring what lies beyond the dominant deterrence rationale of sanctions in the marketplace is also a timely enterprise in the face of the immediate challenges presented by the evolving risks of artificial intelligence to consumer safety and the prospect of improving the capacity of our current regimes to influence the conduct of market actors in ways that are conducive to reinforcing societal trust in experts.

PART IV

Why Tort Law

OVERVIEW

Existing accounts of tort law systematically overlook the intrinsic significance of tort victims by disregarding the plaintiffs' perspective in articulating tort law and its procedure. Courts and commentators alike insist that tort law is about "making victims whole," that tort victims seek "restoration" to their former state before the tort occurred, and that the tort process aims to obtain "monetary compensation" for victims. While these depictions of tort victims and the tort process are certainly the default, they are hardly the whole story. As should be clear by now, the tort process is not always only about reparation. Certainly, those simplifications are appealing in that they neatly fit into the bilateral transactional structure of tort adjudication without any need to account for the substantive role and attitude of the tort victim, who originally and ultimately calls upon the defendant to answer for the wrong committed. However, this accommodation comes at the expense of conceptualizing tort victims as formal and abstract constructs detached from the substantive content of their responses to wrongdoing and from the broader social and cultural context in which tort law is applied by treating them as if they existed in a vacuum isolated from the social context.

Part IV sets the stage for *Relational Retribution* by proposing a shift away from formalistic and abstract depictions of tort victims and the tort process in favor of a substantive and contextualized reading of tort victims and their value-laden responses to wrongdoing, one that brings out a meaning-generative and knowledge-producing role that is articulated through tort law and the tort process and is worth preserving in our democratic societies. It does this by focusing on the significance of both tort victims and courts of law in developing tort law and remaining sensitive to the rich moral insights that claimants' substantive responses to wrongdoing provide when they articulate the tort process that mandates the courts to convene the parties in a public forum and issue reasoned decisions after hearing each side. In advancing this line of thinking, Chapter 9 offers a novel reconstruction of the (legal) power to act punitively in torts that is respectful of the wrongdoer-victim perspective (developed in Part II) and, even more particularly, to the substantive content of the victim's punitive responses to categories of reprehensible wrongdoing. It challenges the assumption that criminal law and the criminal procedure represent the exclusive institutional venues for the imposition of punishment by identifying the content of *Relational Retribution* as a mode of institutional moral communication between the private parties that is proper of the role of the victim in tort law and its bilateral structure. It recognizes the special position of the victim herself to personally provide sufficient reasons for the court to exercise its power and impose a punitive sanction on the reprehensible wrongdoer. Ultimately, the idea underlying Chapter 9's analysis is that, if we care about individuals' ability to engage meaningfully with their peers, we should ensure the availability of legitimate, official channels for institutional expression, among which tort lawsuits certainly qualify.

The pervasive narrative according to which victims solely seek some rectificatory response (restoration) has fueled general skepticism over the functioning of the tort system and, importantly, disparagement of the tort process as a legitimate intermediate structure for participation where (1) other-regarding meaning is constructed and (2) institutional knowledge is generated. Against this widespread skepticism that proposes abandoning tort law for alternative mechanisms of dispute resolution (such as social compensation systems or settlement processes that operate on a routinized model), Chapter 10 argues that the capacity of the tort process to generate other-regarding meaning and institutional knowledge represent compelling reasons to maintain the institution and endeavor to improve it. Tort lawsuits provide, in an important sense, a means for developing and articulating collective standards of conduct. Punitive lawsuits themselves are apt examples of a meaning-producing institution because they embrace the values embodied in the condemnatory legal message that the wrongdoer is not somehow worth more than the victim and is not entitled to treat the victim in a manner that diminishes her relative value. Punitive lawsuits persuasively illustrate how tort responses are able to capture the moral significance of the wrongdoing in a way that communicates the situated meaning of the impact of reprehensible wrongs on the victims and their complex motivations for resorting to tort law and its procedure for private redress. Ultimately, punitive lawsuits are not isolated instances of tort litigation that take place in a vacuum – quite the opposite. Most frequently, they are better understood as occurring in *articulation* with and as *complements* to the actions of other relevant institutional actors in our democratic societies.

9

The Significance of the Tort Victim

The recognition of interplay between tort law and criminal law and, as a consequence, the blurriness of the divide between private law and public law undermines the insistence on arguing in binary terms as if punishment were the exclusive affair of the state and the public law (i.e., criminal law) and compensation of the private individual and the private law (i.e., tort law).[1] As extensively demonstrated up to now, compensation and punishment coexist in torts and there is nothing inherently anomalous, illogical, or inappropriate in including punitive elements in the law of torts.[2] As Peter Cane has eloquently stated, "[r]eparation and retribution are potentially competing moral and social goals, and one of the functions of tort law […] is to embody a socially (and ethically) acceptable compromise between them."[3] The conversation thus calls for a fresh start.

1 For comparative scholarship on the blurred lines between criminal law and tort law, see R. A. Duff, "Torts, Crimes and Vindication: Whose Wrong Is It?," in M. Dyson (ed.), *Unravelling Tort and Crime* (Cambridge University Press, 2014), pp. 146–73 (showing that the distinction and the division of normative labor between tort law and criminal law becomes less clear cut where tort law takes up the vindication of wrongs); M. Dyson, "Tortious Apples and Criminal Oranges," in M. Dyson (ed.) *Comparing Tort and Crime: Learning from Across and Within Legal Systems* (Cambridge University Press, 2015), pp. 416–75, 420 (noting that the allocation of punishment to the criminal law and of compensation to the civil law is not completely stable).

2 For the argument that tort remedies are as much concerned with protecting the interests of plaintiffs (reparative justice) as they are with sanctioning the conduct of defendants (retributive justice), see P. Cane, "Retribution, Proportionality, and Moral Luck in Tort Law," in P. Cane and J. Stapleton (eds.), *The Law of Obligations: Essays in Celebration of John Fleming* (Oxford University Press, 1998), pp. 145–46. This was already advanced in the classic work of Theodore Sedgwick. See T. Sedgwick, *A Treatise on the Measure of Damages* (7th ed.) (Baker, Voorhis & Co., 1880), p. 34 (punitive damages "blends together the interest of society and the aggrieved individual, and gives damages no only to recompense the sufferer, but to punish the offender."). Also, in early English case-law, see *Broome* v. *Cassell & Co Ltd* [1972] AC 1027, 1114 (Lord Wilberforce: "it cannot be lightly taken for granted […] that there is something inappropriate, illogical or anomalous in including a punitive element in civil damages, or, conversely, that the criminal law, rather than the civil law, is […] a better instrument for conveying social disapproval […]."). Moreover, see K. Mann, "Punitive Civil Sanctions: The Middle Ground Between Criminal and Civil Law" (1992) 101 *Yale Law Journal* 1795; Dyson, "Tortious Apples and Criminal Oranges," p. 417 (pointing out that many ancient civil law systems, particularly Roman law, contained penal elements).

3 See Cane, "Retribution, Proportionality, and Moral Luck in Tort Law," p. 146.

A THE (LEGAL) POWER TO BE PUNITIVE

Much of the argument for or against punishment in torts boils down to an argument over the relative virtues and vices of exacting punishment through privately or publicly controlled judicial processes.[4] A first attempt to tackle this quest would be to acknowledge that the vast majority of tort cases where punitive damages are sought involve a range of reprehensible conducts that merit a condemnatory response but that either do not rise to the level of criminal sanction[5] or do meet the threshold for criminal sanction but are rarely successfully prosecuted by the state for priority reasons, lack of resources, inertia, or inherent difficulties tackling certain categories of criminal behavior.[6] As the legality principle precludes criminal procedure for conducts that are not typical crimes and the conducts that are criminal are not all effectively prosecuted, tort law would fill a significant gap by providing victims of those reprehensible wrongdoings a legitimate avenue for the condemnatory message that those conducts are taken seriously.[7] If punitive damages were not available in torts, there wouldn't be any other legitimate avenue to publicly channel and convey that condemnatory message.[8]

Similarly, the widely accepted understanding that the criminal procedure is the only mechanism that provides the proper degree of constitutional and procedural safeguards that the imposition of punishment requires seems to call for qualification. This seems particularly compelling when the most serious punishments, such as long-term incarceration, are being imposed. We certainly have every reason to assure those accused of criminal conduct the highest level of protections (for instance, the beyond reasonable doubt standard of proof) to reduce the chances of criminally convicting innocent defendants. However, when the punishment is a monetary sanction, as in the case of punitive damages in torts, the evidentiary

4 I owe this way of framing the problem to insightful comments from John Witt.

5 Profitable wrongs being the paradigmatic example. For instance, see S. Rowan, "Punishment and Private Law: Some Comparative Observations," in E. Bant, W. Courtney, J. Goudkamp and J. M. Paterson (eds.), *Punishment and Private Law* (Hart Publishing, 2021), p. 68 (showing that in France profitable wrongs have been characterized as "morally condemnable" and "morally shocking").

6 An example of this in the English context is the wrongful eviction of tenants where public authorities are reluctant to criminally prosecute landlords and where exemplary damages are commonly awarded instead. See J. Goudkamp and E. Katsampouka, "An Empirical Study of Punitive Damages" (2018) 38 *Oxford Journal of Legal Studies* 90, 112–13.

7 For the point that punitive damages can remedy the deficiencies of the criminal law, see N. J. McBride, "Punitive Damages," in P. Birks (ed.), *Wrongs and Remedies in the Twenty-First Century* (Clarendon Press, 1996), pp. 175; 192–93; A. Reed, "Exemplary Damages: A Persuasive Argument for Their Retention as a Mechanism of Retributive Justice" (1996) 15 *Civil Justice Quarterly* 130.

8 Note that, for instance, in the United Kingdom, "it is well established that punitive damages may not be awarded […] if other sanctions have already been imposed on the defendant for the conduct concerned," see Goudkamp and Katsampouka, "An Empirical Study of Punitive Damages," 94. Likewise, in Australia, punitive damages "will not be available […] where substantial punishment has been imposed on the defendant by the criminal law," see F. Maher, "An Empirical Analysis of Exemplary Damages in Australia" (2019) 43 *Melbourne University Law Review* 694, 700.

threshold might work differently. In fact, the tort process offers different mechanisms to ensure that monetary sanctions (i.e., the punitive award) are only imposed for reprehensible, wanton, serious, or reckless wrongdoing (for instance, instead of applying the typical "balance of probabilities" for a civil award, a more stringent standard of proof, such as "clear and convincing evidence," can be applied for the punitive award), and the amounts vary in proportion to the seriousness of the wrongdoing and are subject to different controls (for instance, there are mechanisms to guide and review jury awards, opportunities for defendants to appeal, and methods or formulas to inform quantification).[9] Moreover, often underestimated is the actual operation of the typical "balance of probabilities" standard of proof in the tort process when serious wrongdoing is being alleged: The more serious the plaintiff's allegation of the wrongdoers' behavior (e.g., fraudulent scheme, deliberate or reckless physical injury), the harder it becomes to meet the standard since those actions are less likely than negligent ones, meaning that establishing them in court requires more condemning evidence (perhaps something close to "clear and convincing evidence") than the sort needed to establish mere negligence.[10] Another important aspect to keep in mind is that punitive damages in torts are pervasively regarded as an "exceptional remedy" in most jurisdictions around the world.[11]

This is not to suggest that civil proceedings present a superior mechanism for the imposition of monetary sanctions. Rather, my narrow point is that the apparent tension between using the civil proceedings to compensate a private party who has been wronged and using the same proceedings to punish the wrongdoer fades in the context of punitive damages. In this context, the conventional punishment involves exclusively monetary sanctions imposed for reprehensible misbehavior and the tort process has the adaptability to offer reasonable safeguard mechanisms for the proper and proportional determination of the monetary sanction.[12] Skeptics may recall the array of empirical studies demonstrating that punitive damages are imposed exceptionally, and that their amounts are constant and modest (not excessive), which reinforces this point.[13]

9 The fact that judges have many times corrected exorbitant punitive damages jury awards, particularly in the United States, reinforces this point.

10 For a further exploration of this point, see J. Goudkamp and W. Courtney, "Introduction," in E. Bant, W. Courtney, J. Goudkamp and J. M. Paterson (eds.), *Punishment and Private Law* (Hart Publishing, 2021), p. 11.

11 For instance, in England it is well established that the awards of punitive damages are subject to an "if but only if test," according to which punitive damages can be granted only if the compensatory damages awarded do not sufficiently punish and deter.

12 I have explored this point in Section B of Chapter 4.

13 For the referred empirical studies, see Chapter 1. Moreover, see D. Kahneman, O. Sibony and C. R. Sunstein, *Noise. A Flaw in Human Judgment* (William Collins, 2021), p. 190 ("Requests for punitive damages are often denied, and even when they are granted, the awards frequently do not add much to compensatory damage.").

For many, these answers might prove unsatisfactory or at best incomplete since it can still be argued that it is not the purpose of tort law to remedy the deficiencies of the criminal law and that the criminal law should instead expand to criminalize those reprehensible behaviors. Whether more or less criminal law is desirable in a certain society is an important and complex question that I cannot meaningfully address here. But I can affirm instead that, in dealing with that question, we should not constrain our thinking by framing it in dichotomous terms of criminal-law-or-nothing simply because there is nothing structural about the jurisdiction for punishment as belonging exclusively to the criminal law and the criminal procedure. In other words, that a condemnatory response is called for in instances of reprehensible behavior does not necessarily mean that the criminal law (and the criminal process) represents the exclusive venue to address it or that, if the criminal law does not address it, the reprehensible conduct must go unpunished as a consequence.[14] Perhaps this dichotomous framing of the punitive question in our societies has contributed not only to overburdening our criminal justice systems but also inhibited thorough conversation on whether other less restricting areas of the law, such as tort law, may be listed to address condemnatory responses as well.

Instead of fiercely claiming the right to punish for the criminal law, we could perhaps rethink its place and ambit in our societies by debating, for instance, whether it should be reserved for the most serious conducts and for offences that lack direct, identifiable victims, or by simply recognizing the limitations of criminal punishment itself to correct certain behaviors, overcome the scarcity of resources and effectively achieve its goals.[15] Perhaps we should also be more open to the idea of less criminal law.[16] Moreover, the frequency with which corporate misbehavior goes unprosecuted in criminal courts compared to the significant success of punitive damages claims in civil proceedings against corporations (at least in the United States) should at the very least prompt serious inquiry.[17] One of many possible answers is

[14] For a discussion on why should it be for the state to inflict punishment through a system of criminal punishment, see, for instance, D. Husak, "Does the State Have a Monopoly to Punish Crime?," in C. Flanders and Z. Hoskins (eds.) *The New Philosophy of Criminal Law* (Rowman and Littlefield, 2016), p. 97; G. S. Mendlow, "On the State's Exclusive Right to Punish" (2022) 41 *Law and Philosophy* 243, among others. Also see J. Edelman, "In Defence of Exemplary Damages," in C. E. F. Rickett (ed.), *Justifying Private Law Remedies* (Hart Publishing, 2008), p. 232 (arguing that, historically, "in criminal law, punishment has never been the exclusive province of the state.").

[15] For recent criminal law scholarship along these lines, see R. A. Duff, *The Realm of Criminal Law* (Oxford University Press, 2018).

[16] On this point, see D. Husak, *Overcriminalization: The Limits of the Criminal Law* (Oxford University Press, 2007), p. 3 ("The most pressing problem with the criminal law today is that we have too much of it").

[17] For instance, Catherine Sharkey refers to a study that collected data from state courts across the United States showing that individuals sought punitive damages in 10 percent of cases against individuals as compared to 16 percent against businesses. And punitive damages were awarded more frequently in cases that individuals won against businesses (7 percent) than against individuals (4 percent). See C. M. Sharkey, "Punitive Damages Transformed into Societal Damages," in E. Bant, W. Courtney,

that tort law's more fluid "reprehensibility" standard of conduct is better equipped to deal with the unique character of corporate misbehavior, decision-making, and culture because it functions as a generic proxy under which courts can capture and identify different types of grossly unacceptable or morally offensive misconduct that merit a condemnatory response but do not meet the stringent standards that must be met for the state to legitimately exercise its coercive power to initiate prosecution, as is the case for criminal offenses.[18] Furthermore, empirical studies show that victims of crimes committed by corporations are generally dropped out of the equation (and sometimes are even actively excluded) when public prosecutors determine the appropriate criminal fines to levy on guilty corporations.[19] This is just an example to make the broader point that the punitive quest might be more meaningfully addressed by first seeking to better understand the different ways in which the legal system as a whole, be it through the operation of the criminal law or the law of torts, or both in tandem,[20] contributes to ensuring that proper institutional avenues are available to address the condemnatory responses called for by particularly reprehensible conduct.[21]

In the criminal process, the public prosecutor holds the power to charge an alleged offender and initiate the legal proceedings, not the victim.[22] In principle, no private individual can bring a criminal action. Even for crimes that certain criminal justice systems will not prosecute unless the individual victim herself denounces, it is still ultimately up to the public official's discretion whether to prosecute the case or not. Moreover, the scarcity of resources at the state's disposal (e.g., budgetary limits or judicial backlog) forces it to employ its discretion to prioritize which categories of crime will be actively prosecuted and investigated. These important constraining factors mean that the victim depends almost entirely on the public prosecutor's discretion for the activation of the criminal procedure against the alleged offender.

J. Goudkamp and J. M. Paterson (eds.), *Punishment and Private Law* (Hart Publishing, 2021), p. 162. The situation is reversed in the United Kingdom and Australia where punitive damages are more frequently awarded against individuals than against businesses. In the case of Argentina and Chile, punitive damages are only awarded against businesses since they are only available in the consumer context. In the case of Mexico, punitive damages have been so far mainly awarded against businesses (e.g., insurance companies), but, in principle, they could be awarded against individuals as well.

18 This does not imply condoning light-handed application of criminal law to corporations. Quite to the contrary. The point is different: That victims' responses to corporate wrongdoing might be more directly channeled and better addressed through tort law.

19 On this point, see M. E. Diamantis, "Erasing the Victims of Corporate Crime" (August 4, 2023), available online at SSRN: https://ssrn.com/abstract=4531052.

20 Certainly, tort law and criminal law overlap when the same conduct constitutes both a tort and a crime, but their responses differ for they do not address the same wrongs.

21 For an example of scholarship along these lines, see M. H. Weiner, "Domestic Violence and the Per Se Standard of Outrage" (1995) 54 *Maryland Law Review* 183, 189 (arguing that in the context of domestic violence, tort law could play functions that the criminal law is lacking).

22 I offer this overgeneralized depiction of the "typical" workings of criminal justice systems for the sake of simplicity in advancing the overall argument of this section while fully acknowledging that different jurisdictions have their own particularities worth further exploration.

The victim generally plays a minimal role and has virtually no control (i.e., no formal standing) over the criminal proceedings, which are initiated, directed, and further pursued by the public prosecutor in her role as "representative" of the public interest.[23]

It could be argued that the criminal law should not exclusively reserve the power to initiate the criminal action in the hands of public officials by granting victims the opportunity to exercise some control or review over the legal proceedings as well (for instance, by seeking review of the public prosecutor's decision not to prosecute the offender). That would certainly be desirable if it provided a valuable safeguard against arbitrary refusals to prosecute offenders, bias selectivity, or misguided assessments of public interest. However, even if we grant victims the opportunity to exercise some control or review over the initiation of the legal proceedings, the power to prosecute (i.e., to investigate and continue proceedings) remains in the hands of the public prosecutor as the *representative* of the community. The victim's engagement with the prosecutorial process is always limited to *contribute* to the public's interest by guarding against abuse of power or jurisdiction from the state instead of having *separate standing* to bring her private interests forward for vindication. Even if, under certain criminal justice systems (albeit exceptionally), the victim is given an opportunity to have her private interests heard as an independent voice from the state during the different stages of the criminal process (e.g., plea bargaining, sentencing), this prerogative is still contingent on the public prosecutor's discretion to prosecute and investigate the case in the first place. Most importantly, even if all goes as the victim expected, the criminal judgment holds the offender accountable to the public (or the state), not to the individual victim, since the criminal law mostly focuses on punishing the offender to vindicate the public interest (making clear that the conduct is not tolerated as proper of a member of the community) and not the individual victim's rights.[24] The victims' perspectives are purposefully and justifiably excluded from the determination of criminal sanctions.[25] This is why, for

[23] See M. Manikis, "Conceptualizing the Victim in England and Wales and the United States within a Spectrum of Public and Private Interests" (2021) 41(1) *Oxford Journal of Legal Studies* 219 (offering a more nuanced account of the victim in the oscillation of criminal justice between the public/private categories).

[24] See Duff, "Torts, Crimes and Vindication," pp. 146–73 (arguing for both making the vindication of victims' rights more central in criminal law and giving victims a more active role in the criminal process).

[25] The exclusion of the victim's perspective in criminal sanctions has, to some extent, motivated the relatively recent attempts from advocates of restorative justice to open more space for victim participation in the criminal justice system. For instance, see Z. Gabbay, "Justifying Restorative Justice: A Theoretical Justification for the Use of Restorative Justice Practices" (2005) 2 *Journal of Dispute Resolution* 349. Others have instead argued for abandoning punishment in favor of compensation or restitution by transforming the criminal process into something similar to the civil process. See, for example, D. Golash, *The Case against Punishment: Retribution, Crime Prevention, and the Law* (New York University Press, 2005); D. Boonin, *The Problem of Punishment* (Cambridge University Press, 2008).

a simple yet convincing example, criminal fines imposed on the offender go to the state coffers and can only be enforced by the state.

The situation is different under tort law, where the tort victim plays a protagonist role. The tort process, unlike most criminal proceedings, is initiated and further advanced by the victim. The very person who claims to have been wronged in a reprehensible manner (i.e., the plaintiff) is the one who unilaterally holds the power to file the punitive lawsuit against the wrongdoer (i.e., the standing to ask the court to consider the imposition of a punitive award) and thus determines the jurisdiction of the court over the defendant. The private actor possesses the power to subject the defendant to the court's jurisdictional power to issue a reasoned judgment against her (provided the legal conditions are met), without dependence on a public prosecutor to take up the case. Tort victims who experience the value-diminishing reprehensible wrongdoing are specially situated vis-à-vis their wrongdoers to directly address and hold them accountable by seeking, through the articulation of the punitive lawsuit, a condemnatory response that is respectful of the meaning and significance of having been wronged in that reprehensible fashion by that defendant. Recognizing tort victims' authority on whether to respond to those who wrong them in a particularly reprehensible way by filing a punitive lawsuit means acknowledgment not only of their individual autonomy but, most importantly, of their status as equal members of the community in that they can subject reprehensible defendants to publicly answer their legal claim made in torts.[26] The action of filing the punitive lawsuit is thus better understood as a communicative act directly addressing the wrongdoer, which is expressive of the defendant's reprehensible interference with the victim's protected interests and which calls for a condemnatory response for purposes of the victim's self-assertion.[27]

It could be argued that, if the wrongdoer is criminally punished, this would also very well imply recognition of the victim's status as an equal member of the community. However, as already explained, such recognition would be an ancillary effect of the criminal judgment in the sense that the criminal law is mainly concerned with punishing the defendant's behavior vis-à-vis the community but not with vindicating the individual victim's rights violated by the offender. Once again, the imposition of the criminal punishment on the wrongdoer is not carried out in the victim's name. The criminal law offers a form of answerability toward the public (and the state), which aligns well, on one side, with the public prosecutor's role as the *representative* of the public interest in prosecuting the case and, on the other, with the minimal role of victims as *contributing* to the public interest of the community

[26] Similarly, see S. Darwall, "Justice and Retaliation," in *Honor, History and Relationship. Essays in Second-Personal Ethics II* (Oxford University Press, 2013), p. 62 (arguing that victims who have been wronged have a distinctive individual standing to hold their wrongdoers answerable that they can exercise at their discretion).

[27] On *Relational Retribution*, see Chapter 4.

instead of as *advancing* their own private interests in vindication. Tort law offers a unique *relational form of answerability* from the wrongdoer to the victim that the criminal law cannot provide. This is patent in punitive damages understood as *Relational Retribution*, where tort victims seek, playing a certain relational role, a condemnatory response for the mistreatment directly from their wrongdoers (not from a third party or any compensation fund).[28] This relational retributive rationale is reinforced by key features in most jurisdictions: Punitive damages awards are in principle paid in full to the victim (but for some split-recovery mechanisms in the United States which partially allocate them to the victim)[29] and are in principle uninsurable (or their insurability is considered unenforceable as a matter of public policy or is frequently excluded from insurance contracts).[30]

While tort victims possess the relational power to act punitively against the wrongdoer, courts possess the power to impose the actual punitive sanction by issuing a reasoned tort judgment against the defendant.[31] These two aspects are necessarily linked in concatenation: Without victims exercising their power to initiate the tort process and demand the imposition of punitive damages, courts cannot exercise their power to impose the punitive award.[32] At the same time, the victim's power

[28] I explored this relational retributive dynamic in greater detail in Chapter 4.

[29] Note that split-recovery mechanisms have been criticized on many grounds, such as for facilitating abuse in settlement negotiations (e.g., defendant's exercise pressure to convince victims to obtain an inflated amount of compensatory damages in exchange for a promise not to seek punitive damages, thereby preventing the state from receiving their part of the punitive award); for being too costly to administer and enforce; for negatively impacting victims' incentives to sue, among others. For instance, the English Law Commission declined to recommend the enactment of legislation that would divert punitive damages awards from the plaintiff to the state or a public fund (Law Commission, *Aggravated, Exemplary and Restitutionary Damages*, Law Com 247 [1997] 1.142–50, 1.158).

[30] Many states directly prohibit insurability in the United States. In France, the proposed provision to introduce civil penalties also prohibits their insurability (Project de Réforme du Droit de la Responsabilité Civile 2017, subs. 5, art. 1266–61). Likewise, the proposed reform of the Argentinian Consumer Statute 2018 also prohibits the insurability of punitive damages (art. 118). Moreover, in the United States, courts disagree on whether liability insurance for punitive damages is enforceable as a matter of public policy, see generally C. M. Sharkey, "Revisiting the Noninsurable Costs of Accidents" (2005) 64 *Maryland Law Review* 409. Under English law, insurance coverage against punitive damages awards is not considered contrary to public policy (*Lancashire County Council* v. *Municipal Mutual Insurance Ltd* [1997] QB 897, 909); however, it is commonplace that insurance contracts do in fact exclude coverage of such awards, see J. Birds, B. Lynch and S. Paul, *MacGillivray on Insurance Law* (14th ed.) (Sweet and Maxwell, 2018) para. 30.009 n36. For the view that liability insurance prevents the victims of wrongs to hold defendants accountable because the compensation is ultimately paid by the insurance company in many tortious situations, see S. Hedley, "Corrective Justice. An Idea Whose Time Has Gone?," in M. Del Mar and M. Lobban (eds.), *Law in Theory and History: New Essays on a Neglected Dialogue* (Hart Publishing, 2016), p. 305.

[31] On this point, see J. C. P. Goldberg and B. C. Zipursky, *Recognizing Wrongs* (Harvard University Press, 2020), p. 169 (emphasizing that in the United States plaintiffs are not "entitled" to punitive damages even when they can prove culpability).

[32] See generally T. Liau, *Standing in Private Law. Powers of Enforcement in the Law of Obligations and Trusts* (Oxford University Press, 2023) (arguing that standing, a power of the claimant, needs to be better differentiated from the court's powers to issue orders).

to sue is distinct and independent from the court's power to impose the punitive sanction: The mere fact that the victim is exercising her power to sue for punitive damages does not necessarily entail the imposition of a punitive award by the court. Just as in any other request for damages awards, a lawsuit for punitive damages is by no means guaranteed success.[33] The plaintiff must satisfactorily prove to the court (in accordance with the applicable evidentiary rules and procedural standards) that the wrongful behavior denounced is sufficiently reprehensible to deserve the imposition of a punitive award. The court has no duty to grant the punitive award; its duty is to consider the plaintiff's argument for the imposition of the punitive award and only proceed to grant it if the required conditions are met.[34] To clarify, once the legal proceedings are initiated, the plaintiff is entitled to a reasoned judgment from the court, but that does not necessarily mean the judgment has to be favorable: It is ultimately within the courts' (discretionary) power to pronounce its reasoned judgment for or against the defendant. Moreover, even if the court judgment does in fact rule against the defendant, it does not follow that all the damages requested by the plaintiff will be granted: It will be up to the court to decide the specific remedies to be granted under the legal conditions, whether injunctive, compensatory, or punitive. To sum up, once the civil proceedings have been activated and continued, the court's duty is to consider the reasons presented for the imposition of the punitive award requested by the plaintiff, not to grant it no matter what. The courts' jurisdictional duty is to judge the case before them: to respond to the plaintiff's tortious claim by issuing a reasoned judgment to the case (one that follows precedent and statutory rules).

Once the power to be punitive in torts is understood accordingly, the often-raised objections that punitive damages privatize punishment, that it is not the business of the individual citizen to punish reprehensible wrongdoing, and that the benefit of a punitive sanction cannot be allocated to the private actor all resonate as simplistic and unconvincing. Similarly, the well-trodden fears repeatedly expressed by scholars regarding the inherent risk of punitive damages as an instrument for legitimizing morally indefensible notions of vengeance or as turning a public punishment into a form of private retaliation prove less threatening than had been proclaimed.[35] Indeed, at the heart of the punitive lawsuit is the state providing tort victims who have been wronged with a form of relational answerability from their wrongdoers to

33 See O. Herstein, "How Tort Law Empowers" (2015) 65 *University of Toronto Law Journal* 99, 112–13.

34 For the arguments that "the victim is doing more than delivering the wrongdoer to the court for punishment; she is personally presenting reasons to the court for the punishment of the wrongdoer," see A. J. Sebok, "Punitive Damages: From Myth to Theory" (2007) 92 *Iowa Law Review* 957, 1029.

35 This fear has been expressed by many, for instance, see J. Gardner, *From Personal Life to Private Law* (Oxford University Press, 2018), pp. 1–4; J. Penner, "Punishments and Penalties in Private Law, with Particular Reference to the Law Governing Fiduciaries," in E. Bant, W. Courtney, J. Goudkamp and J. M. Paterson (eds.), *Punishment and Private Law* (Hart Publishing, 2021), pp. 117, 127; and K. Barker, "Punishment in Private Law – No Such Thing Anymore," in E. Bant, W. Courtney, J. Goudkamp and J. M. Paterson (eds.), *Punishment and Private Law* (Hart Publishing, 2021), p. 46.

them that is respectful of the substantive meaning and significance of having been wronged in a reprehensible manner. It is the state that channels the claim for private redress through the operation of an adversarial legal process, where the tortious narratives are substantially controlled by the litigating parties and overseen by an impartial judge.[36] This scheme can hardly be understood as a morally objectionable act of private revenge or, as some have suggested, an archaic or barbaric approach to torts that distorts the legal system that has properly displaced private retaliation through the criminal law.[37] Once again, plainly associating private revenge or retaliation with victims' punitive responses to wrongdoing pursue through tort litigation is unfounded and misleading.[38] As extensively discussed in Part II, retaliation is not necessarily connected to accountability and does not involve any claim for recognition of individual authority in that it need not purport to hold a defendant *answerable* to the victim in the way *Relational Retribution* does.[39] Importantly, recall that, under *Relational Retribution*, not only retributive (just desert) but also recognitional (affirmation of self-worth) aims operate simultaneously when tort victims pursue punitive responses to instances of reprehensible wrongdoing. Punitive damages, conceived as a *just practice* reinforcing societal values, individual autonomy, and self-worth, do not involve retaliation, vengeance, or revenge.

Moreover, if we take seriously the fact that tort victims may understandably experience moral outrage (or betrayal aversion) for having been wronged in particularly reprehensible manners, it would be more respectful of that powerful empirical insight to focus on understanding tort victims' punitive responses to wrongdoing rather than to directly suppress them as irrational, misleading, risky, or misplaced. Indeed, it might be our collective responsibility to strive for better understanding them and to secure legitimate institutional avenues to properly channel and address them.[40] We should be open to the possibility that the risk of emotions "backfiring," identified by many scholars as a danger of validating retributive responses through torts, could perhaps be greater if we keep plainly disregarding them or pretending that they are always misplaced or irrational. The risk could be instead mitigated by addressing them carefully, respectfully, and properly – the underlying idea being that providing official venues to legitimately channel such claims might

[36] On this point, see Goldberg and Zipursky, Recognizing Wrongs, p. 265 (the provision of tort law is "the fulfillment of a duty owed by government to victims of legal wrongs to provide them with an avenue of redress against wrongdoers.").

[37] On this point, see J. Gardner, "Crime: In Proportion and Perspective," in A. Ashworth and M. Wasik (eds.), *Fundamentals of Sentencing Theory* (Oxford University Press, 1998), pp. 31–32.

[38] Similarly, see Goldberg and Zipursky, Recognizing Wrongs, p. 65 ("being serious about wrongs need not lead to the valorization of vengeance"). I have explored this point in Section B of Chapter 3.

[39] On *Relational Retribution*, see Chapter 4.

[40] On a related point, see J. M. Darley, "Citizens' Sense of Justice and the Legal System" (2001) 10(1) *Current Directions in Psychological Science* 10 (suggesting that, in the criminal law context, discrepancies between the law and the moral retributive-justice principles that people use may cause people to feel alienated from authority and to reduce their voluntary compliance with the law).

in the long run discourage people from resorting to noninstitutional alternatives for expression.[41] Contrariwise blocking the communicative act of filing a punitive lawsuit against their wrongdoers would prevent tort victims of an institutional avenue (1) to legitimately address what it means to have been wronged in a reprehensible manner by that particular wrongdoer, (2) to relationally hold the wrongdoer to account by denouncing their own rejection of the wrongdoer's mistreatment and, as a consequence, reaffirming their self-worth vis-à-vis the wrongdoer, and (3) to obtain private redress from the wrongdoer in the form of a punitive award imposed by the court that is burdensome enough to the defendant to give material force to the condemnatory message. In other words, blocking recourse to punitive damages would deprive tort victims of an institutional venue where they can be treated as equals vis-à-vis their wrongdoers and where, importantly, victims and wrongdoers must take each other seriously. Moreover, ruling out any consideration of the victim's punitive motivation in the tort process would insulate wrongdoers from the human impact of their reprehensible wrongdoing and, as a consequence, prevent them from gaining a fuller understanding of the moral dimension of the wrong they committed.

By redirecting our efforts toward better comprehending tort victims' punitive responses to reprehensible wrongdoing, we would find ourselves in a more suitable position to learn about the circumstances of wrongdoing under which it would be proper for tort victims to demand a punitive response.[42] Subsequently, we might learn more about when it would be proper for the state to provide tort victims with a legitimate avenue to meaningfully address condemnatory responses. Tort law and the tort process offer a legitimate avenue that can certainly be of use. As it will be explored in Chapter 10, the tort process enables the parties to prove or disprove the claim that the wrongdoer's behavior calls for a punitive response, facilitating the evaluation of the pertinence of the victim's retributive motivations.

B WHY DO VICTIMS SUE?

The central role allocated to the victim in the inherently bilateral structure of tort litigation requires the victim to take the initiative and actively sue the wrongdoer. The tort victim has a personal stake in the question of whether, and how, her legal claim for private redress is addressed in the courtroom. However, existing accounts of tort law have systematically overlooked the intrinsic significance of tort victims' motivations by disregarding altogether the fundamental reasons why victims invoke the protection of

41 See Goldberg and Zipursky, Recognizing Wrongs, p. 113 (suggesting that implementing a system of tort law is a political duty of the State toward its citizens who are forbidden by the State to take justice into their own hands).

42 Which allows in turn for acknowledgement of the cultural differences regarding the wrongful behaviors that are deemed sufficiently reprehensible to demand a condemnatory response from their victims in different places and times.

tort law – that is, why do victims ultimately sue.[43] This is partly explained by tort scholars' longstanding inattentiveness to the victim's perspective and, particularly, to the substantive content of the distinctive responses to different categories of wrongdoing. As extensively discussed in Parts I and II, tort scholars have been largely reluctant to acknowledge openly the punitive component of tort victims' responses to reprehensible wrongdoing that demand some sort of condemnatory response and, consequently, unwilling to explore deeply the retributive motivations that authenticate them. In fact, rather than empirically exploring the substantive content of victims' motivations that lead them to resort to tort law and the tort process in the first place, the commonplace understanding by courts and commentators (but for few exceptions) is that the fundamental role of the law of torts is to "make victims whole" by providing them financial compensation.[44] This rectificatory stance has (over)emphasized compensation at the expense of serious consideration of other noncompensatory responses (such as punitive damages) that coexist in the law of torts. The underlying claim is that viewing tort responses only through formal compensatory lenses obscures what is truly at stake when victims demand and courts impose damages awards.[45]

That the tort system offers a rationalistic approach that translates injury, pain, suffering, and other intangible harms into sums of money does not necessarily mean that claimants solely or even primarily seek monetary compensation in response to wrongdoing inflicted upon them.[46] Such an assumption misapprehends the tort plaintiff's motivational compound. After all, no sum of money returns someone who has been

[43] But see, for example, D. Engel, "The Myth of the Litigious Society: Why We Don't Sue" (Chicago University Press, 2016) (addressing the question of why victims do not sue).

[44] Note that civil recourse theory power allocation reconstruction goes beyond "making whole," but shares with other theories the lack of sufficient engagement with the substantive content of the responses – I have explored this claim in more detail in Section F of Chapter 2. For the view that the aim of tort law is not to repair harm wrongly done but to articulate and enforce primary obligations to others, see G. C. Keating, *Reasonableness and Risk. Right and Responsibility in the Law of Torts* (Oxford University Press, 2023).

[45] This is certainly no novelty. Others have suggested this before. See, for example, G. H. L. Fridman, "Punitive Damages in Tort" (1970) 48(3) *Canadian Bar Review* 373, 404 (arguing that tort law may serve many purposes, such as laying down certain standards of conduct which the community is expected to observe – which if accepted means the notion of compensation must be regarded as secondary in importance); D. G. Owen, "Deterrence and Desert in Tort: A Comment" (1985) 73 *California Law Review* 665, 667 (noting that tort law might rectify private wrongs, but it is "often public in its spirit and effect."); R. A. Duff, "Repairing Harms and Answering for Wrongs," in J. Oberdiek (ed.), *Philosophical Foundations of Tort Law* (Oxford University Press, 2014), p. 221 (arguing that claimants often seek an accounting and apologetic recognition of wrongdoing that does not fit neatly with the logic of cost allocation), among others.

[46] See generally M. J. Radin, "Compensation and Commensurability" (1993) 43 *Duke Law Journal* 56; R. L. Abel, "The Real Tort Crisis. Too Few Claims" (1987) 48 *Ohio State Law Journal* 443 (criticizing tort law for its commodifying features). For a similar line of thinking in the context of intergenerational reparative claims, see R. Kumar, "Why Reparations?," in J. Oberdiek (ed.), *Philosophical Foundations of the Law of Torts* (Oxford University Press, 2014), p. 203 (arguing that "[i]t is not a general feature of a person having been wronged that what she is entitled to is best understood as 'compensation.'").

injured to their former position, unless their injury was purely monetary.[47] However, monetary damages might still well serve the expressive end of marking the moral significance of harms and wrongs even when they cannot repair those harms or undo those wrongs. In fact, tort victims often demand responses that go beyond private rectification, particularly when the defendant's wrongful conduct is reprehensible, wanton, egregious, or humiliating, as is the case when punitive damages are sought. They seek instead responses from tort law that better match the moral wrong caused to them by conveying the significance and meaning of the wrongdoing.[48] Tort victims are sometimes after a "moral response" to discrete instances of objectionable wrongdoing. They may want affirmation of worth and dignity (i.e., affirmation that their lives and autonomy are important and have value). Sometimes what is sought is communication of condemnation of reprehensible behavior that violates other-regarding values. Other times it is a public forum to voice the moral significance of the wrongdoing, and affirmation that justice and equality matter in our society.[49] The plaintiff's motivational compound may involve any combination of these and other considerations.

It has already been established that, when the defendant's wrongful conduct is particularly egregious or humiliating, the victim requires "something else" to remedy the harm done. Admittedly, compensatory awards that cover the costs of the harm could very well suffice, especially when the defendant's conduct was not grossly negligent and solely induced economic loss, but we cannot simply assume that this general response is suitable in every case,[50] as the appropriate response is contingent in that it certainly depends on the type of tort (e.g., whether it has affected property, bodily integrity, dignity, autonomy), the particular circumstances of wrongdoing (e.g., whether it was negligent, reckless, intentional, humiliating, outrageous), and the significance the wrongdoing has for the private parties involved (wherein lies its moral wrong: How the manner of the defendant's interference with the victim's protected interests is

47 See generally D. Laycock, "The Death of the Irreparable Injury Rule" (1990) 103 *Harvard Law Review* 687.

48 On this point, see T. G. Okimoto and T. R. Tyler, "Is Compensation Enough? Relational Concerns in Responding to Unintended Inequity" (2007) 10(3) *Group Processes & Intergroup Relations* 399, 401 (arguing that even if the victim is compensated, she may still feel disrespected and undervalued, suggesting that "[t]he provision of compensation alone for an injury, even when it is viewed as favorable, will not be an adequate response to the harm.").

49 Asserting that plaintiffs often sue to ascertain truth, express anger, or achieve moral vindication through the formal recognition of their opponent's wrongdoing, see, for example, D. Engel, "The Oven Bird's Song: Insiders, Outsiders and Personal Injuries in an American Community" (1984) 18 *Law & Society Review* 551, 558–62. Also see generally S. E. Merry and S. S. Silbey, "What Do Plaintiffs Want? Re-Examining the Concept of Dispute" (1984) 9 *Justice System Journal* 151.

50 On this point, see G. C. Keating, "Is the Role of Tort to Repair Wrongful Losses?," in D. Nolan and A. Robertson (eds.), *Rights and Private Law* (Hart Publishing, 2012), p. 391 (arguing that "[i]t is often but not always the case that restoration of the right requires reparation."). See A. Bernstein, "Q: What Is Tort? A: Categorical Hurt" (2021) 14(2) *Journal of Tort Law* 261 (displaying sensitivity to the plaintiff's personal experience of injury) and "The Communities that Make Standards of Care Possible" (2002) 77 *Chicago-Kent Law Review* 735 (for the view that all who make decisions in tort actions are human beings subject to variations on hurt that can include rage, anxiety, bias, humiliation and despair).

connected to the inherent value attributed to them in the particular circumstances of the wrongdoing), an assertion that is borne out by the available empirical evidence.[51] Tort victims search for responses that are sensitive not only to what happened as an outcome of the wrongful behavior (i.e., the harm suffered) but also to why it was done to them, the manner in which it was done, and how the wrongdoers themselves esteem the wrong they committed and its victims. They seek responses that connect the wrongdoer to the victim by acknowledging the particular circumstances of the wrongdoing and the correlative motivations of the victim in a more holistic fashion.

In the specific context of punitive damages, exploring why victims would actively pursue punishment for the wrongdoing they experienced directs our attention toward the *value* attributed by the victim to the interests affected (or invaded) by the defendant's wrongful conduct. The victims' motives for redress provide the key to what gives content to the punitive response because they are connected to the nature of the defendant's conduct toward the victim and to the attribution of value the victim does to the interest invaded by that defendant. A more meaningful understanding of punitive damages thus arises from comprehending who we are and how we make sense of the circumstances of deliberate, reckless, humiliating, or outrageous wrongdoing that represents a threat to our personal autonomy, individual dignity, bodily integrity, or even life. Indeed, "compensation" and "punishment" are two different manners to respond to wrongdoing that befalls us. Psychological research shows that, when we are confronted with reprehensible wrongdoing that affects incommensurable interests such as our individual dignity, bodily integrity, and personal autonomy, we do not seek rectification; instead, we seek a response that helps us communicate our sense of moral outrage at the gravity of the manner in which those protected interests were violated and that allows us to signal our inherent value in order to reinforce the importance of other-regarding interests in our society.[52] In this context, the imposition of a sanction functions as a legitimate vehicle to disseminate the values informed by our deep moral intuitions on the proper regard for others, a function that clearly exceeds the classic private interest in compensation. The claimant is thus better understood as not only pursuing her private interests through tort litigation but also her interest in safeguarding the other-regarding values of the community through legal means. Conversely, if we readily accept "rectification" as a satisfactory explanation of the content of tort responses, we end up not only stripping tort remedies of their true

[51] See S. Ingber, "Rethinking Intangible Injuries: A Focus on Remedy" (1985) 73 *California Law Review* 772, 783–85 (discussing the needs of victims and arguing that monetary awards for nonpecuniary damages do not provide meaningful compensation to the victim of an intangible injury). Moreover, see Keating, Reasonableness and Risk, p. 49 (suggesting that the irreparability of serious injury may justify supra-compensatory damages, such as punitive damages).

[52] For a detailed study on how people respond differently to carelessly inflicted harm, intentionally inflicted harm, and reckless conduct, see J. M. Darley and T. S. Pittman, "The Psychology of Compensatory and Retributive Justice" (2003) 7 *Personality and Social Psychology Review* 324, 336.

meaning (in terms of the underlying values involved) but also treating the victims' responses to wrongdoing as if they were fungible, marginalizing the individual and social importance of articulating the distinctive intrinsic motivations that are elicited according to the varying intensity of the wrongdoing and the diverse nature of the interests invaded.

Under this new light, punitive damages offer a rich range of moral nuance regarding the respect we believe all members of our society are due, respect which private individuals ought to be able to reclaim through the judicial tort process.[53] Indeed, when reprehensible invasions to our personal dignity, physical integrity, or individual autonomy take place in their respective contexts of wrongdoing, they signal a fundamental change in our relationship to others and society. We find ourselves unable to simply ignore either the effect the wrongdoing has on our lives (i.e., our experience of injury) or the implicit, complex meaning of that injury with regards to the values that inform our understanding of the rightful treatment owed to each other in our society.[54] Certainly, this does not mean that compensation has no relevance in the tort victim's motivational compound, but rather that is not the only (exclusive) element and that is not always necessarily present in every instance.[55] Most of the time, the perceived need for compensation overlaps with the perceived need to be punitive.[56] Other times, the need to be punitive predominates in the victim's motivational compound over the need for compensation and vice versa. Tort victims' responses to wrongdoing are complex and textured in that they reflect common sense understandings of other-regarding values, which serve as the basis to establish collective standards of care and behavior. The point is that a more explicit value-driven discourse on the responses of tort victims (i.e., the meaning

53 For the idea of the tort legal process as a forum for accountability, see S. Darwall and J. Darwall, "Civil Recourse as Mutual Accountability" (2011) 39 *Florida State University Law Review* 17, 19–24 (the notion being that the harm I cause to you when my actions violate your right is a form of disrespect, and tort actions are a means whereby you can "respectfully demand respect."). For similar ideas, see generally J. M. Solomon, "Equal Accountability through Tort Law" (2009) 103 *Northwestern University Law Review* 1765; S. Hershovitz, "Treating Wrongs as Wrongs: An Expressive Argument for Tort Law" (2017) 10(2) *Journal of Tort Law* 405.

54 For the argument that "the intentional infliction of a wrong injuries not just the victim but what might be called the 'fabric of society,'" see Darley and Pittman, "The Psychology of Compensatory and Retributive Justice," 330.

55 On this point, see C. J. Robinette, "Harmonizing Wrongs and Compensation" (2021) 80 *Maryland Law Review* 343, 346 (pointing out studies in the United States, particularly in the area of medical practice, which have identified noncompensatory motives for plaintiffs to file tort lawsuits, such as to obtain fuller information about their injury, to determine accountability, or to prevent future injuries). Similarly, see S. Blanchard, "Nominal Damages as Vindication" (2022) 30(1) *George Mason Law Review* 227 (arguing that plaintiffs pursue suits for nominal damages for motives other than money).

56 For a qualitative study of personal injury lawyers in the United States suggesting that compensatory and retributive concerns figure far more prominently in tort law in action than the deterrence concerns emphasized by much of the theoretical and doctrinal literature, see T. Baker, "Blood Money, New Money, and the Moral Economy of Tort Law in Action" (2001) 35(2) *Law and Society Review* 275.

victims construe from the varying circumstances of wrongdoing understood as a threat to their individual autonomy, dignity, physical integrity, or even life) holds considerable potential as a vehicle of more nuanced and layered social messages pertaining to our ultimate concerns and genuine motivations (e.g., the sanctity of life, the deep-seated desire to live autonomously) that should be recognized and embraced.[57] It is time to start giving tort responses consideration that better reflects the plurality of values underlying the significance and meaning that the particular circumstances of wrongdoing hold for the private parties involved as well as for our society as a whole.

The strictly rectificatory narrative is ill-equipped to capture the richness of the much more textured responses that tort victims' pursue by resorting to tort law and the tort process; most of the time it cannot capture the situated meaning of the impact of tortious wrongs on victims (i.e., its account of the actual significance of the wrongdoing for the victim is inadequate) and their complex motivations for seeking redress.[58] Skeptics would probably argue that this reading of tort victims is rather utopian (or romantic) or that the reasons why victims file a tort lawsuit should not matter much to tort law since they are ultimately contingent on the individual victim's cognitive assessment and evaluative judgment of the meaning and significance of the egregious wrong done to her. They might have a point. However, my claim is different. My claim is that it is misguided to assume simply that there is an overwhelmingly predominant motive for filing a tort lawsuit and that this motive is obtaining compensation. This is not only because such a stance overlooks the available empirical insights on tort victims' motivations to sue but also because it depicts the distinctiveness of tort law (and the tort process) as if its sole aim were obtaining monetary compensation for victims, thus diverting scholars' attention away from other substantive aspects of the current practice of tort law (such as the plurality of underlying values that tort responses reflect) that might further vindicate the institution. Narrowing down the margin of legitimate tort responses to strictly rectificatory precludes broader reflection not only on the distinctive substance of different tort responses and the underlying values that they convey, but also on the broader social context in which tort law is applied, ultimately impairing a sound understanding of the subtler interplay of the plurality of values embraced by the different responses to wrongdoing that go beyond restoration and coexist in the law of torts. It prevents us

[57] For the idea that tort law operates as a critical forum for the articulation of public understandings of morality, see D. A. Kysar, "The Public Life of Private Law: Tort Law as a Risk Regulation Mechanism" (2018) 9(1) *European Journal of Risk Regulation* 48, 63.

[58] For an empirical study showing that potential litigants see the decision to sue as much or more about how they understand their relationship to their community and their responsibilities as a citizen as how they evaluate monetary considerations, see G. K. Hadfield, "Framing the Choice Between Cash and the Courthouse: Experiences with the 9/11 Compensation Fund" (2008) 42 *Law and Society Review* 645. Similarly, see T. Relis, *Perceptions in Litigation and Mediation: Lawyers, Defendants, Plaintiffs, and Gendered Parties* (Cambridge University Press, 2009) (offering new insights into the area of litigants' noneconomic goals for litigation).

from better assessing the interconnectedness of the plurality of values that are regularly channeled through the tort process.[59]

Moreover, recent trends to move away from tort law toward alternative compensation schemes that abolish private-law duties of repair and private-law mechanisms for the enforcement of rights raise similar concerns.[60] Referring to the pervasive assessment that tort law poorly performs its compensatory role, commentators question whether there is a compelling reason to address harms we cause to each other through tort law instead of through other alternative schemes such as social compensation funds.[61] These critics basically call into question the capacity and effectiveness of tort law to provide satisfactory compensation to victims and argue for replacing it with alternative compensatory mechanisms that promise more "effective" rectificatory responses to victims. Once again, even if alternative systems of compensation represent a rectificatory response considered satisfactory for certain categories of tort victims (mostly those involving tortious conduct that is not grossly negligent and mostly causes reparable loss), we cannot generalize from these cases that the alternative scheme would be satisfactory for every tort victim, in every context of wrongdoing and in every tort case. For instance, solid evidence suggests that receiving compensation from a compensation fund or a party other than the wrongdoer often fails to satisfy victims of humiliating, outrageous, or reprehensible wrongdoing.[62] As previously described, the picture is much more complex and suggests that tort law litigation's centering on the relation of the parties as doer and sufferer of the same wrong offers a powerful explanation for the continuing existence of tort adjudication as an avenue victims of serious wrongful conduct seek out despite its imperfections (it cannot fully repair harm, it is costly and time-consuming, etc.). As a result, scholarly appeals to the effectiveness and successfulness of tort law in compensating victims as the main criterion for deciding whether to reform or repeal the institution seem fundamentally misguided.[63]

59 But see E. J. Weinrib, *Reciprocal Freedom. Private Law and Public Right* (Oxford University Press, 2022) (arguing against pluralism in torts).

60 New Zealand is the paradigmatic example of a common law jurisdiction with a comprehensive accident compensation scheme (NZ Accident Compensation Act 2001). But note that, after almost 50 years in operation, it has not been replicated in any other major common law jurisdiction but for isolated examples in the United States. Note that the alternatives are many: We could think, for instance, of social funds financed with general taxes or with special taxes on those who carry out certain risky activities, among others.

61 For a classic tort law skeptic, see S. D. Sugarman, "Doing Away with Tort Law" (1985) 73 *California Law Review* 555 (discussing the replacement of personal injury tort law with alternative compensation schemes).

62 On this point, see L. Bender, "Feminist (Re)Torts: Thoughts on the Liability Crisis, Mass Torts, Power, and Responsibilities" (1990) 4 *Duke Law Journal* 848, 877–78.

63 To clarify: This is not to say that compensation funds are unwelcome. There are situations in which they might play a fundamental role. For instance, the European Parliament contemplated the possibility of EU countries using existing or new national sectorial compensation schemes for victims of defective products who fail to obtain compensation in cases where the economic operator is insolvent or no longer exists.

Such an approach not only misunderstands the role of victims in torts (because they are often motivated by more than monetary interests) but also, once again, it mistakenly depicts tort law (and the tort process) as if the institution's sole purpose was obtaining monetary compensation for victims. As discussed in Chapter 4 on *Relational Retribution*, victims often seek the imposition of monetary sanction (i.e., the punitive award) on the principle of holding the wrongdoer accountable for her reprehensible, wrongful behavior in order to communicate moral condemnation and reassert their self-worth vis-à-vis the defendant.[64]

Moreover, this all-or-nothing approach presents a false dichotomy by suggesting that we must rid ourselves of tort law if we decide to introduce nonfault schemes or other alternative compensatory mechanisms. These institutions could be made compatible by, for instance, applying each to different categories of tort cases or to the different needs and choices of the tort victims depending on how the categories are defined in the given legal system.[65] Ultimately, the question is better framed by avoiding the binary construction in favor of an understanding that incorporates the interconnectedness between tort law and other compensatory mechanisms in any given society.[66] For reasons already alluded to, the timeliness of such an enterprise is opportune. Indeed, the potential accountability deficits of the proposed alternatives to tort law adjudication (ones that abolish private-law mechanisms for the enforcement of rights) are particularly relevant to the discussions of the proposals currently being discussed in Europe (and elsewhere) for moving away from a tort liability regime to nonfault social insurance schemes to cover all personal injuries arising from accidents involving artificial intelligence.[67] Such nonfault programs are

64 On *Relational Retribution*, see Chapter 4.

65 Suggesting a hybrid of tort law and other social compensatory mechanisms in certain cases, see D. M. Papayannis, "The Morality of Compensation through Tort Law" (2023) 36(1) *Ratio Juris* 3, 18–22. Also see J. C. Love, "Punishment and Deterrence: A Comparative Study of Tort Liability for Punitive Damages under Non-Fault Compensation Legislation" (1983) 16 *UC Davis Law Review* 231 (suggesting various options for drafting nonfault compensation legislation that would preserve the punitive and deterrent functions of tort law). In addition, see C. J. Robinette, "Party Autonomy in Tort Theory and Reform" (2013) 6 *Journal of Tort Law* 173, 174 (pointing out that the crucial issue that should be engaged by tort scholars "is how to divide tort cases worthy of individualized justice treatment from those better suited to routinized resolution."). Note that even a comprehensive nonfault compensatory scheme like the one put forward in New Zealand for accidental injury does not completely displace tort law in that a victim is not precluded from bringing a civil action for damages with respect to injuries not covered by the scheme.

66 Similarly, see G. C. Keating, "Is Tort Law 'Private'?," in J. Oberdiek and P. B. Miller (eds.), *Civil Wrongs and Justice in Private Law* (Oxford University Press, 2020), pp. 351–71 (arguing that we have diverse institutional devices to respond to accidents that sometimes compete, sometimes complement each other: tort law, administrative schemes, and direct regulation of risk are preeminent among these devices and overlap in various ways).

67 A revival of proposals to replace torts by other mechanisms for compensation is evident in the current scholarly discussions on liability for harms caused by AI systems. On nonfault compensation schemes for autonomous vehicles, see, for example, S. Van Uytsel, *Different Liability Regimes for Autonomous Vehicles: One Preferable Above the Other? Perspectives in Law, Business and Innovation*

based on the premise that by removing the uncertain outcome of legal proceedings, they more "effectively'" secure compensation for victims while at the same time being "less discouraging to innovation." Once again, this approach might work in particular circumstances and sectors, but it hardly seems a satisfactory across-the-board solution for harmful outcomes resulting from the use of AI systems.[68] A more nuanced discussion, in any case, on the positive and negative implications of nonfault approaches is certainly called for.

(Springer, 2021), pp. 67–92. Moreover, see J. Yoshikawa, "Sharing the Costs of Artificial Intelligence: Universal No-Fault Social Insurance for Personal Injuries" (2020) 21(4) *Vanderbilt Journal of Entertainment and Technology Law* 1155; E. Marchisio, "In Support of 'No-Fault' Civil Liability Rules for Artificial Intelligence" (2021) 54(1) SN *Social Sciences* 1.

68 For instance, some have argued that their application should be limited to high-risk uses of AI. See C. Wendehorst, "Strict Liability for AI and Other Emerging Technologies" (2020) 11(2) *Journal of European Tort Law* 150.

10

The Significance of the Tort Process

Rendering the victim's legal power to be punitive in torts (advanced in Chapter 9) under the more nuanced and layered substantive reading of the tort claimant just described demands *resignifying* our understanding of the judicial tort process as a privately controlled institutional framework for addressing not only *compensatory* but also *condemnatory* responses to wrongdoing. It requires conceptualizing the tort process as a legitimate institutional avenue for a variety of different responses to wrongdoing that offers a unique approach to the problem of redressing private wrongs. It means reading the tort process as not only sensitive to the substantive responses of tort victims who engage with it but also, and perhaps most importantly, as attentive to the broader social context in which the wrongdoing takes place and for which the plaintiff's perspective provides an invaluable lens.[1] In what follows, I explore how the tort process offers a legitimate avenue for tort victims to contribute proactively to the construction of other-regarding meaning and the generation of institutional knowledge in our democratic societies. I deal with each separately.

A THE CONSTRUCTION OF OTHER-REGARDING MEANING

Once again, abstractly constructing tort victims in a vacuum without any meaningful connection to the particular circumstances of the wrongdoing they have experienced and the broader social context in which tort law is applied fails to capture in any adequate manner the substantive motivational complex that drives many victims of reprehensible wrongdoing to engage the tort process. These victims mostly act upon a complex, value-laden set of reasons that drive them to demand, by lodging judicial complaints, not only recognition of and private redress for their injuries but also the reaffirmation of the other-regarding values that their wrongdoers disregarded. The tort process, which is controlled by the litigants and overseen by a nonpartisan

1 For the related argument that the point of private law is "to inculcate the private domain with connectedness," see C. Michelon, "The Public Nature of Private Law?" (2020) 7 *Latin American Legal Studies* 231, 242.

public authority, gives private parties the opportunity to question each other's behavior and recognize their mutual answerability in a forum that reaffirms their value as moral equals.[2] The initial effort of the tort victim to file her lawsuit is of central importance because that process provides her with a unique chance to personally convey several distinct messages. One is what the wrong inflicted upon her by the defendant means to her (by exposing what amounts to reprehensible wrongdoing in the specific context of the tort). Another is the moral significance the wrongdoing has had on her life (by offering her own narrative of her experience of injury). The process also allows her to make claims regarding the rightful treatment that she believes she is owed by the defendant and by society at large (by defining the terms of what private redress means). The understanding of the tort victim I have in mind is thus substantive and contextual. It affords a meaning-producing role that unfolds through the articulation of tort law and the tort process.

Comprehending the richness of the varied, distinct, and yet overlapping substantive motives for seeking redress is especially important when considered together with the avenue tort law presents for private individuals to play *reactive* and *proactive* roles in the construction of collective values for the regard of others in society. In other words, by filing the punitive lawsuit, victims *react* not only in defense of established norms, seeking the authoritative declaration of judgments of rights and responsibility in an adversarial judicial process informed by rules of evidence, principle reasoning, statutory rules, and precedent, but also as a positive means to *proactively* take part in the public establishment of collective standards for interpersonal behavior that reflect the community's evolving intuitions concerning risk, trust, and truth that tort law could hardly do without.[3] By voicing the plurality of values involved in her demand, the tort victim infuses tort law with meaning. She instills the law with meaning by expressing her experience of wrongdoing and its significance (i.e., how it has affected the personal beliefs, values, and attitudes that have significant bearing on the way she leads her life).[4] The punitive lawsuit constructs a humanizing narrative in which the tort victim attaches moral

2 See generally S. Darwall and J. Darwall, "Civil Recourse as Mutual Accountability" (2011) 39 *Florida State University Law Review* 17.

3 For the understanding of the tort system as providing "a public forum within which plaintiffs and defendants can tell their stories" and "a public space within which society can debate how tort obligations should be defined," see J. K. Robbennolt and V. P. Hans, *The Psychology of Tort Law* (New York University Press, 2016), p. 4.

4 For the argument that the meaning of injury shapes the experience of injury, see S. Mor, "The Meaning of Injury: A Disability Perspective," in A. Bloom, D. Engel and M. McCann (eds.), *Injury and Injustice: The Cultural Politics of Harm and Redress* (Cambridge University Press, 2018), pp. 27–49 (arguing that "the pain, the suffering, the tragedy, and the misfortune that are associated with bodily injury are not a-contextual bodily experiences, but rather culturally dependent occurrences that call for further interrogation and critique."). Similarly, see A. Bernstein, "Q: What Is Tort? A: Categorical Hurt" (2021) 14(2) *Journal of Tort Law* 261, 269 (stating that "[b]oth compensatory and punitive damages share a commitment to standing, causation, and the complaint as narrative when both insist on a historical instance of hurt suffered by at least one individual.").

significance to the facts leading to her experience of injury. For instance, in making her punitive demand against the defendant, the victim conveys what it means to her to be wronged by reprehensible, reckless, wanton, humiliating, or outrageous behavior. She defends her status as worth the attention of a court of law and the accountability that torts ensure her as an equal member of the community. By denouncing reprehensible wrongdoing, the victim makes clear that her experience of injury cannot be reduced to a mere statistic or an economic consequence of living in a complex society. It instead depicts the wrongdoing as a personal affront to her value as a moral equal, infusing tortious events with social and cultural significance and demanding recognition of the relevance of our interpersonal relationships and obligations of care to one another. In this way, the tort victim generates substantive meaning of other-regarding human interactions, informing legal doctrines and standards (for instance, what amounts to "reprehensible behavior") with the insights provided by her perspective.

Under this light, the punitive lawsuit becomes a meaning-producing mechanism that embraces the values embodied in the request for a condemnatory response (i.e., the punitive award). The punitive lawsuit requires analyzing the sequence of interactions and the seriousness of the wrongdoing, whether the victim's reasonable expectations of safety were disappointed, whether effort was made to conceal the offense, and so on. All these evaluations have a place within the tort process. The tort process thus becomes a legitimate avenue for the tort victim to convey that there are other substantial values at stake (e.g., life and physical integrity are nontradable, the deep-seated desire to live autonomously) that go beyond "money" – recall that compensation is one possible dimension of victims' motivational compound when they take the initiative to activate legal processes in these particular categories of tort cases. Once again, without denying that most tortious events lead to losses for victims, which might increase their need for money.[5]

Through the tort process, the victim plays a significant role in the construction of other-regarding meaning in our society.[6] To perform her role, she requires access to legitimate avenues that allow her to present her account of the tortious event, to convey the wisdom she possesses in the regard of others (shared moral insights), and to face the other party in a process that incorporates mechanisms of control to regulate the competition of narratives on what actually transpired. This tailored character of the tort process bestows courts with greater sensitivity to the wrongful situation and the most relevant aspects and also appreciates the value of lay understandings of the care and respect for others people believe are due, incorporating them into

5 Again, some victims might only seek money.

6 Similarly, see S. V. Shiffrin, "Democratic Law and the Erosion of Common Law," in S. V. Shiffrin and H. Ginsborg (eds.) *Democratic Law* (Oxford University Press, 2021), p. 66, 89 (arguing that the common law makes it possible "to give voice to mutual moral commitments we must make to one another"). Also see M. S. Shapo, "A Social Contract Tort" (1977) 75 *Texas Law Review* 1835, 1844 (understanding tort law as the law of "social cohesion").

the decision-making processes when proper.[7] Viewed in this way, the tort process becomes an intermediate structure for participation, one that allows tort victims themselves to actively engage in the collective construction of the social and cultural significance of both what it means to be wronged by reprehensible wrongdoing and what holding the egregious wrongdoer accountable entails.[8] Skeptics might contend that this reading of the tort process is unrealistic. The tort process is almost always intermediated by lawyers, legal forms, processes, and technical reasoning, all of which limit the opportunity for tort victims to convey their beliefs, values, attitudes, and wisdom. I am sympathetic to the criticism but maintain nonetheless that courts, with all their technocratic institutions, and judges and lawyers, who have their own notion of expert legal reasoning, do not necessarily preclude tort proceedings that allow room for lay insights to be voiced and considered.[9] Moreover, my aim here is not to assess the current functioning of tort processes in particular jurisdictions. Rather, it is to point out the powerful potential of tort processes to balance technical reasoning and expert knowledge with lay values and understandings – potential that may require procedural reforms for realization and that will certainly take a variety of forms depending on and according to the needs of each jurisdiction.

Moreover, preserving the room for such balancing that the tort process provides is now more urgent than ever, as alternative dispute resolution mechanisms that aim to privatize the conflict are increasingly used.[10] "ADR" mechanisms move access to justice away from the trial paradigm for the sake of settlement.[11]

7 Similarly, C. C. Tilley, "Tort Law Inside Out" (2017) 128 *Yale Law Journal* 1320 (seeking to show that tort law reflects community values). Also see M. S. Shapo, *Tort Law and Culture* (Carolina Academic Press, 2003), p. 284 (describing a "role of courts as cultural agents – realigning the law with developments in the economy and with the evolving attitudes of ordinary people.").

8 To clarify, I do not aim to offer a democratic defense of tort litigation. To say that the tort victim through the punitive lawsuit participates in the construction of other-regarding meaning is not to say that she is necessarily engaging in direct law-making or risk regulation or that this is a democratic feature of civil litigation as others have claimed. For a democratic defense of civil litigation, see A. D. Lahav, *In Praise of Litigation* (Oxford University Press, 2017), p. 6 (the core democratic feature of civil litigation is that it "offers the opportunity to present reasoned arguments and proofs before an official adjudicator – a judge or jury – and in the process, a chance to debate the values at stake in the lawsuit.").

9 See Chapter 8 where I have offered further insights on how expert and lay understandings of risk can interact and speak to each other in the context of product liability litigation.

10 On this point, see C. J. Robinette, "Two Roads Diverge for Civil Recourse Theory" (2013) 88 *Indiana Law Journal* 543 (pointing out that most tort cases in the United States are resolved prior to trial, usually by settlement). For the English perspective, see L. Mulcahy and W. Teeder, "Are Litigants, Trials and Precedents Vanishing After All?" (2022) 85(2) *Modern Law Review* 326 (showing that, in England and Wales, the number of appellate court judgments has increased while cases coming into the system and proceeding to trial have decreased).

11 For an insightful account of how bureaucratic settlement procedures minimize or circumvent the idea of a right to redress in American tort law, see J. F. Witt and S. Issacharoff, "The Inevitability of Aggregate Settlement: An Institutional Account of American Tort Law" (2004) 57 *Vanderbilt Law Review* 1571; N. Donahue and J. F. Witt, "Tort as Private Administration" (2020) 105 *Cornell Law Review* 1093. For a timely example along these lines, see A. R. Gluck, E. C. Burch and A. S. Zimmerman,

As a result, tort victim's rights and remedies are mostly defined and controlled by entirely private actors, without providing victims with a meaningful opportunity to hold wrongdoers accountable, to convey the significance of the wrongdoing, or to participate in the reinforcement and redefinition of other-regarding values in a legitimate judicial process.[12] Furthermore, most of these settlement mechanisms depersonalize the tort victim.[13] By putting forward entirely bureaucratic frameworks for settlement characterized by impersonal, mechanized processes for the allocation of monetary damages to resolve a great many tort claims, these mechanisms diminish the relevance of the private right to redress for tort victims and the meaning a personalized judgment conveys. They recommend wariness of defendants overly willing to settle lawsuits against them in haste, even though settlement is often interpreted as a "solution" for the victims and a "victory" for their lawyers.[14] Here I would like to dispel any suggestion that settlements are inherently negative[15] or overwhelmingly disadvantageous for claimants.[16] However, the *Relational Retribution* framing of tortious cases involving reprehensible wrongdoing that justify the imposition of punitive damages considers that the kinds of alternative settlements described above represent a less legitimate forum than a courtroom for plaintiffs' claims to be aired and stories to be told.[17] They almost never reveal the true dimensions of the reprehensible wrongdoing, making conveying an adequately condemnatory message difficult. Most fundamentally,

"Against Bankruptcy: Public Litigation Values versus the Endless Quest for Global Peace in Mass Litigation" (2024) 133 *Yale Law Forum* 525 (describing how Purdue Pharma's resort to bankruptcy procedures to "manage" the opioid litigation crisis in the United States is another example of a decades-long saga of unorthodox civil procedure maneuvers to push cases further away from the trial paradigm in the name of "settlement").

12 Similarly, see S. A. Talesh, "The Privatization of Public Legal Rights: How Manufacturers Construct the Meaning of Consumer Law" (2009) 43(3) *Law and Society Review* 527 (arguing that alternative dispute resolution weakens the impact of consumer protection laws because consumer rights and remedies are being redefined and controlled by private organizations).

13 For the effects of the deformalization of justice through mechanisms of alternative dispute resolution, see generally K. Barker, "Private Law as a Complex System: Agendas for the Twenty-First Century," in K. Barker, K. Fairweather and R. Grantham (eds.), *Private Law in the 21st Century* (Hart Publishing, 2017), pp. 3–28.

14 But note that the availability of punitive damages is one reason why some victims who sue refuse settlement.

15 For instance, there are settlements that take place with judicial oversight.

16 For the view that victims choosing settlement means the tort system is working as it should, see Goldberg and Zipursky, Recognizing Wrongs, pp. 277–78 n4. For the opposite view, see O. Fiss, "Against Settlement" (1984) 93 *Yale Law Journal* 1073, 1085 ("Parties might settle while leaving justice undone.").

17 On this point, see T. R. Tyler, "The Psychology of Aggregation: Promise and Potential Pitfalls" (2015) 64 *De Paul Law Review* 711, 713 (stating that people want, when dealing with judicial authorities, the opportunity to tell their side of the story). Also see J. W. van Prooijen, *The Moral Punishment Instinct* (Oxford University Press, 2018), p. 254 (arguing that victims often appreciate the opportunity to explain what happened to them because "[t]here is a symbolic value in having a voice, as it contributes to victim's feelings of being taken seriously and respected by the decision-maker.").

these alternative settlement mechanisms do not provide meaningful responses to the victims of those reprehensible wrongdoings in that they do not afford them the opportunity to convey the moral significance of the wrongdoing and obtain value-affirmation by demanding the judicial imposition of punishment on the wrongdoer (i.e., punitive damages). It is the legitimacy of a duly comprised and disciplined courtroom that gives material force to the condemnation of the value-diminishing, reprehensible conduct that affronted the victim's self-worth for which *Relational Retribution* calls.[18]

Furthermore, I am not suggesting that tort litigation in its current state is optimal either.[19] I do not pretend that the adversarial tort process is the perfect mechanism for the resolution of private disputes (it has numerous flaws to go with its strengths)[20] or that it could not have negative effects for tort victims.[21] I understand why many have argued that the tort process, apart from being costly and inefficient, could exacerbate in many cases the sentiment of grievous injustice. The process devours time and energy and produces enough stress to overwhelm even stalwart individuals. Moreover, tort law and the judicial tort process are indisputably incapable of assessing the full dimensions of many cases that are brought to it. Sometimes the layers of causation are too complex to be addressed in an adversarial format. The adversarial discovery process also seriously limits the evidentiary information and knowledge that can be solicited.[22] The lack of technical expertise on the part of the adjudicating bodies is also a well-documented downside. These (and other) reasons might explain why many victims of torts choose not to sue their wrongdoers. Yet experience also shows that many tort victims of reprehensible wrongdoing decide to sue in spite of the potentially negative effects and expense. As Leslie Bender argues, "[t]here is a human-social need for dignity, respect, empowerment, and an ideology of fairness that a system of justice provides."[23] My focus here has been on the tort victims who decide, by

18 I have further explored this point in Chapter 4.

19 For instance, see generally J. Langbein, "The Disappearance of Civil Trial in the United States" (2012) 122 *Yale Law Journal* 522 (arguing that Anglo-American common law procedure focused on discovery enables cases to be settled or dismissed without trial).

20 For instance, see M. King, A. Freiberg, B. Batagol and R. Hyams, *Non-Adversarial Justice* (2nd ed.) (The Federation Press, 2014), pp. 2–3 (describing the adversarial process as "[a]ntagonistic and confrontational, with primacy being accorded to negating or destroying the opposition's case rather than to settling the dispute.").

21 Some worry that, even if having one's story heard generates a sense of dignity to victims, the adversarial process can generate serious dignitary harms as well. On this point, see M. A. Shapiro, "The Indignities of Civil Litigation" (2020) 100 *Boston University Law Review* 501 (arguing that while civil litigation can allow plaintiffs to assert their dignity-as-status, it can also be a humiliating affair for plaintiffs too).

22 For instance, see W. Wagner, "When a Corporation's Deliberate Ignorance Causes Harm: Charting a New Role for Tort Law" (2023) 72 *DePaul Law Review* 413 (showing that the ability of corporations to control the information environment relevant to causation in toxic torts impairs tort litigation).

23 See Bender, "Feminist (Re)Torts," 877.

filing a punitive lawsuit, to engage tort law and the tort process with all its virtues and vices. Once again, we should not overlook the fact that, under *Relational Retribution*, it is ultimately the tort victim's prerogative not only to activate the tort process at all but also to see it through.[24] I suspect skeptics will still argue that this description only fits a small number of exceptional tort cases.[25] They might be right. Yet I fail to understand why we should attach less significance to the fewer "exceptional" cases than to most "regular" cases. Why are quantity and regularity so important? Understanding tort law representativeness in solely quantitative terms is misguiding in that it diverts our attention from the less frequent yet more fundamental tort cases, which touch directly on substantive issues of great significance (e.g., reprehensible, reckless, or wanton misbehavior involving defective products, plus defamation, harassment, and privacy invasions, among others). It is these infrequent cases that not only have the potential to elicit meaningful conversations over the nature of our obligations to each other but also to convey powerfully much more nuanced and meaningful social messages about our deepest concerns and genuine motivations. Overlooking the importance of these tortious cases just because they are relatively rare risks misunderstanding the value and actual place of tort law and the tort process in our society. We should be more open to the possibility that the most compelling reasons of all to embrace tort law might be found in those isolated, exceptional cases. In any event, the time has come to look at tort law more qualitatively than quantitatively. It is time to shift the focus of the conversation toward understanding why such cases are much less common and, more importantly, toward improving tort law and the operation of the tort process so it provides tort victims with a legitimate avenue where substantive claims for private redress can be meaningfully addressed.[26]

B THE GENERATION OF INSTITUTIONAL KNOWLEDGE

Apart from the powerful other-regarding meaning that the condemnatory response conveys, the tort victim gives additional expression to the law by publicly exposing in the tort process the underlying context of the reprehensible wrongdoing

[24] See Section A of Chapter 9.

[25] On this point, see generally S. D. Sugarman, "Peter Cane on Torts," in J. Goudkamp, M. Lunney and L. McDonald (eds.), *Taking Law Seriously: Essays in Honour of Peter Cane* (Hart Publishing, 2022), pp. 73–94.

[26] For a scholarly example on devising second-best solutions to tackle evidentiary challenges in the context of toxic torts, see A. D. Lahav, "The Knowledge Remedy" (2020) 98 *Texas Law Review* 1361 (arguing for a "knowledge remedy," which is a court order requiring the defendant to pay for the production of new information about the harm it is alleged to have caused). Note that burden-of-proof shifting and cost-shifting were among the possibilities discussed in Europe in the context of the draft proposals to revise the Product Liability Directive for the digital age; however, rebuttable presumptions of defectiveness and causation were instead proposed.

(i.e., the institutional arrangements in the background).[27] The adversarial tort process, while focusing on the litigating parties' bilateral relationship of wrongdoing and the plaintiff's recourse to private redress, provides an institutional framework for the production of relevant information and knowledge regarding the particularities of the reprehensible wrongdoing and its underlying social and cultural conditions that only the tort victim who experiences it can properly activate and convey. The victim normally possesses information about the harm caused and the seriousness of the wrongdoing that few others can provide. It is the victim herself who is specially situated to expose the underlying institutional arrangements that facilitated the wrongful behavior. She exposes them by requiring that the defendant explain, backed by the jurisdictional power of the court, how the wrong came to pass. Fundamentally, the tort process questions the defendant's behavior. It forces the defendant to justify her conduct to the victim; to explain how and why the wrongdoing took place, and what reasons she may have had for believing it permissible. In these clarifications lies the potential of the tort process to uncover information of public interest regarding structural schemes of reprehensible wrongdoing and other pervasive power dynamics in our society that would otherwise go unknown or neglected.[28] The tort process similarly offers an invaluable avenue for communicating to the greater public emerging threats of wrongdoing that affect the community at large, encouraging public debate and conversation around otherwise hidden instances of wrongful behavior.[29]

For instance, punitive damages verdicts on cases of product liability involving wanton disregard for consumer safety, particularly in the United States, have raised citizen consciousness on the structural dimension of these societal problems and the need for public debate over current laws and potential reforms to address them.[30] As a result, significantly more attention is required from the legislature and regulatory agencies. The idea is that allowing tort litigation of these cases, while providing

[27] Pointing out the broader context of the reprehensible wrongdoing, see, for example, *Rowlands* v. *Chief Constable of Merseyside Police* [2006] EWCA Civ 1773; [2007] 1 WLR 1065 [42] (reflecting that awarding punitive damages would express the Court's disapproval of the conduct of both the individual police officer and the police force as an institution).

[28] For early views on this, see A. M. Linden, "Tort Law as Ombudsman" (1973) 51 *Canadian Bar Review* 155, 156. For a recent discussion on problem articulation, norm amplification, and intergovernmental signaling as the ancillary benefits of tort, see Kysar, "The Public Life of Private Law," 48–65. Note that civil recourse theorists have recognized that insisting "[t]hat tort law is private law is not to deny that tort law's operation has public dimensions or that its operation has implications for public policy." See Goldberg and Zipursky, Recognizing Wrongs, p. 72.

[29] On this point, see Robbennolt and Hans, The Psychology of Tort Law, p. 4 (stating that "tort verdicts provide information – about community standards, safety, vindication, and other topics – to other audiences as well.").

[30] For a similar viewpoint, see C. C. Tilley, "Private Law, Public Law, and the Production of American Virtue" (2020) 115 *Northwestern University Law Review Online* 270, 273 (demonstrating that tort litigation "produces a distinct kind of virtue that is crucial complement to the systemic reforms at the heart of public law.").

an immediate satisfactory response to the specific victim pursuing the punitive judgment, might spark a legislative or administrative response that with time hastens a solution to the underlying social problem, reducing the amount of similar tort litigation in the long run. Certainly, this does not mean to say that tort judicial judgments can or should do all the work or assume the role of legislatures or regulatory agencies. Quite the contrary. It only means that, in certain types of punitive lawsuits, judicial processes (e.g., discovery, fact-finding, etc.) gather information that can lead to knowledge of otherwise unknown or neglected egregious scheme of wrongdoing that has a public interest dimension. This knowledge may indirectly prompt legislatures and regulatory agencies to consider the underlying cause and play a *complementary* role in addressing it using their constitutional competencies.[31] It basically means not overlooking what happens in courts as they are institutional venues where potentially relevant knowledge is created. For instance, punitive tort litigation discovery and fact-finding have prompted deliberation on the desirability of criminalizing certain behaviors. At the same time, it has assisted criminal law professionals identify crimes that would otherwise go unknown to public prosecutors. Importantly, by providing valuable insights into how exactly the reprehensible wrongdoing came about, tort litigation has also prompted deliberation on the desirability of regulating certain activities.[32] Additionally, the punitive judgment creates a precedent for future similar cases, and in this way, tort law and tort doctrine gradually evolve.

As already acknowledged, the limitations of tort law and the judicial tort process to assess the full dimensions of tort cases are unarguable – again, the difficulties in addressing complex layers of causation, the limited evidentiary information and knowledge that can be produced in an adversarial discovery process, the lack of technical expertise, and regulatory-like remedies are all very well-known challenges. For their part, legislators and regulatory agencies are limited as well. Regarding technical competence, regulatory agencies lack the resources and knowledge to keep up with scientific and technological developments more often than is generally believed, not to mention the resources necessary to compensate for the underreporting and deception employed by certain manufacturers – factors that are even more patent in the rapidly changing landscape of the new challenges raised by AI-enabled products and other technological developments for which neither courts nor legislators or regulatory agencies (and in the context of generative AI, not even the developers themselves) possess sufficient expertise or knowledge to

[31] For scholarship illustrating the uneasy relationship between the role and function of the judiciary and the legislator, see R. Weaver and D. A. Kysar, "Courting Disaster: Climate Change and the Adjudication of Catastrophe" (2017) 93(1) *Notre Dame Law Review* 295.

[32] A telling example is the Johnson & Johnson litigation over ovarian cancer caused by talcum powder containing asbestos, which sparked initiatives to review the regulation of "cosmetics" in the United States. See C. Cep, "Johnson & Johnson and a New War on Consumer Protection," The New Yorker, September 12, 2022.

properly tackle.[33] Moreover, political and corporate interests, to take one example, often have greater sway with legislators and regulatory agencies than with courts.[34] Judges and juries operate, in principle, in an institutional context that is purposively designed to be insulated from, independent of, and unaccountable to the political branches.[35] Indeed, much of the evidence supporting the affirmations just made comes directly from the discovery process conducted during tort litigation.[36]

Courts, legislative bodies, and administrative agencies interact in direct and indirect manners.[37] Judges and courts are not better suited than legislators and regulatory agencies to solve the complex social problems underlying tort litigation. Still, seeing that regulatory agencies and legislators also face their own limitations, the judicial tort process plays an invaluable *complementary* role in highlighting the underlying social conditions of reprehensible wrongdoing that might call for more public attention and discussion. For instance, the tort process allows for detailed consideration of the specific context of reprehensible wrongdoing in which alleged harms were caused that may prove useful to the regulator deciding how the problem should be addressed. Despite the limitations of the tort process to produce complete or comprehensive information, it nonetheless represents an important source of awareness about emerging trends of reprehensible wrongdoing. By considering specific product defects identified by the plaintiff on a case-by-case basis (rather than the a priori abstract treatment that regulators are expected to perform), courts generate detailed information about the context of an injury, which might provide important clues to regulators that help reduce risks and alert them to emerging ones. After all, the courts' reliance on experts is much more localized (and concrete) than that of regulators. Without judicial decisions, those patterns of reprehensible wrongdoing that the tort victim undertakes to reveal and sanction through a punitive complaint might go unknown (or remain hidden). Consequently, regulators would likely leave it unattended for a longer period of time, during which wrongdoers would continue their behavior, exposing more victims to similar harm for possibly decades.

33 I have further explored this point in Section B of Chapter 8.

34 For instance, corporate efforts to influence the drafting of laws and regulations are well documented in the United States. See L. Drutman, *The Business of America is Lobbying: How Corporations Became Politicized and Politics Became More Corporate* (Oxford University Press, 2015).

35 For the view that judges are "non-insiders" who stand outside the agency system and the political process, see J. L. Sax, *Defending the Environment: A Strategy for Citizen Action* (Alfred A. Knopf, 1971).

36 On this point, see W. Wagner, "When All Else Fails: Regulatory Risky Products through Tort Litigation" (2007) 95 *Georgetown Law Journal* 693, 711 (asserting that the extent of manufacturers' internal knowledge about product risks [e.g., asbestos, tobacco, Dalkon Shield] is often uncovered and publicly exposed as a result of tort litigation).

37 On this point, see F. C. Zacharias, "The Politics of Torts" (1986) 95 *Yale Law Journal* 698. For an insightful account on how courts and agencies working together can pave the way for the regulator in the realm of competition law, see A. Kuenzler, "Third-Generation Competition Law" (2023) 11(1) *Journal of Antitrust Enforcement* 133.

Product liability punitive litigation offers a paradigmatic example of these dynamics by providing a unique vehicle for revealing reprehensible corporate misbehavior and holding manufacturers accountable for misrepresenting or withholding critical facts concerning the adverse effects of their products from public view.[38] In the course of the litigation, courts often identify dangerous activity unknown to the regulator or learn that a design defect is more serious than it appears on the surface.[39] Courts may also indirectly, through a series of similar product liability decisions, prompt legislatures and regulatory agencies to address the underlying cause.[40] This is not to suggest that regulators should rest or rely on tort litigation. Quite the contrary. Once again, the point is that legislatures, agencies, and courts should operate as *complements*, not as substitutes of one another.[41] For instance, product liability punitive litigation and the implementation and enforcement of risk regulation have different but complementary roles to play in protecting consumer safety. Surely, regulatory agencies should strive to prevent significant harm from happening by exercising their information gathering and control functions properly. This becomes particularly relevant in those cases of reprehensible wrongdoing where victims do not know they have been harmed by corporate misbehavior and, as a consequence, tort litigation is unlikely to take place (or it takes place too late).[42] Regulatory action is crucial in monitoring corporate misbehavior, taking action to prevent the materialization of significant harm, and, in the unfortunate event where harms have already manifested, establishing channels for victims to pursue private redress through courts. For its part, product liability punitive litigation, understood as a *retributive sanction* that denounces violations of societal trust (betrayals of consumers' safety expectations) by reasserting the consumers' self-worth vis-à-vis callous corporate behavior, offers a valuable tool for holding corporate offenders accountable for unanticipated instances of reprehensible wrongdoing, for voicing the plurality of substantive values that inform consumers' understanding of unacceptable risk in our society, and for providing victims with a legitimate avenue for a relational retributive response to the wrong suffered.[43] That the complaint is seconded by condemnation from the state apparatus reasserts the egregious nature of the corporate misbehavior

38 For a detailed analysis of the role of punitive damages in the mass-market context, see Chapters 6, 7, and 8.

39 For the argument that tort litigation plays an indispensable role in lowering information-related barriers to regulating risky products, see Zacharias, "The Politics of Torts," 715.

40 Ibid 698. For example, litigation was critical to focus regulatory attention on the weight loss pill Ephedra and the sleeping pill Halcion and uncover internal company knowledge about their potential harms. See Wagner, "When All Else Fails," 711.

41 On the entanglement of modern tort law with direct regulation of risk, see G. C. Keating, *Reasonableness and Risk. Right and Responsibility in the Law of Torts* (Oxford University Press, 2023).

42 Similarly, see G. C. Hazard (Jr.), "The Futures Problem" (2000) 148 *University of Pennsylvania Law Review* 1901 (pointing out the challenges of evaluating toxic tort cases where injuries only manifest years later).

43 I have further explored this notion in Chapter 7.

and in so doing reinforces the other-regarding standards of society. Importantly, by exposing unknown corporate misbehavior in a highly contextualized setting, product liability punitive litigation produces valuable knowledge and information about technological and other hazards from a diversity of expert inputs and lay consumer understandings, providing us with, in Mary L. Lyndon's words, a "social learning mechanism."[44] Under this more holistic reading, regulatory action and product liability punitive litigation interact and learn from each other in an ongoing feedback loop fashion.[45]

Moreover, as discussed in Chapter 8, direct risk regulation tends to prioritize expert assessments and de-emphasize lay perspectives. For instance, in the context of product safety, regulators exhibit a conscious preference for probabilistic approaches to risk regulation that mostly involve expert-driven risk-utility reasoning. The fact is that laypeople's judgments about risk often capture values that experts find difficult to represent adequately within their technical approaches.[46] While the experts' assessments of regulators are certainly important, lay understandings of risk, those of ordinary consumers, also matter and often matter equally. Again referring back to Chapter 8, the assumption that risk assessments should be exclusively assigned to experts (manufacturers, regulators) needs (at least partial) revision since we have found no compelling reason to believe that expert opinion should always outweigh layperson understandings.[47] The underlying idea is that a genuine system of protection of consumer safety should both respond to expert assessments of risk (manufacturers, risk regulators) and strive to generate dialogue between the experts and lay peoples' understandings of risk. One way of doing this is by maintaining avenues for ordinary consumers to participate in the social definition of risk in society. Certainly, regulatory activities should solicit and incorporate greater layperson feedback, but it is also important to look at complementary avenues for participation. In that sense, product liability punitive litigation offers a complementary avenue whose judicial endorsement confers certain legitimacy and allows consumers to participate to some extent in the legal norms surrounding risk in our society. It allows ordinary consumers to engage actively in the construction of the social significance of risk that gives force to the public intuitions charged with managing it.[48] Product liability

44 See M. L. Lyndon, "Tort Law and Technology" (1995) 12 *Yale Journal on Regulation* 137, 176 (arguing that courts' procedural structure makes them "an important social learning mechanism").

45 I have explored this point in Section B of Chapter 8.

46 To clarify, the argument is that experts generally use a narrow model that exclusively targets aggregate welfare and that lay judgments could help identify other relevant values worth expert attention, not that we should reject a formally structured expert approach to risk assessment altogether.

47 The underlying idea is that lay citizens legitimately represent the public interest in safety in that their incentives are in principle not compromised with those of the private corporation.

48 For instance, see P. Slovic, "Trust, Emotion, Sex, Politics, and Science: Surveying the Risk-Assessment Battlefield" (1999) 19 *Risk Analysis* 689, 689 (arguing that more public participation in both risk assessment and risk decision making would improve the quality of analysis and increase the legitimacy of the decisions).

punitive litigation serves as an intermediate structure for participation in the sense that it makes litigants' views publicly available to regulators and the society at large.

I respect the argument that, instead of relying on the democratically questionable legitimacy of court verdicts (in that courts are in general nonrepresentative institutions) to inform the underlying social and cultural conditions of wrongdoing that call for public attention and discussion, we should perhaps focus our efforts on seeking to draw more widely from the population by facilitating and fostering citizen participation in more democratically accountable venues, such as the legislative or regulatory processes.[49] This would certainly be desirable, yet powerful reasons to commend tort litigation as a *complement* still stand. One of these reasons is that, for the average citizen to be effectively heard in those venues (i.e., to be able to exercise some effective pressure toward regulatory or legislative reform), some sort of organizational power in the form of additional political, societal, economical, and other technical resources would be required, whereas the judicial tort process can be effectively activated by an individual citizen seeking private redress. In the vast majority of tort cases, individual victims lack the power and organizational structure to translate their demands into legislative or executive action, so resorting to courts appears to be the most readily available venue to voice their claims. One counterargument could be that the cost (and uncertainty) of tort litigation represents an insurmountable obstacle for the average citizen. Granted. However, the expense of litigation is not a fundamental obstacle. It is a systemic problem of tort litigation that we can (and should) tackle by introducing legal reforms that facilitate access to courts for those who lack the economic resources to do it themselves.[50] Among other proposals to such an end are waiving or lowering court fees, making available public subsidies for civil legal aid (attorneys) and discovery costs (e.g., experts, transcripts). Another counterargument could be that, even if the costs of litigation are eventually alleviated, the pronounced asymmetry of power and information typical in most cases of corporate reprehensible wrongdoing would still pose a significant obstacle for claimants seeking the evidence needed to make their punitive cases in court.

49 For discussions regarding the legitimacy and suitability of civil courts as risk regulators, see generally E. R. De Jong, "Tort Law and Judicial Risk Regulation: Bipolar and Multipolar Risk Reasoning in Light of Tort Law's Regulatory Effects" (2018) 9 *European Journal of Risk Regulation* 14; M. A. Loth, "The Civil Court as Risk Regulator: The Issue of Its Legitimacy" (2018) 9 *European Journal of Risk Regulation* 66, 66–78. From a different angle, see A. J. Ley, "The Costs and Benefits of American Policy-Making Venues" (2014) 48 *Law and Society Review* 91 (using field interviews and three case studies of an environmental dispute to show that the judiciary can provide an institutional venue for public input that is sometimes more inclusive than other venues and produces positive-sum outcomes where other venues cannot).

50 On this point, see J. M. Feinman, "Unmaking and Remaking Tort Law" (2005) 5 *Journal of High Technology Law* 61 (arguing for removing victims' obstacles to reach courts systemically). On lowering entrance barriers, see J. Resnik, "The Functions of Publicity and of Privatization in Courts and Their Replacements (from Jeremy Bentham to #MeToo and *Google* Spain)," in B. Hess and A. K. Harvey (eds.), *Open Justice: The Role of Courts in a Democratic Society* (Nomos, 2019).

This challenge might be exacerbated in cases where victims are confronted with the daunting task of identifying and proving that harm was caused by AI-enabled products, given their complexity and the sheer amount of unretrievable data used to construct them. To that end, putting in place procedural rules that are more sensitive to the information and power asymmetries of the litigant parties would certainly be desirable (for example, requirements for more equitable distribution of the burden of proof considering the party with better access to relevant information, for greater use of early-stage discovery to allow claimants to gather information to respond to motions to dismiss, and many others).[51] One possible counter-response to these arguments would be that some of the organizational and other barriers for citizen participation and involvement in the regulatory and legislative processes might also be alleviated.[52] Absolutely, such barriers should also be revised.[53] Notwithstanding, a powerful reason to recommend tort litigation as *complementary* means for seeking redress still exists. Neither regulators nor legislators have a legal duty to hear out and respond to citizen demands the way judges do. Indeed, once the tort process is activated by the tort plaintiff, judges are duty-bound to decide the case before them by either accepting or rejecting the plaintiff's claim for redress through a reasoned legal judgment based on the evidence produced, judicial precedents, and legal rules and principles. As Douglas Kysar argues, the entitlement of the tort plaintiff to a response once she brings a legal issue to the court's attention is a unique feature of tort law that recommends it.[54]

◊ ◊ ◊

CONCLUDING REMARKS

Tort law provides a channel for the expression of important values in our society. Properly understanding the tort victim's legal power to make punitive demands through the tort process requires seeing beyond restoration or empowerment. It means paying close attention to the substantive content of the victim's retributive

[51] For a recent example of the legal recognition of presumptions of defectiveness of the product and of the causal link between the defectiveness of the product and the harm, see Directive (EU) 2024/2853 of the European Parliament and of the Council of 23 October 2024 on liability for defective products and repealing Council Directive 85/374/EEC, art. 10. Note that disclosure of the evidence that is necessary to uphold a claim might sometimes be limited by the protection of third parties' trade secrets and confidentiality.

[52] For a recent proposal to foster popular participation in agency decision-making, see generally M. Sant'Ambrogio and G. Staszewski, "Democratizing Rule Development" (2021) 98 *Washington University Law Review* 793.

[53] See, for example, B. Emerson, *The Public's Law: Origins and Architecture of Progressive Democracy* (Oxford University Press, 2019) (arguing that the administrative state should provide regulation and social services through deliberative procedures).

[54] See Kysar, "The Public Life of Private Law," 54.

responses to reprehensible wrongdoing in order to understand better social expectations of how victims should be treated as equals vis-à-vis their wrongdoers and the appropriate institutional venues for the articulation of relational answerability when private disputes arise. The tort process, where judgments of rights and responsibility are central, is a distinct forum where accountability is assigned, harms are aired, stories are told, and collective standards of conduct and levels of care are enforced, refined, challenged, and redefined as our societies evolve. The tort process provides a channel for private individuals to appeal to the other-regarding values they esteem of great social importance in a judicial forum for which other legitimate, effective avenues are extremely scarce.

Tort victims are specially situated to convey the moral significance and impact of the defendant's reprehensible wrongful behavior on their lives and expose the underlying social and cultural implications of the wrongdoing. The explicit value-driven consideration of the tort victim's responses (i.e., the meaning they construe from circumstances of wrongdoing that represent a deliberate threat to their individual autonomy, dignity, physical integrity, or even life) powerfully conveys the nuances and layers of varied social messages regarding our ultimate concerns and true motivations. As a community, we ought to devote more attention to the advantage of using tort law, in addition to providing ex post compensatory and noncompensatory remedies, to contribute proactively to the process of constructing other-regarding meaning and generating institutional knowledge in our society. The tort process offers a legitimate space for voicing the plurality of substantive values that inform our understandings of what we owe to each other as members in the community and our collective intuitions on risk, trust, and truth that reflect the mettle of our interpersonal relationships with one another. Hopefully, the substantive and contextual reading of the tort victim offered by *Relational Retribution* will spark constructive conversations on the proper place of tort law and tort litigation in our societies. These conversations will not only bring out the need to preserve the rich moral insights provided by tort law's sensitivity to the substantive responses of tort victims who engage the tort process, but also, rather than simply abandoning or replacing it, provide clues for improving its operation in concerted articulation with other relevant *complementary* institutions charged with accounting for harm in our democratic societies.

Conclusion

Reconciling Torts and Retribution

Torts and Retribution embarked on a multifaceted journey in search of an analytical retributive framework to conceptualize punitive damages across jurisdictions by articulating a justificatory account of the retributive character of tort law embedded in punitive damages that is sorely needed. Taking retribution in torts seriously necessarily demands reassessing widely accepted assumptions underlying the understanding of tort law as an exclusively private rectificatory mechanism. *Torts and Retribution* did this by freshly examining alternative yet persuasive readings of classic tort law assumptions. It has been argued that the time has come to abandon structural and formal readings of the tort victim and the tort process by giving tort responses due respect that more accurately reflects the significance and substantive meaning of the circumstances of the wrongdoing for both the private parties involved and society as a whole.

By rethinking punitive damages from a holistic perspective that effectively links wrongdoers and victims, *Torts and Retribution* offers a novel retributive reconstruction of punitive damages, coined *Relational Retribution*, that is sensitive to the context within which the tort occurred. The notion of *Relational Retribution* unlocks the underlying logic of punitive damages – a notion that comfortably suits both the bilateral structure of tort law and the proactive role traditionally allocated to the victim in tort litigation. *Relational Retribution* shifts the focus away from exclusive attention on the reprehensibility of the defendant's conduct as deserving of punishment in order to include consideration of the perspective of the victim's correlative retributive motivations for punishment and, in the process, it directs attention to the richness of the value-driven reactions of lay citizens to instances of reprehensible wrongdoing. Drawing from promising findings in the fields of cognitive and social psychology in addition to studies from the social sciences on human behavior and decision-making and insights related to the "reactive attitudes" discussed by moral philosophers, *Relational Retribution* brings to light the underlying values that motivate the retributive reactions of the victims of reprehensible wrongdoing. Significantly, this approach acknowledges the human emotions at the core of the retributive motivations (such as moral outrage and aversion to betrayal) that are triggered when people confront certain types of deliberate misbehavior, such as actions that threaten or undermine their autonomy of action, or that deliberately cause serious harm (e.g., the inherent disparagement of the victim's worth conveyed by the defendant's cyberbullying or workplace harassment, or the manufacturer's deliberate prioritization of private gain over preventing significant harm to consumers). *Relational Retribution* compellingly demonstrates that victims' retributive motivations to punish wrongdoers through punitive damages do not only tie into the reprehensible character of the wrongdoing, but they also, and most importantly, involve the self-identity of victims who have been wronged, their status as moral agents, and the meaning they construe from the circumstances of value-diminishing reprehensible wrongdoing that represents a deliberate threat to their individual autonomy, individual dignity, physical integrity, or even life. The focus of *Relational Retribution* on the underlying relationship between defendant and plaintiff makes it possible to untangle and tease out the correlative retributive motivations of those victims who seek *condemnation* and *value affirmation* for seriously disrespectful actions through punitive awards.

As the preceding pages exhaustively demonstrate, neither purely conceiving the imposition of punishment in terms of just deserts nor solely focusing on the objective of deterring future misbehavior fully encapsulate the motivations that lead people to demand punitive damages. *Torts and Retribution* argues that people seek punitive damages for principled reasons to communicate their commitment to the other-regarding values affected in reprehensible tortious situations involving either interpersonal invasions of dignitary interests or collective violations of societal trust in the marketplace. Punitive damages are thus better understood as a mode of moral communication between private parties that exists because punitive damages provide a condemnatory institution for holding wrongdoers accountable, affirming the victim's intrinsic worth, and reinforcing the importance of other-regarding values in our society.

In this light, punitive damages represent an institution that meaningfully conveys the complex other-regarding values of society that are not satisfactorily or convincingly addressed by either criminal or public law. Moreover, the judicial endorsement of the substantive values brought to the fore by private actors in successful punitive damage claims reaffirms the victim's equal moral value vis-à-vis the wrongdoer and communicates to society at large that the wrongdoer is not in any way worthier than the victim or entitled to treat her poorly. Rendering the power to the tort victim to demand the imposition of a sanction under this new substantive light resignifies our understanding of the judicial tort process as a privately controlled institutional framework for addressing not only compensatory but also condemnatory responses to reprehensible wrongdoing. Overall, this view situates the tort judicial process as a legitimate and complementary avenue for tort victims to actively participate in defining the content of the fundamental values we wish to cultivate in our society. The tort process offers a legitimate space for voicing the plurality of substantive values that inform our understandings of what we owe to each other as members in the community and our collective intuitions on risk, trust, and truth that reflect the mettle of our interpersonal relationships with one another. Punitive lawsuits themselves are apt examples of a meaning-producing institution because they embrace the values embodied in the condemnatory legal message that the wrongdoer is not somehow worth more than the victim and is not entitled to treat the victim in a manner that diminishes her relative value. Accordingly, understanding tort victim's punitive responses to reprehensible wrongdoing requires looking beyond rectification and formal empowerment; it means recognizing that tort victims are not actors behaving rationally in a vacuum but are rather laden with substantive values embedded in the broader social context. Punitive lawsuits persuasively illustrate how tort responses are able to capture the moral significance of the wrongdoing in a way that communicates the situated meaning of the impact of reprehensible wrongs on the victims and their complex motivations for resorting to tort law and its procedure for private redress. Ultimately, punitive lawsuits are not isolated instances of tort litigation that take place in a vacuum – quite the opposite. Most frequently, they are better understood as occurring in articulation with and as complements to the actions of other relevant institutional actors in our democratic societies. This is why it makes little sense to think about tort law and its procedure in isolation.

THE VALUE OF INTRINSIC MOTIVATIONS

Torts and Retribution takes seriously the uneasy yet unavoidable observation of tort law's retributive dimension. It starts with the observation that, despite the widely accepted understanding of punitive damages as combining "retribution and deterrence," the large body of sophisticated scholarship on the deterrent aspect of the institution has not been matched by similar efforts to account for its dominant retributive facet. In accounting for the ongoing practice of punitive damages, scholars have (over)emphasized the wrongdoer's behavior and, as a consequence, failed to give victims' retributive responses the attention they deserve. This focus has devoted too much attention to the deterrent aspect of punitive damages (i.e., the argument that punishment ought to be calibrated to achieve deterrence). While deterrence may well be the value most cited in legalist accounts, accredited research in the social sciences has clearly shown that deterring future wrongdoing does not figure significantly among the primary motivations that drive punitive responses when individuals are confronted with specific instances of reprehensible behavior. Conversely, the available empirical findings demonstrate that the retributive dimension of punitive damages aligns more closely with moral intuitions than with the deterrent motive.

The study of moral outrage and betrayal aversion brings to light the underlying values at the core of the retributive motivations that are triggered when people confront certain types of reprehensible misbehavior, in particular those that undermine their autonomy of action or cause serious harm. A more meaningful understanding of punitive damages can thus be found in the rich value-laden lay intuitions that drive people to punish certain behaviors through tort law. Moral outrage and betrayal aversion possess, in certain tortious settings, a logic and structure that makes them appropriate responses to instances of reprehensible wrongdoing. Studies demonstrate that moral outrage and betrayal aversion are two powerful retributive motivations behind "reactive attitudes" to punish those who wrong us in a reprehensible fashion that obey their own rationality.

These retributive motivations hold meaning; they express other-regarding values and comprise a significant, as yet missing element in the predominant understanding of punitive damages. To integrate the insights of retributive motivations, purely rationalistic approaches to punitive damages might well be complemented with a more expansive approach that leaves room for the respectful consideration of emotive-intuitive responses. In this expanded logic, punitive damages should be re-elaborated so that the denser, deeper, and richer retributive motivations of individual tort victims to certain serious acts of disrespect are properly addressed. This is not to say that tort law should categorically consider retributive motivations as legitimate. It means that unreflectively denying, suppressing, or directly ignoring the widely acknowledged emotional component that our retributive responses express as powerful forms of moral communication leaves a crucial factor out of the equation.

Even when they do not fit in rational models of deterrence, emotive-intuitive responses play a function in our society that transcends the individual who experiences them and performs a function that benefits the community. The collective control they express and exercise in the community cannot be rendered in terms of individual rational behavior. Under economic readings of deterrence, tort victims' retributive motivations, rooted in emotive-intuitive responses, are mostly deemed irrational in the sense that tort victims would be better served by always making detached, calculated decisions in their own best interest – recall the rational actor depiction of plaintiffs. Tort victims would be acting irrationally, in defiance of their self-interest, by launching a tort lawsuit and seeking punitive damages (which often involve significant cost, effort, uncertainty, and suffering for victims) against, for instance, a callous corporation or a defamatory colleague mainly to condemn its behavior and affirm their own self-worth, including reaffirmation of the other-regarding values violated by seriously disrespectful actions. Such individual actions (e.g., filing the punitive lawsuit), however, are very often good for society: We all want to live in a world in which defamatory behavior is held to account and callous corporate behavior for profit is denounced, does not reward offenders, or goes unnoticed. In that sense, retributive motivations powerfully override economic rationality. Tort lawsuits are not substituting for the victim's retributive reactions (they do not substitute the intuitive-emotive responses to reprehensible wrongdoing); rather they are a legitimate means for properly channeling them in a controlled and proportionate manner. We are all better off in a society in which legitimate channels for such accounting exist.

THE ROAD AHEAD: JOINT CONVERSATIONS

In times where the discussion over the place of punishment in private law seems fluid and dynamic across civil law and common law jurisdictions (and capable of evolving even in legal systems where it is flatly rejected), *Torts and Retribution* extends an invitation to both tort and criminal law scholars worldwide to join a conversation about the forms of punishment in our democratic societies that fall outside the confines of criminal law and procedure. This invitation to rethink the place and ambit of punishment in our societies coincides with current debates over the state's exclusive authority to impose punishment through its system for criminal sanction. Ultimately, by challenging the traditional understanding that situates the monopoly of punishment exclusively in criminal law in a criminal-law-or-nothing dichotomy, *Torts and Retribution* elicits a much-needed conversation on whether other areas of the law, particularly tort law, may be enlisted as complementary mechanisms to express condemnatory responses. Importantly, in times when new technologies are giving rise to new forms of significant wrongdoing (for instance, cyberbullying, AI-generated defamation, algorithmic discrimination, invasion of privacy caused by exploitative tactics employed by digital platforms) and distinct types of harms both tangible (e.g., losing an economic benefit due to algorithmic discrimination, suffering a physical injury from the malfunctioning of an AI-enabled surgical tool) and intangible (including addiction, depression, diminished self-esteem, and different kinds of privacy violations) that the law must urgently grasp and properly address, *Torts and Retribution* extends an invitation to legal scholars more broadly, ones working in a wide variety of fields, such as contract law, trust law, consumer law, antitrust law, intellectual property law, privacy law, anti-discrimination law, and regulatory law, to join the conversation about the rich potential of tort law and the tort process as a *complementary* mechanism to counteract the structural power imbalances patent in the new digital economy and work toward better addressing the current challenges posed by artificial intelligence (and other new technologies) to citizens' safety, privacy, dignity, and psychological integrity. Tackling these important issues calls for closely concerted articulation with other fields, disciplines, and relevant institutions and practices meant to ensure safety and mitigate risk in our society. All have a significant place in this conversation, but for that conversation to begin, we must first overcome the theoretical boundaries that keep them separated. Hopefully, *Torts and Retribution* will contribute not only to rethinking the classic confines of tort law but also to reconceptualizing tort law and the tort process as an integral part of the broader social and cultural context in which it operates.

Bibliography

Abel R, "The Real Tort Crisis – Too Few Claims" (1987) 48 *Ohio State Law Journal* 443.

Abrams K and Keren H, "Who's Afraid of Law and the Emotions?" (2010) 94 *Minnesota Law Review* 1997.

Ackerman F and Heinzerling L, *Priceless: On Knowing the Price of Everything and the Value of Nothing* (The New Press 2004).

Ames D L and Fiske S T, "Intentional Harms Are Worse, Even When They're Not" (2013) 24(9) *Psychological Science* 1755.

Anderson E S and Pildes R H, "Expressive Theories of Law: A General Restatement" (2000) 148 *University of Pennsylvania Law Review* 1503.

Alstott L, "A Fine Is Not a Price: Insights for Law," in J Hanson (ed), *Ideology, Psychology, and Law* (Oxford University Press 2012) 185–92.

Arlen J and Kornhauser L A, "Battle for Our Souls: A Psychological Justification for Corporate and Individual Liability for Organizational Misconduct" (2023) 3 *University of Illinois Law Review* 673.

Arvind T T and Gray J, "The Limits of Technocracy: Private Law's Future in the Regulatory State," in K Barker, K Fairweather and R Grantham (eds), *Private Law in the 21st Century* (Hart Publishing 2017) 237–55.

Ausness R C, "Danger Is My Business: The Right to Manufacture Unsafe Products" (2014) 67 *Arkansas Law Review* 827.

Baker T, "Blood Money, New Money, and the Moral Economy of Tort Law in Action" (2001) 35(2) *Law and Society Review* 275.

Bandes S A, "Feeling and Thinking Like a Lawyer: Cognition, Emotion and the Practice and Progress of Law" (2021) 89 *Fordham Law Review* 1.

Bandes S A, "Introduction," in S A Bandes (ed), *The Passions of Law* (New York University Press 2000) 1–15.

Bant E, "Culpable Corporate Minds" (2021) 48 *University of Western Australia Law Review* 352.

Bant E and Paterson J M, "Systems of Misconduct: Corporate Culpability and Statutory Unconscionability" (2021) 15 *Journal of Equity* 63.

Barker K, "Punishment in Private Law – No Such Thing Anymore," in E Bant, W Courtney, J Goudkamp and J M Paterson (eds), *Punishment and Private Law* (Hart Publishing 2021) 35–62.

Barker K, "Private Law as a Complex System: Agendas for the Twenty-First Century," in K Barker, K Fairweather and R Grantham (eds), *Private Law in the 21st Century* (Hart Publishing 2017) 3–28.

Barker K, "Private and Public: The Mixed Conception of Vindication in Torts and Private Law," in S G A Pitel, J W Neyers and E Chamberlain (eds), *Tort Law: Challenging Orthodoxy* (Hart Publishing 2013) 59–93.
Baron J, "The Effect of Normative Beliefs on Anticipated Emotions" (1992) 63 *Journal of Personality and Social Psychology* 320.
Baron J, "Tradeoffs among Reasons for Action" (1986) 16 *Journal for the Theory of Social Behaviour* 173.
Baron J and Ritov I, "Intuitions about Penalties and Compensation in the Context of Tort Law" (1993) 7 *Journal of Risk and Uncertainty* 17.
Beever A, "Justice and Punishment in Tort: A Comparative Theoretical Analysis," in C E F Rickett (ed), *Justifying Private Law Remedies* (Hart Publishing 2008) 249–98.
Beever A, "The Structure of Aggravated and Exemplary Damages" (2003) 23 *Oxford Journal of Legal Studies* 87.
Bender L, "Feminist (Re)Torts: Thoughts on the Liability Crisis, Mass Torts, Power, and Responsibilities" (1990) 4 *Duke Law Journal* 848.
Benforado A and Hanson J D, "The Cost of Dispositionism: The Premature Demise of Situationist Law and Economics" (2005) 64 *Maryland Law Review* 24.
Bennett Moses L, "Regulating in the Face of Sociotechnical Change," in R Brownsword, E Scotford and K Yeung (eds), *The Oxford Handbook of Law, Regulation and Technology* (Oxford University Press 2017) 573–96.
Bentham J, "Principles of Penal Law," in J Bowring (ed), *The Works of Jeremy Bentham* (Russell & Russell 1962) 365–580.
Berman M N, "Proportionality, Constraint, and Culpability" (2021) 15 *Criminal Law and Philosophy* 373.
Bernstein A, "Q: What Is Tort? A: Categorical Hurt" (2021) 14(2) *Journal of Tort Law* 261.
Bernstein A, "The Communities that Make Standards of Care Possible' (2002) 77 *Chicago-Kent Law Review* 735.
Berryman J, "Reconceptualizing Aggravated Damages: Recognizing the Dignitary Interest and Referential Loss" (2004) 41 *San Diego Law Review* 1521.
Best E K, "Atypical Actors and Tort Law's Expressive Function" (2012) 96 *Marquette Law Review* 461.
Bilz K, "Testing the Expressive Theory of Punishment" (2016) 13(2) *Journal of Empirical Legal Studies* 358.
Binder G, "Victims and the Significance of Causing Harm" (2008) 28 *Pace Law Review* 713.
Birds J, Lynch B and Paul S, *MacGillivray on Insurance Law* (14th ed.) (Sweet and Maxwell 2018).
Blanchard S, "Nominal Damages as Vindication" (2022) 30(1) *George Mason Law Review* 227.
Boonin D, *The Problem of Punishment* (Cambridge University Press 2008).
Borghetti J-S, "Taking EU Product Liability Law Seriously: How Can the Product Liability Directive Effectively Contribute to Consumer Protection?" (2023) 1 *French Journal of Legal Policy* 136.
Borghetti J-S, Santos Silva M, Fairgrieve D, García P, Keirse A, Machnikowski P, Rajneri E, Schmon C, Ulbeck V, Vallone V and Zech H, "Relevance of Risk-benefit for Assessing Defectiveness of a Product: A Comparative Study of Thirteen European Legal Systems" (2021) 29(1) *European Review of Private Law* 91.
Borghetti J-S, "Punitive Damages in France," in H Koziol and V Wilcox (eds), *Punitive Damages: Common Law and Civil Law Perspectives* (Springer 2009) 55–73.
Boyd W, Kysar D A and Rachlinski J J, "Law, Environment, and the 'Nondismal' Social Sciences" (2012) 8 *Annual Review of Law and Social Science* 183.

Bradford A, *Digital Empires, The Global Battle to Regulate Technology* (Oxford University Press 2023).
Brennan W J (Jr), "Reason, Passion, and 'The Progress of the Law'" (1988) 10 *Cardozo Law Review* 3.
Bronsteen J, Buccafusco C and Masur J, "Happiness and Punishment" (2009) 76 *University of Chicago Law Review* 1037.
Brooks T, *Punishment: A Critical Introduction* (Routledge 2021).
Bublick E M, "Mathias v Accor Economy Lodging, Inc (2003): Judge Richard A. Posner's Message and Method on Punitive Damages," in J Goudkamp and E Katsampouka (eds), *Landmark Cases in the Law of Punitive Damages* (Hart Publishing 2023) 281–302.
Buell S W, "Retiring Corporate Retribution" (2020) 83 *Law and Contemporary Problems* 25.
Busch C, "Rethinking Product Liability Rules for Online Marketplaces: A Comparative Perspective" (July 31, 2021) Available at SSRN: https://ssrn.com/abstract=3784466.
Burrows A, "Damages and Rights," in D Nolan and A Robertson (eds), *Rights and Private Law* (Hart Publishing 2012) 275–308.
Burrows A, *Remedies for Torts and Breach of Contract* (3rd ed.) (Oxford University Press 2004).
Burrows A, "Reforming Exemplary Damages: Expansion or Abolition?" in P Birks (ed), *Wrongs and Remedies in the Twenty First Century* (Oxford University Press 1996) 153–74.
Burrows A, "The Scope of Exemplary Damages" (1993) 109 *Law Quarterly Review* 358.
Büyüksagis E, Ebert I, Fairgrieve D, Meurkens R C and Quarta F, "Punitive Damages in Europe and Plea for the Recognition of Legal Pluralism" (2016) 1 *European Business Law Review* 137.
Calabresi G, "The Complexities of Torts: The case of Punitive Damages," in M Stuart Madden (ed), *Exploring Tort Law* (Cambridge University Press 2005) 333–51.
Calabresi G, "Some Thoughts on Risk Distribution and the Law of Torts" (1961) 70 *Yale Law Journal* 499.
Calabresi G, "Civil Recourse Theory's Reductionism" (2013) 88 *Indiana Law Journal* 449.
Calabresi G, "A Broader View of the Cathedral: The Significance of the Liability Rule, Correcting A Misapprehension" (2014) 77 *Law and Contemporary Problems* 1.
Calabresi G and Bobbit P, *Tragic Choices* (W.W. Norton & Company 1978).
Calabresi G and Melamed A D, "Property Rules, Liability Rules, and Inalienability: One View of the Cathedral" (1972) 85 *Harvard Law Review* 1089.
Calhoun C, "Cognitive Emotions?" in C Calhoun and R C Solomon (eds), *What Is An Emotion? Classic and Contemporary Readings* (Oxford University Press 1984) 327–42.
Calnan A, "Ending the Punitive Damage Debate" (1995) 45 *DePaul Law Review* 101.
Cane P, "Searching for United States Tort Law in the Antipodes" (2011) 38 *Pepperdine Law Review* 257.
Cane P, "Mens Rea in Tort Law" (2000) 20 *Oxford Journal of Legal Studies* 533.
Cane P, "Retribution, Proportionality, and Moral Luck in Tort Law," in P Cane and J Stapleton (eds), *The Law of Obligations: Essays in Celebration of John Fleming* (Oxford University Press 1998) 141–74.
Cane P, *The Anatomy of Tort Law* (Hart Publishing 1997).
Cappelletti M, "Comparative Reflections on Punishment in Tort Law," in J-S Borghetti and S Whittaker (eds), *French Civil Liability in Comparative Perspective* (Hart Publishing 2019) 329–52.
Cardi W J, Penfield R D and Yoon A H, "Does Tort Law Deter Individuals? A Behavioral Science Study" (2012) 9 *Journal of Empirical Legal Studies* 567.
Carlsmith K M, "The Roles of Retribution and Utility in Determining Punishment" (2006) 42 *Journal of Experimental Social Psychology* 437.
Carlsmith K M and Darley J M, "Psychological Aspects of Retributive Justice" (2008) 40 *Advances in Experimental Social Psychology* 193.

Carlsmith K M, Darley J M and Robinson P H, "Why Do We Punish? Deterrence and Just Deserts as Motives for Punishment" (2002) 83 *Journal of Personality and Social Psychology* 284.
Chamallas M and Wriggins J, *The Measure of Injury: Race, Gender, and Tort Law* (New York University Press 2010).
Chapman B and Trebilcock M, "Punitive Damages: Divergence in Search of a Rationale" (1989) 40 *Alabama Law Review* 741.
Cherry M and Flanagan O (eds), *The Moral Psychology of Anger* (Rowan and Littlefield International 2017).
Coase R, "The Problem of Social Cost" (1960) 3 *Journal of Law and Economics* 1.
Colby T B, "Clearing the Smoke from Phillips Morris v. Williams: The Past, Present and Future of Punitive Damages" (2008) 118 *Yale Law Journal* 392.
Colby T B, "Beyond the Multiple Punishment Problem: Punitive Damages as Punishment for Individual, Private Wrongs (2003) 87 *Minnesota Law Review* 583.
Coleman J C, "The Structure of Tort Law" (1988) 97 *Yale Law Journal* 1233.
Cooter R D, "Expressive Law and Economics" (1998) 27 *Journal of Legal Studies* 585.
Cooter R D, "Punitive Damages, Social Norms, and Economic Analysis" (1997) 60 *Law and Contemporary Problems* 73.
Cooter R D, "Punitive Damages for Deterrence: When and How Much?" (1989) 40 *Alabama Law Review* 1143.
Cooter R D, "Prices and Sanctions" (1984) 84 *Columbia Law Review* 1523.
Cooter R D, "Economic Analysis of Punitive Damages" (1982) 56 *Southern California Law Review* 79.
Cooter R D and Sugarman S D, "A Regulated Market in Unmatured Tort Claims: Tort Reform by Contract," in W Olson (ed), *New Directions in Liability Law* (Academy of Political Science in conjunction with the Manhattan Institute for Policy Research 1988) 174–85.
Cooter R D and Porat A, *Getting Incentives Right: Improving Torts, Contracts, and Restitution* (Princeton University Press 2014).
Cooter R D and Rubinfeld D L, "Economic Analysis of Legal Disputes and Their Resolution" (1987) 27 *Journal of Economic Literature* 1067.
Cosmides L and Tooby J, "Cognitive Adaptations for Social Exchange," in J H Barkow, L Cosmides and J Tooby (eds), *The Adapted Mind: Evolutionary Psychology and the Generation of Culture* (Oxford University Press 1992) 163–227.
Craswell R, "Deterrence and Damages: The Multiplier Principle and Its Alternatives" (1999) 97 *Michigan Law Review* 2185.
Croley S P and Hanson J D, "Rescuing the Revolution: The Revived Case for Enterprise Liability" (1993) 91 *Michigan Law Review* 683.
Dagan H, "Pluralism and Perfectionism in Private Law" (2012) 112 *Columbia Law Review* 1409.
Dagan H and Zipursky B C, "Introduction: The Distinction between Private Law and Public Law," in H Dagan and B C Zipursky (eds), *Research Handbook on Private Law Theory* (Edward Elgar 2020) 1–20.
Damasio A, *Descartes' Error: Emotion, Reason, and the Human Brain* (Penguin 2005).
Darley J M, "Citizens' Sense of Justice and the Legal System" (2001) 10(1) *Current Directions in Psychological Science* 10.
Darley J M and Pittman T S, "The Psychology of Compensatory and Retributive Justice" (2003) 7 *Personality and Social Psychology Review* 324.
Darwall S, *Honor, History and Relationship. Essays in Second-Personal Ethics II* (Oxford University Press 2013).
Darwall S, "Bipolar Obligation," in R Shafer-Landau (ed), *Oxford Studies in Metaethics* (Oxford University Press 2012) 332–57.

Darwall S and Darwall J, "Civil Recourse as Mutual Accountability" (2011) 39 *Florida State University Law Review* 17.
Deci E L, Koestner R M and Ryan R A, "Meta-Analytic Review of Experiments Examining the Effect of Extrinsic Rewards on Intrinsic Motivation" (1999) 125 *Psychological Bulletin* 627.
De Jong E R, "Tort Law and Judicial Risk Regulation: Bipolar and Multipolar Risk Reasoning in Light of Tort Law's Regulatory Effects" (2018) 9 *European Journal of Risk Regulation* 14.
Del Olmo P, "Punitive Damages in Spain," in H Koziol and V Wilcox (eds), *Punitive Damages: Common Law and Civil Law Perspectives* (Springer 2009) 137–54.
De Sousa R, "From the Rationality of Emotion," in R C Solomon (ed), *What is an Emotion? Classic and Contemporary Readings* (Oxford University Press 2003) 248–57.
De Sousa R, *The Rationality of Emotions* (MIT Press 1987).
Dheu O and De Bruyne J, "Artificial Intelligence and Tort Law: A 'Multi-faceted' Reality" (2023) 2–3 *European Review of Private Law* 261.
Diamantis M E, "Erasing the Victims of Corporate Crime" (August 4, 2023) Available at SSRN: https://ssrn.com/abstract=4531052.
Dobbs D B, *Dobbs Law of Remedies: Damages, Equity, Restitution* (2nd ed.) (West Publishing 1993).
Dolinko D, "Some Thoughts about Retributivism" (1991) 101(3) *Ethics* 537.
Donahue N and Witt J F, "Tort as Private Administration" (2020) 105 *Cornell Law Review* 1093.
Douglas M and Wildavsky A, *Risk and Culture* (University of California Press 1982).
Drutman L, *The Business of America is Lobbying: How Corporations Became Politicized and Politics Became More Corporate* (Oxford University Press 2015).
Duff R A, *The Realm of Criminal Law* (Oxford University Press 2018).
Duff R A, "Torts, Crimes and Vindication: Whose Wrong Is It?" in M Dyson (ed), *Unravelling Tort and Crime* (Cambridge University Press 2014) 146–73.
Duff R A, "Repairing Harms and Answering for Wrongs," in J Oberdiek (ed), *Philosophical Foundations of Tort Law* (Oxford University Press 2014) 212–29.
Duff R A, *Punishment, Communication, and Community* (Oxford University Press 2001).
Duff R A, *Trials and Punishments* (Cambridge University Press 1991).
Dworkin R, *Law's Empire* (Harvard University Press 1986).
Dyson M, "Tortious Apples and Criminal Oranges," in M Dyson (ed), *Comparing Tort and Crime: Learning from Across and Within Legal Systems* (Cambridge University Press 2015) 416–75.
Edelman J, "In Defence of Exemplary Damages," in C E F Rickett (ed), *Justifying Private Law Remedies* (Hart Publishing 2008) 225–48.
Edelman J, Colton S and Varuhas J (eds), *McGregor on Damages* (20th ed.) (Sweet & Maxwell 2017).
Eisenberg T, Hannaford P L, Heise M, LaFountain N, Ostrom B, Wells M T and Munsterman G T, "Judges, Juries and Punitive Damages: Empirical Analyses Using the Civil Justice Survey of State Courts 1992, 1996 and 2001 Data" (2006) 3 *Journal of Empirical Legal Studies* 263.
Eisenberg T and Engel C, "Assuring Civil Damages Adequately Deter: A Public Good Experiment" (2014) 11 *Journal of Empirical Legal Studies* 301.
Eisenberg T, Rachlinski J J and Wells M T, "Reconciling Experimental Incoherence with Real-World Coherence in Punitive Damages" (2002) 54 *Stanford Law Review* 1239.
Ellis D, "Fairness and Efficiency in the Law of Punitive Damages" (1982) 56 *Southern California Law Review* 1.

Emerson B, *The Public's Law: Origins and Architecture of Progressive Democracy* (Oxford University Press 2019).
Encarnacion E, "Resilience, Retribution, and Punitive Damages" (2022) 100 *Texas Law Review* 1025.
Engel D, *The Myth of the Litigious Society: Why We Don't Sue* (University of Chicago Press 2016).
Engel D, "The Oven Bird's Song: Insiders, Outsiders and Personal Injuries in an American Community" (1984) 18 *Law and Society Review* 551.
Engstrom N F and Rabin R L, "Pursuing Public Health through Litigation: Lessons from Tobacco and Opioids" (2021) 73 *Stanford Law Review* 285.
Epstein R, "The Risks of Risk/Utility" (1987) 48 *Ohio State Law Journal* 469.
Essert C, "Thinking Like a Private Lawyer" (2018) 68 *University of Toronto Law Journal* 166.
Fairgrieve D and Goldberg R, *Product Liability* (3rd ed.) (Oxford University Press 2020).
Fairgrieve D, Howells G, Møgelvang-Hansen P, Straetmans G, Verhoeven D, Machnikowski P, Janssen A and Schulze R, "Product Liability Directive," in P Machnikowski (ed), *European Product Liability-An Analysis of the State of the Art in the Era of New Technologies* (Intersentia 2017) 17–108.
Feigenson N R, "Can Tort Juries Punish Competently?" (2003) 78 *Chicago-Kent Law Review* 239.
Feinberg J, "The Classic Debate," in J Feinberg and J Coleman (eds), *Philosophy of Law* (6th ed.) (Wadsworth Publishing 1999) 799–803.
Feinberg J, *Doing and Deserving: Essays in the Theory of Responsibility* (Princeton University Press 1970).
Feinberg J, "The Expressive Function of Punishment" (1965) 49 *Monist* 397.
Feinman J M, "Unmaking and Remaking Tort Law" (2005) 5 *Journal of High Technology Law* 61.
Feldman Y and Lobel O, "The Incentives Matrix: The Comparative Effectiveness of Rewards, Liabilities, Duties, and Protections for Reporting Illegality" (2010) 88 *Texas Law Review* 1151.
Feldman Y and Teichman D, "Are All 'Legal Dollars' Created Equal?" (2008) 102 *Northwestern University Law Review* 223.
Feldthusen B, "Punitive Damages: Hard Choices and High Stakes" (1998) 1998(4) *New Zealand Law Review* 741.
Fischer K W and Tangney J P, "Self-Conscious Emotions and the Affect Revolution: Framework and Overview," in J P Tangney and K W Fischer (eds), *Self-Conscious Emotions: The Psychology of Shame, Guilt, Embarrassment, and Pride* (Guilford Press 1995) 3–22.
Fischhoff B, Slovic P and Lichtenstein S, "Weighting the Risks: Which Risks Are Acceptable?" in P Slovic (ed), *The Perception of Risk* (Taylor & Francis 2000) 126–42.
Fiske A P and Tetlock P E, "Taboo Trade-Offs: Reactions to Transactions that Transgress the Spheres of Justice" (1997) 18 *Political Psychology* 255.
Fiss O, "Reason in All Its Splendor" (1990) 56 *Brooklyn Law Review* 789.
Fiss O, "Against Settlement" (1984) 93 *Yale Law Journal* 1073.
Fletcher G P, "The Place of Victims in the Theory of Retribution" (1999) 3 *Buffalo Criminal Law Review* 51.
Frankel T T, *Fiduciary Law* (Oxford University Press 2010).
Fridman G H L, "Punitive Damages in Tort" (1970) 48(3) *Canadian Bar Review* 373.
Gabbay Z, "Justifying Restorative Justice: A theoretical Justification for the Use of Restorative Justice Practices" (2005) 2 *Journal of Dispute Resolution* 349.

Galanter M and Luban D, "Poetic Justice: Punitive Damages and Legal Pluralism" (1993) 42 *American University Law Review* 1393.

Gamonal Contreras S and Pino Emhart A, "The Role of Human Dignity in Private Law: An Interpretation from the Concept of Dignity as Status" (2022) 43 *Revista de Derecho Privado* 45.

García Matamoros L V and Herrera Lozano M C, "El Concepto de los Daños Punitivos o Punitive Damages" (2003) 5(1) *Revista Estudios Socio-Jurídicos* 211.

Gardner J, *From Personal Life to Private Law* (Oxford University Press 2018).

Gardner J, "What Is Tort Law For? Part I. The Place of Corrective Justice" (2011) 30 *Law and Philosophy* 1.

Gardner J, "Torts and Other Wrongs" (2011) 39 *Florida State University Law Review* 43.

Gardner J, "Crime: In Proportion and Perspective," in A Ashworth and M Wasik (eds), *Fundamentals of Sentencing Theory* (Oxford University Press 1998) 31–52.

Geistfeld M A, "Strict Products Liability 2.0: The Triumph of Judicial Reasoning Over Mainstream Tort Theory" (2021) 14(2) *Journal of Tort Law* 403.

Geistfeld M A, *Principles of Products Liability* (3rd ed.) (Foundation Press 2020).

Geistfeld M A, "Punitive Damages, Retribution, and Due Process" (2008) 81 *California Law Review* 263.

Gerber M M and Jackson J, "Retribution as Revenge and Retribution as Just Deserts" (2013) 26(1) *Social Justice Research* 61.

Gerhart P M, *Tort Law and Social Morality* (Cambridge University Press 2010).

Gigerenzer G, "Moral Intuition=Fast and Frugal Heuristics," in W Sinnott-Armstrong (ed), *Moral Psychology: Vol. 2. The Cognitive Science of Morality: Intuition and Diversity* (MIT Press 2008) 1–26.

Gigerenzer G, *Reckoning with Risk: Learning to Live with Uncertainty* (Penguin 2002).

Gigerenzer G and Todd P M, "Fast and Frugal Heuristics: The Adaptive Toolbox," in S Stich (ed), *Simple Heuristics that Make us Smart* (Oxford University Press 1999) 3–34.

Gilles M, "'A Force Created': The U.S. Chamber of Commerce and the Politics of Corporate Immunity" (2023) 72 *DePaul Law Review* 139.

Gilles S G, "On Determining Negligence: Hand Formula Balancing, the Reasonable Person Standard, and the Jury" (2001) 45 *Vanderbilt Law Review* 813.

Gilliker P, *Vicarious Liability in Tort: A Comparative Perspective* (Cambridge University Press 2010).

Gluck A R, Burch E C and Zimmerman A S, "Against Bankruptcy: Public Litigation Values versus the Endless Quest for Global Peace in Mass Litigation" (2024) 133 *Yale Law Forum* 525.

Gneezy U and Rustichini A, "A Fine is a Price" (2000) 29 *Journal of Legal Studies* 1.

Golash D, *The Case Against Punishment: Retribution, Crime Prevention, and the Law* (New York University Press 2005).

Goldberg J C P and Zipursky B C, *Recognizing Wrongs* (Harvard University Press 2020).

Goldberg J C P and Zipursky B C, "The Fraud-on-the-Market Tort" (2013) 66 *Vanderbilt Law Review* 1755.

Goldberg J C P and Zipursky B C, "Civil Recourse Revisited" (2011) 39 *Florida State University Law Review* 273.

Gordon R M, *The Structure of Emotions: Investigations in Cognitive Philosophy* (Cambridge University Press 1987).

Goudkamp J, "Exemplary Damages," in G Virgo and S Worthington (eds), *Commercial Remedies: Resolving Controversies* (Cambridge University Press 2017) 318–40.

Goudkamp J and Courtney W, "Introduction," in E Bant, W Courtney, J Goudkamp and J M Paterson (eds), *Punishment and Private Law* (Hart Publishing 2021) 3–32.

Goudkamp J and Katsampouka E, "Punitive Damages: Ten Misconceptions," in E Bant, W Courtney, J Goudkamp and J M Paterson (eds), *Punishment and Private Law* (Hart Publishing 2021) 187–224.

Goudkamp J and Katsampouka E, "Punitive Damages and the Place of Punishment in Private Law" (2021) 84(6) *Modern Law Review* 1257.

Goudkamp J and Katsampouka E, "Form and Substance in the Law of Punitive Damages," in A Robertson and J Goudkamp (eds), *Form and Substance in the Law of Obligations* (Hart Publishing 2019) 331–52.

Goudkamp J and Katsampouka E, "An Empirical Study of Punitive Damages" (2018) 38 *Oxford Journal of Legal Studies* 90.

Goudkamp J and Nolan D, *Winfield & Jolowicz on Tort* (20th ed.) (Sweet & Maxwell 2020).

Gray D, "Punishment as Suffering" (2010) 63 *Vanderbilt Law Review* 1617.

Greco C, "The Poly Implant Prothèse Breast Prostheses Scandal: Embodied Risk and Social Suffering" (2015) 147 *Social Science and Medicine* 150.

Green L, "Tort Law: Public Law in Disguise" (1959–60) 38 *Texas Law Review* 257.

Green E, Coon D and Bornstein B H, "The Effects of Limiting Punitive Damages Awards" (2001) 25(3) *Law and Human Behavior* 217.

Greenleaf S, *A Treatise on the Law of Evidence* (2nd ed.) (Little and J. Brown 1848).

Gromet D M, "Psychological Perspectives on the Place of Restorative Justice in Criminal Justice Systems," in M E Oswald, S Bieneck and J Hupfeld-Heinemann (eds), *Social Psychology of Punishment of Crime* (Wiley-Blackwell 2009) 39–54.

Guttel E, Harel A and Lavie S, "Torts for Nonvictims: The Case for Third-Party Litigation" (2018) 2018(3) University of Illinois Law Review 1049.

Hacker P, "The European AI Liability Directives – Critique of a Half-Hearted Approach and Lessons for the Future" (2023) 51 *Computer Law and Security Review* 105871.

Hadfield G K, "Framing the Choice between Cash and the Courthouse: Experiences with the 9/11 Compensation Fund" (2008) 42 *Law and Society Review* 645.

Hammesfahr R W and Nugent L S, *Punitive Damages: A State-by-State Guide to Law and Practice* (Thomson West 2012).

Hampton J, "Correcting Harms versus Righting Wrongs: The Goal of Retribution" (1992) 39 *University of California Law Review* 1659.

Hampton J, "An Expressive Theory of Retribution," in W Cragg (ed), *Retributivism and Its Critics* (Franz Steiner Verlag Wiesbaden GmbH 1992) 1–25.

Hampton J, "A New Theory of Retribution," in R G Frey and C W Morris (eds), *Liability and Responsibility* (Cambridge University Press 1991) 377–414.

Hampton J, "The Retributive Idea," in J G Murphy and J Hampton (eds), *Forgiveness and Mercy* (Cambridge University Press 1988) 111–61.

Hampton J, "Forgiveness, Resentment and Hatred," in J G Murphy and J Hampton (eds), *Forgiveness and Mercy* (Cambridge University Press 1988) 35–87.

Hanna N, "Say What? A Critique of Expressive Retributivism" (2008) 27 *Law and Philosophy* 123.

Hans V P, *Business on Trial: The Civil Jury and Corporate Responsibility* (Yale University Press 2000).

Hanson J D, "Introduction: Ideology, Psychology, and Law," in J Hanson (ed), *Ideology, Psychology, and Law* (Oxford University Press 2012) 3–31.

Hanson J D and Kysar D A, "Taking Behavioralism Seriously: The Problem of Market Manipulation" (1999) 74 *New York University Law Review* 630.

Hanson J D and Kysar D A, "Taking Behavioralism Seriously: Some Evidence of Market Manipulation" (1999) 112 *Harvard Law Review* 1420.

Hanson J D and Kysar D A, "Taking Behavioralism Seriously: A Response to Market Manipulation" (2000) 6 *Roger Williams University Law Review* 259.

Hanson J D and Logue K D, "The Costs of Cigarettes: The Economic Case for Ex Post Incentive-Based Regulation" (1998) 107 *Yale Law Journal* 1163.

Hanson J D and Yosifon D, "The Situational Character: A Critical Realist Perspective on the Human Animal" (2004) 93 *Georgetown Law Journal* 1.

Harel A, "Public and Private Law," in M D Dubber and T Hörnle (eds), *The Oxford Handbook on Criminal Law* (Oxford University Press 2014) 1040–63.

Hart H L A, *Punishment and Responsibility: Essays in the Philosophy of Law* (2nd ed.) (Oxford University Press, 2008).

Hastie R and Viscusi W K, "What Juries Can't Do Well: The Jury's Performance as a Risk Manager" (1998) 40 *Arizona Law Review* 901.

Hazard G C (Jr.), "The Futures Problem" (2000) 148 *University of Pennsylvania Law Review* 1901.

Hedley S, "The Rise and Fall of Private Law Theory" (2018) 134 *Law Quarterly Review* 214.

Hedley S, "Corrective Justice – An Idea Whose Time Has Gone?" in M Del Mar and M Lobban (eds), *Law in Theory and History: New Essays on a Neglected Dialogue* (Hart Publishing 2016) 305–26.

Heider F, *The Psychology of Interpersonal Relations* (Martino Fine Books 2015).

Heilbroner R, *In the Name of Profit* (Doubleday 1972).

Hershovitz S, "Treating Wrongs as Wrongs: An Expressive Argument for Tort Law" (2017) 10(2) *Journal of Tort Law* 405.

Hershovitz S, "Tort as a Substitute for Revenge," in J Oberdiek (ed), *Philosophical Foundations of the Law of Torts* (Oxford University Press 2014) 86–100.

Hershovitz S, "Corrective Justice for Civil Recourse Theorists" (2011) 39 *Florida State University Law Review* 107.

Herstein O, "How Tort Law Empowers" (2015) 65 *University of Toronto Law Journal* 99.

Hieronymi P, "Articulating an Uncompromising Forgiveness" (2001) 62 *Philosophy Phenomenological Research* 529.

Hoffman D A and O'Shea M P, "Can Law and Economics Be Both Practical and Principled?" (2002) 53 *Alabama Law Review* 335.

Holmes O W, *The Common Law* (Little Brown 1923).

Honoré T, *Responsibility and Fault* (Hart Publishing 1999).

Horwitz M J, "The History of the Public/Private Distinction" (1982) 130 *University of Pennsylvania Law Review* 1423.

Howells G, "Product Liability – A History of Harmonisation," in D Fairgrieve (ed), *Product Liability in Comparative Perspective* (Cambridge University Press 2005) 202–18.

Howells G, "The Relationship between Product Liability and Product Safety – Understanding a Necessary Element in European Product Liability through a Comparison with the U.S. Position" (2000) 39 *Washburn Law Journal* 305.

Howells G and Owen D G, "Products Liability in America and Europe," in G Howells, I Ramsay and T Wilhelmsson (eds), *Handbook of Research on International Consumer Law* (2nd ed.) (Edward Elgar 2018).

Howells G, Twigg-Flesner C and Wilhelmsson T, *Rethinking EU Consumer Law* (Routledge 2017).

Huang P H, "Diverse Conceptions of Emotions in Risk Regulation" (2008) 156 *University of Pennsylvania Law Review* 435.

Husak D, "Retributivism and Over-Punishment" (2022) 41 *Law and Philosophy* 169.

Husak D, "Why Legal Philosophers (Including Retributivists) Should be Less Resistant to Risk-Based Sentencing," in J W de Keijser, J V Roberts and J Ryberg (eds), *Predictive Sentencing: Normative and Empirical Perspectives* (Hart Publishing 2019) 33–50.

Husak D, "Kinds of Punishment," in H M Hurd (ed), *Moral Perplexities and Legal Puzzles: The Work of Larry Alexander* (Cambridge University Press 2018) 23–38.

Husak D, "Does the State Have a Monopoly to Punish Crime?" in C Flanders and Z Hoskins (eds), *The New Philosophy of Criminal Law* (Rowman and Littlefield 2016) 95–110.

Husak D, *Overcriminalization: The Limits of the Criminal Law* (Oxford University Press 2008).

Husak D, "Strict Liability, Justice, and Proportionality," in A P Simester (ed), *Appraising Strict Liability* (Oxford University Press 2005) 81–104.

Hylton K N, "A Theory of Wealth and Punitive Damages" (2008) 17 *Widener Law Journal* 927.

Hylton K N, "Punitive Damages and the Economic Theory of Penalties" (1998) 87 *Georgetown Law Journal* 421.

Hylton K L and Miceli T J, "Should Tort Damages be Multiplied?" (2005) 21 *Journal of Law Economics & Organization* 388.

Ingber S, "Rethinking Intangible Injuries: A Focus on Remedy" (1985) 73 *California Law Review* 772.

Jansen N and Rademacher L, "Punitive Damages in Germany," in H Koziol and V Wilcox (eds), *Punitive Damages: Common Law and Civil Law Perspectives* (Springer 2009) 75–86.

Javela J J, Mercadillo R E and Ramírez J M, "Anger and Associated Experiences of Sadness, Fear, Valence, Arousal, and Dominance Evoked by Visual Scenes" (2008) 103 *Psychological Review* 663.

Jolls C, Sunstein C R and Thaler R, "A Behavioral Approach to Law and Economics" (1998) 50 *Stanford Law Review* 1471.

Kahan D M, "Two Conceptions of Emotion in Risk Regulation" (2008) 156 *University of Pennsylvania Law Review* 741.

Kahan D M, "The Cognitive Illiberal State" (2007) 60 *Stanford Law Review* 115.

Kahan D M and Braman D, "More Statistics, Less Persuasion: A Cultural Theory of Gun-Risk Perceptions" (2003) 151 *University of Pennsylvania Law Review* 1291.

Kahan D M, "Trust, Collective Action, and Law" (2001) 81 *Boston University Law Review* 333.

Kahan D M, "Punishment Incommensurability" (1998) 1 *Buffalo Criminal Law Review* 691.

Kahan D M, "What Do Alternative Sanctions Mean?" (1996) 63 *University of Chicago Law Review* 591.

Kahn P W, *The Cultural Study of Law: Reconstructing Legal Scholarship* (The University of Chicago Press 1999).

Kahneman D, *Thinking Fast and Slow* (Penguin 2011).

Kahneman D and Frederick S, "Representativeness Revisited: Attribute Substitution in Intuitive Judgment," in T Gilovich, D Griffin and D Kahneman (eds), *Heuristics and Biases: The Psychology of Intuitive Judgment* (Cambridge University Press 2002) 49–81.

Kahneman D, Sibony O and Sunstein C R, *Noise. A Flaw in Human Judgment* (William Collins 2021).

Khaneman D, Schkade D and Sunstein C R, "Shared Outrage and Erratic Awards: The Psychology of Punitive Damages" (1998) 16 *Journal of Risk and Uncertainty* 49.

Kahneman D and Tversky A, "Prospect Theory: An Analysis of Decision under Risk" (1979) 47 *Econometrica* 263.

Kahneman D, Ritov I and Schkade D, "Economic Preferences of Attitude Expressions? An Analysis of Dollar Responses to Public Issues" (1999) 19 *Journal of Risk and Uncertainty* 203.

Kaminski M E, "Regulating the Risks of AI" (2023) 103 *Boston University Law Review* 1347.

Kant I, *The Science of Right* (W Hastie Trans 2010).

Keating G C, *Reasonableness and Risk. Right and Responsibility in the Law of Torts* (Oxford University Press 2023).
Keating G C, "Is Tort Law 'Private'?" in J Oberdiek and P B Miller (eds), *Civil Wrongs and Justice in Private Law* (Oxford University Press 2020) 351–72.
Keating G C, "Is Cost-Benefit Analysis the Only Game in Town?" (2018) 91 *Southern California Law Review* 195.
Keating G C, "Is the Role of Tort to Repair Wrongful Losses?" in D Nolan and A Robertson (eds), *Rights and Private Law* (Hart Publishing 2012) 367–406.
Keating G C, "Pressing Precaution Beyond the Point of Cost-Justification" (2003) 56 *Vanderbilt Law Review* 653.
Keeton W P, Dobbs D B, Keeton R E and Owen D G, *Prosser and Keeton on Torts* (5th ed.) (West Publishing, 1984).
Kelman M, "Moral Realism and the Heuristics Debate" (2013) 5 *Journal of Legal Analysis* 339.
Kelman M, *The Heuristics Debate* (Oxford University Press 2011).
Kennedy D, "New Approaches to Comparative Law: Comparativism and International Governance" (1997) 1997 *Utah Law Review* 545.
Kessler F, Contracts of Adhesion – Some Thoughts about Freedom of Contract (1943) 43 *Columbia Law Review* 629.
King M, Freiberg A M, Batagol B M and Hyams R L, *Non-Adversarial Justice* (2nd ed.) (Federation Press 2014).
Kircher J J and Wiseman C M, *Punitive Damages: Law and Practice* (2nd ed., 2 vols) (Clark Boardman Callaghan, 2023).
Kleinig J, "What Does Wrongdoing Deserve?" in M Tonry (ed), *Retributivism Has a Past: Has It a Future?* (Oxford University Press 2011) 46–62.
Knetsch J, "France" (2022) 11 *European Tort Law Yearbook* 174.
Koch B A, "Punitive Damages in European Law," in H Koziol and V Wilcox (eds), *Punitive Damages: Common Law and Civil Law Perspectives* (Springer 2009) 197–209.
Koehler J J and Gershoff A D, "Betrayal Aversion is Reasonable" (2005) 28 *Behavioral and Brain Sciences* 556.
Koehler J J and Gershoff A D, "Betrayal Aversion: When Agents of Protection Become Agents of Harm" (2002) 90 *Organizational Behavior and Human Decision Processes* 244.
Koening T and Rustad M, "His and Her Tort Reform: Gender Injustice in Disguise" (1995) 70 *Washington Law Review* 1.
Kolber A J, "The Subjective Experience of Punishment" (2009) 109 *Columbia Law Review* 182.
Komesar N, "Injuries and Institutions: Tort Reform, Tort Theory, and Beyond" (1990) 64 *New York University Law Review* 60.
Königs P, "The Expressivist Account of Punishment, Retribution, and the Emotions" (2013) 16 *Ethical Theory and Moral Practice* 1029.
Korzec R, "Dashing Consumer Hopes: Strict Products Liability and the Demise of the Consumer Expectations Test" (1997) 20 *Boston College International and Comparative Law Review* 227.
Kotler M A, "Utility, Autonomy and Motive: A Descriptive Model of the Development of Tort Doctrine" (1990) 58 *University of Cincinnati Law Review* 1231.
Koziol H, "Punitive Damages – A European Perspective" (2008) 68 *Louisiana Law Review* 751.
Kuenzler A, "Third-Generation Competition Law" (2023) 11(1) *Journal of Antitrust Enforcement* 133.
Kuenzler A, "Competition Law Enforcement on Digital Markets – Lessons from Recent EU Case Law" (2019) 7(2) *Journal of Antitrust Enforcement* 249.

Kuenzler A, *Restoring Consumer Sovereignty: How Markets Manipulate Us and What the Law Can Do About It* (Oxford University Press 2017).

Kumar R, "Why Reparations?" in J Oberdiek (ed), *Philosophical Foundations of the Law of Torts* (Oxford University Press 2014) 193–210.

Kusch M, "Towards a Political Philosophy of Risk: Experts and Publics in Deliberative Democracy," in T Lewens (ed), *Risk: Philosophical Perspectives* (Routledge 2007) 131–55.

Kysar D A, "The Public Life of Private Law: Tort Law as a Risk Regulation Mechanism" (2018) 9(1) *European Journal of Risk Regulation* 48.

Kysar D A, *Regulating From Nowhere: Environmental Law and the Search for Objectivity* (Yale University Press 2010).

Kysar D A, "The Expectations of Consumers" (2003) 103 *Columbia Law Review* 1700.

Kysar D A, "Preferences for Processes: The Process/Product Distinction and the Regulation of Consumer Choice" (2003) 118 *Harvard Law Review* 525.

Lahav A D, "The Knowledge Remedy" (2020) 98 *Texas Law Review* 1361.

Lahav A D, *In Praise of Litigation* (Oxford University Press 2019).

Lamb S, "The Psychology of Condemnation: Underlying Emotions and Their Symbolic Expression in Condemning and Shaming" (2003) 68 *Brooklyn Law Review* 929.

Landes W M and Posner R A, *The Economic Structure of Tort Law* (Harvard University Press 1987).

Langbein J, "The Disappearance of Civil Trial in the United States" (2012) 122 *Yale Law Journal* 522.

Latin H, "'Good' Warnings, Bad Products, and Cognitive Limitations" (1994) 41 *University of California at Los Angeles Law Review* 1193.

Latin H, "Activity Levels, Due Care, and Selective Realism in Economic Analysis of Tort Law" (1987) 39 *Rutgers Law Review* 487.

Laux J, Wachter S and Mittelstadt B, "Trustworthy Artificial Intelligence and the European Union AI Act: On the Conflation of Trustworthiness and Acceptability of Risk" (2024) 18 *Regulation & Governance* 3.

Laycock D, "The Death of the Irreparable Injury Rule" (1990) 103 *Harvard Law Review* 687.

Laycock D and Hasen R L, *Modern American Remedies: Cases and Materials* (5th ed.) (Aspen Publishing 2018).

Lee J Y, "Money Norms" (2017) 49(1) *Loyola University Chicago Law Journal* 57.

Legrand P, "The Impossibility of 'Legal Transplants'" (1997) 4 *Maastricht Journal of European and Comparative Law* 111.

Lens J W, "Product Recalls: Why is Tort Law Deferring to Agency Inaction?" (2016) 90 *St. John's Law Review* 329.

Lens J W, "Justice Holme's Bad Man and the Depleted Purposes of Punitive Damages" (2003) 101 *Kentucky Law Journal* 789.

Lerner A M, "From Socrates to Damasio, from Langdell to Kandel: The Role of Emotion in Modern Legal Education," in P Maharg and C Maughan (eds), *Affect and Legal Education. Emotion in Learning and Teaching the Law* (Routledge 2011) 148–73.

Lerner J S, Goldberg J H and Tetlock P E, "Sober Second Thought: The Effects of Accountability, Anger, and Authoritarianism on Attributions of Responsibility" (1998) 24 *Journal of Personality and Social Psychology* 563.

Lerner M J, *The Belief in a Just World: A Fundamental Delusion* (Springer 1980).

Lessig L, "The Regulation of Social Meaning" (1995) 62 *University of Chicago Law Review* 94.

Ley A J, "The Costs and Benefits of American Policy-Making Venues" (2014) 48 *Law and Society Review* 91.

Liau T, *Standing in Private Law. Powers of Enforcement in the Law of Obligations and Trusts* (Oxford University Press 2023).
Lichtenstein S, Slovic P, Fischhoff B, Layman M and Combs B, "Judged Frequency of Lethal Events" (1978) 4 *Journal of Experimental Psychology: Human Learning and Memory* 551.
Linden A M, "Tort Law as Ombudsman" (1973) 51 *Canadian Bar Review* 155.
Lo Giudice D, *Daños Punitivos* (El Derecho 2024).
López Herrera E, *Los Daños Punitivos* (Abeledo Perrot 2008).
Loth M A, "The Civil Court as Risk Regulator: The Issue of Its Legitimacy" (2018) 9 *European Journal of Risk Regulation* 66.
Love J C, "Punishment and Deterrence: A Comparative Study of Tort Liability for Punitive Damages under Non-Fault Compensation Legislation" (1983) 16 *UC Davis Law Review* 231.
Lyndon M L, "Tort Law and Technology" (1995) 12 *Yale Journal on Regulation* 137.
Maher F, "An Empirical Analysis of Exemplary Damages in Australia" (2019) 43 *Melbourne University Law Review* 694.
Manikis M, "Conceptualizing the Victim in England and Wales and the United States within a Spectrum of Public and Private Interests" (2021) 41(1) *Oxford Journal of Legal Studies* 219.
Mann K, "Punitive Civil Sanctions: The Middleground between Criminal and Civil Law" (1992) 101 *Yale Law Journal* 1795.
Marchisio E, "In Support of 'No-Fault' Civil Liability Rules for Artificial Intelligence" (2021) 54(1) *SN Social Sciences* 1.
Markel D, "How Should Punitive Damages Work?" (2009) 157 *University of Pennsylvania Law Review* 1383.
Markel D, "Retributive Damages: A Theory of Punitive Damages as Intermediate Sanction" (2009) 94 *Cornell Law Review* 239.
Markel D and Flanders C, "Bentham on Stilts: The Bare Relevance of Subjectivity to Retributive Justice" (2010) 98 *California Law Review* 907.
Martínez Alles M G, "Reducing Inequality in Consumer Transactions: The Significance of Aggravated Vulnerabilities," in K E Davis and M Pargendler (eds), *Legal Heterodoxy in the Global South* (Cambridge University Press 2025) 77–111.
Martínez Alles M G, "Punitive Damages in Argentina and Mexico: Rethinking the Scope of the Public Policy Exception," in C Vanleenhove and L Meurkens (eds), *The Recognition and Enforcement of Punitive Damages Judgments across the Globe: Insights from Various Continents* (Eleven International Publishing 2023) 129–47.
Martínez Alles M G, "La Dimensión Sancionadora del Derecho de Daños. Los Daños Punitivos," in D M Papayannis (ed), *Manual de Responsabilidad Extracontractual* (Suprema Corte de Justicia de la Nación de Mexico 2022) 601–47.
Martínez Alles M G, "La Dimensión Retributiva del Derecho de Daños: La Perspectiva de la Víctima," in J A García Amado and D M Papayannis (eds), *Dañar, Incumplir y Reparar. Ensayos de Filosofía del Derecho Privado* (Palestra 2020) 107–31.
Martínez Alles M G, "Tort Remedies as Meaningful Responses to Wrongdoing," in J Oberdiek and P B Miller (eds), *Civil Wrongs and Justice in Private Law* (Oxford University Press 2020) 231–52.
Martínez Alles M G, "Punitive Damages: Reorienting the Debate in Civil Law Systems" (2019) 10(1) *Journal of European Tort Law* 63.
Martínez Alles M G, "Moral Outrage and Betrayal Aversion: The Psychology of Punitive Damages" (2018) 11 *Journal of Tort Law* 245.
Martínez Alles M G, "¿Para Qué Sirven los Daños Punitivos? Modelos de Sanción Privada, Sanción Social y Disuasión Óptima" (2012) 5 *Revista de Responsabilidad Civil y Seguros* 55.

Martínez Alles M G and Nazareno P, "Desafíos Constitucionales de los Daños Punitivos: Los Problemas del Ne Bis in Idem," in S Legarre, L S Grosman, J C Rivera (h) and J S Elías (eds), *Tratado de los Derechos Constitucionales* (Abeledo Perrot 2014) 688–731.
Masur J, Bronsteen J and Buccafusco C, "Retribution and the Experience of Punishment" (2010) 98 *California Law Review* 1463.
Matravers M, "The Place of Proportionality in Penal Theory: Or Rethinking Thinking about Punishment," in M Tonry (ed), *Of One-Eyed and Toothless Miscreants: Making the Punishment Fit the Crime?* (Oxford University Press 2019) 76–96.
McBride N J and Bagshaw R, *Tort Law* (6th ed.) (Pearson Education 2018).
McBride N J, "Punitive Damages," in P Birks (ed), *Wrongs and Remedies in the Twenty-First Century* (Oxford University Press 1996) 175–202.
McCormick C T, *Handbook on the Law of Damages* (West Publishing 1935).
McDonald D C, Greene J and Worzella C, *Day Fines in American Courts: The Staten Island and Milwaukee Experiments* (National Institute of Justice, Department of Justice 1992).
McGeer V, "Civilizing Blame," in D J Coates and N A Tognazzini (eds), *Blame. Its Nature and Norms* (Oxford University Press 2013) 162–88.
McMichael B J and Viscusi W K, "Bringing Predictability to the Chaos of Punitive Damages" (2022) 54 *Arizona State Law Journal* 471.
Mendlow G S, "On the State's Exclusive Right to Punish" (2022) 41 *Law and Philosophy* 243.
Mendlow G S, "Is Tort Law a Form of Institutionalized Revenge?" (2011) 39 *Florida State University Law Review* 129.
Menyhárd A, "Punitive Damages in Hungary," in H Koziol and V Wilcox (eds), *Punitive Damages: Common Law and Civil Law Perspectives* (Springer 2009) 87–102.
Merry S E and Silbey S S, "What Do Plaintiffs Want? Re-Examining the Concept of Dispute" (1984) 9 *Justice System Journal* 151.
Merryman J H and Pérez-Perdomo R, *The Civil Law Tradition: An Introduction to the Legal Systems of Europe and Latin America* (3rd ed.) (Stanford University Press 2007).
Meurkens R C, *Punitive Damages: The Civil Remedy in American Law, Lessons and Caveats for Continental Europe* (Kluwer 2014).
Meurkens L and Nordin E (eds), *The Power of Punitive Damages. Is Europe Missing Out?* (Intersentia 2012).
Michaels R, "The Functional Method of Comparative Law," in M Reimann and R Zimmermann (eds), *The Oxford Handbook of Comparative Law* (Oxford University Press 2006) 339–82.
Michelon C, "The Public Nature of Private Law?" (2020) 7 *Latin American Legal Studies* 231.
Micklitz H W, "Risk, Tort and Liability," in S Grundmann, H Micklitz and M Renner (eds), *New Private Law Theory: A Pluralistic Approach* (Cambridge University Press 2021) 272–97.
Miller D T and Vidmar N, "The Social Psychology of Punishment Reactions," in M J Lerner and S C Lerner (eds), *The Justice Motive in Social Behavior* (Springer 1981) 145–72.
Moore M S, *Placing Blame: A Theory of the Criminal Law* (Oxford University Press 1997).
Moore M S, "Victims and Retribution: A Reply to Professor Fletcher" (1999) 3 *Buffalo Criminal Law Review* 65.
Mor S, "The Meaning of Injury: A Disability Perspective," in A Bloom, D Engel and M McCann (eds), *Injury and Injustice: The Cultural Politics of Harm and Redress* (Cambridge University Press 2018) 27–49.
Morgan F W, "The Evolution of Punitive Damages in Product Liability Litigation for Unprincipled Marketing Behavior" (1989) 8 *Journal of Public Policy & Marketing* 279.

Morgan J, "Reflections on Reforming Punitive Damages in English Law," in L Meurkens and E Nordin (eds), *The Power of Punitive Damages. Is Europe Missing Out?* (Intersentia 2012) 183–207.
Morgan P, "Vicarious Punishment: Vicarious Liability for Exemplary Damages?" in E Bant, W Courtney, J Goudkamp and J M Paterson (eds), *Punishment and Private Law* (Hart Publishing 2021) 287–318.
Morris C, "Punitive Damages in Tort Cases" (1931) 44 *Harvard Law Review* 1173.
Mulcahy L and Teeder W, "Are Litigants, Trials and Precedents Vanishing After All?" (2022) 85(2) *Modern Law Review* 326.
Murphy J, "Anomalies in Tort Law: A Cause for Concern?" (2023) 86 *Modern Law Review* 872.
Murphy J, "The Nature and Domain of Aggravated Damages" (2010) 69 *Cambridge Law Journal* 353.
Murphy J G, *Getting Even: Forgiveness and Its Limits* (Oxford University Press 2005).
Murphy J G, "Two Cheers for Vindictiveness" (2000) 2 *Punishment and Society* 131.
Murphy J G, "Retributive Hatred: An Essay on Criminal Liability and the Emotions," in R G Frey and C W Morris (eds), *Liability and Responsibility* (Cambridge University Press 1991) 351–76.
Murphy J G, "Forgiveness and Resentment" (1982) 7 *Midwest Studies in Philosophy* 503.
Murphy J G and Hampton J (eds), *Forgiveness and Mercy* (Cambridge University Press 1988).
Nagareda R A, *Mass Torts in a World of Settlement* (University of Chicago Press 2007).
Nolan D, "Against Strict Product Liability," in D Nolan (ed), *Questions of Liability. Essays on the Law of Tort* (Hart Publishing 2023) 392–426.
Nolan D, "Tort and Public Law: Overlapping Categories?" (2019) 135 *Law Quarterly Review* 272.
Nolan D and Robertson A (eds), *Rights and Private Law* (Hart Publishing 2012).
Note, "The Assessment of Punitive Damages against an Entrepreneur for the Malicious Torts of His Employees" (1961) 70 *Yale Law Journal* 1296.
Note, "Exemplary Damages in the Law of Torts" (1957) 70 *Harvard Law Review* 517.
Note, "Exemplary Damages against Corporations" (1942) 30 *Georgetown Law Journal* 294.
Nussbaum M C, *Anger and Forgiveness: Resentment, Generosity, Justice* (Oxford University Press 2016).
Nussbaum M C, *Hiding from Humanity: Disgust, Shame and the Law* (Princeton University Press 2006).
Nussbaum M C, *Upheavals of Thought: The Intelligence of Emotions* (Cambridge University Press 2001).
Oatley K, Keltner D and Jenkins J M, *Understanding Emotions* (2nd ed.) (Wiley-Blackwell 2006).
Oberdiek J, *Imposing Risk: A Normative Framework* (Oxford University Press 2017).
Okimoto T G and Tyler T R, "Is Compensation Enough? Relational Concerns in Responding to Unintended Inequity" (2007) 10(3) *Group Processes and Intergroup Relations* 399.
Oman N B, "The Honor of Private Law" (2011) 80 *Fordham Law Review* 31.
Otero Crespo M, "Punitive Damages Under Spanish Law: A Subtle Recognition?," in L Meurkens and E Nordin (eds), *The Power of Punitive Damages. Is Europe Missing Out?* (Intersentia 2012) 283–302.
Owen D G, "Aggravating Punitive Damages" (2010) 158 *University of Pennsylvania Law Review PENNumbra* 181.
Owen D G, "The Evolution of Products Liability Law" (2007) 26 *The Review of Litigation* 955.
Owen D G, "Risk-Utility Balancing in Design Defect Cases" (1997) 30 *University of Michigan Journal of Law Reform* 239.

Owen D G, "Deterrence and Desert in Tort: A Comment" (1985) 73 *California Law Review* 665.
Owen D G, "Civil Punishment and the Public Good" (1982) 56 *Southern California Law Review* 103.
Owen D G, "Problems in Assessing Punitive Damages against Manufacturers of Defective Products" (1982) 49 *University of Chicago Law Review* 1.
Owen D G, "Punitive Damages in Products Liability Litigation" (1976) 74 *Michigan Law Review* 1257.
Owen D G and Davis M J, *Owen & Davis on Products Liability* (4th ed.) (Thomson West 2014–2021).
Papayannis D M, "The Morality of Compensation through Tort Law" (2023) 36(1) *Ratio Juris* 3.
Penner J, "Punishments and Penalties in Private Law, with Particular Reference to the Law Governing Fiduciaries" in E Bant, W Courtney, J Goudkamp and J M Paterson (eds), *Punishment and Private Law* (Hart Publishing 2021) 105–30.
Pereira Fredes E, "Un Alegato a Favor de las Consideraciones Punitivas en el Derecho Privado" (2015) 7 *Revista de Derecho Escuela de Postgrado* 61.
Perry R, "Income-Dependent Punitive Damages" (2018) 95 *Washington University Law Review* 835.
Perry R, "The Role of Retributive Justice in the Common Law of Torts: A Descriptive Theory" (2006) 73 *Tennessee Law Review* 163.
Perry S R, "The Moral Foundations of Tort Law" (1992) 77 *Iowa Law Review* 449.
Persad G C, "Risk, Everyday Intuitions, and the Institutional Value of Tort Law" (2010) 62 *Stanford Law Review* 1445.
Persad G C, "When, and How, Should Cognitive Bias Matter to Law" (2014) 32 *Law and Inequality* 31.
Peteffi da Silva R and Pickersgill Walker M, "Punitive Damages: United States Conceptualization of the Doctrine and Case Law Analysis of Santa Catarina Court of Appeals" (2016) 74 *Seqüência (Florianópolis)* 295.
Peterson M A, Sarma S and Shanley M G, *Punitive Damages: Empirical Findings* (Institute for Civil Justice Rand 1987).
Pildes R H and Anderson E S, "Slinging Arrows at Democracy: Social Choice Theory, Value Pluralism, and Democratic Politics" (1990) 90 *Columbia Law Review* 2121.
Pillsbury S H, Emotional Justice: Moralizing the Passions of Criminal Punishment (1989) 74 *Cornell Law Review* 655.
Pino Emhart A, "No Sólo Quieren Dinero: La Función Expresiva de la Responsabilidad Extracontractual," in R Barría Díaz, A Ferrante and L C San Martín Neira (eds), *Presente y Futuro de la Responsabilidad Civil* (Thomson Reuters 2017) 159–76.
Pizarro R D, "Daños Punitivos," in A Kemelmajer De Carlucci (ed), *Derecho de Daños: Libro en Homenaje al Prof. Félix Trigo Represas* (La Rocca 1993) 287–337.
Polinsky A M, "Are Punitive Damages Really Insignificant, Predictable, and Rational? A Comment on Eisenberg et al.," (1997) 26 *Journal of Legal Studies* 663.
Polinsky A M and Shavell S, "The Uneasy Case for Product Liability" (2010) 123 *Harvard Law Review* 1437.
Polinsky A M and Shavell S, "Punitive Damages: An Economic Analysis" (1998) 111 *Harvard Law Review* 869.
Posner R A, "Emotion Versus Emotionalism in Law," in S A Bandes (ed), *The Passions of Law* (New York University Press 2000) 309–29.
Posner R A, "The Economic Approach to Law" (1975) 53 *Texas Law Review* 757.
Posner R A, "A Theory of Negligence" (1972) 1 *Journal of Legal Studies* 29.

Priel D, "Tort Law for Cynics" (2014) 75(5) *Modern Law Review* 703.

Priest G, "The Invention of Enterprise Liability: A Critical History of the Intellectual Foundations of Modern Tort Law" (1985) 14 *Journal of Legal Studies* 461.

Priest G, "The Best Evidence of the Effect of Products Liability Law on the Accident Rate: Reply" (1982) 91 *Yale Law Journal* 1386.

Priest G, "A Theory of the Consumer Product Warranty" (1981) 90 *Yale Law Journal* 1297.

Rabin R L, "Law for Law's Sake" (1996) 105 *Yale Law Journal* 2261.

Rachlinski J J, "Heuristics, Biases, and Philosophy" (2007) 43 *Tulsa Law Review* 865.

Radin M J, "Compensation and Commensurability" (1993) 43 *Duke Law Journal* 56.

Radzik L, "Book Review: Recognizing Wrongs" (2021) 131(3) *Ethics* 610.

Radzik L, "Tort Processes and Relational Repair," in J Oberdiek (ed), *Philosophical Foundations of the Law of Torts* (Oxford University Press 2014) 231–48.

Raphael D D and Macfie A L (eds), *The Glasgow Edition of the Works and Correspondence of Adam Smith: The Theory of Moral Sentiments* (Oxford University Press 1976).

Reed A, "Exemplary Damages: A Persuasive Argument for their Retention as a Mechanism of Retributive Justice" (1996) 1996 *Civil Justice Quarterly* 130.

Reimann M, "Liability for Defective Products at the Beginning of the Twenty-first Century: Emergence of a Worldwide Standard?" (2003) 51 *American Journal of Comparative Law* 751.

Relis T, *Perceptions in Litigation and Mediation: Lawyers, Defendants, Plaintiffs, and Gendered Parties* (Cambridge University Press 2009).

Resnik J, "The Functions of Publicity and of Privatization in Courts and their Replacements (from Jeremy Bentham to #MeToo and Google Spain)," in B Hess and A K Harvey (eds), *Open Justice: The Role of Courts in a Democratic Society* (Nomos 2019) 177–252.

Rice D A, "Exemplary Damages in Private Consumer Actions" (1969) 55 *Iowa Law Review* 307.

Ripstein A, *Private Wrongs* (Harvard University Press 2016).

Ripstein A, *Equality, Responsibility and the Law* (Cambridge University Press 2012).

Ripstein A, "Civil Recourse and Separation of Wrongs and Remedies" (2011) 39 *Florida State University Law Review* 163.

Ripstein A, "Tort Law in a Liberal State" (2007) 1 *Journal of Tort Law* 1.

Ripstein A and Zipursky B C, "Corrective Justice in an Age of Mass Torts," in G J Postema (ed), *Philosophy and the Law of Torts* (Cambridge University Press 2001) 214–49.

Robbennolt J K and Hans V P, *The Psychology of Tort Law* (New York University Press 2016).

Roberts A and Richardson M, "Privacy, Punishment and Private Law," in E Bant, W Courtney, J Goudkamp and J M Paterson (eds), *Punishment and Private Law* (Hart Publishing 2021) 83–104.

Robinette C J, "Harmonizing Wrongs and Compensation" (2021) 80 *Maryland Law Review* 343.

Robinette C J, "Party Autonomy in Tort Theory and Reform" (2013) 6 *Journal of Tort Law* 173.

Robinette C J, "Two Roads Diverge for Civil Recourse Theory" (2013) 88 *Indiana Law Journal* 543.

Rosenvald N, *As Funções da Responsabilidade Civil: a Reparação e a Pena Civil* (2nd ed.) (Atlas 2014).

Ross E A, *Sin and Society: An Analysis of Latter-Day Iniquity (1907)* (Reprint) (Cornell University Library 2009).

Rousseau D M, Sitkin S B, Burt R S and Camerer C, "Not So Different After All: A Cross-Discipline View of Trust" (1998) 23 *Academy of Management Review* 393.

Rowan S, "Punishment and Private Law: Some Comparative Observations," in E Bant, W Courtney, J Goudkamp and J M Paterson (eds), *Punishment and Private Law* (Hart Publishing 2021) 63–82.

Rubenstein W B, "On What A 'Private Attorney General Is – And Why It Matters'" (2004) 57 *Vanderbilt Law Review* 2129.
Rustad M L, "Torts as Public Wrongs" (2011) 38 *Pepperdine Law Review* 433.
Rustad M L, "Happy No More: Federalism Derailed by the Court that would be King of Punitive Damages" (2005) 64 *Maryland Law Review* 461.
Rustad M L, "In Defense of Punitive Damages in Products Liability: Testing Tort Anecdotes with Empirical Data" (1992) 78 *Iowa Law Review* 1.
Rustad M L and Koenig T, "The Historical Continuity of Punitive Damages: Reforming the Tort Reformers" (1993) 42 *The American University Law Review* 1269.
Sage N, "Relational Wrongs and Agency in Tort Theory" (2021) 41 *Oxford Journal of Legal Studies* 1012.
Salvador Coderch P, "Punitive Damages" (2000) 1 *InDret* 1.
Sant'Ambrogio M and Staszewski G, "Democratizing Rule Development" (2021) 98 *Washington University Law Review* 793.
Sax J L, *Defending the Environment: A Strategy for Citizen Action* (Knopf 1971).
Scarso A P, "Punitive Damages in Italy," in H Koziol and V Wilcox (eds), *Punitive Damages: Common Law and Civil Law Perspectives* (Springer 2009) 103–13.
Schlueter L L, *Punitive Damages* (8th ed.) (LexisNexis 2020).
Schroeder E T, "Note. A Tort by Any Other Name? In Search of the Distinction between Regulation through Litigation and Conventional Tort Law" (2005) 83 *Texas Law Review* 897.
Schwartz A, "Proposals for Products Liability Reform: A Theoretical Synthesis" (1998) 97 *Yale Law Journal* 353.
Schwartz A, "The Case against Strict Liability" (1992) 60 *Fordham Law Review* 819.
Schwartz B, "Crowding Out Morality: How the Ideology of Self-Interest Can Be Self-Fulfilling," in J Hanson (ed), *Ideology, Psychology, and Law* (Oxford University Press 2012) 160–84.
Schwartz G T, "Empiricism and Tort Law" (2002) 4 *University of Illinois Law Review* 1067.
Schwartz G T, "Mixed Theories of Tort Law: Affirming Both Deterrence and Corrective Justice" (1997) 75 *Texas Law Review* 1801.
Schwartz G T, "Reality in the Economic Analysis of Tort Law: Does Tort Law Really Deter?" (1994) 42 *University of California Law Review* 377.
Schwartz G T, "The Myth of the Ford Pinto Case" (1991) 43 *Rutgers Law Review* 1013.
Schwartz V E and Appel C E, "Exporting United States Tort Law: The Importance of Authenticity, Necessity, and Learning from Our Mistakes" (2011) 38 *Pepperdine Law Review* 2.
Schwartz V E and Lorber L, "Twisting the Purpose of Pain and Suffering Awards: Turning Compensation into 'Punishment'" (2002) 54 *Southern California Law Review* 47.
Sebok A J, "Normative Theories of Punitive Damages: The Case of Deterrence," in J Oberdiek (ed), *Philosophical Foundations of the Law of Torts* (Oxford University Press 2014) 312–28.
Sebok A J, "Punitive Damages: From Myth to Theory" (2007) 92 *Iowa Law Review* 957.
Sebok A J, "What Did Punitive Damages Do? Why Misunderstanding the History of Punitive Damages Matters Today" (2003) 78 *Chicago Kent Law Review* 163.
Sedgwick T, *A Treatise on the Measure of Damages* (7th ed.) (Baker, Voorhis & Co. 1880).
Shapiro M A, "The Indignities of Civil Litigation" (2020) 100 *Boston University Law Review* 501.
Shapo M S, *Tort Law and Culture* (Carolina Academic Press 2003).
Shapo M S, *Products Liability and the Search for Justice* (Carolina Academic Press 1993).
Shapo M S, *The Duty to Act – Tort Law, Power, & Public Policy* (University of Texas Press 1978).

Shapo M S, "A Social Contract Tort" (1977) 75 *Texas Law Review* 1835.

Sharkey C M, "Punitive Damages Transformed into Societal Damages," in E Bant, W Courtney, J Goudkamp and J M Paterson (eds), *Punishment and Private Law* (Hart Publishing 2021) 155–86.

Sharkey C M, "Economic Analysis of Punitive Damages: Theory, Empirics, and Doctrine," in J Arlen (ed), *Research Handbook on the Economics of Torts* (Edward Elgar 2013) 486–511.

Sharkey C M, "Crossing the Punitive-Compensatory Divide," in B H Bornstein, R L Wiener, R Schopp and S L Willborn (eds), *Civil Juries and Civil Justice: Psychological & Legal Perspectives* (Springer 2008) 79–104.

Sharkey C M, "Revisiting the Noninsurable Costs of Accidents" (2005) 64 *Maryland Law Review* 409.

Sharkey C M, "Punitive Damages as Societal Damages" (2003) 113 *Yale Law Journal* 347.

Shavell S, "Strict Liability versus Negligence" (1980) 9 *Journal of Legal Studies* 1.

Sherwin E, "Comments on Stephen Smith's Duties, Liabilities and Damages" (2012) 125 *Harvard Law Review Forum* 164.

Sherwin E, "Interpreting Tort Law" (2011) 39 *Florida State University Law Review* 227.

Sherwin E, "Compensation and Revenge" (2003) 40 *San Diego Law Review* 1387.

Shiffrin S V, "Democratic Law and the Erosion of Common Law," in S V Shiffrin and H Ginsborg (eds), *Democratic Law* (Oxford University Press 2021) 65–89.

Shuman D W, "The Psychology of Compensation in Tort Law" (1994) 43 *Kansas Law Review* 39.

Silva L, "Is Anger a Hostile Emotion?" (2024) 15 *Review of Philosophy and Psychology* 383.

Sinanis N, "Aggravation in Tort before 1763" (2022) 43 *Journal of Legal History* 24.

Simons K W, "Response, Retributivists Need Not and Should Not Endorse the Subjectivist Account of Punishment" (2009) 109 *Columbia Law Review* 1.

Slovic P, "Perception of Risk," in P Slovic (ed), *The Perception of Risk* (Taylor and Francis 2000) 219–31.

Slovic P, "Trust, Emotion, Sex, Politics, and Science: Surveying the Risk-Assessment Battlefield" (1999) 19 *Risk Analysis* 689.

Smith S A, *Rights, Wrongs, and Injustices: The Structure of Remedial Law* (Oxford University Press 2020).

Smith S A, "Duties, Liabilities, and Damages" (2012) 125 *Harvard Law Review* 1727.

Solomon J M, "Equal Accountability through Tort Law" (2009) 103 *Northwestern University Law Review* 1765.

Solomon R C, "From Emotions and Choice," in R C Solomon (ed), *What Is an Emotion? Classic and Contemporary Readings* (Oxford University Press 2003) 224–35.

Solomon R C, "Justice v. Vengeance: On Law and the Satisfaction of Emotion," in S A Bandes (ed), *The Passions of Law* (New York University Press 2000) 121–48.

Solomon R C, *The Passions: Emotions and the Meaning of Life* (Hackett Publishing 1993).

Spring V L, Cameron C D and Cikara M, "The Upside of Outrage" (2018) 22(12) *Trends in Cognitive Sciences* 1067.

Srinivasan A, "The Aptness of Anger" (2018) 26(2) *Journal of Political Philosophy* 123.

Stapleton J, *Three Essays on Torts* (Oxford University Press 2021).

Stapleton J, "Products Liability in the United Kingdom: The Myths of Reform" (1999) 34 *Texas International Law Journal* 45.

Stark F, "Tort Law, Expression, and Duplicative Wrongs," in J Oberdiek and P B Miller (eds), *Civil Wrongs and Justice in Private Law* (Oxford University Press 2020) 441–62.

Steel S, "Deterrence in Private Law," in H Psarras and S Steel (eds), *Private Law and Practical Reason: Essays on John Gardner's Private Law Theory* (Oxford University Press 2023) 123–42.

Steel S, "Damages without Loss" (2023) 139 *Law Quarterly Review* 219.

Steel S, "On the Moral Necessity of Tort Law: The Fairness Argument" (2021) 41 *Oxford Journal of Legal Studies* 192.

Steele J, "Satisfying Claims? Money, Tort, and 'Consumer Society'" (2011) 20 *Social & Legal Studies* 516.

Stevens R, "Private Law and the Form of Reasons," in A Robertson and J Goudkamp (eds), *Form and Substance in the Law of Obligations* (Hart Publishing 2019) 119–48.

Stevens R, *Torts and Rights* (Oxford University Press 2007).

Strawson P F, "Freedom and Resentment," in G Watson (ed), *Free Will* (Oxford University Press 1982) 59–84.

Sugarman S D, "Peter Cane on Torts," in J Goudkamp, M Lunney and L McDonald (eds), *Taking Law Seriously: Essays in Honour of Peter Cane* (Hart Publishing 2022) 73–92.

Sugarman S D, "Doing Away with Tort Law" (1985) 73 *California Law Review* 555.

Sunstein C R, "Moral Heuristics and Risk," in T Lewens (ed), *Risk: Philosophical Perspectives* (Routledge 2007) 156–70.

Sunstein C R, "Moral Heuristics" (2005) 28(4) *Behavioral and Brain Sciences* 531.

Sunstein C R, "On the Psychology of Punishment" (2004) 11 *Supreme Court Economic Review* 171.

Sunstein C R, *Risk and Reason: Safety, Law, and the Environment* (Cambridge University Press 2002).

Sunstein C R, "The Law of Fears" (2000) 115 *Harvard Law Review* 1119.

Sunstein C R, "Cognition and Cost-Benefit Analysis" (2000) 29 *Journal of Legal Studies* 1059.

Sunstein C R, On the Expressive Function of Law (1996) 144 *University of Pennsylvania Law Review* 2021.

Sunstein C R, Hastie R, Payne J W, Schkade D A and Viscusi W K, *Punitive Damages: How Juries Decide* (The University of Chicago Press 2002).

Sunstein C R, Kahneman D and Schkade D, "Assessing Punitive Damages (with Notes on Cognition and Valuation in Law)" (1998) 107 *Yale Law Journal* 2071.

Sunstein C R, Schakade D A and Kahneman D, "Do People Want Optimal Deterrence?" (2000) 29 *Journal of Legal Studies* 237.

Sunstein C R and Shih J M, "Damages in Sexual Harassment Cases," in C A MacKinnon and R B Siegel (eds), *Directions in Sexual Harassment Law* (Yale University Press 2004) 324–44.

Tadros V, *The Ends of Harm: The Moral Foundations of Criminal Law* (Oxford University Press 2011).

Talesh S A, "The Privatization of Public Legal Rights: How Manufacturers Construct the Meaning of Consumer Law" (2009) 43(3) *Law and Society Review* 527.

Taliadoros J, "The Roots of Punitive Damages at Common Law: A Longer History" (2016) 64 *Cleveland State Law Review* 251.

Tenbrunsel A E and Messick D M, "Sanctioning Systems, Decision Frames, and Cooperation" (1999) 44 *Administrative Science Quarterly* 684.

Tettenborn A, "Punitive Damages – A View from England" (2004) 41 *San Diego Law Review* 1551.

Thaler R H and Susntein C R, *Nudge: Improving Decisions about Health, Wealth and Happiness* (Penguin 2008).

Thompson S D, "Liability of Corporations for Exemplary Damages" (1895) 41 *Central Law Journal* 308.

Tilbury M, "Aggravated Damages" (2018) 71 *Current Legal Problems* 215.

Tilley C C, "Private Law, Public Law, and the Production of American Virtue" (2020) 115 *Northwestern University Law Review Online* 270.

Tilley C C, "Tort Law Inside Out" (2017) 128 *Yale Law Journal* 1320.

Tonry M, "Is Proportionality in Punishment Possible, and Achievable?" in M Tonry (ed), *Of One-Eyed and Toothless Miscreants: Making the Punishment Fit the Crime?* (Oxford University Press 2019) 1–29.

Tonry M, "Preface," in M Tonry (ed), *Of One-Eyed and Toothless Miscreants: Making the Punishment Fit the Crime?* (Oxford University Press 2019) vii–x.

Tversky A and Kahneman D, "The Framing of Decisions and Psychology of Choice" (1981) 211 *Science* 453.

Tversky A and Kahneman D, "Judgment under Uncertainty: Heuristics and Biases" (1974) 185 *Science* 1124.

Twerski A D and Henderson J A (Jr), "Manufacturers' Liability for Defective Product Designs: The Triumph of Risk-Utility" (2009) 74 *Brooklyn Law Review* 1061.

Twigg-Flesner C, "Guiding Principles for Updating the Product Liability Directive for the Digital Age" (2021) *ELI Innovation Paper Series*.

Tyler T R, "The Psychology of Aggregation: Promise and Potential Pitfalls" (2015) 64 *De Paul Law Review* 711.

Van Boom W H, Borghetti J-S, Bloch Ehlers A, Karner E, Nolan D, Oliphant K, Scarso A, Ulfbeck V and Wagner G, "Product Liability in Europe," in H Koziol, M D Green, M Lunney, K Oliphant and Y Lixin (eds), *Product Liability: Fundamental Questions in a Comparative Perspective* (De Gruyter 2017) 255–356.

Van Dijk E, Mulder L B and Kwaadsteniet E W, "For the Common Good? The Use of Sanctions in Social Dilemmas," in P A M Van Lange, B Rockendbach and T Yamagishi (eds), *Reward and Punishment in Social Dilemmas* (Oxford University Press 2014) 70–84.

Van Prooijen J-W, *The Moral Punishment Instinct* (Oxford University Press 2018).

Van Uytsel S, *Different Liability Regimes for Autonomous Vehicles: One Preferable Above the Other? Perspectives in Law, Business and Innovation* (Springer 2021).

Vanleenhove C and Meurkens L (eds), *The Recognition and Enforcement of Punitive Damages Judgments across the Globe: Insights from Various Continents* (Eleven International Publishing 2023).

Varuhas J N E, *Damages and Human Rights* (Hart Publishing 2016).

Varuhas J N E, "The Concept of 'Vindication' in the Law of Torts: Rights, Interests and Damages" (2014) 34(2) *Oxford Journal of Legal Studies* 253.

Vidmar N and Miller D T, "Social Psychological Processes Underlying Attitudes toward Legal Punishment" (1980) 14 *Law and Society Review* 565.

Viscusi W K, "Pricing Lives for Corporate and Governmental Risk Decisions" (2015) 6(2) *Journal of Benefit-Cost Analysis* 227.

Viscusi W K, "The Challenge of Punitive Damages Mathematics" (2001) 30 *Journal of Legal Studies* 313.

Viscusi W K, "Corporate Risk Analysis: A Reckless Act?" (2000) 52 *Stanford Law Review* 547.

Viscusi W K, "The Social Costs of Punitive Damages against Corporations in Environmental and Safety Torts" (1998) 87 *Georgetown Law Journal* 285.

Viscusi W K, "Why There Is No Defense of Punitive Damages" (1998) 87 *Georgetown Law Journal* 381.

Viscusi W K, *Reforming Products Liability* (Harvard University Press 1991).

Von Hirsch A, *Censure and Sanctions* (Oxford University Press 1996).

Von Hirsch A, "Proportionality in the Philosophy of Punishment" (1992) 16 *Crime and Justice* 5.

Von Hirsch A, Roberts J V, Bottoms A E, Roach K and Schiff M (eds), *Restorative Justice and Criminal Justice: Competing or Reconcilable Paradigms?* (Hart Publishing 2003).

Von Hirsch A and Shworth A, *Proportionate Sentencing* (Oxford University Press 2005).
Wagner G, "Liability Rules for the Digital Age – Aiming for the Brussels Effect" (2022) 13(3) *Journal of European Tort Law* 191.
Wagner G, "Robot, Inc.: Personhood for Autonomous Systems?" (2019) 88 *Fordham Law Review* 591.
Wagner G, "Punitive Damages," in J Basedow, K J Hopt, R Zimmermann and A Stier (eds), *The Max Planck Encyclopedia of European Private Law* (Oxford University Press 2012) 1403–6.
Wagner W E, "When a Corporation's Deliberate Ignorance Causes Harm: Charting a New Role for Tort Law" (2023) 72 *DePaul Law Review* 413.
Wagner W E, "When All Else Fails: Regulatory Risky Products through Tort Litigation" (2007) 95 *Georgetown Law Journal* 693.
Walen A, "Retributive Justice," in E N Zalta and U Nodelman (eds), *The Stanford Encyclopedia of Philosophy* (Winter Edition 2023) Available at https://plato.stanford.edu/archives/win2023/entries/justice-retributive/.
Weaver R and Kysar D A, "Courting Disaster: Climate Change and the Adjudication of Catastrophe" (2017) 93(1) *Notre Dame Law Review* 295.
Weiguo Qu Z W, "Betrayal Aversion in the Source of Risk: Research Methods and Influencing Factors" (2019) 9(4) *Advances in Psychology* 717.
Weimer M, "The Origins of 'Risk' as an Idea and the Future of Risk Regulation" (2017) 8(1) *European Journal of Risk Regulation* 10.
Weiner M H, "Domestic Violence and the Per Se Standard of Outrage" (1995) 54 *Maryland Law Review* 183.
Weinrib E J, *Reciprocal Freedom. Private Law and Public Right* (Oxford University Press 2022).
Weinrib E J, *Corrective Justice* (Oxford University Press 2012).
Weinrib E J, "Civil Recourse and Corrective Justice" (2011) 39 *Florida State University Law Review* 273.
Weinrib E J, "Two Conceptions of Remedies," in C E F Rickett (ed), *Justifying Private Law Remedies* (Hart Publishing 2008) 3–32.
Weinrib E J, "Punishment and Disgorgement as Contract Remedies" (2003) 78 *Chicago-Kent Law Review* 55.
Weinrib E J, *The Idea of Private Law* (Oxford University Press 1995).
Weinrib E J, "Understanding Tort Law" (1989) 23 *Valparaiso University Law Review* 485.
Wendehorst C, "Strict Liability for AI and other Emerging Technologies" (2020) 11(2) *Journal of European Tort Law* 150.
Wheeler M E, "A Proposal for Further Common Law Development of the Use of Punitive Damages in Modern Product Liability Litigation" (1989) 40 *Alabama Law Review* 919.
White G E, "The Emergence and Development of a Law of Torts, 1870–1930" (2014) 11 *University of St. Thomas Law Journal* 463.
Whittam S, "Mind the Compensation Gap: Towards a New European Regime Addressing Civil Liability in the Age of AI" (2022) 30 *International Journal of Law and Information Technology* 249.
Witt J F, *The Accidental Republic: Crippled Workingmen, Destitute Widows, and the Remaking of American Law* (Harvard University Press 2006).
Witt J F and Issacharoff S, "The Inevitability of Aggregate Settlement: An Institutional Account of American Tort Law" (2004) 57 *Vanderbilt Law Review* 1571.
Wogalter M S, Brems D J and Martin E G, "Risk Perception of Common Consumer Products: Judgments of Accident Frequency and Precautionary Intent" (1993) 24 *Journal of Safety Research* 97.

Yaffe G, *The Age of Culpability: Children and The Nature of Criminal Responsibility* (Oxford University Press 2018).

Yoshikawa J, "Sharing the Costs of Artificial Intelligence: Universal No-Fault Social Insurance for Personal Injuries" (2020) 21(4) *Vanderbilt Journal of Entertainment and Technology Law* 1155.

Zacharias F C, "The Politics of Torts" (1986) 95 *Yale Law Journal* 698.

Zedner L, "Reparation and Retribution: Are They Reconcilable?" (1994) 57 *Modern Law Review* 228.

Zipursky B C, "Palsgraf, Punitive Damages, and Preemption" (2012) 125 *Harvard Law Review* 1757.

Zipursky B C, "A Theory of Punitive Damages" (2005) 84 *Texas Law Review* 105.

Zipursky B C, "Punitive Damages after Philip Morris USA v. Williams" (2007) 44 *Court Review* 134.

Index

For EU product safety concerns, contact us at Calle de José Abascal, 56–1°,
28003 Madrid, Spain or eugpsr@cambridge.org.

www.ingramcontent.com/pod-product-compliance
Lightning Source LLC
LaVergne TN
LVHW011807200926
848484LV00005B/1095
9781009567893